Gallery of of Best Cover Letters

A Collection of Quality Cover Letters by Professional Resume Writers

by David F. Noble

Publishing

Gallery of Best Cover Letters
A Collection of Quality Cover Letters by Professional Resume Writers

Copyright © 1999 by David F. Noble

Published by JIST Works, Inc.
8902 Otis Avenue
Indianapolis, IN 46216-1033
Phone 1-800-648-5478
E-mail: editorial@jist.com

Interior Design: Debbie Berman
Layout: Carolyn J. Newland
Cover Design: Aleata Howard
Development Editor: Virginia Noble

Printed in the United States of America

03 02 01 00   5 4 3 2

Library of Congress Cataloging-in-Publication Data

Noble, David F. (David Franklin), 1935-
    Gallery of best cover letters / by David F. Noble.
       p.   cm.
    Includes index.
    ISBN 1-56370-551-6
    1. Cover letters.   I. Title.
    HF5383.N618   1999   99-41503
    808'.06665--dc21   CIP

ISBN 1-56370-551-6

To my mother,

Christena Brightwell Noble,

the letter writer

Acknowledgments

This new collection of professionally written cover letters and resumes was made possible first of all because of the submissions of the writers featured in this book. When I compiled the first Gallery (*Gallery of Best Resumes,* JIST Works, Inc., 1994), I knew these writers only as names on a mailing list from the Professional Association of Résumé Writers, which I had recently joined. Since the publication of that first Gallery and during the preparation of its sequels (*Gallery of Best Resumes for Two-Year Degree Graduates,* JIST, 1996; *Professional Resumes for Executives, Managers, and Other Administrators,* JIST, 1998; and *Professional Resumes for Tax and Accounting Occupations,* CCH Incorporated and JIST, 1999), I joined a second organization—the National Résumé Writers Association (NRWA)—and have met many of the writers at annual meetings of their respective organizations. I am happy once more to showcase the latest work of these professional writers in this new Gallery.

This book became possible also because of Mike Farr, Jim Irizarry, and Bob Grilliot of JIST Works. When I wrote the *Gallery of Best Resumes,* a *Gallery of Best Cover Letters* was the first title I thought of next, but other titles intervened. Bob Grilliot was the one who expressed a market need for this book, Jim Irizarry talked me into doing it, and Mike Farr approved it. I want to thank, too, Tim Orbaugh, Barb Ruess, and Michael Cunningham for their support of this book.

Many thanks to Carolyn Newland for her desktop publishing and careful work in reviewing final proofs, and to Aleata Howard for her aesthetic updating of the cover.

Finally, special thanks are directed to my wife, Ginny, who managed and performed all of the many tasks that were necessary to create yet another Gallery.

Contents

This useful "idea book" of best cover letters has three parts: Best Cover
Letter Tips; a Gallery of 292 cover letters written by 76 professional
resume writers; and an Exhibit of 35 companion resumes, together with
tips for improving resumes. With this book, you not only have a treasury
of quality cover letters and resumes but also learn how to view them as
superior models for your own cover letters and resumes.

This book is for *job searchers* who are applying for new positions, *career
changers* who are looking for professional roles with other employers, *job
changers* who are proactively climbing the corporate ladder, *graduate
students* who are applying for higher levels of employment, and *new
university graduates* who are seeking entry-level positions. The book is
also for experienced workers who are scaling down their work, military
personnel who are returning to civilian life, and women who are returning to the workforce after raising children. Because of the wealth and
spread of quality cover letters in this new Gallery, this book is for *any job
searcher* who wants examples of top-quality documents to create an
outstanding cover letter for himself or herself.

This collection of professionally written cover letters shows you how
to present yourself effectively through a cover letter to a prospective
employer so that you can be more competitive as a job applicant.

Tips for Polishing Cover Letters 14

A quality resume can make a great impression, but it can be ruined quickly by a poorly written cover letter. This section shows you how to eliminate common errors in cover letters. It amounts to a *crash writing course* that you won't find in any other job search book. After you read the following sections, you will be better able to write and polish any letters you create for your job search.

Part 2: The Gallery of Best Cover Letters 25

The Gallery at a Glance 26

How to Use the Gallery 29

This Gallery has thirty-nine sections of professional cover letters for a wide variety of occupations. Regardless of your career or occupation, you should check out all the letters throughout the Gallery for design tips, ways to express ideas, and impressive formats. At the bottom of each cover letter are comments that call your attention to noteworthy features or solutions to problems.

Part 3: Best Resume Tips 325

Best Resume Tips at a Glance 326

Best Resume Tips 327

Best Resume-Writing Strategies 328

In this section, you learn experience-tested, resume-writing strategies, such as how to showcase your skills, knowledge, and achievements.

Best Resume Design and Layout Tips 330

This section shows you effective design techniques, such as how to use *white space* for an uncluttered look; how to make decisions about *fonts* and *typefaces*; how to handle italic and boldfacing; and how to use *graphics elements* like bullets, horizontal lines, vertical lines, and boxes.

Introduction

Like the earlier Galleries in this series, *Gallery of Best Cover Letters* is a collection of quality cover letters from professional resume writers, each with individual views about cover letter writing. Unlike many cover letter books whose selections "look the same," this book contains cover letters that look different because they are *real* cover letters prepared by different professionals for actual job searchers throughout the country. (Certain information in the cover letters and companion resumes has been fictionalized by the writers to protect, where necessary, each client's right to privacy.) Even when several cover letters from the same writer appear in the book, most of these letters are different because the writer has customized each letter according to the background information and career goals of the client for whom the related resume was prepared.

Why a Gallery of Best Cover Letters?

One reason is that error-free cover letters are harder to write than most people imagine. When you put together a resume, you can work with just phrases, clauses, and lists. The common writing dangers are misspellings, errors with capital letters, wordy phrases, and faulty parallelism (for example, not having certain words in a series or list grammatically parallel). When, however, you write a cover letter, you are somewhat obligated to write sentences that hang together in several paragraphs in a meaningful sequence. To write sentences and paragraphs is to enter a minefield filled with all of the potential errors and stylistic weaknesses that an individual with good communication skills can make. And many people who try to write a cover letter do make such errors—often unknowingly.

This *Gallery of Best Cover Letters* shows you, example by example, how to create cover letters that are free of errors and writing weaknesses which could ruin your chances for an interview. By studying the sentences and paragraphs in these letters, you can compare your writing with what you see, and find new ways to express what you want to say to win that interview.

Another reason for having a *Gallery of Best Cover Letters* is that many of the cover letters in cover letter books on bookstore shelves are—there's no other way to say it truthfully—models of bad writing. Often they exhibit not just a stylistic weakness here and there, but grammatical errors that would sabotage your job search if you used those passages verbatim in your own cover letters. To browse through the letters in this book is to walk through a minefield free of mines.

Why Cover Letters by Professional Resume Writers?

Instead of assuming that "one cover letter style fits all," the writers featured in this book believe that a client's past experiences and next job target should determine the type, design, and content of each resume and its related cover letter. The writers interacted with clients to fashion resumes that seemed best for each client's situation at the time, and to create one or more cover letters for job(s) the clients were seeking.

This book features resumes from writers who share several important qualities: good listening skills, a sense of what details are appropriate for a particular resume and its cover letter, and flexibility in selecting and arranging the resume's sections and the cover letter's paragraphs. By "hearing between" a client's statements, the perceptive resume writer can detect what kind of job the client really wants. The writer then chooses the information that will best represent the client for the job being sought. Finally, the writer decides on the best arrangement of the information for that job. With this book, you can learn from these professional writers how to shape and improve your own job search documents. You can create such documents yourself, or, if you want, you can contact a professional writer who, for a fee, might create a custom resume and cover letter for you. See the Appendix, "List of Contributors," for contact information about the professional writers whose works are featured in this book.

Most of the writers of the cover letters in this Gallery are members of the Professional Association of Résumé Writers (PARW). Some of these writers are members also of the National Résumé Writers' Association (NRWA), which was established by a regional PARW chapter in February of 1997. Those who have CPRW certification, for Certified Professional Résumé Writer (again, see the Appendix, "List of Contributors"), received this designation from PARW after they studied specified course materials and demonstrated proficiency in an examination. Those who have NCRW certification, for National Certified Résumé Writer, received this designation from NRWA after a different course of study and a different examination. A few contributors are not currently members of either organization but are either past PARW members or are professional writers in Indiana, Michigan, and Ohio who were invited to submit works for possible selection for previous Galleries.

How This Book Is Organized

Gallery of Best Cover Letters, like the preceding four Galleries, consists of three parts, but the content is switched. Part 1, "Best Cover Letter Tips," contains a discussion of some myths about cover letters, plus strategies for writing cover letters and tips for polishing them. Some of the advice offered here applies also to writing resumes.

Part 2 is the Gallery itself, containing 292 cover letters from 76 writers. These cover letters are grouped according to 38 occupational categories (for these, see the Table of Contents). Within each category the cover letters are arranged alphabetically by occupational title. Note that the occupation title is that of the *target position* the applicant is seeking, not the current or recent title of the applicant. In resumes, job titles have to do with the individual's present and past positions. Cover letters, however, are concerned with a target position. You should keep this fundamental difference in mind as you use this book. (If the target position is not stated clearly in a cover letter, the applicant's current or most recent job was used to determine the occupation category of that letter.)

Even though most of the cover letters have been written with a target position in mind, you can learn much by reading any or all of them. That is, to get the most from this book about writing cover letters, you should look at all of the cover letters in this collection and not just at those related to your particular profession or position interest. All of the cover letters form a hunting ground for ideas that may prove useful to you for developing your own cover letters.

Part 3 presents some resume-writing strategies, design and layout tips, and resume-writing style tips for making resumes visually impressive. These tips contain references to resumes in an Exhibit of 35 resumes at the end of Part 3. Each of these resumes was accompanied by a cover letter that appears in this Gallery. These references are to resumes that illustrate a strategy or a tip, but the references are not exhaustive. If you browse through this Exhibit, you may see other resumes that exhibit the same strategy or tip.

Even though the Exhibit contains only 35 resumes, it offers a wide range of resumes whose features you can use in creating and improving your own resumes. Notice the plural. An important premise of an active job search is that you will not have just one "perfect" resume for all potential employers, but different versions of your resume for different interviews. The Exhibit of resumes, like the Gallery of cover letters, is therefore not a showroom where you say, "I'll take that one." It is a valuable resource of design ideas, expressions, and organizational patterns that can help make your own resume a "best resume" for your next interview.

The Appendix is a "List of Contributors," which contains the names, addresses, phone numbers, and other information of professional resume writers who contributed cover letters and resumes for this book. The list is arranged alphabetically by state and city. Although most of these resume writers work with local clients, many of the writers work with clients by phone, e-mail, and the World Wide Web from anywhere in the United States.

You can use the Occupation Index to look up cover letters by the job being sought. This index, however, should not replace careful examination of all of the cover letters. Many cover letters for some other occupation may have features adaptable to your own occupation. Limiting your search to the Occupational Index may cause you to miss some valuable examples.

Who This Book Is For

Anyone who wants ideas for creating or improving a cover letter can benefit from this book. It is especially useful for active job seekers—those who understand the difference between active and passive job searching. A *passive* job seeker waits until jobs are advertised and then mails copies of the same resume, along with a standard cover letter, to a number of ads. An *active* job seeker believes that both the resume and the cover letter should be modified for a specific job target *after* having talked in person or by phone to a prospective interviewer *before* a job is announced. To schedule such an interview is to penetrate the "hidden job market." Active job seekers can find in the Exhibit's focused resumes a wealth of strategies for targeting a resume for a particular interview. The section "How to Use the Gallery" at the beginning of Part 2 shows you how to use the Gallery for improving your cover letters.

What This Book Can Do for You

Besides providing you with a treasury of quality cover letters and companion resumes whose features you can use in your own letters and resumes, this book can help transform your thinking about these job search documents. If you think that there is one "best" way to create a cover letter or resume, this book will help you learn how to design resumes and cover letters that are best for you as you try to get an interview with a particular person for a specific job.

1

P·A·R·T

Best Cover Letter Tips

Best Cover Letter Tips at a Glance

Best Cover Letter Tips

In an active job search, your cover letter and resume should complement one another. Both are tailored to a particular reader you have contacted or to a specific job target. To help you create the "best" cover letters for your resumes, this part of the book mentions some common myths about cover letters and presents tips for polishing the letters you write.

Myths about Cover Letters

1. **Resumes and cover letters are two separate documents that have little relation to each other.** The resume and cover letter work together in presenting you effectively to a prospective employer. The cover letter should draw attention to the most important information in the resume, the information you want the reader to be certain to see.

2. **The main purpose of the cover letter is to establish friendly rapport with the reader.** Resumes show that you *can* do the work required. Cover letters express that you *want* to do the work required. But it doesn't hurt to display enthusiasm in your resumes and refer to your abilities in your cover letters. The cover letter should demonstrate qualities and worker traits you want the prospective employee to see, such as good communication skills, motivation, clear thinking, good sense, thoughtfulness, interest in others, neatness, and so on.

3. **You can use the same cover letter for each reader of your resume.** Modify your cover letter for each reader so that it sounds fresh rather than canned. Chances are that in an active job search, you have already talked with the person who will interview you. Your cover letter should reflect that conversation and build on it.

4. **In a cover letter, you should mention any negative things about your life experience, work experience, health, or education in order to prepare the reader in advance of an interview.** This is not the purpose of the cover letter. You might bring up these topics in the first or second interview, but only after the interviewer has shown interest in you or offered you a job. Even then, if you feel that you must mention something negative about your past, present it in a positive way, perhaps by saying how that experience has strengthened your resolve to work hard at any new job.

5. **It is more important to remove errors from a resume than from a cover letter, because the resume is more important than the cover letter.** Both your resume and your cover letter should be free of errors. The cover letter is

usually the first document a prospective employer sees. The first impression is often the most important one. If your cover letter has an embarrassing error in it, the chances are good that the reader may not bother to read your resume or may read it with less interest.

6. **An error in a cover letter is not important.** The cost of a cover letter might be as much as a third of a million dollars—even more—if you figure the amount of income and benefits you don't receive over, say, a 10-year period for a job you don't get because of the error that got you screened out.

7. **To make certain that your cover letter has no errors, all you need to do is proofread it or ask a friend to "proof" it.** Trying to proofread your own cover letter is risky, even if you are good at grammar and writing. Once a document is typewritten or printed, it has an aura about it that may make it seem better written than it is. For this reason, you are likely to miss typos or other kinds of errors.

   Relying on someone else is risky too. If your friend is not good at grammar and writing, that person may not see any mistakes either. Try to find a proofreader, a professional editor, an English teacher, a professional writer, or an experienced secretary who can point out any errors you may have missed.

8. **After someone has proofread your letter, you can make a few changes to it and not have it looked at again.** More errors creep into a document this way than you would think possible. The reason is that such changes are often done hastily, and haste can waste an error-free document. If you make *any* change to a document, ask someone to proofread it a final time just to make sure that you haven't introduced an error during the last stage of composition.

9. **It doesn't take long to write a cover letter.** You should allow plenty of time to write and revise . . . and revise . . . a cover letter to get it just right for a particular reader. Most people think that writing is 90 percent of the task of creating a cover letter, and revision is 10 percent. It's really the other way around: writing is closer to 10 percent of the task; revision, 90 percent. That is true if you really care about the cover letter and want it to work hard for you.

10. **It doesn't take long to print the cover letter.** To get the output of a printer looking just right, you may need to print the letter a number of times. Watch for extra spaces between words and sentences; unwanted spaces are usually easier to see in the printed letter than on-screen (if you are using word processing). Fix any problems with vertical alignment between the date at the top of the letter and the complimentary close (an expression like "Sincerely yours") if the date and the closing are not flush with the left margin but are tabbed to the center or the right side of the page. Finally, be sure that you leave enough vertical space for your signature between the complimentary close and your typed name.

Tips for Writing Cover Letters

To write well, you need to know why you are writing, the reader(s) to whom you are writing, what you want to say, how you want to organize what you say, and how you want to say it. Similarly, to write a good cover letter, you should know clearly its purpose, audience, content, organization, and style. The following tips, or strategies, should help you consider these aspects of cover letter writing. Consider using some of these strategies to ensure that your letters are impressive, even outstanding—and thus get the attention you deserve.

Purpose Strategies

1. **Make it clear in your letter that you really want the job.** See Cover Letters 2 and 3. An employer doesn't want to know that you just want a job. An employer wants to know that you *really* want a particular job. If you display a ho-hum attitude in a letter, the chances are that you will receive a ho-hum response, which usually means rejection.

2. **Consider putting a subject line near the beginning of the letter to indicate the target position you are seeking.** See Cover Letters 17, 21, 23, 27, 47, 75, 80, 81, 100, 106, 117, 123, 152, 172, 173, 194, 204, and 205. See Cover Letter 157, which is a thank-you note with a subject line. See Cover Letter 206 in which a cartoon balloon message is functionally a subject line.

3. **If you know that a company has been having employee-turnover problems, show interest in a long-term commitment if that fits your plans.** See Cover Letter 13.

4. **Consider writing the cover letter so that you can use it also as a marketing letter in which you make your job interests and availability known to a number of readers.** See Cover Letter 292.

5. **Consider marketing your services aggressively in your letter.** See Cover Letter 161. See also Cover 169, which prompted a call for an interview *before* the caller had reviewed the resume and application.

Audience Strategies

6. **Make certain that the letter is addressed to a specific person and that you use this person's name in the salutation.** Avoid using such general salutations as Dear Sir or Madam, To Whom It May Concern, Dear Administrator, Dear Prospective Employer, and Dear Committee. (To ensure anonymity, some of the resume writers who have provided sample cover letters for this book have used general salutations.) In an active job search, you should do everything possible to send your cover letter and resume to a particular individual, preferably someone you've already talked with in person or by phone, and with whom you have arranged an interview. If you have not been able to make a personal contact, at least do everything possible to find out the name of the person who will read your letter and resume. Then address the letter to that person.

7. **Don't let your opening statement or one in your first paragraph give the reader a chance to think "No" and read no further.**

   Example: "Perhaps you are looking for a new auditor."

The reader can think "I'm not" and stop reading.

Example: "If you have a need for. . . ."

The reader can think "I don't" without reading further.

Example: "If you think your auditor should be as good at building team-work as he is at building reports, we should talk." (See Cover Letter 8.)

The reader can't disagree with this reasoning and will probably read further.

8. **Sometimes a cover letter will be more successful if the timing is right.** Be alert to a prospective company's needs as determined by seasons, holidays, grants, changes in the economy, and so on. See Cover Letter 15.

9. **Play down experience that may threaten a prospective employer.** See Cover Letter 33, in which an experienced owner/operator (who was also the vice president and general manager) of a former business was afraid that he would be a threat to a less-experienced employer in a new employer-employee relationship.

10. **Make your cover letter target-oriented by researching the prospective company and showing in the letter that you know important information about that company.** See Cover Letters 35 and 56.

11. **For individuals leaving the military and returning to civilian life, emphasize experience perceived as relevant to civilian life.** The reader may not know how to translate military responsibilities into civilian duties. Be sure to present military terms as civilian tasks when the conversion is feasible and strategic. See Cover Letters 40, 44, 69, 138, 162, 166, 197, 198, and 283.

Content Strategies

12. **If you often reply to ads without a person's name and have no way to learn it, consider omitting the salutation and varying the subject line.** See Cover Letter 152.

13. **If your name is unfamiliar or difficult to pronounce, consider putting an aid to pronunciation in parentheses after it.** See Cover Letter 283.

14. **When you are short on professional work experience to qualify for a position, consider related personal and voluntary experiences that may qualify you for the job.** See Cover Letter 276.

15. **If you are responding to a job that has been posted on an online database, include the reference number, if any, if you respond to the posting.** See Cover Letter 283.

16. **Numerals in the opening paragraph can be eye-catching.** See Cover Letters 35, 46, and 101.

Resume Connections

17. **If the intended reader of your resume suggested that you send it, or if you have recently spoken with the person, say this in the first sentence of the cover letter.** Mentioning the person's name is even better. Indicating that the resume was requested helps to get your resume past any "gatekeeper"—the person who opens the mail and makes preliminary routing decisions—and into the hands of the appropriate reader. See Cover Letters 14, 38, 90, 98, 103, 236, 241, 242, 244, 245, and 273.

18. **Similarly, if a third party has suggested that you submit your resume to the reader, mention that at or near the beginning of your cover letter.** See Cover Letters 17, 35, 52, 81, 97, 183, 214, 223, 224, 231, 233, 256, 258, 259, and 261. Even mentioning the third party near the end of the letter may be beneficial. See Cover Letter 282.

19. **Put in your letter important information for which there is no room in the resume.** See Cover Letter 68, which includes community activities not mentioned in the resume.

20. **Try to make the letter match, or correspond in some conspicuous way, to an early, important section of the resume.** See Cover Letter 1. The purpose is to ensure that the reader will see the important information if for some reason the resume doesn't get read, and to help the reader feel at home with an important part of the resume if it is read.

21. **If you don't have a resume and don't have time to make one, try constructing the cover letter as an alternative or substitute for a formal resume.** See Cover Letters 43 and 129. You might even consider making your letter a flyer that you can leave with companies or put on job bulletin boards. In some circumstances, this creative approach may get the kind of attention you are seeking. See Cover Letter 135.

22. **Think of the cover letter as a hook for the resume.** A cover letter is not an end in itself but a means for getting the reader to read the resume. A cover letter should refer at least once to the resume. See Cover Letter 75. A cover letter might refer specifically to the most important part of the resume—the part that you want the reader to see for sure.

23. **A letter can be a cover letter even when you send a resume separately.** See Cover Letter 165.

24. **Create an ASCII (text) version of your cover letter and resume so that you can customize them as needed and e-mail them in response to online ads or post them to online job databases.** See Cover Letter 253 and compare it with 252.

Testimonials

25. **Consider using an important testimonial in a cover letter.** A testimonial is a quotation from a former or current boss, a coworker, or someone else who knows the quality of your work or the strength of your character. Testimonials can be effective in setting your letter or resume apart from other "stock" submissions. If you use testimonials in your cover letters or resumes, be sure to get permission from the sources. See Cover Letters 51, 60, and 225.

Anecdotes

26. **If you have an impressive success story to tell about previous work experience, consider telling the story in your cover letter.** See Cover Letters 65 and 223.

Follow-Up Plans

27. **At the end of the letter, consider keeping control of the follow-up by indicating that you will phone later.** See Cover Letters 5, 8, 17, 20, 23, 26, 27, and many others.

28. **For those who think that calling the prospective employer seems pushy, you can soften the tone of the statement about calling.** See, for example, Cover Letter 158.

Organization Strategies

29. **Consider restating important themes at the end of the letter.** See Cover Letter 16.

30. **Try a change in format for a change of pace within a letter.** See Cover Letters 18, 53, and 206.

31. **For a change, try presenting the information in your cover letter in ascending order of importance to give the impression that the information gets better and better as one reads the letter.** See, for example, Cover Letter 78. (Resumes tend to be written in descending order of importance to capture the attention of the reader near the top of the resume and to ensure that the most important information will be read.)

32. **Consider expressing interest in an interview in one paragraph and saying thank you in another.** The reason is that saying thank you in a separate paragraph gives you another chance to show interest in the reader as a person. See Cover Letter 195.

Style Strategies

Tone

33. **Try not to sound desperate, even a little bit.** The following examples may seem extreme, but try to avoid using any similar statements in your letter:

"I'll take anything you have to offer."
"It makes no difference what kind of job you have."
"I can start immediately."
"I am available for employment right away."
"When's the first pay check?"

34. **It's okay to be enthusiastic in a cover letter. See Cover Letters 62 and 67.**

35. **Consider beginning the letter with a quotation that sets the tone of the letter and provides insight for understanding your work, character, attitude, outlook, or whatever else you want to convey.** See Cover Letter 275.

36. **Try you make your tone match your claims for yourself.** For example, if you say that you are an aggressive person, then be aggressive in what you say in your letter. See Cover Letters 203 and 207.

37. **If you want to appear aggressive, keep your letter short.** Aggressive people don't have the time to write long letters, just as they don't have the time to sit in long meetings. Aggressive people have a knack for saying it all quickly and then moving on. See, for example, Cover Letter 240. It's short, but it says everything and says it persuasively. It's hard to imagine a reader who wouldn't want to interview this candidate.

Persuasiveness

38. **Consider making your cover letter not only informative but also persuasive.** See Cover Letters 5, 26, 53, 54, and 105.

39. **Strive to make your cover letter hard to ignore.** Your task is easier, of course, if you are a great catch for any company. See Cover Letters 44, 46, 70, 87, 88, and 258.

40. **To grab attention, try making your first sentence a bold assertion.** See Cover Letters 49 and 88.

Tempo

41. **If you want to speed the tempo of reading a cover letter, try using a series of short paragraphs.** See Cover Letter 45. Vital words can keep a reader's momentum moving. See Cover Letter 102.

42. **To increase the tempo, make paragraphs progressively shorter.** See Cover Letter 160.

Font and Text Enhancement

43. **Consider using a combination of bullets and boldfacing for information you think the reader must see.** See Cover Letters 7, 21, 45, 74, 86, 89, 104, 134, 175, 177, 191, 220, 234, 240, and 255. It's hard to keep your eyes away from information that is bulleted and bold.

44. **For a change, consider putting key points in italic.** See Cover Letter 11. In a few instances, using italic for the entire letter may be effective. See, for example, Cover Letter 89.

45. **Consider using decorative bullets that relate to the kind of job you are seeking.** See the airplane bullets in Cover Letter 38.

46. **To catch the attention of the reader, include in a cover letter a graphic that you use in the resume.** See Cover Letter 73 and Resume 10, Cover Letter 114 and Resume 12, and Cover Letter 233 and Resume 27.

Language

47. **Try to make each paragraph fresh and free of well-worn expressions commonly found in cover letters.** See, for example, Cover Letter 8 for an original letter.

48. **Try using an open-ended question in showing interest in an interview**. See Cover Letter 191. Unlike a question that calls for a yes or no answer, an open-ended question places on the reader an unexpressed obligation to say something in response.

Tips for Polishing Cover Letters

You might spend several days working on your resume, getting it "just right" and free of errors. But if you send it with a cover letter that is written quickly and contains even one conspicuous error, all of your good effort may be wasted.

You can prevent this kind of tragedy by polishing your cover letter so that it is free of all errors. The following tips can help you avoid or eliminate common errors in cover letters. If you become aware of these kinds of errors and know how to fix them, you can be more confident about the cover letters you send with your resumes.

Word Processing Tips

1. **Adjust the margins for a short letter.** If your cover letter is 300 words or longer, use left, right, top, and bottom margins of one inch. If the letter is shorter, the width of the margins should increase. How much they increase is a matter of personal taste. One way to take care of the width of the top and bottom margins is to center a shorter letter vertically on the page. A maximum width for a short cover letter of 100 words or fewer might be two-inch left and right margins. As the number of words increases by 50 words, you might decrease the width of the left and right margins by two-tenths of an inch.

2. **If you write your letter with word processing or desktop publishing software, use left-justification to ensure that the lines of text are readable with fixed spacing between words.** The letter will have a "ragged right" look along the right margin, but the words will be evenly spaced horizontally. Be wary of using full justification in an attempt to give a letter a printed look. You can make your letter look worse with some extra wide spaces between words. Resume writers who are experienced with certain typesetting procedures—like kerning, tracking, and hyphenating words at the end of some lines—can sometimes use full justification effectively for variety in their documents.

Using Pronouns Correctly

3. **Use *I* and *My* sparingly.** When most of the sentences in a cover letter begin with *I* or *My*, the writer may appear self-absorbed, self-centered, or egotistical. If the reader of the letter is turned off by this kind of impression (even if it is a false one for you), you could be screened out without ever having an interview. Of course, you will need to use these first-person pronouns because most of the information you put in your cover letter will be personal. But try to avoid using *I* and *My* at the beginnings of sentences and paragraphs.

4. **Refer to a business, company, corporation, or organization as "It" rather than "they."** Members of the Board may be referred to as "they," but a company is a singular subject requiring a singular verb. Note this example:

   > New Products, Inc., was established in 1980. It grossed over a million dollars in sales during its first year.

5. **If you start a sentence with *This*, be sure that what *This* refers to is clear.** If the reference is not clear, insert some word or phrase to clarify what *This* means. Compare the following lines:

   > My revised application for the new position will be faxed to you by noon on Friday. You indicated by phone that *this* is acceptable to you.

   > My revised application for the new position will be faxed to you by noon on Friday. You indicated by phone that this *method of sending the application* is acceptable to you.

   A reader of the first sentence wouldn't know what *This* refers to. Friday? By noon on Friday? The revised application for the new position? The insertion after *This* in the second sentence, however, tells the reader that *This* refers to the use of faxing.

6. **Use *as follows* after a singular subject.** Literally, *as follows* means *as it follows*, so the phrase is illogical after a plural subject. Compare the following lines:

Incorrect:	My plans for the day of the interview are as follows:
Fixed:	My plans for the day of the interview are these:
Correct:	My plan for the day of the interview is as follows:
Better:	Here is my plan for the day of the interview:

   In the second set, the improved version avoids a hidden reference problem—the possible association of the silent "it" with *interview*. Whenever you want to use *as follows*, check to see whether the subject that precedes *as follows* is plural. If it is, don't use this phrase.

Using Verb Forms Correctly

7. **Make certain that subjects and verbs agree in number.** Plural subjects require plural forms of verbs. Singular subjects require singular verb forms.

Most writers know these things, but problems arise when subject and verb agreement gets tricky. Compare the following lines:

Incorrect: My education and experience has prepared me. . . .
Correct: My education and experience have prepared me. . . .

Incorrect: Making plans plus scheduling conferences were. . . .
Correct: Making plans plus scheduling conferences was. . . .

In the first set, *education* and *experience* are two things (you can have one without the other) and require a plural verb. A hasty writer might lump them together and use a singular verb. When you reread what you have written, look out for this kind of improper agreement between a plural subject and a singular verb.

In the second set, *making plans* is the subject. It is singular, so the verb must be singular. The misleading part of this sentence is the phrase *plus scheduling conferences*. It may seem to make the subject plural, but it doesn't. In English, phrases that begin with such words as *plus*, *together with*, *in addition to*, *along with*, and *as well as* usually don't make a singular subject plural.

8. **Whenever possible, use active forms of verbs rather than passive forms.** Compare these lines:

Passive: My report will be sent by my assistant tomorrow.
Active: My assistant will send my report tomorrow.

Passive: Your interest is appreciated.
Active: I appreciate your interest.

Passive: Your letter was received yesterday.
Active: I received your letter yesterday.

Sentences with passive verbs are usually longer and clumsier than sentences with active verbs. Spot passive verbs by looking for some form of the verb *to be* (such as *be*, *will be*, *have been*, *is*, *was*, and *were*) used with another verb.

A trade-off in using active verbs is the frequent introduction of the pronouns *I* and *My*. To solve one problem, you might create another (see Tip 3 in this list). The task then becomes one of finding some other way to start a sentence.

9. **Be sure that present and past participles are grammatically parallel in a list.** See Tip 55 in Part 3. What is true about parallel forms in resumes is true also in cover letters. Present participles are action words ending in *-ing*, such as *creating*, *testing*, and *implementing*. Past participles are action words usually ending in *-ed*, such as *created*, *tested*, and *implemented*. These are called *verbals* because they are derived from verbs but are not strong enough to function as verbs in a sentence. When you use a string of verbals, control them by keeping them parallel.

10. **Use split infinitives only when *not* splitting them is misleading or awkward.** An *infinitive* is a verb preceded by the preposition *to*, as in *to create*, *to test*, and *to implement*. You split an infinitive when you insert an adverb

between the preposition and the verb, as in *to quickly create*, *to repeatedly test*, and *to slowly implement*. About 50 years ago, split infinitives were considered grammatical errors, but opinion about them has changed. Many grammar handbooks now recommend that you split your infinitives to avoid awkward or misleading sentences. Compare the following lines:

Split infinitive:	I plan to periodically send updated reports on my progress in school.
Misleading:	I plan periodically to send updated reports on my progress in school.
Misleading:	I plan to send periodically updated reports on my progress in school.

The first example is clear enough, but the second and third examples may be misleading. If you are uncomfortable with split infinitives, one solution is to move *periodically* further into the sentence: "I plan to send updated reports periodically on my progress in school."

Most handbooks that allow split infinitives also recommend that they not be split by more than one word, as in *to quickly and easily write*. A gold medal for splitting an infinitive should go to Lowell Schmalz, an Archie Bunker prototype in "The Man Who Knew Coolidge" by Sinclair Lewis. Schmalz, who thought that Coolidge was one of America's greatest presidents, split an infinitive this way: "*to instantly and without the least loss of time or effort find. . . .*"[1]

Using Punctuation Correctly

11. **Punctuate a compound sentence with a comma.** A compound sentence is one that contains two main clauses joined by one of seven conjunctions (*and, but, or, nor, for, yet,* and *so*). In English, a comma is customarily put before the conjunction if the sentence isn't unusually short. Here is an example of a compound sentence punctuated correctly:

    I plan to arrive at O'Hare at 9:35 a.m. on Thursday, and my trip by cab to your office should take no longer than 40 minutes.

    The comma is important because it signals that a new grammatical subject (*trip*, the subject of the second main clause) is about to be expressed. If you use this kind of comma consistently, the reader will rely on your punctuation and be on the lookout for the next subject in a compound sentence.

12. **Be certain not to put a comma between compound verbs.** When a sentence has two verbs joined by the conjunction *and*, these verbs are called *compound verbs*. Usually, they should not be separated by a comma before the conjunction. Note the following examples:

    I *started* the letter last night *and finished* it this morning.

---

[1] Sinclair Lewis, "The Man Who Knew Coolidge," *The Man Who Knew Coolidge* (New York: Books for Libraries Press, 1956), p. 29.

I *am sending* my resume separately *and would like* you to keep the information confidential.

Both examples are simple sentences containing compound verbs. Therefore, no comma appears before *and*. In either case, a comma would send a wrong signal that a new subject in another main clause is coming, but no such subject exists.

Note: In a sentence with a series of three or more verbs, use commas between the verbs. The comma before the last verb is called the *serial comma*. The serial comma is optional; many writers of business documents omit this comma. For more information on using the serial comma, see resume writing style Tip 70 in Part 3.

13. **Avoid using *as well as* for *and* in a series.** Compare the following lines:

    Incorrect: Your company is impressive because it has offices in
                   Canada, Mexico, as well as the United States.

    Correct: Your company is impressive because it has offices in Canada
                   and Mexico, as well as in the United States.

Usually, what is considered exceptional precedes *as well as*, and what is considered customary follows it. Note this example:

    Your company is impressive because its managerial openings are filled by
    women as well as men.

14. **Put a comma after the year when it appears after the month.** Similarly, put a comma after the state when it appears after the city. Compare the following pairs of lines:

    Incorrect: In January, 1998 I was promoted to senior analyst.
    Correct: In January, 1998, I was promoted to senior analyst.

    Incorrect: I worked in Chicago, Illinois before moving to Dallas.
    Correct: I worked in Chicago, Illinois, before moving to Dallas.

15. **Put a comma after an opening dependent clause.** Compare the following lines:

    Incorrect: If you have any questions you may contact me by phone or
                   fax.
    Correct: If you have any questions, you may contact me by phone or
                   fax.

Actually, many writers of fiction and nonfiction don't use this kind of comma. The comma is useful, though, because it signals where the main clause begins. If you glance at the example with the comma, you can tell where the main clause is without even reading the opening clause. For a step up in clarity and readability, use this comma. It can give you a "feel" for a sentence even before you begin to read the words.

16. **Use semicolons when they are needed.** See resume writing style Tip 71 in Part 3 for the use of semicolons between items in a series. Semicolons are used also to separate main clauses when the second clause starts with a *conjunctive adverb* like *however*, *moreover*, and *therefore*. Compare the following lines:

Incorrect:	Your position in sales looks interesting, however, I would like more information about it.
Correct:	Your position in sales looks interesting; however, I would like more information about it.

The first example is incorrect because the comma before *however* is a *comma splice*, which is a comma that joins two sentences. It's like putting a comma instead of a period at the end of the first sentence and then starting the second sentence. A comma may be a small punctuation mark, but a comma splice is a huge grammatical mistake. What are your chances for getting hired if your cover letter tells your reader that you don't recognize where a sentence ends, especially if a requirement for the job is good communication skills? Yes, you could be screened out because of one little comma!

17. **Avoid putting a colon after a verb or a preposition to introduce information.** The reason is that the colon interrupts a continuing clause. Compare the following lines:

Incorrect:	My interests in your company *are:* its reputation, the review of salary after six months, and your personal desire to hire handicapped persons.
Correct:	My interests in your company *are these:* its reputation, the review of salary after six months, and your personal desire to hire handicapped persons.
Incorrect:	In my interview with you, I would like *to:* learn how your company was started, get your reaction to my updated portfolio, and discuss your department's plans to move to a new building.
Correct:	In my interview with you, I would like to discuss *these issues:* how your company was started, what you think of my updated portfolio, and when your department may move to a new building.

Although some people may say that it is OK to put a colon after a verb like *include* if the list of information is long, it is better to be consistent and avoid colons after verbs altogether.

18. **Understand colons clearly.** People often associate colons with semicolons because they sound alike, but colons and semicolons have nothing to do with each other. Colons are the opposite of dashes. Dashes look backward (see resume writing style Tip 72 in Part 3), and colons usually look forward to information about to be delivered. One common use of the colon does look backward, however. Here are two examples:

My experience with computers is limited: I have had only one course on programming, and I don't own a computer.

I must make a decision by Monday: that is the deadline for renewing the lease for my apartment.

In each example, what follows the colon explains what was said before the colon. Using a colon this way in a cover letter can impress a knowledgeable reader who is looking for evidence of writing skills.

19. **Use slashes correctly.** Information about slashes is sometimes hard to find because *slash* often is listed under a different name, such as *virgule* or *solidus*. If you are not familiar with these terms, your hunt for advice on slashes may lead to nothing.

At least know that one important meaning of a slash is *or*. For this reason, you often see a slash in an expression like ON/OFF. This means that a condition or state, like that of electricity activated by a switch, is either ON or OFF but never ON and OFF at the same time. As you saw in resume writing style Tip 68 in Part 3, this condition may be one in which a change means going from the current state to the opposite (or alternate) state. If the current state is ON and there is a change, the next state will be OFF, and vice versa. With this under-standing, you can recognize the logic behind the following examples:

Incorrect:	ON-OFF switch (on and off at the same time!)
Correct:	ON/OFF switch (on or off at any time)
Incorrect:	his-her clothes (unisex clothes, worn by both sexes)
Correct:	his/her clothes (each sex had different clothes)

Note: Although the slash is correct in *his/her* and is one way to avoid sexism, many people consider this expression clumsy. Consider some other wording, such as "clothes that both men and women wear" or "unisex clothes."

20. **Think twice about using *and/or*.** This stilted expression is commonly misunderstood to mean *two* alternatives, but it literally means *three*. Look at the following example:

If you don't hear from me by Friday, please phone and/or fax me the informa-tion on Monday.

What is the person at the other end to do? The sentence really states three alternatives: just phone, just fax, or phone *and* fax the information by Monday. For better clarity, use the connectives *and* or *or* whenever possible.

21. **Use punctuation correctly with quotation marks.** A common misconcep-tion is that commas and periods should be placed outside closing quotation marks, but the opposite is true. Compare the following lines:

Incorrect:	Your company certainly has the "leading edge", which means that its razor blades are the best on the market.
Correct:	Your company certainly has the "leading edge," which means that its razor blades are the best on the market.

| Incorrect: | In the engineering department, my classmates referred to me as "the guru in pigtails". I was the youngest expert in programming languages on campus. |
| Correct: | In the engineering department, my classmates referred to me as "the guru in pigtails." I was the youngest expert in programming languages on campus. |

Unlike commas and periods, colons and semicolons go *outside* double quotation marks.

Using Words Correctly

22. **Avoid using lofty language in your cover letter.** A real turn-off in a cover letter is the use of elevated diction (high-sounding words and phrases) as a bid to seem important. Note the following examples, along with their straight-talk translations:

| Elevated: | My background has afforded me experience in. . . . |
| Better: | In my previous jobs, I. . . . |

| Elevated: | Prior to that term of employment. . . . |
| Better: | Before I worked at. . . . |

| Elevated: | I am someone with a results-driven profit orientation. |
| Better: | I want to make your company more profitable. |

| Elevated: | I hope to utilize my qualifications. . . . |
| Better: | I want to use my skills. . . . |

In letter writing, the shortest distance between the writer and the reader is the most direct idea.

23. **Check your sentences for an excessive use of compounds joined by *and*.** A cheap way to make your letters longer is to join words with *and* and do this repeatedly. Note the following wordy sentence:

> Because of my background and preparation for work and advancement with your company and new enterprise, I have a concern and commitment to implement and put into effect my skills and abilities for new solutions and achievements above and beyond your dreams and expectations. [44 words]

Just one inflated sentence like that would drive a reader to say, "No way!" The writer of the inflated sentence has said only this:

> Because of my background and skills, I want to contribute to your new venture. [14 words]

If, during rereading, you eliminate the wordiness caused by this common writing weakness, your letter will have a better chance of being read completely.

24. **Avoid using abstract nouns excessively.** Look again at the inflated sentence of the preceding tip, but this time with the abstract nouns in italic:

> Because of my *background* and *preparation* for *work* and *advancement* with your *company* and new *enterprise*, I have a *concern* and *commitment* to implement and put into *effect* my skills and *abilities* for new *solutions* and *achievements* above and beyond your *dreams* and *expectations*.

Try picturing in your mind any of the words in italic. You can't because they are *abstract nouns*, which means that they are ideas and not images of things you can see, taste, hear, smell, or touch. One certain way to turn off the reader of your cover letter is to load it with abstract nouns. The following sentence, containing some images, has a better chance of capturing the reader's attention:

> Having created seven multimedia tutorials with my videocamera and Gateway Pentium computer, I now want to create some breakthrough adult-learning packages so that your company, New Century Instructional Technologies, will exceed $50,000,000 in contracts by 1995.

Compare this sentence with the one loaded with abstract nouns. The one with images is obviously the better attention grabber.

25. **Avoid wordy expressions in your cover letters.** Note the following examples:

> at the location of (at)
> for the reason that (because)
> in a short time (soon)
> in a timely manner (on time)
> in spite of everything to the contrary (nevertheless)
> in the event of (if)
> in the proximity of (near)
> now and then (occasionally)
> on a daily basis (daily)
> on a regular basis (regularly)
> on account of (because)
> one day from now (tomorrow)
> would you be so kind as to (please)

After each of these phrases is a suitable substitute in parentheses. Trim the fat wherever you can, and your reader will appreciate the leanness of your cover letter.

26. **At the end of your cover letter, don't make a statement that the reader can use to reject you.** For example, suppose that you close your letter with this statement:

> If you wish to discuss this matter further, please call me at (555) 555-5555.

This statement gives the reader a chance to think, "I don't wish it, so I don't have to call." Here is another example:

> If you know of the right opportunity for me, please call me at (555) 555-5555.

The reader may think, "I don't know of any such opportunity. How would I know what is right for you?" Avoid questions that prompt yes or no answers, such as, "Do you want to discuss this matter further?" If you ask this kind of question, you give the reader a chance to say no. Instead, make a closing statement that indicates your optimism about a positive response from the reader. Such a statement might begin with one of the following:

> I am confident that
> I look forward to. . . .

In this way, you invite the reader to say yes to further consideration.

2
P·A·R·T

The Gallery of Best Cover Letters

The Gallery
at a Glance

How to Use the Gallery

You can learn much from the Gallery just by browsing through it. To make the best use of this resource, however, read the following suggestions before you begin.

Look at the cover letters in the category containing your field, related fields, or target occupation. Use the Occupation Index to help you find cover letters for certain fields. Notice what kinds of cover letters other people have used to find similar jobs. Always remember, though, that your cover letter should not be "canned." It should not look just like someone else's cover letter but should reflect your own background, unique experiences, knowledge, areas of expertise, skills, motivation, and goals.

Use the Gallery primarily as an "idea book." Even if you don't find a cover letter for your specific position or job target, be sure to look at all the letters for ideas you can borrow or adapt. You may be able to find portions of a letter (the right word, a phrase, a strong sentence, maybe even a well-worded paragraph) that you can use in your own letter but modify with information that applies to your own situation or target field.

Compare some of the beginning paragraphs of the letters. Notice which ones capture your attention almost immediately. In your comparison, notice paragraph length, sentence length, clarity of thought, and the kinds of words that grab your attention. Are some statements better than others from your point of view? Do some paragraphs fit your situation more than others?

Compare some of the closing paragraphs of the letters. What trends do you notice? What differences? What endings are more effective than others? What are the different ways to say thank you? What are the best ways to ask for an interview? How are follow-up plans expressed? What closing paragraphs seem to match your situation best? Continue to note differences in length, the kinds of words and phrases used, and the effectiveness of the content. Jot down any ideas that might be true for you.

If you find this kind of comparative study useful, compare the middle paragraphs across the letters of the Gallery. See how the person introduces herself or himself. Look for a paragraph that seems to be a short profile of an individual. Notice paragraphs devoted to experience, areas of expertise, qualifications, or skills. How does the person express motivation, enthusiasm, or interest in the target position? Which letters use bullets? Which letters seem more convincing than others? How are they more persuasive? Which letters have a better chance of securing an interview?

As you review the middle paragraphs, notice what words and phrases seem to be more convincing than other typical words or phrases. Look for words that you might use to put a certain "spin" on your own cover letter as you pitch it toward a particular interviewer or job target.

After comparing letters, examine the paragraphs of several letters to determine the design or arrangement of each one. For example, the first paragraph of a letter might indicate the individual's job goal, the second paragraph might say something about the person's background, the third paragraph might indicate qualifications, and the last paragraph might express interest in an interview. This letter would then have a Goal-Background-Qualifications-Interview design or pattern. If you review the letters in the Gallery this way, you will soon detect some common cover letter designs. The purpose of doing this is to discover which designs are more effective than others—all so that you can make your cover letter the most effective letter it can be.

By developing a sense of cover letter design, you will know better how to select and emphasize the most important information about you for the job you want to get.

Try comparing the cover letters also for their visual impact. Look for horizontal and vertical lines, borders, boxes, bullets, white space, and graphics. Which cover letters have more visual impact at first glance, and which ones make no initial impression? Do some of the resumes seem more inviting to read than others? Which ones are less appealing because they have too much information, or too little? Which ones seem to have the right balance of information and white space?

After comparing the visual design features, choose the design ideas that might improve your own cover letter. You will want to be selective here and not try to work every design possibility into your letter. Generally, "less is more" in cover letter writing, especially when you integrate design features with content.

The Gallery contains sample cover letters that were prepared by professional resume writers to accompany resumes submitted for this book. In most cases, the names, addresses, and facts have been changed to ensure the confidentiality of the original sender and receiver of the letter. For each letter, however, the essential substance of the original remains intact.

Use the Gallery of cover letters as a reference whenever you need to write a cover letter for your resume. As you examine the Gallery, consider the following questions:

1. **Does the person show a genuine interest in the reader?** One way to tell is to count the number of times the pronouns *you* or *your* appear in the letter. Then count the number of times the pronouns *I*, *me*, and *my* occur in the letter. Although this method is simplistic, it nevertheless helps you see where the writer's interests lie. When you write a cover letter, make your first paragraph *you*-centered rather than *I*-centered.

2. **Where does the cover letter mention the resume specifically?** The purpose of a cover letter is to call attention to the resume. If the letter fails to mention the resume, the letter has not fulfilled its purpose. Besides mentioning the resume, the cover letter might direct the reader's attention to one or more parts of the resume, increasing the chances that the most important part(s) will be seen by the reader. It is not a good idea, however, to put a lot of resume facts in the cover letter. Let each document do its own job. The job of the cover letter is to point to the resume.

3. **Where and how does the letter express interest in an interview?** The immediate purpose of a cover letter is to call attention to the resume, but the *ultimate* purpose of both the cover letter and the resume is to help you get an interview with the person who can hire you. If the letter doesn't display your interest in getting an interview, the letter has not fulfilled its ultimate purpose.

4. **How decisive is the person's language?** This question is closely related to the preceding question. Is interest in an interview expressed directly or indirectly? Does the person specifically request an interview on a date when the writer will be in the reader's vicinity, or does the person only hint at a desire to "meet" the reader some day? When you write your own cover letters, be sure to be direct and convincing in expressing your interest for an interview.

5. **How does the person display self-confidence?** As you look through the Gallery, notice the cover letters in which the phrase "I am confident that…" (or a similar expression) appears. Self-confidence is a sign of management ability and essential job-worthiness. Many of the letters display self-confidence or self-assertiveness in various ways.

6. **Does a letter indicate whether the person is a team player?** From an employer's point of view, an employee who is self-assertive but not a team player can spell T-R-O-U-B-L-E. As you look at the cover letters in the Gallery, notice how the letters mention the word *team*.

7. **How does the letter make the person stand out?** As you read the letters in the Gallery, do some letters present the person more vividly than other letters? If so, what does the trick? The middle paragraphs or the opening and closing paragraphs? The paragraphs or the bulleted lists? Use what you learn here to help you write effective cover letters.

8. **How familiar is the person with the reader?** In a passive job search, the reader will most likely be a total stranger. In an active job search, the chances are good that the writer will have had at least one conversation with the reader by phone or in person. In that case, the letter can refer to any previous communication.

After you have examined the cover letters in the Gallery, you will be better able to write an attention-getting letter—one that leads the reader to your resume and to scheduling an interview with you.

An important note about style and consistency: The 292 cover letters and 35 resumes in this book represent 76 unique styles of writing—the exact number of professional resume writers who contributed to this book. For this reason, you may notice a number of differences in capitalization. To showcase important details, many of the writers prefer to capitalize job titles and other key terms that usually appear in lowercase. Furthermore, the use of jargon may vary considerably—again, reflecting the choices of individual writers and thus making each letter and resume truly "one of a kind."

Variations in the use (or *nonuse*) of hyphens may be noticeable. With the proliferation of industry jargon, hyphens seem like moving targets, and "rules" of hyphenation vary considerably from one handbook to another. In computer-related fields, some terms are evolving faster than the species. Thanks to America Online®, the term *on-line* is more often shown as *online*, but both forms are acceptable. And electronic mail comes in many varieties: *email, e-mail, Email,* and *E-Mail.* But the computer world is not the only one that has variety: both *healthcare* and *health care* appear in the cover letters and companion resumes in this book.

Although an attempt has been made to reduce some of the inconsistencies in capitalization and hyphenation, differences are still evident. Keep in mind that the consistent use of capitalization and hyphenation *within* a cover letter or resume is more important than adherence to any set of external conventions.

Note: To ensure the privacy of their clients, the professional resume writers whose work appears in this book have *fictionalized* the information about their clients. Omitting an address or salutation in a cover letter is another way of protecting a client's privacy. For this reason, some of the letters in this book include generic salutations like "Dear Hiring Manager" or "Dear Sir/Madam." In an actual letter, such a salutation should be replaced with the name of an individual who works at the company to which you are applying.

Note: In some of the comments below the cover letters, the views of the resume writers themselves appear in quotation marks.

William A. Alleva

0000 Honeymoon Lane
Anytown, New York 00000   555/555-5555

Date

Name, Title
Company
Street Address
City, State, Zip

Dear Name:

I am contacting a select number of firms who may be seeking an **Entry-Level Accountant** with a business background. As a highly self-motivated and energetic individual with a strong work ethic, I know the meaning of responsibility and team work. My résumé is enclosed for your perusal.

Highlights of my qualifications that may be of particular interest to you include the following:

- Bachelor of Science in Accounting/Professional Studies.
- Knowledge of general accounting principles, including **financial analysis**, accounts payable/receivable.
- Experience with computers on a range of applications, including Lotus.
- Outstanding research, analytical and problem-solving skills.
- Background in all aspects of customer service and support.

Please let me know if you need additional information. I would welcome your time to explore opportunities within your organization and can assure you that my experience would provide immediate and tangible results.

Thank you for your consideration. I look forward to hearing from you.

Sincerely,

William A. Alleva

Accountant. *Betty Geller, Elmira, New York*
This individual with business experience and strong academic credentials was seeking an entry-level accounting position. The middle three bulleted items echo the resume's Profile.

ROBERT I. BRIGHT

555 South Street
Phoenix, AZ
(000) 000-0000

July 1, xxxx

Donald Trumpet
Communications International
2222 S. South
Phoenix, AZ 49999

Dear Mr. Trumpet:

Thank you for meeting with me to discuss career opportunities at Communications International. The courtesy you extended me only confirms the strong reputation and professionalism that Communications International has earned within the community and abroad.

As we discussed, I feel that my experience and qualifications prepare me to excel at Communications International. A key element of my background is my ability to take a proactive approach in strategizing and planning, which generate tax saving for Communications International as a whole. I approach my work with a strong sense of urgency, work well under pressure, execute time management and organizational skills, and possess strong work ethics. As part of Communications International's professional team, I would work to the maximum of my potential and carry myself in a professional manner at all times.

I would like to reiterate my strong desire to become a part of Communications International and look forward to hearing from you regarding career opportunities.

Sincerely,

Robert I. Bright

Accountant. *Betty Callahan, Vicksburg, Michigan*
A thank-you letter that calls new attention to the applicant's relevant skills and most important worker traits. The final paragraph shows that he really wants to join the firm.

Rose Taylor

3851 Somewhere Ln.

Sierra Vista, AZ 85635

000/000/0000

Email: rtaylor@writeme.com

October 1, xxxx

Dan White
Insurance Adjusters Organization
4514 Commerce St.
Costa, FL 55555

Dear Mr. White:

Please consider this letter of introduction as an expression of my interest in exploring professional opportunities with your organization. I have enclosed my résumé for your review.

At this point in my career, I am seeking to transition my experience into accounting with a dynamic organization that offers an opportunity to utilize my training and develop my knowledge / skills as a professional accountant.

Qualifications I bring to your organization include:

- A career marked by rapid advancement as a result of excellent work habits and strong ethics.
- Track record for significant improvements and innovative solutions.
- Solid technical foundation in accounting fundamentals.

I will work hard to achieve bottom-line results and look forward to discussing how I can contribute to your company's future success. Thank you for your time, consideration and forthcoming response.

Sincerely,

Rose Taylor

Enclosure

3

Accountant. *Rosa St. Julian, Houston, Texas*
Some cover letters are job-oriented. This letter is organization-oriented: in all four paragraphs the writer makes it clear that working for *this* company is a chief interest.

TRONG ON
5555 Drake Avenue ■ Los Angeles, California 55555
(555) 555-5555 / Fax (555) 555-5555 ■ E-mail: xxxxxxt@xxx.com

After researching accounting firms in the Los Angeles area, I believe that I possess the attributes that can make a positive contribution to your organization, and that your firm offers the kind of challenges that I am seeking in developing my accounting skills.

In addition to the obvious skills that are required of accountants — analytical and mathematical strengths, attention to detail, and an ability to work well independently — I possess other strengths that you might find of interest.

To say I am goal-oriented would be an understatement. Since arriving alone in the U.S. at the age of 14, I have enjoyed the satisfaction of knowing that I can accept challenges, remain focused and achieve what I set out to accomplish. During most of my college studies, I worked 30 to 35 hours a week to support my educational goals. As a result of careful personal cash management, I was able to save enough money to resign my last position in order to focus my full-time attention on my final year of studies toward my degree.

I have developed excellent communication skills with people of all cultural backgrounds. As is required in the accounting field, I am able to make complex information understandable to individuals at all required levels as demonstrated by the work I did providing tax preparation assistance this Spring at CSLA. In the workplace, I have always maintained excellent working relationships with clients and coworkers at all levels.

While my enclosed resume outlines my background and academic accomplishments, a personal meeting would better demonstrate the qualifications that I possess. I hope you will consider me a serious candidate for a position with your firm.

Sincerely,

Trong On

enclosure

4

Accountant. *Vivian Van Lier, Valley Glen (Los Angeles), California*
A letter of five paragraphs that refer in turn to this individual's attributes, strengths, goal-orientation, and communication skills, and to the value of "a personal meeting."

WILLIAM GREGSON
3000 Wisteria Drive
Montgomery, Alabama 36000
[334] 555-5555 (Office) - ☎ [334] 555-6666 (Home)
gregsonw@aol.com

December 7, XXXX

Mr. Charles W. Morgan
Chief Financial Officer
Argent Services, Inc.
1200 Ventura Avenue
Suite 100
Montgomery, Alabama 36100

Dear Mr. Morgan:

If you would like to free your senior accounting team for the kind of work they do best, we should talk about my joining the Argent Services' team as your newest accountant.

My résumé can show you just a small sample of the kind of results I can get for your firm and your clients. It also outlines a self-development program, something you probably demand from your accounting staff. However, behind the words you read on the next page is my own professional code:

○ Fixing an accounting problem the client found is the minimum standard; finding and fixing *all* the problems defines excellence.

○ Giving the right answer to accounting questions is the minimum standard; explaining, in simple English, *why* the answers are right, is better.

○ Painstaking attention to detail is the minimum standard; exacting results, delivered *early* enough to capitalize upon their impact, are better.

If my approach appeals to you, I would like to explore how I can serve your firm. May I call your secretary in a few days to arrange an interview for that purpose?

Sincerely,

William Gregson

Enclosure: Resume

5

Accounting Assistant. *Donald Orlando, Montgomery, Alabama*
"This junior accountant had become complaisant in his job—until the firm downsized." The writer focused on the person's "solid approach to new tasks rather his track record."

Alicia Lee Combs

888 SOMERSET DRIVE ◁▷ BLOOMFIELD HILLS, MICHIGAN 48331
248.555.2626

ACCOUNTING PROFESSIONAL

The demands of organizations are more challenging than ever before. With corporate downsizing, business reengineering, and computerized technologies . . . the office administrator is challenged continually. The very good news is . . . I welcome challenges and look forward to implementing new strategies.

As Accounting Manager, I have successfully introduced systems, processes, and methods to increase productivity, improve efficiency, and expand service capabilities. By integrating the capabilities of well-trained staff with sophisticated information technology, I have delivered strong operating results.

Key areas of focus include accounting management, information technology, strategic planning, and human resources. In addition, I have spearheaded a number of business development projects that have contributed to growth and increased profitability.

Although secure in my current position, I am confidentially pursuing new opportunities. In the event you are looking for someone with my credentials, I am enclosing my résumé. I would appreciate your serious consideration and welcome your comments.

Thank you for your time reviewing my credentials. I look forward to speaking with you.

Sincerely,

Alicia Lee Combs

Enclosure: Résumé

6

Accounting Manager. *Lorie Lebert, Novi, Michigan*
A positive letter throughout. The person is challenged by change, has achieved much, is skilled in multiple areas, and does not need a new job but is looking anyway. See Resume 1.

Julius E. Collins
999 Westgate Way
City, State 00000
555-555-5555

November 16, XXXX

Ms. Jane J. Jones
Director of Human Resources
Mega Industries, Ltd.
1234 Industrial Parkway
City, State 00000

Dear Ms. Jones:

As an experienced accountant with over 15 years in the field, I hope to use my skills in an appropriate position with Mega Industries. Your advertisement for an Accounts Payable Manager has caught my interest, and I have enclosed for your consideration a résumé that briefly outlines my qualifications.

Some of the key talents that I can bring to a position with your organization include:

- **General Accounting experience that includes exposure to Accounts Payable, Accounts Receivable, Payroll, and General Ledger. I have also prepared financial reports and projections and participated in budgeting activities.**

- **Experience administering Defined Benefit and Defined Contribution Pension Plans. As an employee of financial institutions, I prepared annual filings and monitored plans for compliance with government regulations. I tracked terminations and new submissions and communicated with plan sponsors, participants, attorneys, accountants, and regulatory authorities.**

- **A mature, disciplined approach to work with the ability to effectively establish priorities and achieve business objectives. I also have supervisory experience in accounting.**

I believe that my experience and professional diligence would allow me to contribute to your success. I would enjoy speaking with you in person to discuss this opportunity, or others, and how I can best serve your needs. Please call me at 555-555-5555 to arrange a meeting. I look forward to talking with you soon.

Thank you.

Sincerely,

Julius E. Collins

Enclosure

Accounts Payable Manager. *Arnold G. Boldt, Rochester, New York*
The writer uses bullets and boldface to highlight the individual's key talents in this response to an ad. Because experience is a key strength, the word *experience* is used throughout.

John Castle
5716 Neely Lane
Montgomery, Alabama 36100
℘ [334] 555-5555

November 27, 19XX

Mr. Marlin Jameson
Saxon Norman LLP
Office of Government Services
Department JA1119
P.O. Box 20011
1101 Wilson Boulevard
Arlington, Virginia 22209

Dear Mr. Jameson:

There has always been an "easy" way to get your policies carried out to increase the bottom line: Put an auditor on your team. And it works – if you have the right auditor. Being the "right" auditor is what I do best. If you think your auditor should be as good at building teamwork as he is at building reports, we should talk.

I recently joined a firm that sought me out to be its asset manager. The job requires both my auditing and accounting skills. Nevertheless, I do best when all my energies, knowledge, and creativity are used to the fullest as an auditor. That is why I am making this confidential application.

My résumé shows a small sample of results I have gotten and can help you learn about my background. But it cannot show you *how* I got payoffs for my organizations. I have always been guided by these few unwavering ideas:

- ☑ Earned trust is everything.
- ☑ Earned trust begins and ends with anticipating and filling needs.
- ☑ Earned trust has nothing to do with caring who gets the credit.

Now I want to use those guidelines and my energies serving your clients. And since words on paper cannot replace face-to-face conversations, I would like to call to set up an interview soon.

Sincerely,

John Castle

Encl.: Résumé

8

Auditor. *Donald Orlando, Montgomery, Alabama*
This letter is strong because in every paragraph the writer successfully presents new and interesting comments, avoiding well-worn expressions commonly found in cover letters.

HARRISON WILLIAMS, CPA

| 8 Shadow Road | New Egypt, New Jersey 08533 | (609) 758-6708 |

Dear Prospective Employer:

As a Certified Public Accountant with a solid systems and procedures background and extensive experience in the commercial real estate industry, I would like to explore the opportunity for employment within your organization. Since 1983, I have been employed by Schroder Real Estate Associates, a New York City registered investment adviser overseeing real estate investments for several corporate and public pension funds.

Focused in the property accounting and reporting areas, I have particular expertise in credit analysis and tax assessment/reporting. Particular achievements include the development of a credit review process for the firm, which I have managed since 1992. In addition to this position, I have been serving as Controller, Property Accounting, since August 1997. In this capacity, I manage other accounting professionals, many of whom are managers.

Since my resume is an overview of my background, I look forward to the opportunity during a personal interview to provide you with further insight into my professional value. Until we meet, thank you for your consideration.

Yours truly,

Harrison Williams, CPA
Enclosure

9

Certified Public Accountant. *Nina K. Ebert, Toms River, New Jersey*
The movement of thought in this letter is from the general to the particular, making clear the person's purpose, areas of expertise, achievements, interest in an interview, and thanks.

LAURIE JONES
1000 N. 25th Avenue
Hollywood, FL 33026
Phone: (954) 000-0000 e-mail: ljones@aol.com

AUTOMOTIVE CONTROLLER

<u>VIA FACSIMILE</u>

TO: Richard Dunn, XYZ Corporation

Dear Mr. Dunn:

I am forwarding the enclosed résumé at the suggestion of Joe Cool in your Accounting Department. I am an automotive controller with over 10 years accounting experience in the automotive industry. My career has been unique, interesting, and unparalleled, and I have achieved a record of fast-track growth. XYZ Corporation impresses me as a progressive organization with vision and opportunity, therefore, I am very interested in investigating career opportunities with you.

Presently an automotive controller with Smith Operations, my responsibilities include, but are not limited to, preparing financial statements, financial reporting, account analysis, cash flow, and compliance. I oversee six managers with 100 employees. Additionally, I am also responsible for turning around troubled dealerships through retraining, automation, streamlining staff, and increasing efficiency.

Some of my successes throughout my career include:

- I collected $700,000+ in old outstanding receivables
- I was instrumental in dealership's rise from #2 to #1 in sales
- I increased computer capacity from 50%-80%, eliminating need for extra personnel
- I initiated and wrote a 400-page accounting policies and procedures manual which has since been inforce by the Internal Audit Department

My strengths include increasing productivity and efficiency through proper training. I am also an excellent troubleshooter/problem solver. I work well with all levels of management and maintain a high standard of professionalism.

May we arrange a time to meet to discuss XYZ's goals and objectives and how my background can help you achieve them? I thank you for your time and consideration of my credentials and appreciate your confidentiality in this matter. I look forward to speaking with you soon and hearing your comments.

Sincerely,

Laurie Jones

Encl.

10

Controller. *Shelley Nachum, Ft. Lauderdale, Florida*
A substantial letter. It expresses in turn the occasion for the letter, the person's present responsibilities, successes (quantified), strengths, interest in an interview, and thanks.

BRADLEY JONES
888 Cross Town Court
City, State 00000
(555) 555-5555
E-mail: BJ0000@college.edu

October 7, XXXX

Mr. Bean Counter, CPA
Managing Partner
Counter & Associates, LLP
1234 Executive Tower
City, State 11111

Dear Mr. Counter:

As a Senior majoring in Accounting at CIT, my long-term goal is to pursue a career as a CPA with a public accounting firm. Currently, I am seeking a co-op assignment beginning in mid-November that will further my professional objectives and fulfill my educational requirements. For this reason, I have enclosed for your consideration a résumé that briefly outlines my qualifications.

Some key points that I would like to bring to your attention include:

- *As a Dean's List student at CIT, I have taken numerous courses in Accounting, Finance, and Business Management. This has exposed me to the various aspects of the Accounting field and prepared me to learn more in a real-world environment.*

- *As Treasurer of the CIT chapter of Alpha Beta Gamma, I have been responsible for maintaining accounting records and for financial reporting to the student government. I also play an integral role in preparing the organization's budget for submission to and approval by the student government.*

- *In addition to helping me defray educational expenses, my employment experiences have taught me personal responsibility and the importance of both teamwork and leadership. I have also gained firsthand insights into manufacturing, food service, and contracting businesses, which I hope will prove helpful in my future role as an Accountant.*

I am confident that as a co-op student, I could make a contribution to your firm and its clients while furthering my understanding of the Accounting profession. I would appreciate the opportunity to meet with you to discuss how my joining your staff would be mutually beneficial. Please call me at (555) 555-5555 to arrange a convenient date and time for an in-person interview. I look forward to speaking with you soon.

Should your firm not have any co-op opportunities available, I would be grateful if you would pass my résumé along to any of your colleagues or clients who might have such an opening.

Thank you.

Sincerely,

Bradley Jones

Enclosure

11

Co-op position for Accounting Major. *Arnold G. Boldt, Rochester, New York*
This senior was looking for a co-op assignment to fulfill graduation requirements. Key points in italic attest to the person's course preparation, fraternity duties, and work experience.

NELLIE S. O'BRIEN

555 Smith Lane
San Jose, NM 00000

(555) 555-5555
nobrien@jose.net

May 15, XXXX

Ms. Hiring Person
Director, Human Resource
The Great Company
Futuristic Road
San Jose, CA 0000

Dear Ms. Person:

I am interested in discussing employment possibilities at The Great Company. Having been promoted rapidly at my current place of employment, I am now limited in professional growth. Therefore, I am exploring new career opportunities.

During the time since I worked at The Great Company, I have kept abreast of the ever-changing business world. One of the most important areas, I believe, is emerging technology.   As co-owner of Snelling Accounting Company, I executed the implementation and operation of a new computer system. My career success is due largely to my ability to excel in a fast-paced environment.

I am not a beginner, but rather a well-seasoned professional with over 20 years of experience building and keeping current with the changes in the business forum. I sincerely believe that, with my experience and desire for personal and professional growth, I will be an asset to The Great Company.

If you need further information, I will gladly respond upon request and would appreciate the opportunity for a personal interview. Thank you for your time and consideration, and I look forward to hearing from you soon.

Very truly yours,

Nellie O'Brien

enclosure

12

General accounting position. *Gwen Haggerty, Delaware, Ohio*
Because of her spouse's death, this "seasoned professional" had to close a successful company and find a job. She sent this letter to the firm where she once worked for 20 years.

CARLOS CAMPOS
111 West Page Drive
City, State 00000
(555) 555-5555
E-mail: CC9999@college.edu

June 25, xxxx

Mr. Percy P. Pennywise, Managing Partner
Pennywise, Poundfoolish, & Associatcs, LLC
1234 Executive Tower
City, State 11111

Dear Mr. Pennywise:

As I am just completing the requirements for my MBA in Accounting at City Institute of Technology, I am exploring potential opportunities with a well-established firm that will lead to a career as a CPA. I hope to join an organization where I can learn and grow within the Accounting profession and build a long-term relationship. With these goals in mind, I have enclosed for your consideration and review a résumé that briefly outlines my credentials.

Some of the key experiences I can bring to an entry level position with your firm include:

- **Administering Accounts Receivable and Payroll for an engineering firm that was also engaged in construction and some custom manufacturing.**

- **Preparing individual tax returns as part of a volunteer program in conjunction with CIT.**

- **Serving as Treasurer of a campus organization, Delta Beta Gamma, which encompassed maintaining financial records and providing financial reports to the auditing CPA and to the national organization.**

- **Proficiency with basic Windows and Microsoft Office applications, as well as a keen interest in technology and high-tech businesses.**

I am confident that my education and experience to date provide me with skills that would be beneficial to your firm and its clients. Given the opportunity to learn and grow within your organization and successfully pursue CPA certification, I believe that I can significantly contribute to your long-term success. I would enjoy speaking with you in person to discuss the possibilities that exist and how I can best serve the needs of your firm and your clients. Please call me at **(555) 555-5555** to arrange a convenient date and time for us to meet. I look forward to opening a dialogue with you soon.

Thank you.

Sincerely,

Carlos Campos

Enclosure

13

Entry-level accounting position for new M.B.A. *Arnold G. Boldt, Rochester, New York*
The person wanted a job with a CPA firm and to achieve CPA certification. Because some candidates get their CPA and leave, this letter shows interest in a long-term commitment.

COST ACCOUNTANT, CPA   1 Accounting Blvd.
                                                    New York, New York 99999
                                                            (000) 000-0000

September 9, XXXX

Mr. Mark Swing, Manager   Hand Carried
Yatesville Country Club
P. O. Box 9999
Yatesville, New York 11111-2222

Dear Mr. Swing:

Wednesday of last week I spoke with you on the telephone concerning the part-time Accounting position.

As you can see from the attached résumé, I have worked in almost every facet of the accounting field. As an internal auditor, I used computer systems to examine and evaluate the company's financial and information systems, management procedures, and internal controls to ensure that records were accurate and controls were adequate to protect against fraud and waste. I have reviewed company operations — evaluating their efficiency, effectiveness, and compliance with corporate policies and procedures, laws, and government regulations. I have handled budgeting, performance evaluation, cost management, and asset management. More specifically, I have experience with accounts receivable, accounts payable, general and tax ledger reports, payroll, and sales tax functions. I am familiar with a number of software packages used to facilitate accounting procedures.

My qualifications and flexible scheduling capabilities would be an asset to Yatesville Country Club. Please contact me for an interview.

Sincerely,

Cost Accountant

Enclosure

14

Part-time accounting position. *Sally McIntosh, Jacksonville, Illinois*
This individual had been out of the workforce for five years to raise children. The letter calls attention to the person's extensive experience, computer skills, and flexible schedule.

Maggie Morris, CPA

5555 Actress Boulevard
Dramatic, Montana 55555
(555) 555-5555 - Office • (555) 555-5556 - Home

January 15, current year

Mike Bryant, CPA
A-Plus Accounting Services
555 Chestnut Lane
Dramatic, MT 55555

Dear Mr. Bryant:

The busy season is here once again, and I'm sure you, like many others, have already counted the days to April 15. I'd like to make this difficult time of year go a little more smoothly for you by offering my accounting expertise on a part-time basis—to help fill in wherever extra help is needed. My expertise is in the area of corporate auditing (both financial and compliance), but I would gladly accept general bookkeeping/accounting work, payroll processing, or research. Although my tax experience is limited, I am a quick study and could certainly serve as an assistant to free valuable time for your tax experts.

As you can see from my enclosed résumé, I am currently employed full time. I would like to supplement my income, however, and would be happy to accept 10-15 hours per week in the evenings and weekends (when I'm sure many of your own employees need to unwind a little). I'm confident of my ability to help you solve some of your company's pressing time problems. My work is accurate, thorough, and punctual. Whether large projects or small—you can count on me to get the job done.

Thank you for considering my qualifications. I would very much appreciate an opportunity to discuss part-time opportunities. Please call me at either number listed above at your convenience. I look forward to talking with you soon.

Sincerely,

Maggie Morris, CPA

Enclosure

15

Part-time accounting position. *Barbie Dallmann, Charleston, West Virginia*
A broadcast letter for a person seeking part-time accounting beyond full-time work. The letter is sent in January when firms need extra help for the tax season. See Resume 2.

JANICE M. RICH
8197 Trailway Lane • Relay, Maryland 21000 • (000) 000-0000

May 10, XXXX

Jackson & Ferns Associates
Attn: Ms. M. E. Cooper
4420 Peach Tree Ave., Suite 1
Atlanta, Georgia 22255

Dear Ms. Cooper:

Enclosed is my resume for your review and consideration for possible employment opportunities in your organization in the area of accounting or office management. I am confident that my broad-based experience in various aspects of finance, accounting, bookkeeping, contract administration, supervision, and management would serve as an asset to your company. A synopsis of my qualifications follows:

- *Over eight years of experience in office management, supervision, training, and managing people.*
- *Over 14 years of diverse accounting experience including accounts payable, accounts receivable, payroll, inventory, and bank reconciliations.*
- *Completed over 98 semester hours in Management at Temple University, Temple, Texas.*
- *Self-motivated; able to set effective priorities to achieve immediate and long-term goals and meet operational deadlines.*

In addition to the above, I have worked with construction managers, project managers, engineers, and technical and support personnel as well as owners and managers of businesses. I am able to establish effective rapport with supervisors and subordinates, and I have "hands-on" knowledge of office procedures.

I strongly believe that my experience, coupled with my education and can-do attitude, will enable me to contribute very quickly to your company's efforts. I would welcome an opportunity to present my career and discuss how it might apply to your hiring needs. I look forward to hearing from you at your earliest convenience.

Sincerely,

Janice M. Rich

Enclosure

16

Project Manager. *Ms. Earl M. Melvin, Columbia, Maryland*
The opening paragraph indicates the person's goal and breadth of experience. Qualifications highlight experience, education, and skills—three themes restated in the last paragraph.

John A. Doe

1234 Any Street   24-Hour Voice Mail: 555.555.5555
City, IN 55555   E-Mail: 0000@xxx.com

October 30, XXXX

Bigfirm, USA
5555 That Street, Suite 7A
Municipality, IN 00000

Attn: Mr. Big, CEO

RE: Senior Accountant Position

Dear Mr. Big:

I was referred to you by John Q. Public, whom I met yesterday at a financial planning seminar
coordinated by Smith & Smith S.C. Mr. Public mentioned that your firm is in the process of
selecting candidates for a new Senior Accountant. Enclosed please find a summary of my
qualifications for your review.

Experienced in financial management of large and small companies, I have developed methods
of evaluating business growth so that goals are met within reasonable time frames. Recently, I
volunteered to analyze the ledgers of a local nonprofit organization in order to identify
effective cost-cutting strategies. Addressing challenges such as this one is a great way for me
to develop new skills while building on those that I have already mastered.

When you have had a chance to look over my credentials, I would welcome the opportunity to
meet with you to discuss this job opening. Next week I will be contacting your secretary to
arrange for an interview. In the interim, if you have any questions or if you would like me to
furnish a list of references, please do not hesitate to call or e-mail me. I look forward to
speaking with you soon.

Very truly yours,

John Doe

Enc.

17

Senior Accountant. *Tina Merwin, Milwaukee, Wisconsin*
This letter displays a subject (RE:) line and a phone number format becoming popular, with periods
as separators (see also Cover Letter 6). The occasion for the letter is a referral.

CHRISTINE CALDWELL
11 Severn Court, Apt. C
Severn, MD 55555
(555) 555-5555

October 1, XXXX

Dear Recruiter,

Your recent advertisement in The Accounting Gazette for a **Senior Accountant** caught my eye. This is exactly the kind of position for which I have been looking. It seems to require the skills and experience I have acquired in my previous work assignments.

My resume is enclosed for your review. I would like to call attention to the similarities between your requirements and my qualifications:

YOUR REQUIREMENTS	MY QUALIFICATIONS
1. Bachelor's degree in Accounting	1. 1995 BS, Accounting Central College of Maryland, Somerville, MD
2. Two years' experience	2. Over 2 years' experience as a Senior Accountant in the Health Care and Pharmaceutical industries
3. Microsoft Excel and Word	3. Microsoft Excel, Word, and MS Project Management

I would appreciate more information concerning this position as well as an opportunity to meet with you to discuss our mutual interests. Please contact me if you require any further background information. With keen interest, I look forward to hearing from you to schedule a meeting. Thank you for your consideration.

Sincerely,

Christine Caldwell

Enc.

18

Senior Accountant. *Susan Guarneri, Lawrenceville, New Jersey*
A letter with two-column format (Your Requirements . . . My Qualifications), which is useful for making evident a match between a position and the applicant's experience and skills.

MATTHEW A. PORTER

8910 Stillwell Avenue, #1234
Lutz, Florida 33549
(813) 000-0000

March 10, 1997

Mr. Richard James
R & J Associates, P. A.
2300 Ashley Drive
Suite 555
Tampa, Florida 33600

Dear Mr. James:

I am interested in exploring your firm's need for a senior-level, corporate accountant. At this juncture of my career, I am pursuing more challenging, professional roles where my broad scope of accounting and MIS experience will bring immediate value to corporate operations.

Highlights of my qualifications include:

- B.S. degree in Accounting from the University of Florida.

- Senior-level management experience emphasizing corporate leadership, P&L accountability, progressive accomplishments and successive advancement.

- Expertise in strategic planning, business operations, automated accounting systems, software applications, and upholding fiscal efficiency.

- Peak performance in orchestrating directives, producing bottom-line results, problem solving, and making prudent decisions.

- Well-developed time management, organizational, communication and interpersonal skills.

Enclosed is my resume, which will provide a more detailed summation of my experience and key accomplishments. If you have a need, I could do an excellent job for you. May we talk?

Sincerely,

Matthew Porter

Enclosure

19

Senior Corporate Accountant. *Diane McGoldrick, Tampa, Florida*
The opening paragraph indicates not only the goal but also the rationale for the change. Qualification highlights include education, experience, expertise, performance, and skills.

KAREN O'KEEFE
150 Serpentine Way
Bridgeton, DE 00000
(555) 555-5555

To those concerned:

As I plan on relocating to the Chicago area, I am exploring career opportunities in public accounting with your firm. For most of the past year, I have been employed as a staff accountant at a CPA/business consulting firm in Delaware, primarily supporting one partner but assisting at all levels to maintain the efficiency of the organization. I believe that with my educational preparation, prior work experience and desire for increased responsibility, I will prove to be a solid contributor to your company's continued success.

A copy of my resume is enclosed for your review, where you will note that much of my background centered on tax accounting. To increase my value, I have researched tax laws on my own initiative to gain a broader understanding for the benefit of our clients. In addition, my major strength in computer applications has facilitated the handling of complex tax planning issues and various other analytical functions. My work with financial statements has thus far involved compilations and reviews, but given the opportunity, I am confident that I can excel in auditing as well.

Should you have a position available for someone with my qualifications, I would greatly appreciate your consideration of me. I will be calling your office within the next week to determine your interest and perhaps arrange a personal interview. In the interim, if you require any additional information, you may contact me at the above phone number.

Sincerely,

Karen O'Keefe

Enclosure: Resume

20

Staff Accountant. *Melanie A. Noonan, West Paterson, New Jersey*
Relocation is the reason for this individual's search for a new job. The target is not a specific position but any position that would match the individual's education, experience, and skills.

RICHARD ALAN MANN

5555 North University Avenue
Daly City, California 95555
(555) 555-5555

May 14, xxxx

Jane Deer, Professional Recruiter
Accounting Firm
One Market Plaza, Suite 555
San Francisco, CA 95555

Re: Staff Accountant / CPA Candidate

With the close of the tax season, your firm is likely planning for next year's demands and evaluating the need for new staff accountants. If so, please consider the enclosed résumé. Qualifications I would bring to your organization include the following:

- **Experience as revenue agent with the IRS:** My four years as a revenue agent with the Internal Revenue Service included intensive training in the Tax Reform Act, TEFRA, fraud awareness and bribery, audits of tax shelters, and quality management, as well as work in the areas of individual, sole proprietorship, partnership, and corporate tax law.

  My performance merited above-average scores on evaluations and resulted in assignment to the more difficult and technically complex cases. Supervisors characterized me as "very cooperative" and willing to participate in other assignments, as evidenced by my volunteer service at taxpayer assistance programs and selection as an automated exam system coordinator for my 10-member examination group.

- **Broad range of additional financial experiences:** As a tax consultant and financial planner with Secure Financial Advisors, I prepared tax returns for business clients and advised individuals on retirement planning, estate planning, college planning, debt management, tax minimization, survivor protection, and income and asset protection. As finance manager for a high-volume automotive dealership, I negotiated contracts, secured financing for customers, and oversaw processing of DMV documentation.

- **Academic preparation:** My continuing education efforts include current enrollment in the Masters in Taxation program at UC Berkeley. I plan to take the Enrolled Agent exam in September and the CPA exam in November. My baccalaureate degree is in Business Administration from St. Mary's College.

I will call next week to ensure your receipt of this material and look forward to learning more about your firm's needs. In advance, thank you for your time.

Sincerely,

Richard A. Mann

Enclosure

21

Staff Accountant. *Susan Britton Whitcomb, Fresno, California*
A strong letter that contains much specific information. Square bullets point to embedded headings in boldface. The person keeps the initiative by being the one to call "next week."

GREGORY L. GRIFFIN
555 Parker Road • Smithfield, New York • 55555
555 • 555-5555

September 12, 1998

Matthew J. Chaucer
Office of the State Comptroller
A. E. Smith Office Bldg.
Albany, NY 12236

Dear Mr. Chaucer:

I am writing in response to your advertisement in the September 10th edition of the *Times Union* for the position of State Accounts Auditor Trainee. I feel that I have excellent supporting qualifications for this position, and would appreciate your careful consideration of my credentials as presented on the enclosed resume.

As my resume indicates, I have a B.S. degree in Accounting as well as experience as a senior tax clerk with the Golden Corporation, where I am responsible for payroll, sales and excise tax returns for the parent company and its subsidiaries. In addition, I also do extensive analysis via Lotus 1-2-3. Prior to this, I was a staff auditor with Easton & Young in Albany, NY. My activities within this position included performing a wide range of auditing functions for banking, manufacturing, not-for-profits, and health care clients.

Equally strong are my organizational, problem-solving and communication skills. I thrive in fast-paced environments that require independent thinking and decisive action. I am ready to meet new challenges and deliver strong results as a valued member of your audit team.

I would welcome the opportunity for a personal interview. If you require any additional information prior to our meeting, please contact me at the above referenced address or telephone number. I look forward to speaking with you soon.

Thank you for your time and consideration.

Sincerely,

Gregory L. Griffin

Enclosure: [resume]

22

State Accounts Auditor Trainee. *Barbara M. Beaulieu, Scotia, New York*
The letter expresses in turn the person's purpose, experience, skills, interest in an interview, and thanks. The individual was offered the position after very competitive interviews.

94 Meadowlark Lane
Cityville, Nevada 55555
(555) 555-5555

March 11, XXXX

McMahon & Paulsen, LLP
Suite 55
South Olsen Street
Cityville, Nevada 55555

Position of Interest – Tax Preparer or Accountant

For the past nine years I have worked for Bigname Tax Co., and from XXXX to the present I have had oversight of fourteen to nineteen tax offices throughout the state. My accomplishments and areas of expertise are outlined on the enclosed resume.

I am exploring opportunities not only in the tax field, but also in other management areas such as general accounting, financial services, human resources, and recruiting of accounting or management personnel. My contributions to the field have been significant, as is evidenced by my focus on bottom-line figures and profitability. Outstanding skills in customer and client services, as well as employee motivation and training, have resulted in measurable successes in account retention and expansion, expense reduction and high revenue generation.

Other assets and strengths include sound decision making, integrity, zest for challenge, and excellent presentation skills. My ability to oversee multiple branches and franchises with ease attests to my overall managerial and organizational style, as well as my emphasis on employee responsibility and empowerment. Obviously, teamwork has been an important component in my vision for success.

I would welcome the opportunity to join a top-flight executive team concerned with productivity, quality customer service and managed growth patterns. You will find my salary requirements to be in line with my experience and level of responsibility. I will be contacting your office to set up an appointment to review my past performance and successes in greater detail. I look forward to our conversation.

Sincerely,

Lars Blanning

Enclosure

Tax Preparer or Accountant. *Beverley Drake, Rochester, Minnesota*
This letter begins with statements about work experience and then indicates in subsequent paragraphs the individual's areas of expertise, skills, strengths, and follow-up plans.

Joseph Financial, CPA

10 Money Terrace
Cash, New Jersey 07040

Home: (201) 555-5555
Office: (212) 444-4444

February 13, xxxx

HR Dept./C
Major Stock Exchange
1000 Stock Road
New York, New York 11111

Dear Hiring Manager:

Please accept this letter and enclosed résumé as expressed interest in the advertised Vice President/Controller position. Since March of xxxx, I have served as Controller of the New XYZ Exchange and previously held the position of Controller at the Coffee, Sugar & Cocoa Exchange during the late 1980s.

During my tenure at the XYZ Exchange, the ZYX Exchange Inc. was acquired, and it was my chief responsibility to merge the financial systems and operations of the two exchanges in an orderly and efficient fashion. I successfully executed a seamless transition, while at the same time, effecting a significant reduction in labor costs. Additional accomplishments and strengths include but are not limited to:

❑ Implementation of a new client-server-based accounting system (Computron), which is similar to that being utilized at your exchange. Served as Chief Architect of the installation, making all major implementation decisions.

❑ Extremely skilled and knowledgeable in accounting systems and software, including Computron, Solomon, Real World, SBT, MCBA, Excel and Lotus 1-2-3.

❑ Executed several conversions and system enhancements that improved, streamlined and maximized efficiency of internal controls, financial reporting and other fiscal management processes.

❑ Knowledgeable in fee structures, auditing and compliance issues.

I believe that my combined experience at both Exchanges speaks for itself and indicates that I would be the ideal candidate for the Controller's position. I would appreciate the opportunity for a personal interview, at your convenience, to discuss this further. My salary requirement is $125,000 plus bonus per year; however, it is negotiable based upon job responsibilities and benefits. If you need any additional information, please feel free to contact me at the above address or telephone number(s).

Thank you very much for your time and consideration. I look forward to hearing from you in the near future.

Sincerely,

Joseph Financial

Joseph Financial

Enclosure

24

Vice President/Controller. *Judith Friedler, New York, New York*
The entire letter is designed to show that the individual is the "ideal candidate" for the position. Shadowed square bullets point to impressive achievements and strengths.

Pollie Ann Naguri

555 Blossom Street
Los Cabrillos, CA 99999
(660) 444-4444

Dear Hiring Manager:

I am the proverbial "right-hand" person, having twice helped CEOs build start-ups into thriving businesses. I accomplished this with top-notch organizational skills, a can-do attitude and plenty of persistence.

For instance, it took plenty of persistence to approach 24 city managers before finally securing a contract that developed into $3.5M in annual sales. In fact, one manager said, "I knew I had to meet you because you weren't going away."

Although I am no stranger to marketing, my interest lies in providing administrative support for a growing company's vision. I have 10 years of such experience, from assisting in the incorporation process to coordinating projects, developing programs and writing procedures.

If you could use someone with proven ability to complement an executive's efforts, I would do an excellent job for your organization.

I look forward to meeting you.

Sincerely,

Pollie Ann Naguri

enclosure: résumé

25

Administrative Consultant. *Ms. Sydney J. Reuben, Menlo Park, California*
The challenge was to qualify this person for a lesser position (from Director to Executive Assistant). The writer therefore stressed support skills in three of the five paragraphs.

CONFIDENTIAL

Susan Bond
1340 Prairie View Road
Missoula, Montana 59800
℘[406] 555-5557

June 7, XXXX

Dr. Charles W. Thayer
Thayer Medical Group
Suite 200
125 Division Street
Missoula, Montana 59802

Dear Dr. Thayer:

Lack of time translates into more than lack of money. When the business of business demands your constant attention, it robs you of practicing the profession you worked so hard to enter. And your patients miss the care only you can give. I think I can help.

My profession is making all that necessary administration transparent—but not invisible—to busy practitioners. But it doesn't stop there. I have the gift for designing, building and running support systems that do more than keep records. My work can contribute to your bottom line.

For the last eight years I have administered a medium-sized organization, bringing it out of inefficiency and confusion and into its most profitable period yet. My employer values what I do. Now, however, I want a new challenge. I would like to put my talents, energy and drive to work for the Thayer Medical Group.

To help you learn more about my track record, I have enclosed a résumé. However, when it comes to discussing something of mutual benefit, nothing tops a face-to-face meeting.

In the next few days, I will be calling to see when your schedule might accommodate an interview. I think we will both find that time well spent.

Sincerely,

Susan Bond

Susan Bond

One enclosure: Résumé

CONFIDENTIAL

26

Administrator of Support Systems. *Donald Orlando, Montgomery, Alabama*
Many cover letters just make assertions. The mood of this letter is persuasive: it argues that the reader needs the person's services and that an interview would be "well spent."

JESSE LANG
1234 Candy Lane South
Anycity, Washington 98000-0000
(555) 123-1212

July 29, XXXX

Mary Smith, Executive Placement
Northwest Energy
7823   164th Avenue
Anycity, Anystate 99999

Dear Ms. Smith:

RE: Executive Assistant, #12-EA position advertised in the July 28 issue of *The Times*

As an experienced Executive Assistant who has successfully supported senior-level management personnel over an 18-year career, I have developed the skills and acquired the knowledge to ensure the highest level of competence, time management, and confidentiality. My ongoing objective is to make my boss' job easier, and I have consistently been successful in doing just that. It is this ability, plus commitments to quality, that make me an excellent candidate for Executive Assistant, #12-EA, currently open at Northwest Energy.

For 14 years I served as an Executive Assistant and Secretary to the Vice President of Campaign and Resource Development for the American Heart Association. Driving the fund-raising for up to $60 million, my supervisor needed — and received   efficient, effective response to up to 30 telephone calls daily, coordination of materials for and activities by loaned executives from all major U.S. businesses, and on-time delivery of up to 100 pieces of correspondence each day.

As your newest Executive Assistant, you can expect the same performance that past employers have praised:

- ❑ Loyalty and service.
- ❑ Competence with intricate attention to detail.
- ❑ Customer service and solid follow-through abilities.
- ❑ Proficient computer and office service skills.
- ❑ Time management and excellent prioritizing and organization strengths.
- ❑ Extensive experience scheduling and coordinating activities, including that of other internal and external customers at all levels of management.

I look forward to discussing in greater detail with you the ways in which I can assist Northwest Energy. I will call you next week to schedule a conversation.

Sincerely,

Jesse Lang
Enclosure: Résumé

27

Executive Assistant. *Carole S. Barns, Woodinville, Washington*
This longtime employee of a major charity was "reorganized" out of a position and felt that she could not find a new job. Her excellent skills—highlighted here—got her many job offers.

Lori D. Harris

152-1 Safi Rd – Fort Hood, TX 76544   **(000) 000-0000**

Dear Sir/Madam:

I am seeking a position with your organization and have enclosed my resume for your review in light of your current or future need for Administrative Support. I have excellent qualifications for this position and would appreciate your careful consideration.

My background is diverse and covers a variety of experiences that would be directly transferable to a position you may have open. Highlights include:

- Experience in administrative support, cash handling, reception, and customer service.

- Computer literacy and ability to operate general office and accounting machines.

- Excellent powers of deductive reasoning and ability to teach by personal involvement and example.

- Professional manner with good interpersonal and communication skills.

- Equally effective as a Leader, Team Member, or Independent Contributor.

If you are looking for someone with my qualifications, or if you are aware of any openings outside your organization, I would appreciate hearing from you.

Thank you, for your time and consideration.

Sincerely,

Lori D. Harris

Enclosure(s)

28

File Record Clerk. *Jackie Sexton, Fort Hood, Texas*
The individual spent much time working for temporary agencies and needed a permanent job. The cover letter was put on disk for the person to customize as needed. See Resume 3.

Dianne T. Meyers

7 Larkspur Lane • Needham, MA 02492 • (555) 555-5555

May 15, xxxx

James P. Donovan
Wingate Assisted Living
673 Rockport Avenue
Wellesley, MA 02481

Dear Mr. Donovan:

I am interested in an opportunity to apply my excellent secretarial skills to your organization. A résumé is enclosed for your consideration.

My versatile background — encompassing over 25 years at Wellesley College and shorter stints in legal, medical, and business fields — enables me to work successfully in many settings. I have a solid track record handling the full array of office tasks and maintaining the smooth flow of business, and my computer skills are up-to-date. In particular, my organizational and interpersonal skills and ability to handle multiple tasks simultaneously are well suited to facilitate operations in your busy office. I am dedicated, hardworking, and committed to enhancing the administrative and clerical functions of your company.

After a long period of service for one institution, I have worked in several short-term assignments which have broadened my experience and increased my flexibility. At this time in my career, I am confident that my skills and experience could benefit your company.

I would welcome the opportunity to discuss this with you further. You may contact me at the phone number above.

Thank you.

Sincerely,

Dianne Meyers

29

Secretary. *Wendy Gelberg, Needham, Massachusetts*
The challenge was to lessen the negative impact of many short-term jobs after a long-term job at Wellesley College, so the writer made the short jobs look positive. See Resume 4.

JANE DOE
000 East Main Blvd.
Somewhere, FL 00000
(000) 000-0000

ADVERTISING EXECUTIVE

Dear Advertising Professional:

As a key player in the competitive world of advertising, I understand that success depends on a strong commitment to client satisfaction, a team approach, and the ability to execute strong marketing and advertising campaigns. Finding new business solutions and opportunities, as well as innovative ideas, is also paramount to increasing the bottom line. I believe my extensive background in account management, account service, media buying, marketing, production, communications, and client relations reflects a commitment to these challenges and to this industry.

Experienced on both the client and agency sides, in the areas of retail, communications, finance, healthcare, media, automotive, and sports marketing, I am proficient in strategic planning and knowledgeable in all phases of print and broadcast production. A great deal of my experience has been in media buying, including developing media plans, negotiating contracts, placement, scheduling, billing, and reconciliation of ads. While at Potamkin Corp. in New York City, I managed a monthly in-house media budget of $250,000-$450,000.

As an account manager, I supervise and direct the account team, manage agency resources, conduct day-to-day orchestration and integration of all aspects of my accounts, and interact extensively with all parties involved in the campaigns. I motivate staff and create an environment that sparks a team approach, resulting in achievement of our goals. My continued success is attributed to my commitment to effective and efficient client service. I have strong communication and organization skills and can successfully handle a number of projects simultaneously while working well under pressure to meet deadlines.

I would appreciate the opportunity to meet with you to discuss your marketing needs and how I could fit into your organization. I have enclosed my résumé for your review and consideration, and I look forward to hearing your comments.

Very truly yours,

Jane Doe

Encl.

30

Advertising Executive. *Shelley Nachum, Ft. Lauderdale, Florida*
The opening paragraph expresses the individual's views about success in advertising and her commitment to that success. The rest of the letter shows her experience, duties, and skills.

CARLA V. SALVADOR

711 Lane Court • City, State 44444 • (555) 555-5555
e-mail: salva@coolnet.com

September 9, XXXX

Mr. Video Musikus
Human Resources Department
MTV
New York, New York 10011

Dear Mr. Musikus:

As a dynamic marketing professional with agency and television news experience, I am seeking an opportunity to combine my advertising and broadcasting skills in a marketing position with an entertainment company. For this reason, I have enclosed for your consideration a résumé that outlines my career.

Some professional highlights that I wish to draw to your attention include the following:

- *Managing a national media campaign that encompassed print and electronic ads, press coverage nationally and in local markets, and a promotional tour by a celebrity spokesman (Fred Famous) which culminated with appearances on "Late Night with Conan O'Brien" and "Live with Regis & Kathie Lee."*

- *Servicing major accounts for campaigns promoting consumer products and business-to-business services and products. This role encompasses functioning as a liaison between the client and the agency's creative departments, as well as handling outside media relations.*

- *Supervising studio and field production crews providing live coverage of major sports events. In addition, I have hands-on experience with a variety of broadcast quality video and audio equipment.*

In summary, I believe that my unique capabilities as a creative thinker who is also a disciplined project manager would allow me to contribute to your ongoing success. I would enjoy speaking with you about the opportunities that exist and how I can best serve your needs. Please contact me by phone or e-mail at the number/address shown above to arrange a convenient time to discuss these matters further. I look forward to talking with you soon.

Thank you.

Sincerely,

Carla V. Salvador

Enclosure

31

Television Advertising Manager. *Arnold G. Boldt, Rochester, New York*
This Senior Advertising Account Executive wanted a marketing position with a TV network, so the writer emphasized the person's marketing and production experience and abilities.

JOSEPH J. MARKO
555 55TH Street ▪ Anytown, NY 55555
(555) 555-5555

September 23, XXXX

ABC Company
555 Smith Street
NYC, NY 10001

Dear Human Resources Manager:

Please accept this letter as an expression of interest in obtaining employment within your company. Enclosed is my résumé for your review.

I have extensive knowledge in working with all power tools, light-duty hydraulic cranes and MIG and ARC welders. I also hold an NYS Electrical and Light-Duty Engines license, along with an NYS Inspection license.

In my current position with ABC Auto, I have acquired extensive knowledge in all phases of auto repair and maintenance. In August of 1997, I was given the responsibility of acting manager for two weeks. During this time, I increased the sales volume from $25,000 to $38,000 and the customer base by 50%.

As a dependable person who enjoys working as a team, I feel I will be a valuable asset to your company. Unfortunately, my current position with ABC Auto will be eliminated in the near future because the business is being sold.

I would like to discuss a position within your company and look forward to hearing from you. Thank you for your time and consideration.

Sincerely,

Joseph J. Marko

Enc. résumé

32

Assistant Manager. *Jackie Connelly, Lindenhurst, New York*
This five-paragraph letter expresses in turn the person's goal, know-how and licensing, skills and managerial experience, work habits and reason for leaving, and interest in an interview.

DANIEL GARDNER

5555 Huston Avenue ▪ Sunshine Valley, California 55555 ▪ (555) 555-5555

[date]

[name of contact]
[title]
[name of organization]
[address]

Dear [name]:

If your company could benefit from a seasoned management professional with expertise in the rental car industry, please review my enclosed resume. You will note that my background encompasses over 20 years of progressively responsible experience in general operations management, staffing and supervision, customer relations, purchasing and marketing.

I was instrumental in spearheading the growth of Supreme Rent-A-Car from a start-up company to annual revenues exceeding $800,000 and a fleet of 100+ vehicles. By identifying a niche market, stressing outstanding customer relations, developing strategic promotional programs and selecting and training a top team, we were able to succeed as an independent operation in the shadow of major competitors. Unfortunately, our lease has expired, and we have had to close our operations.

With my experience and background, I am confident that I can make a meaningful and lasting contribution to your company. I would like to meet with you to discuss this further. Please contact me at your earliest convenience to arrange a personal meeting. I may be reached at (555) 555-5555.

Thank you in advance for your time and consideration.

Respectfully yours,

Daniel Gardner

enclosure: résumé

33

Co-owner, car rental company. *Vivian Van Lier, Valley Glen (Los Angeles), California*
The person feared that as a previous owner he might be a threat to an employer and that 20 years with one company might work against him. He got an excellent position quickly.

FRED B. JONES

333 North Pine Street • Olathe, Kansas 66666 • Work: (913) 555-5555 • Mobile: (913) 555-5555

March 30, XXXX

Mr. Jack Phillips
Richard Petty Driving Experience
Fax: (555) 555-5555

Dear Mr. Phillips:

Please accept this letter of introduction in response to your advertisement for the position of **Race Car Mechanic** with the Richard Petty Driving Experience, as advertised in the *Florida Times* on Sunday, March 22, XXXX. **This position is just what I am looking for!** Please allow me to point out a few of the reasons I am well qualified for the position.

My qualifications <u>include</u>:

- *Over fifteen years' professional experience as a successful Mechanic and Certified Master Technician.*

- *A passion for racing that began at 14 years of age while apprenticing with Robert Smith Pro-Stock Racing and continues to the present with experience as a Racing Mechanic, Crew Chief, Driver, and Sponsor.*

- *An energetic team player with the proven ability to communicate with Drivers, Pit Crew, Sponsors, Coworkers, and Customers.*

Since building my first race motor at age 16, I have gathered extensive practical experience and developed a high level of skill in engine work that includes:

Drive-line • removal • installation • tear down • assembly • inspection • clearancing • valve adjustment • carburetion • tuning • race car suspension setup •

I have achieved a reputation of providing **quality work and ensuring racing driver safety** by utilizing a talent for identifying wear and damage of engine, drive-line and suspension, and all other wear-related parts.

Although presently in Kansas, <u>I plan to relocate to Florida early to mid-summer.</u> My résumé will provide you with additional information for your review. Since this information is only a brief overview of my qualifications, I would appreciate the opportunity to speak with you personally so that we may further discuss how I can meet your particular needs. Please feel free to contact me at the above address or telephone numbers, or at my Florida telephone number (555) 555-5555. I will contact you in a few days to verify your receipt of this information.

Your consideration of my qualifications is greatly appreciated!

Sincerely,

Fred B. Jones

Attachment: Résumé

34

Race Car Mechanic. *Karen D. Wrigley, Round Rock, Texas*
The letterhead with a graphic matches the contact information in the resume. Boldfacing is used to call attention to the person's goal, qualifications, quality of work, and appreciation.

CORY LAWRENCE
5 Clove Road ➤ Staten Island, New York ➤ 55555
555-555-5050 ➤ E-mail: CoryL@yahoo.com

December 28, XXXX

Clyde Flaherty
Director
Personnel Department
Flyaway Services
55 Paulding Plaza
New Hyde Park, NY 55555

Dear Mr. Flaherty:

At the suggestion of my colleague, Mathilde Khan, a Flyaway Services airline pilot based in Dallas, Texas, I am writing to inquire about a flight crew or pilot position with your company. I offer 3 years of professional flight experience with 2,000 total flight hours logged. Competent and knowledgeable in the field of aviation, I have an impeccable flight and safety record. My résumé is enclosed for your review.

Most recently, at Charter Airways, I served as Captain on the BN 2A and First Officer on the DC 3. In this capacity, I received frequent commendations from the passengers for conducting smooth flights. I effectively handled difficult and dangerous situations while maintaining the highest emphasis on safety. Previously, as First Officer at Caribbean Airways, I gained expertise in Cockpit Resource Management. My background includes Flight Instructor experience—I taught 40 students and assisted more than 10 students in obtaining their licenses.

At this point in my career, I am seeking to join a company that offers opportunity for growth and advancement. I have followed your company for the last few years and have been impressed by your dedication to service and excellence. Flyaway Services is a leader in delivery service with a global reach—I would be proud to be a part of Flyaway Services' continued success. I bring to Flyaway Services strong leadership competencies, solid judgment, troubleshooting, and decision-making abilities. I am also young, energetic, and committed to achieving corporate goals.

If you are interested in a self-motivated and highly competent candidate, we should speak. I am willing to relocate and am available for an interview at your convenience. I appreciate your time and look forward to speaking with you.

Sincerely yours,

Cory Lawrence

Enclosure

35

Airline Pilot. *Kim Isaacs, Jackson Heights, New York*
A cover letter should be target-oriented. This candidate "has done his research": he knows about the company's excellent record and interest in "delivery service with a global reach."

MICHAEL LAMBERT
4 Baywood Boulevard
Houston, Texas 55555
(555) 555-0555

Dear Hiring Manager:

I am highly interested in your advertised position and believe my professional experience, background, and hands-on management style can contribute to the success of your organization. I offer:

- Over 9 years' combined airline experience in air freight, terminal operations, customer service, and management.

- Excellent working knowledge of FAA, customs, and company regulations; TACT books, and all required documentation.

- Proficiency in American's CARGOTRACE and FOMS computerized systems for monitoring cargo scheduling, preparing manifests, tracing shipments, loading aircraft, and checking aircraft capacities.

- Accomplished skills in Scandinavian Airlines System PBR and PALCO computerized programs for monitoring and tracking luggage, reservations, flights, and other customer-oriented information.

- A team player with the ability to motivate others while achieving consistently high levels of customer satisfaction.

Based on this brief summary and the details in my enclosed résumé, I am certain I would be a strong match for your requirements.

I hope to hear from you in the near future to arrange an interview and discuss in person how my qualifications and experience can meet the needs of your organization and contribute to its profitability.

Thank you for your consideration.

Sincerely,

Michael Lambert

Enclosure: Résumé

36

Cargo International Agent (CIA). *Carol Rossi, Brick, New Jersey*
The person was applying for an internal position for a company that used many acronyms and abbreviations. Those known to the company are used here without explanation.

Morton N. Downer
214 Waltham Trace
Prattville, Alabama 36000
✆ [334] 555-5555 (Home) ◇ [334] 555-6666 (Office)

July 20, XXXX

Mr. Harry Lee
Chief Pilot
Artisan Products, Inc.
P. O. Box 4840
Montgomery, Alabama 36100

Dear Mr. Lee:

When Sammy Black mentioned that you might want to add a pilot to your staff, I thought I might be an ideal match for Artisan. Of course, you would need someone with outstanding pilot skills. And I am one of those few, senior, active duty Air Force officers rewarded for what I love to do: constantly prove my flying skills to the toughest critic I know – myself. But I also realize that corporate pilots must be "ambassadors" for their companies. If that combination of skills and outlook appeals to you, I would like to join your team as a corporate pilot.

My very brief résumé will help you learn about my qualifications. But résumés, particularly pilots' résumés, can't show the ability to put people at ease or to represent an organization just the way the CEO would want it represented. Flying skills and social skills are best discovered in face-to-face meetings.

May I call in a few days to see when your schedule could accommodate an interview?

Sincerely,

Morton N. Downer

One enclosure: Résumé

37

Corporate Pilot. *Donald Orlando, Montgomery, Alabama*
How would you like to have a Top Gun for your Corporate Pilot? To show that this pilot isn't "all skills," this letter calls attention to his social or "people" skills. See Resume 5.

P.O. Box 555
Somewhere, USA 55555
Current Date

Jim Smith, HR Manager
Aircraft Services Corporation
5555 Aviation Way
Somewhere, USA 55555

Dear Mr. Smith:

This letter is a follow-up to our conversation last Thursday regarding the company's plans to establish a comprehensive training program for its maintenance technicians.

As we discussed, I have over seven years' experience in the area of training, half of which involved setting up and monitoring training programs for inspectors, maintenance supervisors, and technicians. At that time, I supervised 27 inspectors and designed and monitored training programs for approximately 400 technicians annually. These programs involved both in-house as well as formalized, classroom training off-site. In addition to my management duties, I also personally conducted many of the training sessions.

In order to establish an effective training program for ASC, I believe the following would be necessary:

✈ Thoroughly evaluate each employee's training, experience, and background to gain a comprehensive picture of available skills and areas of deficiency.

✈ Examine the company's current needs as well as future plans in order to design training programs that timely satisfy all existing and future technical requirements.

✈ Design both short- and long-term training plans for each individual and make arrangements for in-house classes as well as formalized group training so that training can be accomplished in the most efficient, economical manner possible.

✈ Establish a system by which training is monitored to maintain compliance with the company's forecasted needs.

My background seems ideally suited for a training development position, and I very much appreciate your consideration. I've enclosed a résumé for your files and look forward to talking with you in greater detail very soon. Thank you again for your consideration.

Sincerely,

John D. Waterman

Enclosure

38

Director of Maintenance. *Barbie Dallmann, Charleston, West Virginia*
The individual was overqualified, so the writer focused on the person's "plan of action for the position." Theme bullets (airplanes) mark the main steps of this plan. See Resume 11.

✈ ✈ ✈ Jane C. Flight ✈ ✈ ✈

2000 Aero Avenue North
Oriska, ND 58585
701-252-8111

March 28, xxxx

Mr. George Smith
Dakota Airlines
12345 Airport Road
Bismarck, ND 58444

Dear Mr. Smith:

I love people and genuinely enjoy serving them. With excellent communications, interpersonal relations, and leadership qualifications, acquired as a substitute teacher and sales associate, I guarantee that I can surpass your goals and objectives in your search for the right Flight Attendant. Therefore, it is with enthusiasm that I am writing to apply for the **Flight Attendant** position with Dakota Airlines. Our match would be a win-win situation. I have enclosed a résumé and completed application form for your review.

To introduce myself and illustrate the win-win situation in which my personality, experience, and qualifications correspond to your needs, let me highlight the following qualifications:

Travel–I have been a frequent traveler and throughly enjoy it. Unlike many people, I enjoy airports, hotels, and suitcases. Also, I am willing to relocate.

Flexibility–As a substitute teacher for 15 years, I know what *on call* means and having to be ready to go. I have no home responsibilities to interfere.

Personality–My warm, friendly personality is very approachable. I deal comfortably with strangers. A high-energy level is evident on first impression.

Appearance–I possess a vivacious attitude and appearance. Your travelers would enjoy the fun, upbeat service I would provide.

Physical Fitness–On strength tests at a local health club, I scored off the charts, beyond excellent, for leg and bench presses. I enjoy keeping fit through sporting activities.

Other Qualifications–Proficient sign language user; mathematical aptitude; mature dependability; and adaptability to new environments.

My résumé is a good summary, but I feel that it is during a personal interview that my potential to be of service to Dakota Airlines would be fully demonstrated. A meeting, at your convenience, can be arranged by contacting me at the above-listed number. I look forward to speaking with you.

Sincerely,

Jane C. Flight

Enclosures

39

Flight Attendant. *Mary Laske, Fargo, North Dakota*
Enthusiasm is evident throughout this letter for a teacher/salesperson who wanted to be a flight attendant. The Other Qualifications show that she is a mature adult and not just a kid.

JOHN WAYNE WILLIAMS

(913) 555-5555 ● 3333 East 132ⁿᵈ Street ● Olathe, Kansas 66666

June 22, XXXX

In-flight Recruiting
Vanguard Airlines
555 Mexico City Street
Kansas City, MO 66666

Dear In-flight Recruiting Authority:

In response to your ongoing recruitment, I am writing to express my desire to secure employment with *Vanguard Airlines.* My enclosed résumé will provide you with a summary of my qualifications for the position of *Flight Attendant*.

As my résumé indicates, I have *over ten years of successful experience as a Flight Crew Member with the U.S. Army*. The opportunity to provide in-flight safety and service to all types of passengers has been very rewarding. Although my more recent experience has been that of a Career Counselor for the U.S. Army, dealing with the public and meeting individual needs and desires daily have enhanced my ability to work as a commercial Flight Attendant.

Vanguard is a new and dynamic airline with unique challenges. *My military and flight crew experience uniquely qualifies me* to meet these challenges with success. It would be a dream come true to be part of the Vanguard team and provide the utmost quality of safety and service to the traveling public.

My tenure with the U.S. Army will end this August. I am excited about the prospect of accepting new responsibilities as a Flight Attendant with Vanguard Airlines! Since my résumé is only a brief overview, I would appreciate the opportunity of an interview where we can further discuss my qualifications. I will call this week to verify your receipt of this information. Please feel free to contact me at my address or telephone number, or my current work number (913) 333-3333. I look forward to speaking with you in the near future.

Your consideration of my qualifications is greatly appreciated!

Sincerely,

John W. Williams

Enclosure: résumé

40

Flight Attendant. *Karen D. Wrigley, Round Rock, Texas*
A military background is often perceived as a lack of experience with civilians, so the writer emphasized the individual's recent Career Counselor experience as working with the public.

JOHN J. LAWRENCE
5555 Delta Drive
City, State 12121
(555) 555-5555
e-mail: jjlaw@aol.com

Dear Hiring Authority:

As a skilled residential construction professional, I am seeking a new career opportunity with a dynamic home builder in the Charlotte area. My intentions are to permanently relocate to North Carolina within the next few months, and I will be visiting Charlotte on April 23 - 25 to investigate opportunities. Accordingly, I have enclosed for your review a résumé that briefly outlines my qualifications.

Some of the key talents that I can bring to a position with your organization include:

- **Superb Project Management capabilities. As a general contractor, I have built over 40 homes in the past ten years. This has included purchasing materials, hiring and managing subcontractors, dealing with building code and permit issues, and interacting with home buyers to shepherd them through the process.**

- **Extensive hands-on experience in all facets of home building from framing to finish work. I began my career as an apprentice mason and learned the construction business literally from the ground up.**

- **The ability to "think on my feet" and make design modifications in the field, when appropriate. Often I have been able to save time--and money-- by making decisions in the field that solved problems and achieved the buyers' overall objectives.**

- **A practical approach to construction with a constant eye toward maintaining budgets and controlling costs, without sacrificing quality.**

I believe that my knowledge and expertise would allow me to contribute to your continued success in a Project Manager, Construction Supervisor, or Foreman role. I would enjoy speaking with you in person to discuss the possibilities that exist and how I could serve your needs. Again, I will be in Charlotte on **April 23 - 25** and will take the liberty of contacting you while I am in town. In the meantime, you may call me at **(555) 555-5555** should you wish to arrange a meeting. I look forward to talking with you soon.

Thank you.

Sincerely,

John J. Lawrence

Enclosure

41

General Contractor. *Arnold G. Boldt, Rochester, New York*
Boldfacing emphasizes project management skills and the date of a trip to North Carolina. A record of 40 homes built, hands-on experience, and design-change savvy are key strengths.

DAVID MORRIS
1 Bridge Circle
City, State 77777
(555) 555-5555

August 14, xxxx

Mr. Homer H. House
Director of Human Resources
Home Construction, Inc.
1234 Residential Road
City, State 66666

Dear Mr. House:

As an ambitious and motivated individual with A.A.S. degrees in Construction and Industrial Design, I hope to secure a position in the residential contracting industry that will utilize my skills and offer professional growth opportunities. With this in mind, I have enclosed for your consideration a résumé that outlines my qualifications.

Some of the talents that I can bring to a position with your firm include:

- *Practical hands-on experience with residential construction. At SUNY North, I participated in a project that involved building a house from foundation to finish carpentry. This taught me a great deal about all the aspects of residential construction. I also have work experience that included remodeling office space for a human service agency.*

- *Experience reading blueprints and translating drawings into three-dimensional structures, as well as using a wide array of hand and power tools in the field and in shop settings.*

- *A disciplined approach to academics and work. Throughout my academic career, I have held part-time and full-time jobs to offset some of my expenses and augment my experience. At the Art Institute of Rivertown, I have been able to maintain Dean's List performance while also working.*

In summary, I believe that I can make a meaningful contribution to your continued success, given the opportunity to learn and grow within your organization. I would enjoy meeting with you in person to discuss the possibilities that exist and how I could best serve your needs. I will contact you within the next few days to answer any questions and schedule an interview at your convenience. I look forward to speaking with you soon.

Thank you.

Sincerely,

David Morris

Enclosure

42

Residential Construction Manager. *Arnold G. Boldt, Rochester, New York*
This graduate had two associate degrees: one in construction management and the other in design. The writer wrote a letter for each. This is the construction letter with talents in italic.

NICHOLAS GIORDANO
850 Mannington Avenue
Richmond, VA 00000
(555) 555-5555

Dear General Contractor:

If you are looking for a dependable and conscientious subcontractor to manage your construction and remodeling projects, please consider my qualifications. I am an effective team leader, fully insured and capable of any type of installation. I have knowledge of a wide array of building materials and am familiar with costing procedures.

Highlights of my career are the following:

19XX to present	Subcontractor for Corwin Industries of Norfolk, VA, a major firm specializing in the interior construction of retail home centers and superstores. Assumed progressive responsibility for most of their large account work, which generated revenues of approximately $1.4 million for the company.
	Managed installations at 31 of the 90 Mega Home Center stores contracted for all over the country. Also managed similar projects for other large retailers in addition to numerous restaurants, schools and commercial buildings. Hired and oversaw up to 24 union laborers for two to three projects running simultaneously.
19XX to 19XX	Subcontractor for RC Contracting, Hopewell, VA. Developed expertise in fine detail carpentry while working on homes valued at over $500,000 in affluent communities.
19XX to 19XX	Part Owner of GDM Contracting, Richmond, VA. Managed a staff of eight. Specialized in carpentry, kitchen and bath installations.

As my present employer is in the process of relocating out of state, I am writing with the thought that your firm may be interested in my value and contributions. In addition to the experience briefly described above, I also offer my expertise in:

- all phases of construction
- licensed electrical and plumbing
- painting and wall covering
- masonry, demolition and concrete work
- specialized wall and ceiling finishes

Throughout my career, I have maintained a proven track record of completion within specified time frames and budgets. I can attribute my success to careful planning prior to and during projects, as well as excellent interpersonal relationships at all levels. My recommendations for cost saving steps have been readily accepted, resulting in increased efficiency and minimized need for change orders.

It would be my pleasure to meet with you at your convenience to discuss a subcontractor agreement that I am sure would have a positive impact on your bottom line. May I hear from you soon?

Sincerely,

Nicholas Giordano

43

Subcontractor. *Melanie A. Noonan, West Paterson, New Jersey*
This letter, which does not refer to a resume, is a resume substitute. The first paragraph serves as an Objective and a Profile, the highlights are like a Work History, and so on.

Harold Jemson

1112 Norton Road ◆ Trapp Air Force Base, Illinois 62225 ◆ ℘ [618] 555-5555

May 28, XXXX

Mr. John W. Woodall
Senior Executive Vice President
PJM
Box ENR-195
340 East 93rd Street, Suite 12B
New York, NY 10128

Dear Mr. Woodall:

From the first day I started managing projects, my customers always cited a single standard: Bring it in on time and on budget. I never thought those criteria—as good as they are—were good enough. If you agree that well-managed projects should boost productivity before, during, and long after construction, we should talk. Specifically, I want to translate that vision into reality by joining your team as Vice President for Construction.

I have been working as a project manager with the broadest responsibilities for several years. My employer, the United States Air Force, consistently rewards me for my work. However, I think I can make an even better contribution elsewhere.

To help you learn more about my track record, I have enclosed my résumé. A résumé can illustrate capabilities you can use, but it cannot show you *how* I get consistent results my customers like. I bind myself to this professional creed:

> ◆ It is the *customer's* project. I do what it takes to please him now and in the future.
> ◆ Contractors, subcontractors and craftsmen are also "customers." I must stay close to them if the right things are to be in the right place at the right time.
> ◆ Saving time is not good enough; "banking" time is the minimum requirement.

I am ready to put my drive, energy, and experience to work for you. May I call in a few days to explore the possibility of an interview?

Sincerely,

Harold Jemson

One enclosure: Résumé

44

Vice President for Construction. *Donald Orlando, Montgomery, Alabama*
The writer of this letter met two challenges: to portray this person as a credible leader by showing *how* he built his reputation, and to reveal clearly his suitability for civilian work.

Elaine A. Martin

568 Main Street
Forest Park, New York 00000
(555) 555-5555

Dear Hiring Professional:

If your department needs a capable, self-motivated professional in customer service, sales support or administration, you may be interested in my qualifications:

- ▶ **Delivering consistently outstanding service**
- ▶ **Fostering strong customer relations to ensure satisfaction**
- ▶ **Contributing to sales growth and business success**
- ▶ **Training, guiding and motivating others**
- ▶ **Excellent performance record recognized by all supervisors**

My record is one of increased and varied responsibilities. Accustomed to fast-paced environments where deadlines are priority, I am extremely well organized, efficient and capable of managing multiple assignments efficiently to ensure smoothly running department operations.

In addition, I have excellent communication and problem-solving skills as evident in my ability to develop strong relationships easily with customers, coworkers, management, and others. A dedicated professional with a strong work ethic, I am always willing to go "the extra mile" to achieve business goals.

If my background matches your needs, I would welcome an interview to discuss the contributions I would make to your team. In terms of salary requirements, I understand that flexibility is important and am willing to work within your organization's target range for a professional with my experience.

Thank you for your consideration. I look forward to speaking with you soon.

Very truly yours,

Elaine A. Martin

Enclosure

45

Customer Service Administrator. *Louise Garver, Enfield, Connecticut*
The tempo of this cover letter seems quick because of the series of equally short paragraphs.
Right-pointing, half-diamond bullets call attention to qualifications in boldface.

SHARON M. HOFFMANN
391 North 18th Avenue
Redmond, Washington 00000
(555) 555-5555

January 31, XXXX

Lois McLaughlin
Vice President of Sales
Dynamic Resources
2010 Corporate Plaza
Seattle, WA 00000

Dear Ms. McLaughlin:

Please accept this letter and attached resume as an expression of my interest in the Customer Service Manager position you had advertised recently in the Seattle Courier. As you review my qualifications, you will see that I have the ability to deliver 110% toward enhancing your company's competitive edge through exceptional account support.

My greatest enjoyment comes from helping people, and I have a special talent for gaining customers' confidence, especially if their problems have not been dealt with satisfactorily in the past. I will do anything in my power to personally deal with customer issues until they are resolved, exhausting all resources before directing them to others for matters beyond my control. That to me is the true meaning of customer service that organizations owe to their clients in return for their patronage and loyalty. If you have the desire and commitment to strengthen this aspect of your business, I think we should meet.

Throughout my years in service-oriented positions, I have developed excellent rapport with my management and coworkers, encouraging open dialogue and getting everyone, regardless of their personality types or priorities, to work together toward a common goal. I make it my business to learn all I can about a company's products, procedures and alternative solutions so that I can deal with customers from a standpoint of knowledge. In addition, I am very well organized and thorough in my documentation of transactions, which simplifies retrieval and saves time.

If your available opportunity fits my qualifications, I would be very pleased to learn more about it. I am looking forward to an interview soon.

Yours very truly,

Sharon M. Hoffmann

Encl. Resume

46

Customer Service Manager. *Melanie A. Noonan, West Paterson, New Jersey*
If a reader has any interest in customer service, this letter is hard to ignore. The person proposes 110% effort, problem resolution, customer loyalty, and paper trails. See Resume 7.

Beverly R. Preston

2608 Wayland Avenue
Charlottesville, Virginia 00000
(000) 000-0000

June 30, XXXX

Mr. John L. Witherspoon
Director of Human Resources
XYZ Manufacturing Company
1801 Main Street
Charlottesville, VA 00000

Re: Customer Service Manager

Dear Mr. Witherspoon:

Enclosed is my résumé which outlines the strengths I would bring to a customer service management position. I am currently exploring employment options in which I might use the knowledge and skills accumulated in my years of service to a major commercial manufacturing company. At this time I would appreciate your keeping this information confidential.

My background includes building and growing a customer service department from ground up, including the hiring and training of employees. I personally handle a number of our major accounts and have consistently maintained a record of high customer service. My problem-solving approach is one of asking the right questions and staying behind issues until they are resolved. My working relationships with clients and employees are excellent. By coordinating the successful conversion of the department from manual to computer, cross-training employees, and creating detailed job descriptions for each position, I have increased efficiency and productivity.

I am enthusiastic about exploring opportunities with XYZ Manufacturing Company and look forward to talking with you. Please call me at (000) 000-0000 to set up a time to meet. I have enclosed a copy of my résumé in scannable format in the event you scan résumés into your database.

Best regards,

Beverly R. Preston

Customer Service Manager. *Betty H. Williams, Richmond, Virginia*
The strategy of the writer was to show that the individual could do more than just serve customers: she could train employees, create job descriptions, and increase productivity.

Cyd Percin

555 Peaceful Lane
Pleasanton, CA 99999
(510) 555-5555

Dear Hiring Manager:

Could you use a professional on your team who can transform an irate, disgruntled customer into a grateful and loyal patron?

I can, I did, and hopefully I won't have to do it again—but if your customer's dissatisfied, you can be assured that I would apply my considerable resourcefulness to the situation.

Case in point: It was holiday time in the floral business, and things were about as hectic as they could get. The customer wanted flowers with a balloon sent to someone in Georgia. The FTD florist, being just as busy as I was in Santa Monica, neglected to send the balloon with the flowers. The customer was so angry, I could hardly understand what she was yelling on the phone. So I calmed her down, negotiated with the florist in Georgia, then told the customer we were sending 3 roses and a balloon with a note of apology at no charge.

Result: The recipient loved the additional gift, the sender was ecstatic, and she became a long-standing customer.

People have told me that I have three important qualities that enable me to deal with sensitive situations: sincerity, objectivity, and ingenuity.

I would like to bring these and many other important qualities to your organization.

Sincerely,

Cyd Percin

enclosure: résumé

48

Customer Service Professional. *Ms. Sydney J. Reuben, Menlo Park, California*
The person had to close an 18-year massage practice for health reasons and had excellent customer service skills. This letter was so effective, she got job offers from the letter alone.

555 One Way
First Town, OH 55555
Current Date

Mr. Bill Watkins
ABC Company
555 Second Place
First Town, OH 55555

Dear Mr. Watkins:

Success in business is vitally linked to success with people, and that's where I excel. Team building and motivating to exceed performance standards is one of my specialties. Smoothing the rough edges of customer conflict resolution is another. Combining these skills with a record of solid operational management experience, I believe, makes me an ideal candidate for the position of Manager of Customer Service.

ABC Company has long been a customer service leader in our community, with an outstanding reputation for excellence. The success of your management team over the past five years clearly demonstrates solid leadership with a vision for the future. I very much want to be a part of your team. I can confidently offer myself as a seasoned professional with a consistent record of success. My learning and retention abilities are excellent; my desire to achieve is genuine; my commitment to quality is documented.

My résumé is enclosed for your review. I would appreciate a personal interview at your convenience. If I can provide further information, background materials, or letters of reference, please let me know. I appreciate your confidential handling of my application and look forward to hearing from you soon.

Sincerely,

Craig McDonald

Enclosure

49

Manager of Customer Service. *Barbie Dallmann, Charleston, West Virginia*
The letter begins with a bold assertion to grab attention. If you tailor this letter to your own situation, you can use the letter as a broadcast or marketing letter for your own job search.

HOLLAND H. SMITH
1842 Deer Street, Somewhere, USA
555-888-3333

January 31, XXXX

Michael T. Brown
Director of Quality Control
Nordstrom's
615 Olive Street
Chicago, IL 66666

Dear Mr. Brown:

Ensuring Quality Control requires an experienced staff with the expertise to analyze an independent contractor's ability to do the job correctly for the best price. As head of the Design Department, maintaining quality control standards has been my responsibility for the past sixteen years. I possess an innate ability to assess a contractor's employees, equipment and quality standards. My commitment is to quality while remaining price conscious.

Additional strengths include my:

- ability to handle many tasks at one time and meet every deadline, even when those deadlines occur hourly;

- motivation and desire to complete all projects in a timely manner; and

- ability to remain respectful, patient, and level-headed under pressure.

I utilize a real-world, hands-on approach to business and am confident of my ability to make a significant contribution to Nordstrom's. I look forward to discussing this opportunity with you in a personal interview and will give you a call early next week to arrange a mutually convenient time.

Sincerely,

Holland H. Smith

Enclosure

50

Head of Design Department. *Cynthia Kraft, Valrico, Florida*
A tightly constructed letter with indications of experience, expertise, and commitment to quality; bulleted additional strengths; and retention of control and initiative for following up.

Introducing
Jill S. Design
10101 JM Lake Road #314 ▪ Minnetonka, MN 55333 ▪ (612) 444-4444

Interior Designer

"Jill is an enthusiastic and talented young woman with a clear goal of becoming a professional Interior Designer. Jill has a thorough knowledge of color, texture, and principles of design. Her energy and motivation come from a true enjoyment of the profession."

Janice Nelson
President, Design Room 530, Snow, ND

April 2, xxxx

Mr. Troy Johnson
Johnson's Furniture Gallery
1203 East County Road East
High Hills, MN 55111

Dear Mr. Johnson:

Please consider this letter of introduction as an expression of my interest in exploring employment opportunities with your organization. I have enclosed my résumé for your review.

I am accustomed to a fast-paced environment where deadlines are priority and handling multiple jobs simultaneously is the norm. I enjoy a challenge and work very hard to attain my goals. My experience has helped me develop excellent communication skills and self-confidence, as well as the realization of the importance of customer satisfaction.

I would appreciate meeting with you to discuss how I might contribute positively to your team. I look forward to speaking with you further.

Sincerely,

Jill S. Design

Enclosure

51

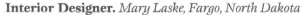

Interior Designer. *Mary Laske, Fargo, North Dakota*
A cover letter for a recent graduate who worked part-time while in college. This letter was successful because of the testimonial from the president of the company where she worked.

PATRICIA P. GOODWRITER
555 E. Grant Avenue
Greentown, California 55555-5555
(000) 000-0000

January 21, XXXX

Mr. Joe Bigwig
Assistant Vice President of University Relations
USA University
555 College Way
Big City, CA 55555

Dear Mr. Bigwig:

Mary Jane Peabody suggested that I contact you regarding the **Director of Corporation and Foundation Giving** position. I think that you will agree that my previous experience recovering hospital funds is a perfect match for this position.

Although I have enjoyed a long, successful career, the infusion of large corporations into hospital ownership has made my previous target industry extremely competitive, and I now would like to redirect my efforts and skills into another fund-acquisition arena. I could not think of a better sector than the University community to contribute my skills. In addition, I would gain the personal reward of contributing to the advancement and growth of educational institutions. I understand that writing grants for various departments within the University is the key function of this position, and I believe that the skill set developed through my past fund-acquisition efforts applies to successful grant writing.

Some details of these skills, which support my résumé, are outlined below:

- **Research and Analysis:** Searching federal and state government bulletins and regulations and industry journals, conducting personal interviews with funding source representatives, attending seminars to find new sources of funding, and analyzing patient profiles and comparing to funding requirements to create matches.

- **Writing:** Preparing *Position Statements* justifying eligibility for funding, and writing appeals to administrative law judges of the Social Security Administration supporting patients' eligibility.

- **Management and Reporting:** Establishing record-keeping methods and materials, internal reporting systems, and follow-up procedures for funding-in-process.

It may also be important for you to know that I completed the "Grant Writing I" course earlier this month taught by Carol Taylor at the Non-Profit Resource Center of Greenville County. I am additionally enrolled in the February "Grant Writing II - Advanced Grant Writing" course to fine-tune my grant writing skills.

I would like to meet with you to further discuss my candidacy for this position. You can reach me at (000) 000-0000, and I look forward to hearing from you to set a date and time to meet.

Thank you for your time and consideration.

Sincerely,

Patricia P. Goodwriter
Enclosure: Résumé

52

Director of Corporation and Foundation Giving. *Denise C. Ross, Anaheim, California*
The first paragraph indicates the reasons for the letter (the open position and the referral), and the second explains the need for a job change (the restructuring of hospital ownership).

LEON I. SWATCH

111 – 33rd **Boulevard** ▪ **Anytown, OR 99999** ▪ **555 / 123-4567**

January 30, XXXX

Timothy Jones, President
Downtown Development Corporation
1313 Fifth Avenue, Suite 1700
Anytown, OR 99999

Dear Mr. Jones:

As a resident of the downtown community and an advocate of historical preservation, I have a committed interest in the future direction of the neighborhood and the significance it holds for the people who live, work, and visit there, as well as its overall impact on the City of Anytown. As an entrepreneurial management professional, I fully understand the need for collaborative efforts to ensure a healthy business community and a supportive environment which can create and sustain jobs. I have the skills — and the enthusiasm — to lead all of those efforts as Executive Director of the newly formed Downtown Development Corporation.

In my current role as Regional Operations Manager for a privately held, $750 million, worldwide company, I work closely and cooperatively with many of the major businesses in the Greater Anytown area. As a result, I am keenly aware of the region's labor and economic conditions. Past positions have consistently placed me in organizing, fund-raising, or presentation roles in public forums for profit and nonprofit organizations. Let me highlight some of the ways in which I can significantly contribute to the Downtown Development Corporation:

YOUR REQUIREMENTS	MY QUALIFICATIONS
▪ Business Development & Collaborative Management	▪ I have grown revenues in the Northwest Region of Solid Sales — which manages outsourced tasks for major corporations around the world — to $15 million by constantly seeking additional sources of revenue for my clients and by negotiating contracts for win-win partnerships. Working with a high level of autonomy, I have the authority and ability to approach my clients entrepreneurially, seeking creative and profitable solutions. I understand and value the art of compromise.
▪ Organizing & Fund-Raising	▪ As Director of Operations for a major California ticket service and Assistant to the Director of a nonprofit music group, I was responsible for organizing events from initial bid to ticketing, equipment planning and procurement, staffing, advertising, on-site operations during the events, and final collection and resolution. I've coordinated and participated in fund-raising activities for numerous benefits. I'm a natural in front of audiences and cameras.
▪ Project Development & Implementation	▪ My success as Director of Operations for a ticket service in business development, growth, and project management led the owner to hire me to broker the sale of his company. Among successes in my present role, I improved productivity and reduced data errors by implementing software changes

I look forward to meeting with you to discuss in greater detail how I can assist in the leadership and growth of the Downtown Development Corporation. I'll call you next week to discuss the next step in the selection process.

Sincerely,

Leon I. Swatch
Enclosure: Résumé

53

Executive Director. *Carole S. Barns, Woodinville, Washington*
A persuasive letter that makes the individual seem *the* person for the position. Two-column format, which matches qualifications with requirements, is a welcome change of pace.

ABLE DIRECTOR
1212 Pond Road   St. Louis, Missouri 99999   555/555-5555

June 10, XXXX

Local Charitable Organization
P. O. Box 9999
St. Louis, Missouri 33333

Dear Search Committee:

This is in response to your ad which appeared in the *St. Louis Post-Dispatch* for Local Charitable Organization Executive Director. As a lifelong resident of St Louis, I am very interested in this position. I would like to utilize my leadership, organizational, management, and fund-raising skills for the betterment of this community.

As you can see from the enclosed résumé, I have a vast amount of experience which would benefit the Local Charitable Organization. My fund-raising abilities are extensive. Aside from the usual church and school volunteer fund-raising, I have been involved with area civic organizations for years. With the ABCDE Campaign I have solicited funds annually and met or exceeded my assigned goals. Alpha Alpha Alpha Sorority, a strictly charitable group, sponsors four to five underprivileged children at SLSB each year, providing clothing, other necessities, and seasonal and birthday parties. Through the Business Education Association, which is the business/school partnership for our school district, I served on the committee to determine the business/school relationships. With AMBUCS I have used my sales and fund-raising skills to solicit items for the annual auction. I have also served on the Board for many years and have been involved in fund-raising expenditure decisions.

My salary has been within industry norms for each of my positions, and I assume that you can offer a competitive salary, as well as challenge and opportunity.

I am looking forward to an interview and can be reached at the above telephone number.

Sincerely,

Able Director

Enclosure

54

Executive Director. *Sally McIntosh, Jacksonville, Illinois*
The second paragraph is used to convince the reader. First the main point (about much experience) is stated twice. Then come six examples in descending order of importance.

JOY J. BASTIN

111 West View Avenue
Danville, Kentucky 40422
Local Phone (606) 555-5555
University Phone (502) 555-5555

Personnel Manager
Kentucky Historical Society
PO Box 1792
Frankfort, Kentucky 40602   28 October XXXX

Dear Sir or Madam:

In response to your October 18, 1998, advertisement, please consider my resume in your search for a **MEMBERSHIP/VOLUNTEER COORDINATOR**.

My understanding of this position is fourfold: 1) To develop and operate programs, 2) To plan and implement recruitment policy, 3) To keep current members and volunteers involved, and 4) To maintain membership records. In my opinion, these duties will require a candidate with excellent planning and organizational skills, someone who is able to <u>consistently motivate others</u>. A successful coordinator will be creative, energetic, and flexible. Additionally, good writing and listening skills will be essential.

As outlined in my resume, I plan to graduate in December with a Political Science major. I have had extensive training in management and strategy, motivation, and the study of leadership. With my minor in Special Education, I have learned about good communication and how to plan and implement programs. We were taught how to keep things "fresh" in order to maintain strong interest, which I know will be tremendously useful in your position.

What I lack in work experience, I more than make up for with enthusiasm, dedication, and energy. As someone who enjoys a challenge, I work tirelessly to achieve my goals. I am ready and able to positively contribute to your members and volunteers.

I have also expressed interest in your **MUSEUM EDUCATOR/CHILDREN'S PROGRAM COORDINATOR** position, and feel my background and personality uniquely qualify me for both. I would appreciate the opportunity to meet so that we may discuss in person how I would be of value to you.

Thank you for your consideration. I look forward to hearing from you soon.

Sincerely,

Joy Bastin

Enclosure (1)

55

Membership/Volunteer Coordinator. *Debbie Ellis, Danville, Kentucky*
This letter is for a new graduate applying for an entry-level position to develop programs and recruit members and volunteers. The letter is an attempt to overcome little experience.

Rachel Marie Pasquel

905 Winter Way   Rockland, New York 12345
Home Phone (123) 456-7890

July 10, XXXX

Ms. Michelle Saprano
Superintendent
ABC Union Free School District
Main Street
Bloomfield, New York 12345

Dear Ms. Saprano:

Please accept this letter of interest and enclosed resume as application for the Art Teacher position with the ABC Union Free School District as advertised in the *Post Journal*. I am currently working full-time as the Art Teacher for Samaritan Private School but am seeking to put my teaching skills to work for a public school district. The New York State Board of Regents has rated the ABC Union Free School District in the top 10 districts in New York State for its commitment to teaching the fine arts. Additionally, the *Chronicle for Elementary through Secondary Education* printed a feature article on June 14, XXXX, praising your school district for "…(its) dedication to involving the entire community in the educational instruction of its youngsters." These are the values that I am seeking in a future employer.

At Samaritan, I teach art history, aesthetics, and techniques to 250 children in kindergarten through eighth grade. I have incorporated weekly and monthly themes, art masters, and multi-grade-level projects into my lesson plans. To further the children's interest in art, I have organized seasonal art shows both in the school and throughout the community and have created an after-school art enrichment program. I have been recognized for these programs by the *Daily Times* as an Outstanding Capital District Teacher based on the recommendations by several community families.

Prior to teaching at Samaritan, I held the position of Preschool Art Teacher at Toddler's Day Care Center to introduce youngsters to the world of art. Lesson plans focused on the development of fine motor skills through the learning of shapes, colors and sizes applied to the world around them.

Additionally, I completed my Student Teaching during the spring of XXXX in your Red Mill Elementary School with Mr. Sampson. You may remember my teaching skills when you observed me teaching an "architecture" project to a first grade class. A copy of your written evaluation is also enclosed. Your ending remark stated that I "truly enjoy teaching and my enthusiasm carries over to the students." During the last 3 years, I have embraced that observation and have worked hard to keep that enthusiasm fresh and exciting for both my students and myself.

Now I am seeking the opportunity to teach a broader spectrum of learning abilities in a public school setting. I welcome the chance to elaborate further on my qualifications in person and to become reacquainted with the ABC Union Free School District. I will contact you next week to schedule a time with your review committee for an initial interview. Thank you in advance for your consideration.

Sincerely,

Rachel M. Pasquel

56

Art Teacher. *Elizabeth M. Daugherty, East Greenbush, New York*
Getting an art teaching position was highly competitive, so this person reminded the Superintendent of an earlier written evaluation. The writer researched school district values.

Sanja Muzdek-Bulling
6045 Paces Woods Court
Lawrenceville, Georgia 30244   (770) 846-0332

Dear Hiring Professional:

Having recently moved from Europe to Georgia, I am seeing an opportunity to continue my career in the field of education. As a part of lifelong education, adult education is my choice for professional and personal growth and fulfillment. I sincerely believe that through lifelong education any goal can be attained on a personal or social level.

After graduation from the University of Belgrade, I was immediately recruited by the University as an Assistant Professor and continued my professional growth by obtaining a Master of Science degree. During the eleven years as a faculty member, I was engaged in teaching students and designing programs for educational models for adult learners. Like many other countries, Yugoslavia had inherited a great deal of illiteracy and was caught in the technical/industrial advance, thus creating many adult learners.

My doctorate, which is its final phase, addresses the particular spectrum of needs of the adult learner in today's environment. For this reason, I am seeking an opportunity with an educational institute to continue my contribution to this fascinating subject and to grow professionally and academically

Sincerely,

Sanja Muzdek-Bulling

Enclosure

57

Assistant Professor. *Kimberly Wright, Buford, Georgia*
In the final phase of doctoral work, this individual was beginning to look for a new position in adult education. The middle paragraph is autobiographical and is like a brief narrative.

HARRY P. SOMEONE, Ph.D.

000 Down St. • Philomath, Oregon 00000 • (W) 000-000-0000 (H) 000-000-0000 • Email: Harry@tight.org

Paul Winters
Search Committee of the Board of Trustees
USA Farming School
9999 Crowley Dr.
Alameda, CA 99999

Dear Mr. Winters,

Enclosed is my curriculum vitae for your review. I am confident that my professional experience in the area of Agricultural Education will serve as an asset to your organization.

I am a well-qualified Assistant Professor with a proven track record of success in:

- Generating funding for major international projects
- Launching highly rated agricultural programs
- Developing currently implemented international teaching programs
- Teaching at the secondary and postsecondary levels

Beginning my career in 1973, I have progressed through several increasingly responsible teaching positions achieving all university goals, within budget. My greatest talent lies in my ability to quickly grasp new concepts and methodologies at any level. I have extensive international working experience and am easily adaptable.

Having proved what I am able to produce, I'd like to do a lot more for the USA Farming School. It is my goal to serve in a capacity where I can contribute to the education of our youth. I look forward to speaking with you in greater detail about my qualifications. Thank you for your time and consideration.

Very truly yours,

Harry P. Someone

Enclosures

58

Assistant Professor. *Rosa St. Julian, Houston, Texas*
Readers pressed for time might read just the first line of each paragraph. That would work well in this letter, for each first line contains positive information. Bullets highlight successes.

Janice G. Marvin

555 Mt Leaf Court, Verona, Virginia 55555   555 • 555 • 5555

August 10, XXXX

Rogers University
1000 Rogers UniversityDrive
Virginia Beach, Virginia 23464-9826

Attention: Human Resource Department
          Barbara Ross

Dear Miss Ross,

It is with considerable interest that I enclose my résumé for the position of Director of Admissions - School of Counseling and Human Services listed on the Rogers University Job Opening Notice. I wish to express my strong interest in this position, which appears to be an exciting career opportunity. I believe my résumé designates that I am well qualified for this position.

My career in teaching and continuing education have equipped me with the ability to develop, implement, and coordinate recruitment activities. I have leadership skills and am committed to working in a team environment of management, marketing and publication. I have excellent interpersonal skills and the ability to interact with all types of individuals.

At present I am serving an Internship in Counseling, Advising, and Administration of Student Services at Rogers University. In the fall I will undertake the writing of my dissertation toward obtaining an Ed.D. at The Adam Washington University.

I would welcome the opportunity to meet with you personally to discuss the contributions that I could make to Rogers University. Thank you for your consideration, and I look forward to hearing from you.

Sincerely yours,

Janice G. Marvin

59

Director of Admissions. *Anne G. Kramer, Virginia Beach, Virginia*
A letter with four short paragraphs that express in turn the person's interest in the posted position, her skills, her internship and doctoral work, and her interest in an interview.

Mary Jane Billings

111 Currency Avenue
Bucks, NY 55555
(555) 555-5555
MJB111@bol.com

Dear Hiring Committee,

Does your school system need an experienced **Elementary School Teacher** for the upcoming school year? With 18 years' experience, including several different grade levels and all subjects, perhaps I can be of service.

My resume is enclosed for your review. Some of the qualifications and professional knowledge I can offer are:

1. Education	- **NY Certification, Elementary School Teacher (Lifetime License)**
	- **BS, Elementary Education,** Bucks State College, Bucks, NY
2. Experience	- **18 years' experience at the Elementary Level**
	- Teaching Science, Language Arts, Math, Music and Art
	- With socioeconomically and racially mixed students
3. Leadership	- Take-charge teacher, relied upon to "get things done"
	- Extensive planning, coordination and organization skills
4. Personality	- Creative, self-motivated individual able to develop curriculum
	to meet the needs and interests of multicultural students

If you are seeking a teaching professional who can stimulate elementary students' interests and focus their intensity and curiosity, then I am the person you want. I enjoy a challenge, and I work diligently and cooperatively to attain my goals. Perhaps even more important, I am concerned about the students, parents and community residents whom I serve, as well as the teachers and administrators with whom I interact daily.

In order to explore your prospective needs, I will call your office next week concerning any questions you may have and to arrange a meeting if that seems appropriate to you. Of course, you may contact me directly at any time. Thank you for your consideration.

Sincerely,

Mary Jane Billings

Enclosure

> " Stimulating, creative and innovative lessons …she makes it look easy."
> - Staff Evaluation, Bucks Central Grammar School.

60

Elementary School Teacher. *Susan Guarneri, Lawrenceville, New Jersey*
The numbered list with a label for each number makes it easier to remember this person's qualifications. She retains control for calling later. The testimonial is a strong ending.

Mary E. Lamb

Current Address: Permanent Address:
000 Merriweather Lane   00 Cloudy Avenue
Sunny, OH 00000   Moon, ME 00000
(555) 555-5555   (555) 555-5555

(Date)

(School)
(Attn:)
(Address)
(Address)

Dear (Name):

My interest in contributing to the enhancement of elementary education within your public school system has prompted my forwarding the enclosed resume for your review and consideration.

I will complete my Bachelor of Science in Education in May XXXX and am seeking an elementary position working with children with special needs. I will be certified in multiple areas and feel I am well rounded to deal with any situation. I have worked with both underprivileged and at-risk children and have multiage experience.

You will find me to be a very creative and enthusiastic teacher with the patience and caring so vital in working with children with special needs. I have developed and implemented reading, writing, and math programs which effectively motivate accomplishment through both individual and group projects in a safe and comfortable learning environment. I have presented at both the NCTE and Maine State "Bright Ideas" Conference, and am committed to pursuing personal and professional growth.

I am confident of my ability to stimulate and motivate children with special needs toward personal growth and achievement. I would welcome the opportunity to meet with you to discuss your current staffing requirements. In the interim, if any additional information is required, please contact me at the above address or phone number.

Sincerely,

Mary E. Lamb

enc.

61

Elementary School Teacher. *Peggy Weeks, Battle Creek, Michigan*
This letter highlights the individual's impressive achievements, which are evident in the third paragraph. Though not yet a graduate, the person displays confidence. See Resume 8.

TAYLOR R. ROBINSON

5 Turtle Road • Poughkeepsie, NY 00000 • (555) 555-5555

March 24, XXXX

Mr. John Smith
Assistant Superintendent
Overlook Elementary School
123 Overlook Street
Poughkeepsie, NY 00000

Dear Mr. Smith:

I am a certified elementary teacher and coach who would like to explore teaching opportunities within your school district. Currently, I am pursuing my master's degree in Special Education from the State University of New York. For the past year, I have been substitute teaching and just recently accepted a long-term sick leave position.

As you will see, throughout my college career I handled many responsibilities. In addition to my academics, I was very involved with athletics, sought to help fellow students, and volunteered much of my time to improve campus life. I always remained focused on my educational goals and successfully managed all the responsibilities that I willingly accepted. It is this same sense of commitment and high level of participation that I would bring to your school district.

I am enthusiastic and positive about my career potential and look forward to the challenges ahead. I have thoroughly enjoyed both student teaching and substitute teaching. I performed with a high degree of self-confidence--gaining an appreciation for the rigors of teaching, meeting the busy day and unexpected challenges with ease, and always achieving my objectives. The teaching experience which already I have obtained only confirms that I made the right career choice for myself.

I am eager to grow in my profession and would appreciate the opportunity of discussing my qualifications in greater detail. Thank you for your time and consideration. I look forward to hearing from you.

Sincerely,

Taylor Robinson

Enclosure

62

Elementary School Teacher. *Kristin Mroz Coleman, Poughkeepsie, New York*
The first paragraph introduces this master's degree candidate and indicates her goal, and the second shows her self-management skills. The rest expresses her eagerness and thanks.

LINDA ANN FISHER

111 Clover Drive
Macon, Georgia 77777
(333) 333-3333

July 5, 0000

Ms. Virginia James, Director of Human Resources
Chatham County Board of Public Education
Post Office Box 0000
Savannah, Georgia 33333

Dear Ms. James:

Please find my résumé enclosed in response to your job announcement for an Environmental Education Naturalist.

As the résumé will illustrate, my record is one of increased responsibility, variety in job assignments, and solid performance. Though my employment is in the field of forestry, my interest in education and public relations has always been significant. To help fund my education, I worked as both a lifeguard and camp counselor. During the school year, I substituted as time allowed and gave private swim lessons to children. I have prepared and presented a special program for elementary students in my hometown on forestry and the environment, and I am currently participating in Georgia Foresters Association Forestry Awareness Week offering educational programs to students visiting a national park. Educating others on our environment has long been my vision.

I believe I have the credentials to meet your immediate needs and the aptitude to grow with the position, and I look forward to discussing your needs and my ability to meet them. Until then, thank you for your consideration.

Sincerely,

Linda Ann Fisher

63

Environmental Education Naturalist. *Carol Lawrence, Savannah, Georgia*
This person was relocating to an area of the country where jobs in her field of forestry were scarce. The writer therefore stressed those skills that applied to the target field of education.

Mary Cross
8 River Bend Lane
City, State 99999
(555) 555-5555

October 8, XXXX

Mr. Ed U. Cator
Director of Admissions
University of Suburban
1234 College Drive
Suburban, State 54545

Dear Mr. Cator:

After a rewarding career as a School Counselor, I am seeking a part-time or consulting position that will utilize my extensive experience advising students applying to college. I believe that my knowledge and expertise could benefit your university in an admissions interviewing or admissions counseling role.

Some of the relevant experiences I have gained during my 26-year career include:

- **Assisting high school seniors in selecting colleges that are appropriate to their academic and professional goals. In addition, I have written letters of recommendation for college applicants and provided advice on completing college applications.**

- **Delivering presentations to parents and students on topics related to college placement, financial aid, and other career planning issues.**

- **Coordinating "Open House" events allowing student attendees to interface with representatives from various local colleges.**

- **Participating in the launch of a School-to-Work program for high school students, which encompassed job shadowing, co-op assignments, and internships with local employers.**

- **Counseling individuals on a wide array of personal, academic, career, and college issues, including substance abuse, interpersonal conflicts, and career goals.**

Enclosed for your reference is a résumé outlining my background. I am confident that my skills are transferable to a college admissions environment and that I can assist you in fulfilling your mission. I would enjoy meeting with you to explore the potential opportunities and discuss how I can best serve the needs of your office. Please call me at (555) 555-5555 to arrange a convenient date and time for us to begin a dialogue. I look forward to speaking with you soon.

Thank you.

Sincerely,

Mary Cross

Enclosure

64

College Admissions Counselor. *Arnold G. Boldt, Rochester, New York*
A letter for a retired school counselor who was seeking a part-time or consulting position as a college admissions interviewer. Bulleted items are experiences that relate to the transition.

Helen Ridgeway

21 Spruce Hill Terrace • Belleville, Illinois 62221
(618) 555-5500 Ext. 374 (W) • (618) 555-5555 (H)

March 18, xxxx

Tim Scott, Athletic Director
Southern University
35 University Avenue
Nashville, Tennessee 37355

Dear Mr. Scott:

I feel prepared to fulfill my goal of coaching at a Division I school. As the Head Basketball Coach for a successful junior college program, I can tell you that my strengths include the ability to:

- Recruit and coach quality players
- Rebuild team unity with pride and passion
- Prepare student-athletes to consistently perform at high levels
- Instill habits that breed success on and off the court

Along with my staff and players, we created a winning tradition at Troy Community College (TCC), where losing was considered the norm. TCC had compiled a 14-125 record from 19xx to 19xx. Recruiting was a unique and immediate challenge, and in our first year we turned things around with a 22-4 record.

Since I started in 1992, we have averaged more than 20 wins per season while accumulating a record of 108-45. TCC finished second in our region this year, our third consecutive 20+ win season. Because of the success we have had with rebuilding, our program has been showcased as a model for other schools to follow. I am extremely proud of that.

I am also proud of my coaching philosophy, one that challenges players to unlock their own potential. The players I recruit share my genuine passion for the game, and together we develop a team spirit that carries us beyond the basic skills of basketball.

Before you make any hiring decisions, we should discuss your needs and my coaching skills in greater detail. I look forward to meeting with you and can be available at your earliest convenience.

Thank you for your consideration and reply.

Sincerely,

Helen Ridgeway
Enc.

65

Division I Basketball Coach. *John A. Suarez, Troy, Illinois*
This letter is upbeat because the record of this person is upbeat. Her strengths are demonstrated by her turning a losing sports program into a showcase program. See Resume 9.

Norma Samuels
43 Oakland Avenue • Dedham, MA 02026 • (555) 555-5555

September 10, xxxx

Dr. Stephen Nash
Director of Personnel
Anytown Public Schools
123 Main Street
Anytown, MA 00000

Dear Dr. Nash:

If you are interested in a dynamic and creative teacher with the ability to challenge and motivate students of all backgrounds and ability levels, please consider the enclosed résumé for the position of high school history teacher.

My background includes a combination of business and teaching experience. As a business owner, I hired, trained, and supervised many teenagers in several suburban retail businesses. As a teacher for the past six years, I have worked with a diverse population of students from middle school through college. By combining a solid grounding in the academic material with a highly creative flair, I have been effective adapting the curriculum and modifying my teaching style to accommodate different ability and interest levels. I have been successful with behaviorally challenging students as well as with academically serious students, and those in between.

I am committed to creating a safe learning environment that encourages young people to share ideas, think creatively, take risks, and make rational choices. I would welcome the opportunity to apply my commitment and my skills to benefit the Anytown Public Schools and look forward to speaking with you. You can contact me at (555) 555-5555.

Thank you for your consideration.

Sincerely,

Norma Samuels

66

High School History Teacher. *Wendy Gelberg, Needham, Massachusetts*
This person lacked traditional classroom experience. The writer therefore focused on those skills, experiences, and views that would appeal to school administrators and students.

ALEXANDRA DAVIS

601 Main Street • Farmington, NY 00000
H (555) 555-5555 • W (555) 555-5555

November 10, XXXX

Mr. John Smith
Senior Manager
Famous Hair Care Company
New York, NY 00000

Dear Mr. Smith:

Thank you for your interest in me for the International Education Manager position which you currently have available. I was very interested to read of this opportunity, as my background and qualifications match the defined objectives and expectations which you require for the position. With my respect and enthusiasm for this profession, I believe I could positively contribute to your endeavors.

I am excited about the opportunity for continued professional growth where I can expand my knowledge base. In return, I can offer Famous Hair Care top-notch skills as an educator and a balanced background that includes extensive and diverse experience within the U.S. haircare market. Additionally, I would bring with me:

- Over 10 years of professional experience as a hairstylist and 5 years as a business owner.

- Proven skills in training/educating others and 7 years' experience promoting Famous products.

- A demonstrated ability to easily convey and establish credibility and confidence with individuals or large groups, due to a professional image, genuine enthusiasm, and extensive industry knowledge.

My current position includes extensive and frequent travel to all areas of the country, and I view this as an integral part of the job. Enclosed is a copy of my resume detailing my background and qualifications as well as other information which may be useful. I am tentatively planning a two-week trip to New York beginning on May 10. I look forward to visiting and discussing how my skills and training might be of benefit to Famous Hair Care's goals and objectives. Should you have any questions regarding my candidacy, please feel free to call. In the interim, thank you for your attention, consideration, and forthcoming response.

Sincerely,

Alexandra Davis

Enclosure

67

International Education Manager. *Kristin Mroz Coleman, Poughkeepsie, New York*
The word "Manager" is a clue that the education here is not school education but product education for practitioners in the hair care industry. Enthusiasm is evident throughout.

TONI TAYLOR WYNDHAM

4812 Old Lexington Road ✦ Camden, SC 00000   (000) 000-0000

September 13, XXXX

Mr. Richard Nichols
Camden Chamber of Commerce
P.O. Box 1412
Camden, SC 00000

Dear Mr. Nichols,

Please accept this letter in response to your need for a **Lifelong Learning Facilitator**. The enclosed resume outlines my qualifications, which closely parallel your requirements for this position. Please notice that my resume reflects academic or work experience that fulfills each of the qualifications mentioned in your advertisement.

For the sake of space, my resume does not reflect the community activities I have been involved in. They include the following:

✦ American Heart Association (provided vocal talent for fund-raising efforts)
✦ Breast Cancer Foundation (helped coordinate and assisted with fund-raising)
✦ Special Olympics (provided support and encouragement to participants in games and activities)
✦ Adopt-a-Highway (involved in program to help contribute to cleaner environment)

My personal commitment to Camden and its citizens, combined with my inexhaustible enthusiasm, would enable me to contribute significantly to the goals of the Chamber. I love working with people and helping people and have strived to develop the kind of skills which would enable me to be a positive force for the community. Please be assured that you'll find me to be both dedicated and hardworking. I can pledge in advance that if granted this opportunity, you'll be adding an effective, enthusiastic member to a team that I know is going to continue to accomplish wonderful things for the Camden community.

Thank you, in advance, for your consideration. I look forward to meeting with you to discuss this opportunity further. I may be reached at (000) 000-0000.

Sincerely,

Toni Taylor Wyndham

Enclosure

68

Lifelong Learning Facilitator. *Gwen P. Noffz, Greenwood, South Carolina*
The resume had no room for community activities, so the writer lists them as bulleted items in the letter. The person sent four resumes and got four interviews and three job offers!

BENJAMIN STARR

101 Able Way
San Francisco, California 55555
(000) 000-0000

October 12, XXXX

Dean J. Sadd
College of Law and Government
General University
1000 Center Court
San Francisco, California 94000-9156

Dear Dean Sadd,

I would like to pursue the possibility of joining the faculty of the College of Law and Government at General University. The enclosed résumé contains information pertaining to my background, experience, and capabilities.

As a military career Judge Advocate, I have extensive litigation experience. Working in the role of prosecutor and defense counsel, I have personally tried more than 350 cases. Senior Supervisor duties have given me the opportunity to mentor junior attorneys in preparation and trial procedures. Most recently, as a sitting judge, I presided over more than 450 bench and jury cases, including felonies and misdemeanors.

My background includes considerable experience in teaching and trial advocacy training. While an instructor at the Naval Justice School—the functional equivalent of a professor of law—I lectured extensively on the Rules of Evidence and did substantial work in curriculum development. I also directed or participated in numerous trial advocacy seminars in both the Navy and California Eastern School of Law.

Having recently completed my military career, I would be genuinely enthusiastic at the prospect of joining the law school faculty. I have the skills, experience, and energy to assume a leading role to enhance student needs while enabling General University to meet its goals.

Thank you in advance for your consideration. I will contact your office shortly to arrange a time to meet.

Sincerely,

Benjamin Starr

Enclosure: Résumé

69

Law School Faculty Member. *Anne G. Kramer, Virginia Beach, Virginia*
A letter for a military Judge Advocate who returned to civilian life and wanted to teach in a law school. The second and third paragraphs indicate considerable teaching experience.

KEVIN ROUSSEAU
27 Washington Place, Portsmouth, NH 00000
(555) 555-5555

May 23, XXXX

Dr. Gerald Anderson
Portsmouth Board of Education
105 Eagle Street
Portsmouth, NH 00000

Dear Mr. Anderson:

If you are seeking an experienced, talented educator who can facilitate the teaching of mathematics through hands-on applications, please allow me to introduce myself. As you will note from my resume, I have taught for over nine years in the Manchester school system and have been successful in providing a strong foundation and challenge to a broad range of upper elementary students, both remedial and gifted.

I have extensive training and experience in EWT preparation and holistic scoring methods, reinforcing my classroom instruction with frequent teacher-made practice tests. I expect the best from my students, encouraging them to use their higher-order thinking skills in solving mathematical problems, which has resulted in impressive achievements on standardized tests.

My superiors have recognized me as a thoroughly prepared, well-organized and highly motivated professional who stays abreast of current educational theory and practice. I am especially empathic to children with learning difficulties or social problems. I adapt my techniques to reach them and am willing to tutor them on my own time if they need additional help.

Throughout my years of teaching, I have always maintained excellent working relationships with parents, colleagues and administrators. Currently, I am serving on the school core team, where I am looked to by my peers for my judgment on both budget and program decisions.

I would appreciate your review of my credentials and the opportunity to interview for a possible opening in your school. Thank you for any consideration you may extend.

Sincerely,

Kevin Rousseau

Enclosure: Resume

70

Mathematics Teacher. *Melanie A. Noonan, West Paterson, New Jersey*
This letter is for a gifted teacher of remedial and gifted students. The first four paragraphs make it clear that this person is an exceptional teacher who should be interviewed.

JOY J. BASTIN

111 West View Avenue
Danville, Kentucky 40422
Local Phone (606) 555-5555
University Phone (502) 555-5555

Personnel Manager
Kentucky Historical Society
PO Box 1792
Frankfort, Kentucky 40602

28 October XXXX

Dear Sir or Madam:

I read with a great deal of interest your advertisement for the position of **MUSEUM EDUCATOR/CHILDREN'S PROGRAMS COORDINATOR** in the Sunday, October 18, edition of the *Lexington Herald Leader*. Please accept this letter and the enclosed resume as my application for the position.

You have expressed interest in candidates with strong communication skills, the ability to work well with children, and a degree in education. As you will find outlined in my resume, I will soon be graduating from Murray State University with a major in Political Science and a minor in Special Education. Additionally, I have both the interest *and* the experience working with children, and possess *excellent* communication and organizational skills. I will bring to the job my enthusiasm and energy, as well as my dedication, strong work ethic, and the deep desire to succeed. I have earned the reputation for being a self-starter, a quick learner, and a team player. I am eager to complete my education, to find the best opportunity, and to put the techniques and ideas I have been studying for so long to work!

Although it is difficult to convey my depth of interest in the form of a letter, I hope that I have done so. I would appreciate the opportunity to meet with you in person so that we might further discuss my background and how I would be of value to your organization. You may contact me at either my local or university telephone, or the above address.

I am very appreciative of your time spent reviewing my material, and look forward to your reply.

Sincerely,

Joy Bastin

Enclosure (1)

71

Museum Educator/Children's Program Coordinator. *Debbie Ellis, Danville, Kentucky*
This is the second cover letter for an individual applying for two different positions at the same location (see Cover Letter 55). Qualifications center in the minor in Special Education.

FIONA R. HERTZBERG

Phone: (555) 555-5555
E-mail: fhertzberg@msn.com

555 Westminster Road
Brooklyn, New York 55555

May 29, XXXX

Anne Sunners
Director/Counselor for Students with Disabilities
Office of Academic Advising and Student Services
5555 University of Omaha
Omaha, NE 55555

Dear Ms. Sunners:

It was a pleasure speaking with you regarding employment opportunities at the University of Omaha. As we discussed, I am interested in providing Orientation and Mobility or liaison services to students with disabilities. Please consider my qualifications if a suitable opening becomes available. I have enclosed several copies of my résumé, so feel free to give them to colleagues who may be interested.

Throughout my professional career, I have learned that the availability of Orientation and Mobility services can mean the difference between success or failure for students with disabilities. It often determines whether a student travels safely to and from school or work. I have dedicated my career to giving students the opportunity for success through Orientation and Mobility and Gross Motor training. Consider the following:

- 25 years of progressive experience in the field of Orientation and Mobility.

- Published writer and speaker on Orientation and Mobility topics.

- Lifelong commitment to helping individuals with physical challenges and multiple disabilities.

- Rapid and thorough assessment of Orientation and Mobility needs and development of plans to help students achieve their goals.

Although my current position is secure, I am exploring new professional challenges at college campuses. I am eager to relocate for the right career opportunity. Since the University of Omaha has approximately 500 registered students with disabilities, I am confident that my professional services would be beneficial to the students.

If you are interested in a results-oriented and dedicated professional with strong credentials, please call me at (555) 555-5555. I am available for a telephone interview or an in-person meeting at your convenience. Thanks again for your time and assistance.

Sincerely yours,

Fiona R. Hertzberg

Enclosures

72

Orientation and Mobility Services Provider. *Kim Isaacs, Jackson Heights, New York*
The person wants to provide orientation and mobility services to university students with disabilities. There were no such services, but she makes clear a need for them.

Lorraine Johnson   23 Larkin Boulevard, Patchogue, NY 11772
516-555-5555   ◆   lojo@sprintmail.com

June 14, xxxx

Mr. Raymond Fell
Superintendent
Patchogue-Medford School District
32 South Ocean Avenue
Patchogue, NY 11772

Dear Mr. Fell:

Will the Patchogue-Medford School District have a need for an experienced physical education teacher this fall? If so, as a permanently certified physical education teacher with a specialty in adaptive physical education and fourteen years of background with the St. Louis, New York City, and Merrick school systems, I should meet your requirements.

With combined expertise in physical education and adaptive physical education, I have had many opportunities to function in a variety of educational settings. Working in city schools was a rigorous training ground and gave me hard-earned training in hands on class management, districtwide curriculum development, and IEP creation. Working with a diverse group of children has been rewarding, and I have created positive change in many of my students' academic and personal lives.

Whatever the circumstances, I always strive to achieve daily goals, to plan activities that enhance the students' academic curriculum, and to instill a love for physical fitness and accomplishment. In today's age of "video" kids who lack opportunity for fitness and are becoming ever more sedentary, I impart a real understanding of the role of athletics and physical fitness in the world in which they live. My students learn that physical well-being enhances their performance at school *and* at play. They learn to welcome and enjoy the benefits of physicality, individual achievement, and team play.

Please consider this letter as an expression of my sincere interest in pursuing any vacancies that may arise in the district. I will create an energizing and productive learning environment that will promote a genuine interest in physical and personal student achievement. I know that I can make a valuable contribution to your students' education, and I look forward to hearing from you.

Sincerely,

Lorraine Johnson

enclosure

73

Physical Education Teacher. *Deborah Wile Dib, Medford, New York*
The graphic is eye-catching for this experienced teacher who left teaching to start a family and now wants to return. The third paragraph gives her views on teaching. See Resume 10.

KAREN R. FRANKLIN
3333 Primrose Parkway
City, State 00000
555-555-5555
e-mail: krfrank@schools.org

April 6, XXXX

Ms. Ella M. Terry, Principal
School Road Elementary School
1234 School Road
Syracuse, New York 13232

Dear Ms. Terry:

As a dynamic teacher with Reading and Elementary Education certification, I am seeking a full-time Reading position for the XXXX-XX school year. Enclosed for your consideration is a résumé that briefly outlines my professional credentials.

Some of the unique talents that I can bring to a teaching role in your district include:

- **Experience working with diverse populations, which have included emotionally disturbed, ADHD, physically challenged, and hearing impaired students. I have developed and implemented IEP's and participated in the CSE process.**

- **A strong proficiency with Information Technology in the classroom with the ability to effectively integrate leading-edge technology into instructional programs.**

- **The ability to maintain an open line of communication with parents to keep them involved in the educational process. I have used newsletters and weekly progress reports, along with face-to-face conferences, to develop and sustain this rapport.**

- **Familiarity with a broad range of early intervention and remedial strategies in Reading and Math. These have included Reading Recovery, Math Their Way, and The Writing Process, among many others.**

As you assess your staffing needs for the XXXX-XX school year, please keep me in mind for a **Reading Resources** position. I would enjoy meeting with you in person to discuss how I could best serve your district's needs and contribute to the educational success of your students. Please contact me at (555) 555-5555 to arrange an in-person interview. I look forward to speaking with you soon.

Thank you.

Sincerely,

Karen R. Franklin

Enclosure

74

Reading Specialist. *Arnold G. Boldt, Rochester, New York*
The focus is on the bulleted list of talents in boldface, which draws attention to this list. The abbreviations, titles, and jargon give the impression of one pro writing to another pro.

Susan K. Schumm
0000 S. County Line Road
Hebron, Indiana 00000
(555) 555-5555

May XX, XXXX

Mr. XYZ, Principal
ABC High School
0000 Learning Avenue
Valparaiso, Indiana 00000

RE: *Secondary Education Teacher*

Dear Mr. XYZ:

Please consider the enclosed resume as an application for a *Secondary Education Teacher* position for the academic year of XXXX-XXXX. Your school corporation came to my attention through my extensive research of quality schools in the Valparaiso area. I am very interested in being actively involved in a creative education environment combined with a family-oriented community. Enclosed please find my resume for your perusal.

I have a strong work ethic and effective rapport-building skills, and am confident that I can make a positive contribution to the goals and objectives at **ABC High School**. I would welcome an opportunity to introduce myself and to discuss how my qualifications can best meet your needs at **ABC High School**. If you should need any additional information, please do not hesitate to contact me.

Thank you for your time and consideration in reviewing this application. I look forward to your response.

Sincerely,

Susan K. Schumm

Encl.

75

Secondary Education Teacher. *Susan K. Schumm, Hebron, Indiana*
This letter is short because the writer believes that readers should be able to read the letter quickly and then want to read the resume. The letter should hook readers for the resume.

HENRY WELLMAN

3331 Garden Street
Northampton, MA 00000
(555) 555-5555

Dear _____:

Children represent the future of our country, and nothing could be more rewarding to me professionally than to play an active role in educating tomorrow's leaders and citizens.

Along with my background in secondary education and certification, I have acquired extensive experience at regional schools, teaching all subjects with a particular concentration in social studies. As an educator, my approach is to foster an energetic, open atmosphere that promotes questions and engages students in the learning process.

Teaching is my passion, and it is continually reinforced by the results I have experienced in my work with students. Given the opportunity, I am confident in my ability to make a difference in the lives of students in your district as well. Additionally, I possess a well-rounded background that includes prior experience in business as well as in military service.

After you have reviewed my credentials, I would welcome a personal interview to discuss my qualifications in greater detail. I offer the necessary training, dedication and personal qualities to serve as an excellent educator in assisting your school district to reach its objectives.

Thank you for your consideration. I look forward to our conversation.

Very truly yours,

Henry Wellman

Enclosure

76

Social Studies Teacher. *Louise Garver, Enfield, Connecticut*
With experience in business and military service, as well as a background in secondary education, the letter must show commitment to education. The first three paragraphs do that.

Lu K. Heung

1111 – 11th Street NW ◆ Anytown, NY 99999 ◆ 555 / 555-5555 ◆ lukheung@u.newyork.com

October 15, XXXX

Henry Smyth, Recruiter
Troner Consulting
Suite 1700
1400 Park Avenue
New York, NY 99999

Dear Mr. Smyth:

With a passion for learning, the motivation to succeed, strong interpersonal and communications skills, and a particular talent for using technology to develop effective and cost-efficient solutions, I believe I have the qualifications to join the Troner Consulting team of professionals.

I graduated last month from the University of New York with two Bachelor of Science degrees — Chemical Engineering and Chemistry — earned in a five-year program. Between my fourth and fifth years, I spent 12 months in Japan doing research with professors in the Kinetic Reactions Laboratory of Tokyo University. A variety of jobs — most requiring data collection, research, analysis, and the ability to work easily with others — financed my education, one I was determined would be paid entirely through my own efforts.

Throughout my life, my curiosity for all things technical, my desire for exploration of the unknown, and an acceptance of new concepts and ideas consistently have opened doors that broaden my knowledge and experience. Among those opportunities was the yearlong research project in Japan. Armed only with enthusiasm, an educational background in chemical engineering, a solid base of research techniques, and a beginning understanding of business strategies, I sought the job and won it. While I did not speak Japanese before going, I have an affinity for languages (fluent in my native Vietnamese and English and conversationally fluent in French) and soon picked it up. I am now comfortable speaking Japanese in both casual and business conversation. I further enhanced my language strengths by teaching English as a Second Language to Japanese students and business people.

Currently, I am working as a research assistant with the dean of the University of New York's School of Engineering and a chemical engineering professor in their investigation of thin film protective coating in microfluidic devices and microelectronic mechanical systems. My contribution to the project is winding down, and I am now drafting a preliminary report.

An ability to successfully interface between the technical and the nontechnical, clearly focused communication skills, and an ability to understand customer needs and translate them into workable solutions are all talents I would like to put to use for Troner Consulting and its clients. I look forward to discussing my strengths and potential contributions in greater detail with you soon.

Sincerely,

Lu K. Heung
Enclosure: Résumé

77

Chemical Engineer and Consultant. *Carole S. Barns, Woodinville, Washington*
A letter for a Vietnamese refugee with two bachelor's degrees, research expertise, and exceptional language skills. The writer focused on his strong work ethic and multiple talents.

BENJAMIN HALL

101 Williams Road   Beekman, NY 00000   (555) 555-5555

August 5, XXXX

Mr. William Mroz
442 Schuyler Avenue
Poughkeepsie, NY 00000

Dear Mr. Mroz:

I am a Design Engineer with extensive industry experience, expert AutoCAD knowledge, and a strong insight into value-added engineering. Although secure in my current position, I am confidentially exploring new professional challenges and opportunities.

As you will see, I have made numerous contributions to my present employer. These accomplishments are derived from my exceptional interpersonal and communication skills, strong attention to detail, powerful work ethic, and sincere dedication to company objectives. I take pride in designing and creating quality products that are cost-effective, and work diligently at distinguishing them as successful endeavors.

Throughout my tenure with LED, I have been consistently praised for making design recommendations and system implementations that prevented customers from experiencing major manufacturing problems and downtime. My team approach involves working with other members toward a common vision in order to initiate action and deliver results. During my career I have developed strengths in strategic planning, team building, and project management. Combining these skills with my solid foundation in creative design and fabrication techniques has enabled me to enhance job performance and respond effectively to constantly changing business needs. My character, ability to build partnerships, and endless ideas and enthusiasm will also prove to be invaluable assets to your organization.

Should you have any questions regarding my candidacy, please feel free to call. In the interim, thank you for your attention, consideration, and forthcoming response.

Sincerely,

Benjamin Hall

Enclosure

78

Design Engineer. *Kristin Mroz Coleman, Poughkeepsie, New York*
A strong letter for a person whose information keeps getting better and better (note the growing length of paragraphs). It's hard to think the reader won't call for an interview.

MITCHELL FORBEST

1211 Smith Way
Vero, Virginia 55555
800 • 456 • 1234

February 7, XXXX

Mark Thomas
Mark J. Thomas, II Consulting Engineers
900B Warner Boulevard
Newview, Virginia 55555

Dear Mr. Thomas,

I am writing to present my credentials for the position of **ENGINEERING CONSTRUCTION INSPECTOR** as advertised in the *Pilot*. I am very much interested in a career opportunity to work in the field of construction engineering and design, where I can apply my background toward reaching mutually beneficial goals.

The enclosed résumé summarizes my background in HVAC, plumbing construction observation, shop drawing review, and cost estimating. I am a mature, personable individual with the ability to get along with people. I have excellent problem-solving skills, and given the opportunity, I would be an immediate and long-term asset to your firm. I continue to expand my knowledge in the field of engineering by taking course work leading to a master's degree in electrical engineering.

My potential to be of service to your organization can be more fully demonstrated in a personal interview. I will contact you next week about the possibility of arranging a meeting at your convenience.

Thank you for your time and consideration.

Sincerely yours,

Mitchell Forbest

79

Engineering Construction Inspector. *Anne G. Kramer, Virginia Beach, Virginia*
The first paragraph indicates the purpose of the letter. The second paragraph carries all the freight in showing the person's background, areas of expertise, skills, and further education.

Bret O. Boyson
2222 Castlemont Trail
Menlo Park, CA 99999

May xx, xxxx

P. C. Butler
Executive Manager
Employment Unlimited, Inc.
222-B Collingwood Avenue
San Jose, CA 99999

Dear P. C. Butler:

ENGINEERING TECHNICIAN

Is your employment agency searching for a qualified professional to fill a position similar to the above? If so, you may wish to consider a candidate with over 20 years of administrative expertise and a broad experience in customer service. In addition, I have considerable experience with employee training and computer usage.

You may find some of my successes of interest. For example:

- Currently performing as Acting Manager, on a weekly rotation, to relieve the Managers at 5 stores, for this 7-day-a-week business, plus replace managers for vacation periods.

- Conceived of a unique, new marketing/pricing plan that is now being implemented company-wide.

- Reduced delinquent accounts, at one store in XXXX, from 39% to only 9%, in less than 90 days.

Enclosed is a copy of my résumé for your evaluation. I would welcome an opportunity to discuss my qualifications with you. I will call you in a few days to discuss this further.

Sincerely,

Bret O. Boyson

Enclosure

80

Engineering Technician. *Carl L. Bascom, Fremont, California*
In this letter a subject line follows the salutation, and the first paragraph refers to experience and areas of expertise. Later bullets point to a chief duty and two achievements.

Marcus Ballantine
5555 Shadow Hills - Apt #66
Santa Clara, CA 99999
(444) 888-7777

September xx, xxxx

Mr. Ansel Proctor
Vice President
Human Resources
Mail Stop #X-333
Leon Enterprises, Inc.
7777 Drucilla Drive
San Jose, CA 99999

Dear Mr. Proctor:

PROCUREMENT ENGINEER

You were referred to me by La Donna Murphy, an Operations Manager with your company. She noted you are searching for a qualified professional to fill the above position in your organization, and encouraged me to submit a résumé. You may wish to consider a candidate with over 13 years of engineering experience with a particular focus on procurement engineering. In addition, I have considerable experience in planning, organizing and implementing workshops and training programs for hands-on electrical engineering applications.

Enclosed is a copy of my résumé for your evaluation. I have a serious interest in a focused position such as this, and will call you in a few days to discuss this further.

Sincerely,

Marcus Ballantine

Enclosure

P.S. For your convenience, a special scannable résumé is enclosed, in addition to the standard résumé.

81

Procurement Engineer. *Carl L. Bascom, Fremont, California*
Another letter in which a subject line follows the salutation. In this two-paragraph letter, the reason for the letter is stated first; then procurement engineering is presented as a specialty.

DORIS SILVER
5000 Northwest 9th Street
Sunrise, Florida 33024
(954) 000-0000

Dear Manager:

For the past seven years, I have been working for the Internal Revenue Service where I have gained extensive skills, knowledge and experience in areas such as finance, collections, tax law, and customer relations. My goal is to relocate to the North Carolina area and transition out of the government sector into private industry where an organization, such as yours, can capitalize on my background.

My positions, in short, involved managing a large volume of taxpayer cases where I conducted client interviews and provided business counseling to assist taxpayers in complying with tax laws. I extensively researched and analyzed information that would lead to prompt and proper case resolution, interacting with all levels of management, Power of Attorneys and the general public. My responsibilities also included asset location and liquidation, code enforcement, and compliance.

My proudest accomplishment was the IRS Volunteer Income Tax Assistance Program, which I managed for Dade County. As a volunteer myself, I coordinated the program, as well as I trained 110 volunteers in basic tax preparation, staffed, scheduled and marketed the 27 sites.

Prior to the IRS, I worked for Citicorp Savings where I serviced 150-200 calls daily. I resolved disputes, problems, and billing questions for account holders and received excellent reviews for my proficiency, speed and courtesy. Subsequently, I was promoted to Team Leader to resolve the more difficult cases.

My greatest strength is my ability to manage multiple tasks or large caseloads simultaneously. I am also proficient in decision making, problem solving, negotiations, and communication. Furthermore, I am bilingual in English and Spanish.

I would like to explore career opportunities with your organization to see how my diversified background can fit in with your needs. My résumé is enclosed for your review, and I look forward to hearing your comments. I am available for interviews at any time. Thank you for your time.

Sincerely,

Doris Silver

Encl.

82

Analyst, Internal Revenue Service. *Shelley Nachum, Ft. Lauderdale, Florida*
For the stream of thought, look for the person's goal; positions; proudest accomplishment; proficiency, speed, and courtesy; greatest strength; ability; diversified background; and resume.

Gary W. Hooper

0000 Gentleman's Lane
Nashville, Tennessee 00000

Knoxville: (000) 000-0000
Nashville: (000) 000-0000

February 5, XXXX

Chase Financial Corporation
Attn: Human Resources
000 West Harper Road
Cleveland, OH 00000

Dear Sirs:

Please accept this letter and the enclosed resume as application for the **Banking Account Executive (Tennessee)** position advertised in the February 2, XXXX, edition of *The Knoxville News-Sentinel.*

As a professional in equipment leasing, financing, and sales for over 25 years, I have a career that covers a variety of services and products, including transportation and heavy equipment. More specifically, I have:

♦ Marketed lease and finance programs to equipment vendors within a specific trade area to solicit new business opportunities.

♦ Maintained positive performance of my commercial loan portfolio through new loan growth and constant monitoring of present loans.

♦ Developed strong interpersonal, communication, and leadership skills through constant negotiation and attention to detail.

In addition to my leasing and finance experience, I gained a strong background in banking as a former Assistant Vice President for the Bank of Whoville. The Banking Account Executive position with Chase Financial Corporation seems to be an ideal match between my leasing, finance, and banking experience and your position requirements.

Based on the background and experience required for this position, the annual base salary I require would be in the $45,000 to $60,000 range, plus commission and benefits.

I would appreciate your serious consideration of my credentials, and I look forward to hearing from you.

Sincerely,

Gary W. Hooper

Enclosure

83

Banking Account Executive. *Carolyn Braden, Hendersonville, Tennessee*
This person wanted to move back to the Knoxville area. To emphasize his background in equipment leasing and financing, the writer used bullets to point to sales, loans, and skills.

MR. LAUREN J. KAMPSEN
13 CONWAY STATION • NILES VALLEY, PA 11111
(OOO) 123-4567 (H)
(555) 444-3333 (W)

April 2, XXXX

Mr. Richard W. Linch
V. P. of Personnel
National Bank
22 South Water Street
Niles Valley, PA 11111

Dear Rich:

I've been quite interested in reading about National Bank's expansion in *The Gazette* recently. As you know, I sold Senior Care & Rehabilitation Center last Spring and have been seeking an opportunity to return to the banking industry where my administrative and financial skills can be utilized to the fullest. Being a member on National Bank's board has also enabled me to gain firsthand knowledge of its organization. Therefore, I have decided to take advantage of the time, now, to forward my résumé to you for consideration of my background to see if there may be an opportunity to join your team of professionals.

My experience in banking spans more than 20 years where I started as a trainee with Branch Financing Services. Continuing with added responsibilities, I was placed in key leadership roles. Positions I have held include loan officer, treasurer, branch manager, and vice president (at both the assistant and executive levels). In my final position with Federal Credit Union, I held full accountability for the operations of five branch offices and overseeing the activities of subordinate executives. During this time, I made significant contributions to the development, recommendation, implementation, and administration of organizational policies and goals. Following my career in banking, I went on to become the owner and administrator of Senior Care & Rehabilitation Center, which brings me full-circle.

If you are seeking someone with my experience in operations who is an aggressive manager with keen skills in improving profitability, then I would like to be considered. I would appreciate an opportunity to discuss my qualifications in detail. As I stated earlier, I am ready to return and make a career investment in National Bank. You can reach me at the office if you would like to schedule a personal interview.

Thank you for your time.

Sincerely,

Lauren J. Kampsen

84

Branch Manager. *Deborah S. Edwards, Wellsboro, Pennsylvania*
The person had a background in banking, left that field to be owner/operator of a nursing home, sold that company, became its business manager, and wanted to return to banking.

Susan F. Meade

1858 Maple Road
Roanoke, Virginia 00000
home: (000) 000-0000 ◆ voice mail: (000) 000-0000

July 30, XXXX

Elizabeth W. Peters
President and CEO
New Community Bank
P. O. Box 111
Roanoke, Virginia 00000

Re: Branch Manager

Dear Ms. Peters:

I am interested in exploring opportunities with New Community Bank in a branch manager or similar management position. My experience and expertise are with smaller banks that place a high priority on personalized service. With the recent purchase of ABC Bank by VVV First Savings Bank, I have found that my position as branch manager and loan officer at the West End location does not involve as much customer contact as I would like.

As you will see from the enclosed résumé, I began my banking career as a teller at Eastern Seaboard Bank in Virginia Beach. I was being trained for a CSR position when my family relocated to Roanoke. At VVV Bank, I began as a teller and was promoted to CSR, Assistant Branch Manager, and Branch Manager. In December XXXX I became an Assistant Vice President. My branch has consistently exceeded expectations, and my staff and I are frequently commended for the high quality of personal service we provide our customers. My strengths include staff training and management and building cohesive, effective team environments.

I would welcome the opportunity to meet with you. Please expect a call from me August 3. Note that I have also enclosed a copy of my résumé in scannable format in the event that you scan résumés into your database.

Sincerely,

Susan F. Meade

85

Branch Manager. *Betty H. Williams, Richmond, Virginia*
The first paragraph shows the person's goal and reason for a change, the second summarizes her history of promotions and strengths, and the third indicates her follow-up plans.

Robert Gardiner
777 Division Avenue
New York, New York 00000
(555) 555-5555

Dear _____:

Like many other recent graduates, I am searching for an opportunity to use my professional skills while contributing to a company's growth and success. Unlike some others, however, I don't believe that a new bachelor's degree is enough of a qualification in today's competitive marketplace.

Therefore, I have worked hard to supplement my education with hands-on experience in financial services and other businesses giving me a broad range of skills necessary to begin a career as a Business Analyst, Analyst or Consultant. Through my work experiences and academic studies, I have developed the qualifications that would make me an asset to your company:

- **Financial services:** Demonstrated initiative in identifying and securing valuable professional experience as one of only 40 selected out of 2,000 applicants to participate in the highly competitive Internship Program with Asset Management Company.

- **Business sense:** Established and managed a successful business requiring the ability to develop new business and address customer needs to ensure consistent service satisfaction resulting in business growth.

- **Research, analytical and problem-solving strengths:** A flexible thinker, I chose an educational program that required careful analysis and examination of factors with rigorous insistence on logic. I have the ability to research, assess and synthesize information, as well as look at problems from many different perspectives to arrive at creative solutions.

- **Communications:** Written reports and research papers as well as presentations were an ongoing part of my college course work as well as in my employment experiences. While interning at Prudential, I prepared and delivered a well-received presentation at a Unit annual meeting.

Additionally, I supported myself while attending college through various positions in business management, customer service, sales and other environments involving extensive public contact, teamwork and client relations. If you foresee the need for a capable professional with the ability, education, experience, and attitude to make a difference to your organization, then we should meet to discuss your needs and how I may contribute. Thank you for your consideration. I look forward to our conversation.

Sincerely,

Robert Gardiner

Enclosure

86

Business Analyst. *Louise Garver, Enfield, Connecticut*
This letter says, "With me, you get more than just another guy with a new degree: you get a head-start professional." Bullets point to this graduate's achievements and skills.

DAVID LAWRENCE
688 Main Street • Huntington, West Virginia 00000 • (555) 555-5555

Dear _____:

As a manufacturing and operations executive, I have consistently delivered strong performance results through my contributions in cost reductions, internal controls and technology solutions. The comparison below outlines some of my accomplishments as a Chief Financial Officer in relationship to the position requirements at your company.

Your Requirements	My Qualifications
Full range of finance, accounting and treasury experience; operational focus; strong internal controls.	Built and led strong finance organizations, creating solid infrastructures and strengthening internal controls. Instituted formal budgeting, forecasting, cash management, and other management processes. Proven record for designing growth strategies and financial consolidations to achieve business objectives.
	Recruited by Halstead Company to provide expertise in acquisitions, financing and MIS and to orchestrate an IPO. Comprehensive background in all areas of finance, accounting and treasury. Recognized for strengths as a consensus/team builder and effective arbitrator/negotiator.
Mergers and acquisitions experience.	Acquired extensive experience in the analysis of new business opportunities and with mergers and acquisitions throughout career history. Effectively merged and streamlined 2 divisions which resulted in substantial savings and positioned company for future growth.
	Spearheaded acquisition of several operating businesses with sales ranging from $1 to $220 million, which included personally handling all negotiations, performing due diligence, developing tax structure, and coordinating legal and accounting activities.
MIS background.	Led installation of state-of-the art MIS technology in different companies. Improved inventory management, boosted sales and cut annual operating expenses through MIS technology implementation.

I would welcome a personal interview to discuss how my experience would contribute to the achievement of your company's objectives for growth and success.

Very truly yours,

David Lawrence

Enclosure

87

Chief Financial Officer. *Louise Garver, Enfield, Connecticut*
The first paragraph sets the theme and introduces the two-column list of qualifications that match requirements. The case is so strong that interest in an interview is *under*played.

Winston G. Pauly
1567 Brittany Lane
Montgomery, Alabama 36106
[334] 555-5555 (Home); [334] 555-6666 (Office)

June 23, XXXX

Mr. Charles W. Morgan
Senior Vice President
L-Mark, Inc.
1100 East 4th Street
Suite B
Chattanooga, Tennessee 37403

Dear Mr. Morgan:

If you feel, as I do, that talent equals the power to make more profits, I have an idea that might help both of us. I'd like to fit my talents and energies into the L-Mark team as your Chief Financial Officer. That's the logical next step in a plan I started years ago.

My goal is to offer a leading company more than the technical skill it takes to gather financial data and do basic analyses. I started by getting my CPA, purposefully specializing in an industry known for volatility.

Then I undertook to master – by hard practice – every aspect of operations. And I never stopped making time to learn how to take advantage of financial opportunities on a broad scale. From negotiating fair contracts to adding value to products, I focused on judging risk prudently. I know the impact of monetary decisions on the future of a firm. In short, I've done more than make money. I understand the art of *how* to make money by serving the needs of the clients.

Now I'm ready to put all my experience, energy and drive to work for our mutual advantage. As a first step I've enclosed a résumé to help you learn more about my track record. I would like to follow up by hearing about your specific needs firsthand. In a few days, may I call to explore opportunities of mutual benefit?

Sincerely,

Winston G. Pauly

Encl.: Résumé

88

Chief Financial Officer. *Donald Orlando, Montgomery, Alabama*
This cotton broker wanted to "make a major leap to serve as a CFO." To link the person's skills from a narrow field to a broader one, the writer emphasized transferable talents.

ARTHUR VANDALYKER
55 Silver Avenue • Moon Silver, New Jersey xxxxx • (xxx) xxx-xxxx

(Date)

Mr. Dan Petersonn
XYZ Associates
1 Main Street
Hackensack, New Jersey xxxxx

Dear Mr. Petersonn:

I have enclosed a summary of my career and accomplishments for your consideration and review for the position of Controller/C.F.O. within your organization.

As you will note, I have accumulated a broad range of financial and operations management experience and have enjoyed substantial growth as a direct result of my efforts. Additionally, I am confident that my background clearly matches your needs, as I have the type of accounting, financing and M.I.S. experience necessary to profitably manage an organization such as yours.

I am interested in playing an active role in an organization that will provide advancement opportunities in which a person with my determination, experience and management ability will be utilized to the greatest advantage.

In addition, my background includes the following:

- ***Demonstrated achievement in the sourcing and negotiating of financing with a proven ability to restructure organizations to maximize existing credit.***
- ***Strong leadership talents, with the ability to motivate staff and build cohesive, goal-oriented teams.***
- ***Thorough understanding of M.I.S. and its critical importance in operational effectiveness.***

Salary requirements are flexible depending on the total compensation package. I am enthusiastic about exploring the prospect of contributing to your organization and would appreciate the opportunity to speak with you concerning the aforementioned position. I can be reached at the telephone number listed above to answer any questions or to arrange a meeting.

I look forward to speaking with you soon and thank you for your consideration.

Sincerely,

ARTHUR VANDALYKER

Enclosure

89

Controller/CFO. *Alesia Benedict, Rochelle Park, New Jersey*
Except for the person's address and phone number in the letterhead, the entire letter is in italic.
Bullets and bold italic ensure that the additional background information is seen.

LINDA FISHER

111 Clover Drive • *Macon, Georgia 77777* • *(333) 333-3333*

May 19, 0000

Mr. James Harvey
Great National Bank
Post Office Box 0000
Macon, Georgia 55555

Dear Mr. Harvey:

Thank you for taking time from your busy schedule to discuss employment opportunities at Great National Bank with me. I have completed the application which you forwarded to me and have enclosed it, along with my résumé, with this letter.

As we discussed, though I presently have no experience in banking, I am very interested in pursuing this field as a career move. Interestingly, my employment in the field of forestry has exposed me to a side of banking about which many know little. As a forestry consultant, I dealt with land management issues of large timber tracts owned by various banks as a source of investment. I understand the importance of maintaining positive customer relations with both the client (which were bank officers in this instance) and the landowners, and through these efforts I have developed excellent interpersonal and communication skills. I also understand the importance of community involvement in the banking industry and am quite comfortable with that concept. In fact, it is another reason I find banking an attractive career move. Over the last two years, I have prepared and presented a special program for elementary students in my hometown on forestry and the environment, taught bible school, served as a lifeguard, and presented educational programs during Forestry Awareness Week at a nearby national park.

If given the opportunity of working with Great National Bank, I can assure you that I will put forth every effort to achieve a satisfactory outcome to any assignment given me. I look forward to meeting with you.

Sincerely,

Linda Fisher

90

Entry-level banking position. *Carol Lawrence, Savannah, Georgia*
Another letter for the person of Cover Letter 63 but for a different kind of job. Her skills were applicable in a variety of fields. This letter shows how these skills apply to banking.

Michael K. Wan

8541 Smith Street
Garden Grove, California 55555
555-555-5555

October 20, 1999

Ms. Ronnie Smith
First National Bank, Inc.
123 Shelby Avenue
Garden Grove, California 55555

Dear Ms. Smith:

Please consider this letter of introduction as an expression of my interest in exploring employment opportunities within your organization. Enclosed is my resume for your review.

I recently obtained my BA degree with concentration in Finance. While pursuing my education, I also held a position at United Commercial Bank, where I used my financial knowledge in helping customers and supporting essential operations. I am looking forward to greater challenges and am eager to apply my knowledge and skills to contribute to your bottom-line objectives. The qualifications I bring to your organization are:

- Proven expertise in credit and financial analysis
- A strong financial academic background with a consistently high GPA
- Working knowledge of a professional banking environment
- Dedication and self-motivation with a strong desire to succeed in the financial field

I would appreciate the opportunity to personally expand upon my background, as well as learn about your specific requirements. I am confident that my enthusiasm, educational achievements and professional experience will be of value to your organization. Thank you for your consideration, and I will follow up with you next week.

Sincerely,

Michael K. Wan

Enclosure

91

Entry-level banking position. *Kim Little, Victor, New York*
A letter for a recent graduate who has already had some banking experience. The writer shows with bullets how this person brings more than just a new degree to the workplace.

DANIEL L. HILGER

115 Round Top Road
Sunningdale, PA 11111
000-000-0000 (H)
555-555-5555 (W)

September 22, XXXX

Mr. Jay Leatherman
VP Finance
Laurel Health Systems
32-36 Central Avenue
Wellsboro, PA 16901

Dear Mr. Leatherman:

I am submitting the enclosed résumé for consideration for the finance director's position which appeared in *The Daily Review* on September 18. My background as finance director with not-for-profit organizations has given me the expertise that would contribute to the continued success of Laurel Health Systems.

My background has been focused in the areas of fiscal management with extensive experience in preparing and administering budgets of as much as $4 million, third-party billing, federal and state reporting, contracts bidding / negotiations, administration of client and resident accounts, A/P, A/R, payroll, and employee benefits administration. I have also supervised and directed employees in the day-to-day operations of a finance office. In each of the positions I have held, I have delivered strong operating results through efficiency improvements and cost reductions. While working for Residential Services, Inc., in Carrington, SC, I was instrumental in improving overall accounting system efficiencies which resulted in a reduction of processing time and a decrease in outstanding receivables. Workers compensation costs were drastically cut by 50% by implementing tight claims and risks management.

I believe my background would provide you with the experience you require for this position, and I would like to apply these talents and technical skills as finance director for Laurel Health Systems. Please call me to arrange a time when we could speak about this opportunity in detail. You may reach me at the telephone number listed above. Thank you for considering my qualifications to become a part of your organization.

Sincerely,

Daniel L. Hilger

Enclosure

92

Finance Director. *Deborah S. Edwards, Wellsboro, Pennsylvania*
In this response to an ad, the middle paragraph supports the first paragraph and sets up the last paragraph. The middle paragraph shows areas of expertise, duties, and achievements.

Phillip Seers

2222 Sunny Lane
San Lucas, CA 94066

Home: (666) 555-5555
Office: (555) 666-6666

Dear Recruiter:

Do you have a client who would be interested in a Finance Executive *and* a General Manager *and* an Operations Chief?

Wearing those three hats for the past three years, I have garnered accomplishments in many areas, including Human Resources, Sales & Marketing, and Information Systems. My most recent challenge involved securing funding without third-party debt for two new business units and reducing outstanding debt by $2.7 million to sustain the company's rapid expansion.

While developing financial and organizational infrastructures, I have established solid relationships with financial institutions, venture capitalists and clients, including some of Silicon Valley's giants.

I look forward to talking to you about your clients in need of someone with my broad financial and general business experience.

Sincerely,

Phillip Seers

enclosure: résumé

93

Finance Executive. *Ms. Sydney J. Reuben, Menlo Park, California*
A short and simple letter for an individual with much experience and many achievements. The writer italicizes *and* twice in the first sentence to emphasize the person's versatility.

JOHN B. ANDERSON
700 North Street
Chicago, IL 60000

Residence: 312.555.1212
Office: 847.555.1212
E-mail: xxxxxxx@xxxx.xxx

Date

Name
Title
Company
Address
City, State, Zipcode

Dear:

I am writing in response to your advertisement for the position of Finance Manager that appeared in Sunday's *Chicago Tribune*. My extensive background and qualifications are very much in line with the requirements outlined for this position. I appreciate your review of my enclosed résumé.

In brief, I am a self-motivated, highly responsible professional who brings:

- Sixteen years of accomplished experience in the areas of accounting, finance, information systems and project management, of which the last five years have been in the wireless telecommunications industry and included direct involvement in the construction of new personal communications systems.

- Keen understanding and utilization of automated financial systems, most notably, the Corporate-Wide Financial Accounting System, and a strong knowledge base in accounting processes to provide solid support to a company's total financial operation.

- Proven leadership acumen underscored by ability to effectively manage complex projects and to recruit and supervise high-performance teams.

- Dynamic analytical, organizational and communication skills; work well under time constraints and with others to achieve a common goal.

- Significant postgraduate education and continued professional development course work demonstrating a constant willingness to learn and take on new challenges.

The strength of my experience and knowledge would serve as a positive addition to your organization. I welcome meeting with you to discuss more specifically what your needs are, and how I can be a valued member of your safety team.

Thank you for your consideration. I look forward to hearing from you.

Sincerely,

John B. Anderson

enclosure

94

Finance Manager. *Cathleen M. Hunt, Chicago, Illinois*
At the end of the first paragraph, the show of appreciation for the reader's review of the resume subtly puts the reader under the obligation to read it as well as the cover letter.

GARY ANDRICH

111 Gomer Court   Toms River, New Jersey 08533   (732) 992-9999

Dear Prospective Employer:

Either I am a smart businessman, or luck has been on my side.   I, for one, doubt that luck has much to do with the success of one's career.

Inherent management and communications skills are my strengths, with extensive experience in finance, personnel training and development, marketing and account development, and sound decision making. Smart planning, honesty and integrity have furthered my career. Per your request, I would like to earn an annual salary in the range of $50,000 to $60,000.

Since my résumé provides an overview of my background, I look forward to the opportunity to provide you with further insight into my professional value during a personal interview.

Thank you for your consideration.

Yours truly,

Gary Andrich
Enclosure

95

Finance Manager. *Nina K. Ebert, Toms River, New Jersey*
The cover letter begins with a rigged Either/Or statement in which denial of the truth of the Or part implies that the Either part (a self-compliment) is true—a clever start for attention.

Elizabeth B. Sharpe

5555 Golden Way   Tel (666) 666-6666
Woodside, CA 99999   Fax (666) 888-8888

Dear Hiring Manager:

Would you be interested in a Finance Professional who also has excellent customer service and interpersonal skills? Now, add a broad business background, and you have a truly well-rounded team member.

With nearly 20 years' experience in financial analysis and internal auditing for Silicon Valley and aeronautics companies, I have extensive knowledge of procurement, government contracting requirements, and legal/contract practices.

I am self-motivated and self-directed, yet very effective working cross-functionally at all levels within an organization, and able to provide strong and sensitive leadership for staff members.

If you could use someone with my financial and business expertise, I would do an excellent job for your organization.

Sincerely,

Elizabeth B. Sharpe

enclosure: résumé

96

Finance Professional. *Ms. Sydney J. Reuben, Menlo Park, California*
In this letter the second paragraph supports the first by showing the breadth of the person's financial and business background and experience. The third shows management skills.

NATHAN BARRY
7 Schoolhouse Lane
Lancaster, OH 00000
(555) 555-5555

December 1, XXXX

Edward Hayes
Controller
Farmstead Dairies, Inc.
P.O. Box 800
Mt. Sterling, OH 00000

Dear Mr. Hayes:

In speaking recently with Troy Garrison, CFO of Farmstead Dairies, I learned of your opening for a financial control manager. He suggested I send you my resume in consideration for this position. It may interest you to know that with my extensive experience in the food industry, I have developed numerous personal relationships with many of the same customers we have in common.

My reputation is outstanding for avoiding delinquencies by exercising sound judgment as to establishing sale terms and credit lines, offering a choice of payment options, and rapidly intervening in the early stages of problems. As you are well aware, the gross margins for perishable food products are very slim, making it crucial to be paid for all products sold. If your organization can use someone who can ensure a positive impact on your bottom line without compromising sales, perhaps we should talk.

I can be available for an interview at your convenience.

Sincerely,

Nathan Barry

Enclosure: Resume

97

Financial Control Manager. *Melanie A. Noonan, West Paterson, New Jersey*
A letter prompted by a friend's suggestion. The clue to the applicant's work style is "sound judgment." He knows how to avoid trouble and to be profitable with slim margins.

RÉSUMÉ CONNECTION   Career Management Resources for Job Transition

June 27, XXXX

Mr. J. Robert Dalton
Human Resources Director
Citizens Bank & Trust
10 North Union Street
Twin Tiers, PA 11111

Dear Bob:

As a follow-up of our telephone conversation today, I am forwarding the enclosed résumé for the new operations position you are currently developing. I think you will want to consider this friend of mine whom I am recommending as a strong candidate for the position because of his solid background and exceptional skills in the areas of lending and branch operations.

I am not at liberty to disclose his identity at this time. He is currently employed with one of your competitor's organizations in another area of Pennsylvania and does not want to jeopardize his position there. I can tell you, however, that he is exploring other opportunities due to the transition and merger taking place within the organization he is currently working for. He feels that it may be time for a change, although he would like to remain in credit administration.

You will note from his résumé that besides his expertise in operations, he also has outstanding experience administering portfolios of as much as $22 million; he has been involved with leading branch personnel within a two-county area; and he is effective in planning, directing, budgeting and cost control. In short, I believe Citizens Bank & Trust would gain a valuable resource in adding him to their growing organization.

I'll call you next week to see how you would like to proceed in setting up an appointment for a personal interview. If you would prefer to move this along sooner, just let me know, and I'll see what can be arranged. Thank you for your time. As always, it's a pleasure to be of service.

Sincerely,

Deborah S. Edwards, NCRW/CPRW

Enclosure

33 Waln Street • PO Box 361 • Wellsboro, PA 16901 • (570) 724-3610
319 Main Street • Towanda, PA 18848 • (570) 265-9459

98

Portfolio Administrator. *Deborah S. Edwards, Wellsboro, Pennsylvania*
A confidential cover letter for a confidential resume in which the letter writer is the intermediary between the target company and the writer's client, whose name is withheld.

Shannon Markles
1404 Willow Rock Road
Montgomery, Alabama 36106
☎ [334] 555-6797

October 5, XXXX

Ms. Geraldine Battle
Manager
Argent Bank
500 Arba Street
Montgomery, Alabama 36104

Dear Ms. Battle:

I want to make it easy for you to increase your team's productivity and service.

When I started in the secondary market six years ago, I soon realized that it was up to me to become a recognized expert in the field. The résumé I have attached gives you a brief overview of what I have done. But it cannot show you *how* I improved my ability to serve the companies I worked with.

Simply put, I decided to go beyond mastering every skill involved in selling existing mortgages. I made it my business to know the competition, to know the best appraisers, to know the needs of the lending institutions. I also started my own "professional development program," taking courses at a local college. Finally, I learned the business by making time to help others get the job done.

My company likes what I do. However, I want to work in Atlanta and return to the secondary marketing specialist field with Argent Bank.

Perhaps the easiest way to start toward that goal is with face-to-face conversation. May I call in a few days to see when your schedule can fit in an interview?

Sincerely,

Shannon Markles

One enclosure: Résumé

99

Secondary Market Specialist. *Donald Orlando, Montgomery, Alabama*
This letter begins and ends with the theme of making it easy for the target bank to become more profitable. The middle paragraph shows how the would-be enabler became expert.

Bradley R. Kemmer
101 Square Boulevard — Monroe, Michigan 46623
313.555.8998

Senior Finance Executive

Corporate finance is no longer just a "numbers" game. As a Financial Manager at Ford Motor Corporation, my responsibilities have extended far beyond finance to include strategic and tactical business planning, marketing, new product development, sales administration, manufacturing, and general operating management within the corporation's emerging and high-growth business units. Results have been significant.

Most significant is my ability to work across diverse divisions (marketing, sales, manufacturing, product development, information systems), linking finance with operations to facilitate expansion, reorganization, and operating improvements.

My management style is direct and decisive, yet flexible in responding to the constantly changing demands of my staff, management teams, and the marketplace. I have earned a reputation for not only the strength of my financial expertise, but for my ability to communicate and coordinate cooperative efforts through cross-functional business teams.

Currently, I am confidentially investigating new career opportunities, thus my interest in your company. I would welcome the opportunity to meet and talk with you about mutual objectives.

I look forward to speaking with you.

Sincerely,

Bradley R. Kemmer

Enclosure: Résumé

100

Senior Finance Executive. *Lorie Lebert, Novi, Michigan*
A letter for a Finance Executive whose many strengths extend beyond finance. A recurrent theme is his ability to relate finance to many other business operations. See Resume 6.

TIMOTHY DE SALVA
1000 NW 21st Street
Plantation, FL 33024
(954) 000-0000; (305) 000-0000

Dear Financial Manager:

After 17 years of employment with one of the largest privately held medical equipment manufacturing companies, with $750 million in global sales, I have made the commitment to move on in my career. I am confident that my broad based experience in **Treasury Management** will serve as an asset to your organization. The enclosed résumé will provide you with a brief outline of my experience and accomplishments.

I am currently Cash and Risk Manager for Colman Corporation with many diversified responsibilities. In addition to managing day-to-day cash and risk management activities, I am accountable for currency hedging, developing and implementing insurance programs, equipment leasing, developing and maintaining bank relationships and negotiating lines of credit, and developing strategies to minimize and/or reduce interest rate risk. Some of my accomplishments include:

- Structuring specific global financing transactions, dividends, intercompany loans, acquisitions, and subsidiary recapitalization generating $1 million in savings

- Implementing a Foreign Exchange Management Program with $100 million in currency exposure, minimizing currency risk

- Introducing an international insurance Controlled Master Program, generating $500,000 in premium savings

I believe I have the knowledge, skills, and experience necessary to be an effective manager — one who can make a significant contribution to your bottom line. Thus, if a current or anticipated opening exists in your organization for a senior treasury manager, I would welcome the opportunity to speak with you further about my credentials. Because my employer is not aware of my intentions, I would appreciate your confidentiality in this matter.

Thank you for your time and consideration, and I look forward to speaking to you soon.

Sincerely,

Timothy De Salva

Enclosure

101

Senior Treasury Manager. *Shelley Nachum, Ft. Lauderdale, Florida*
Numerals in the opening paragraph are eye-catching. The second paragraph shows breadth of responsibilities and expertise, and the bullets point to quantified achievements.

DEBBIE SMITH, C.P.A.
14 S.W. 125th Avenue, Miami, Florida 33330 (305) 000-0000

Dear Executive:

If your organization can benefit from a dynamic senior financial officer, then the enclosed résumé will interest you.

Dedication, hard work, and superb skills have made my accounting/finance career one of fast track growth. In only 12 years, my career has taken me from a Senior Auditor to a Senior Vice President/CFO. I am excited about the rewarding role I had in taking a company public and the preparation involved in doing so. Subsequently, I was one of three officers to complete a 2-week "road show" throughout the United States.

I am skilled in designing and implementing comprehensive programs of audit, financial and internal controls. My experience also encompasses, but is not limited to, strategic planning, investor relations, financial analysis, financial reporting, funding strategies, budgeting, and negotiations. As mentioned above, having taken a company public, I have experience in Due Diligence and Initial Public Offerings.

Additionally, a key part of my function is developing long-term business relationships - both domestically and internationally. Besides relating with investors, I am a liaison with the OCC, SEC, Federal Reserve Bank, and State of Florida Department of Revenue.

As an effective manager, I have the ability to hire and train the key personnel to accomplish my goals. I am bilingual in English and Spanish and computer proficient in a variety of current applications.

Thank you for your time and review of this highly confidential document. I look forward to hearing your comments.

Very truly yours,

Debbie Smith, CPA

Encl.

102

Senior Vice President of Finance/CFO. *Shelley Nachum, Ft. Lauderdale, Florida*
The tempo of this letter is quick because of the relatively short paragraphs and the use of vital words (*dynamic, superb, fast-track, excited, key, bilingual,* and *highly confidential*).

Arlo M. Prescott

555 Broadway
White Plains, New York 55555
(555) 555-5555

Dear Sir/Madam:

As you suggested in your recent phone call, I am enclosing a copy of my resume for your consideration. I would like to call your attention to the skills and achievements in my background that are most relevant to the position you described.

As a veteran banking professional, I understand that success depends on a strong commitment to *customer satisfaction* and a constant focus on the *bottom line*. My career in both retail management and commercial lending includes 16 years with my present organization, Mamaroneck Bank/York Trust Corp. Five of those years have been as Senior Vice President/Regional Manager. I presently supervise 375 employees at 35 locations.

In XXXX I exceeded all corporation sales objectives including a significant improvement in the efficiency ratio of the region.

Recent accomplishments as Senior Vice President/Regional Manager include the following:

- Achieved recognition as the highest producing region in the bank for produ/cts sold per platform FTE, average consumer loans per branch, and small business loans for the entire company.

- Credited by outside financial consultants as maintaining the highest average transaction per teller and the lowest unit labor costs.

- Worked extensively with merger consolidation efforts to devise cost-saving mechanisms and standards. Established operating efficiency standards and maximized profits.

- Chosen for numerous special projects and leadership teams including membership in the Company Acquisition Coordination Group and membership in the Skills Pool Strategy Team, a human resource program that encompassed 360-degree feedback among all staff members.

I approach my work with a strong sense of urgency, working well under pressure and change. I feel that my combined leadership and coaching skills, along with sales management and business development, would serve as an asset to a position within your organization. I am a forward thinker and a team player who has a strong commitment to my organization and my staff.

Thank you for your consideration. I look forward to discussing how I can contribute to your organization.

Sincerely,

Arlo M. Prescott
Enclosure

103

Senior Vice President/Regional Manager. *Beverly Baskin, Marlboro, New Jersey*
Indicating that the resume was requested helps to get it past the "gatekeeper"—the person who opens and routes the mail—and into the hands of the intended or appropriate reader.

ROBERT R. KINCAID
222 Middle Road
City, State 13421
555-555-5555

April 10, XXXX

Mr. J. P. Moneybags, President
First National Bank
123 Bank Street
City, State 00000

Dear Mr. Moneybags:

As a banking professional with an extensive track record of success, I read with great interest your recent ad for a Vice President of Commercial Lending. I believe that I have a wealth of talents that could benefit your institution in this role and have enclosed for your consideration a résumé that briefly outlines my credentials.

Some of the capabilities that I can bring to this position with your bank include:

- **Maintaining a commercial loan portfolio that includes wholesale distributors, medical practices, an industrial rigging firm, retail stores, and other businesses.**

- **Managing a $105 million mortgage portfolio that represented 75% of the bank's total loans.**

- **Supervising Branch Managers, with accountability for business development and profit performance at the individual branches.**

- **Directing special projects that have included construction and ultimate launch of new branches, and renovations to existing facilities.**

- **Exceptional customer rapport and community involvement, which are integral parts of doing business in suburban and rural markets.**

I am convinced that my knowledge, expertise, and professionalism would allow me to effectively meet the challenges of this commercial lending role or other management positions where I could serve your needs. I would enjoy meeting with you in person to discuss the possibilities that exist. Please call me at (555) 555-5555 to arrange a convenient date and time for us to open a dialogue. I look forward to speaking with you soon.

Thank you.

Sincerely,

Robert R. Kincaid

Enclosure

104

Vice President of Commercial Lending. *Arnold G. Boldt, Rochester, New York*
Lending and managing are two dominant themes of this letter. They are evident especially in the bulleted items in boldface and expressed explicitly in the last main paragraph.

Norman Ellington
1442 Norris Lane
Montgomery, Alabama 36117
℘[334] 555-5555

August 16, XXXX

Mr. J. J. Stimpson
President
First Bank of Commerce
1400 Aurora Drive
Montgomery, Alabama 36100

Dear Mr. Stimpson:

Years ago, on my first day as a loan teller, I adopted my own rule of success: Do what promotes peace of mind in every depositor and every member of our banking family. Now I am the Vice President of Operations at Northern Bank. But I still hold to those proven standards. It means that I will not promise more than I can deliver. And it requires me to give my all. If that work ethic appeals to you and The First Bank of Commerce, I would like to talk with you about joining your team.

To help you learn more about my track record, I have attached a brief résumé. The accomplishments are only selected examples, but they do illustrate my focus on providing peace of mind.

For my employees, peace of mind means I must show them that excellent performance leads to promotion. Senior management knows they can count on me to translate their vision into actions that build profitability. Customers – from depositors to other bank employees – know my people strive to solve problems *before* they occur.

Please consider this letter and my résumé as the first phase in an undertaking that promises mutual benefit. However, words on paper can't replace face-to-face conversations. May I call in a few days to see when your schedule will allow an interview?

Sincerely,

Norman Ellington

One enclosure: Résumé

105

Vice President of Operations. *Donald Orlando, Montgomery, Alabama*
Peace of mind is the thread on which the first three paragraphs are strung. Providing peace of mind for clients and peers is the guiding rule of this individual's successful work ethic.

Thomas N. Investigator

000 Detective Street • Anywhere, Michigan 00000
(000) 000-0000

January 1, XXXX

Recruitment Center
P.O. Box 5555
Anywhere, Virginia 00000-0000

RE: Central Intelligence Agency Employment

I am interested in exploring employment opportunities with the Central Intelligence Agency (CIA). The enclosed résumé is in accordance with the instructions stated in the CIA's *Job Kit and Resume Preparation Guide*. I would like to be considered for all possible positions. An acceptable salary would be in the mid-$20K range.

Qualifications I bring to your agency include:

- Proven performance in fast-paced and high-stress working environments
- Strong analytical skills with exceptional attention to detail
- Highly motivated and aggressively take on great responsibility
- Planned and implemented over 100 strategic missions with a 100% success rate
- Hands-on experience with classified documentation
- Experienced in intelligence report writing, including in-depth reports on high-interest areas of operation

My record is one of great responsibility, dedication, and solid accomplishments. I am confident that my experience and abilities can make a valuable contribution to the CIA. I am available for immediate employment and willing to relocate.

Should any questions arise regarding the information on my résumé, please do not hesitate to contact me. I look forward to hearing from you in the near future.

Sincerely,

Thomas Investigator

Enclosure

106

Intelligence Specialist. *Maria E. Hebda, Trenton, Michigan*
A customized letter for a recent graduate who had done intelligence work while in the Navy. The individual found the CIA job posting and *Job Kit* on the World Wide Web.

MARY E. MANAGER

35 Tree Lined Terrace   Oak, IL 60000   (847) 555-1234

April 24, 1998

Ms. Sheila McIntyre
Director
Physicians Practice Group
54 Healing Way
Clinic Springs, IL 66666

Dear Ms. McIntyre:

Please accept this letter and enclosed résumé in response to your recent advertisement for Administrative Manager of your Northwest Medical Facility. My background and experience closely parallel the requirements outlined for this position.

Highlights of my career include:

- Ten years of management experience in fast-paced, high-pressure health care environments with responsibility for overseeing department operations, personnel, quality assurance and organizational development.
- Dynamic team leadership qualifications; solid track record of recruiting, training and developing quality, competent staff; effective in prioritizing and delegating tasks.
- Strong interpersonal skills; relate well with medical professionals, management, agencies, outside vendors and consumers.
- Knowledge of budgets, payroll, inventory and management information systems.

In my most recent position with Health Care Plus, I gained added exposure to Medicare billing and acquired an in-depth understanding of the program's regulations and requirements.

Now, I am interested in exploring new, professional opportunities and would welcome meeting with you to discuss my qualifications in greater detail. I am confident that the extent of my experience would make a positive addition to your medical management team.

Thank you for your time and consideration.

Sincerely,

Mary E. Manager

enclosure

107

Administrative Manager. *Cathleen M. Hunt, Chicago, Illinois*
The bulleted career highlights are self-authenticating by being in agreement. That is, all of the first three bulleted items seem true because the first two items make the third credible.

KENNETH SMITH
1591 Main Street
Rochester, New York 55555
(716) 555-5555

December 29, 1999

Mr. William Simmons
Human Resource Director
Genesee Hospital
40 Alexander Street
Rochester, New York 00000

Dear Mr. Simmons:

My interest in continuing my professional career in the health care field has prompted me to inquire about employment within your organization. Enclosed is my resume for your review.

For over 8 years, I have dedicated myself to the health care field, primarily in an administrative or financial capacity. Briefly, my qualifications include:

♦ All phases of accounting, billing, and insurance procedures
♦ Developed supervisory and customer service skills
♦ Ability to effectively meet deadlines while adhering to strict guidelines

My resume is a good summary, but I would welcome the opportunity to meet with you to more fully discuss my qualifications, as well as learn about your long-term goals. I am confident that my enthusiasm, knowledge and experience would be a benefit to your organization.

Thank you for your attention, and I look forward to speaking with you.

Sincerely,

Kenneth Smith

Enclosure

108

Administrator. *Kim Little, Victor, New York*
The letter is kept brief, and the resume is called a "good summary." The reason is the individual's point that what really matters is an interview for learning about each other.

HELEN P. NELSON, M.N.
11111 – 111st Street SE • Anytown, MI 99999 • 555 / 555-5555

July 5, XXXX

Grady Livermoore, M.D., F.A.C.S.
Anytown Colorectal Practice
12121 - 12th Street
Anytown, MI 99999

Dear Dr. Livermoore:

With receipt of a Master of Nursing degree in June, I am qualified as an Adult Acute Care Nurse Practitioner, preparing for board certification as an A.R.N.P., and seeking a collaborative role with general or colorectal surgeons. As the field of Acute Care Nurse Practitioner is fairly new, I am contacting you to highlight the advantages a surgeon gains in utilizing the services of an A.R.N.P., as well as to advise you of my experience, expertise, and availability.

The ACNP program prepares Accredited Registered Nurse Practitioners to provide billable, comprehensive, and risk-appropriate management of medically vulnerable patients with serious illness in a variety of care settings. The ACNP curriculum at the University of Michigan consists of advanced clinical practice and nursing science, built on a core of intensive physiology, pathophysiology, and pharmacology.

Insurance companies recognize the reimbursement value of our services because we are qualified to:

- Conduct independent health assessments;
- Order and interpret diagnostic tests;
- Diagnose and manage health problems and disease-related symptoms;
- Prescribe and evaluate drugs and treatment; and
- Coordinate care during transitions in settings.

While services of an RN are necessary for your practice, they are nonrevenue producing. The services of an A.R.N.P. – simply put – are

My nursing background is extensive and includes 15 years in both leadership and staff roles, 11 of which were in operating rooms with general, vascular, thoracic, gynecological, and colorectal surgical patients. For the past 5 years, I have served as a Surgical Case Manager at Northeast Hospital. I completed my ACNP general surgery rotation at the University of Michigan Medical Center and my colorectal surgery rotation at General Hospital. In both residencies, I served as First Assist in the operating room and managed preoperative and postoperative patients. Additionally, I performed flexible signoidoscopy and colonoscopy procedures.

Enclosed for your review is my Curriculum Vitae, which details both my experience and expertise, as well as my operating room and clinical background and training. I will call you within the next 10 days to schedule a meeting, at which time I can share additional information on my unique abilities, the skills of Adult Acute Care Nurse Practitioner, and the insurance reimbursement procedures for A.R.N.P.s.

Sincerely,

Helen P. Nelson
Enclosure

109

Adult Acute Care Nurse Practitioner. *Carole S. Barns, Woodinville, Washington*
This individual was concerned that many doctors would not know the financial value of hiring someone with her credentials. Her billable services could add to the bottom line.

TOM FITNESS
Box 8
Corporate, ND 58000

Home (701) 555-5555   Work (701) 666-6666

OCCUPATIONAL HEALTH AND SAFETY PROFESSIONAL
CORPORATE AND COMMUNITY FITNESS
more than nine years of experience

April 2, xxxx

Fitness Clinic, Ltd.
Human Resources
P.O. Box 555
Corporate, ND 58000-5555

Dear Human Resources Director:

While many of your candidates for the *Case Manager/Employee Health Coordinator* position
may have the Registered Nursing License you request, I am able to offer more. My background
may be exactly what you are looking for.

I can offer you:

> **Solid Development Experience:** I successfully developed and implemented an
> Occupational Health Department from ground level, responding to the changing health
> care needs of business and industry. I look forward to meeting this challenge again.

> **Marketing Expertise:** I now work directly with some of North Dakota's major
> manufacturing firms in striving for a safer work environment.

> **Industry Knowledge:** I keep updated and am very knowledgeable on all the latest issues
> regarding work site occupational health through continuing education and research, as
> indicated on my résumé. I am recognized as a community leader in health and wellness
> programs, one who can match services with needs.

I would appreciate the opportunity to meet with you to discuss how my skills could meet your
needs for this position. Since your position offers an opportunity and location that are very
appealing to me, my salary requirements are flexible.

Sincerely,

Tom Fitness

Enclosure

110

Case Manager/Employee Health Coordinator. *Mary Laske, Fargo, North Dakota*
The writer "included the top qualifications the organization was requesting and related them
to his background." The person got an interview and is now an employee of the company.

JoanClaire May, R.D.H.

555 West Right Street
Elmira, NY 00000
(555) 000-0000

Dear Doctor:

I would like to offer the enclosed résumé as an application for a possible position with your practice as a full-time dental hygienist.

I have an excellent background in all facets of dental hygiene care, as well as experience with a wide range of patients including those with mental and physical disabilities. I am particularly meticulous concerning charting and documentation, and I am fully able to handle general office duties as well. I maintain excellent rapport with patients, and I particularly enjoy the challenge of helping to ease the anxiety many patients bring to the chair, turning their visits into a positive experience "at the dentist's."

Please consider my credentials and experience in your search for a qualified, enthusiastic addition to your professional staff. I can be reached at the above address and phone to arrange for a personal interview at your convenience. I will be happy to furnish references; however, until a mutual interest is established, I would request that you do not contact my present employer.

Thank you for your time and consideration of my qualifications. I hope to hear from you soon.

Sincerely,

JoanClaire May, R.D.H.

Enclosure

111

Dental Hygienist. *Betty Geller, Elmira, New York*
This letter focuses on two themes: dental skills and people skills. She has the training and experience to perform well as a hygienist. She can make people *like* being at the dentist!

Eleanor Fong, CPHM

35-21 45th Avenue, Bayside, NY 11360 ■ phone / fax 516-555-5555 ■ efong@aol.com

June 14, xxxx

Mr. Lucas Dorman
Vice President of Operations
Technology Associates Corporation
52 North Service Road
Islandia, NY 11788

Dear Mr. Dorman:

You have advertised for a Director of Procurement. As a resource management and purchasing professional with a track record of achievement in expense reduction, corporate partnership agreements, and revenue enhancement, I have credentials that meet your requirements.

Current responsibilities include the direction of all corporate purchasing functions for Long Island Jewish Medical Center, a multihospital system (four hospital divisions, three nursing homes, and home care/emergency outreach clinics) controlling an operating budget of $1 million with over $70 million purchasing volume.

As a former purchasing manager and materials manager for North Shore University Hospital Medical Center, I initiated highly effective purchasing value analysis and savings programs that produced $3.5 million in savings over a two-year period. In both positions I was instrumental in negotiating innovative corporate partnership agreements with a number of key vendors. The bottom-line savings generated in my tenure with these health care facilities has been in the millions of dollars.

Mr. Dorman, my accomplishments are transferable to any industry that requires quality and service coupled with a keen eye on the bottom line. You will find me to be a take-charge team builder and win-win negotiator. I do not accept failure, and "It cannot be done" is not in my vocabulary. My commitment to imaginative cost containment and proactive resource management has gained me an industry-wide reputation of excellence.

My resource management skills, team-building abilities, ingenuity and passion for excellence would absolutely make me an asset to Technology Associates. I have enclosed my resume for your review (in both traditional and computer scannable versions). If you require a results-oriented resource, purchasing, or materials manager who can direct profitable programs, manage a sizable budget, and reduce expenses without reducing services, then we should meet to discuss the ways that I can help you achieve your project and company goals.

Sincerely,

Eleanor Fong, CPHM

112

Director of Procurement. *Deborah Wile Dib, Medford, New York*
The person wanted to move from health care to an expanding industry. The writer therefore stressed cross-industry skills. The person now works as a university Procurement Director.

ANNE M. LUDWIG

123 Midway Road
Upton, New Jersey 55555
200 • 555 • 5555

February 2, XXXX

Janice A. Merck, Employment Manager
Upton General Medical Center
123 East Ferry Street
Engleton, New Jersey 55555

Dear Ms. Merck:

Please accept this letter and confidential résumé as an application for HIV Case Manager advertised in *The Ledger*. I believe you will find me to be a mature, compassionate and efficient individual well qualified to provide the skills you require for a career with Upton General Medical Center.

Detailed on my résumé is a successful background as HIV Counseling/Testing Site Coordinator and Public Health Nurse Supervisor in East Windsor, New Jersey. Duties include coordinating and managing a staff of HIV/AIDS counselors and counseling HIV-positive clients. Many of the clients were minorities, drug users, gay, bisexual, or highly sexually active individuals. This work requires a high degree of cultural and ethnic sensitivity. I have also worked as an emergency care provider with the American Red Cross as an Advanced First Aid and CPR instructor gaining valuable experience in first-responder care. My credentials and achievements are a matter of record and include expertise and in-depth knowledge of the social services system about HIV/AIDS services in New Jersey, basic life support, and triage.

It would be exciting to serve your community and HIV-infected individuals in a hospital-based primary care clinic. With excellent people skills, I enjoy challenge and work hard to attain goals. My professional abilities include nursing care, treatment, case management, administration, counseling, and education. At present a C.S.W. license is pending.

I look forward to hearing from you in the very near future to schedule an interview at your convenience. The opportunity to meet and explore the contributions I can make will be most welcome.

Sincerely,

Anne M. Ludwig, R.N.

113

HIV Case Manager. *Anne G. Kramer, Virginia Beach, Virginia*
The end of the first paragraph is like a brief Profile. The second paragraph shows that the person can do the work required, and the third paragraph makes it clear that she wants to.

Maria D. Rodriguez, LPN
22 River Road, Patchogue, NY 11772
phone / fax 516-555-5555

June 14, xxxx

Dolores Martino, RN
Director of Nursing
North Shore University Hospital
Manhasset, NY 11030

Dear Ms. Martino:

As a recent recipient of an LPN license and a professional with a wide background in healthcare-related employment, I am interested in discussing the contribution I can make to the nursing staff at North Shore University Hospital.

Although a recent graduate, I have a background that encompasses a wide range of healthcare experience including private duty nursing, medical office assistance, and work with severely impaired children. I am sure that with my professional accomplishments, motivation and sense of responsibility, I can quickly become a productive member of your staff.

This background has given me the training and work ethic necessary to fulfill the rigorous requirements of employment as an LPN. As an experienced professional, I can certainly do an excellent job with all patient care, medical coordination and follow-up. Daily work as an adult student in a demanding program and as a professional in demanding fields has sharpened my assessment skills and prioritization abilities, important criteria for a strong LPN.

Total commitment to the patients in my care and to the achievement of the objectives of the hospital/facility and medical staff is my primary focus. You will find me to be quick to learn and eager to initiate self-directed work when appropriate. The enclosed resume highlights the skills that you may find useful to your staff. I hold a deep commitment to excellence and will make every effort to fulfill your requirements.

Sincerely,

Maria Rodriguez

114

Licensed Practical Nurse. *Deborah Wile Dib, Medford, New York*
In a field flooded with applicants, this recent adult grad got a position in two weeks as charge nurse in a home for elderlies. The graphic is also in the resume. See Resume 12.

Zofia Majewski, RN
14 Charlotte Street
Milwaukee, WI 00000
(555) 555-5555

Dear Nurse Recruiter:

If the staffing requirements at your facility include a skilled orthopedic nurse, I would appreciate your consideration of me. I am a licensed Registered Nurse with six years of prior orthopedic nursing practice in my native country of Poland. My broad range of clinical skills is highlighted on the enclosed resume.

Currently, I am employed by a physicians' group specializing in gynecology and internal medicine but have kept up-to-date in the orthopedic field through volunteer work on the Orthopedic Floor at Waukesha Memorial Hospital. While assisting patients with general care duties, helping them with ROM/breathing exercises, and training them to walk on crutches, I have also had a lot of opportunity to observe various surgical procedures and therapies, as well as learn of new splinting materials.

I am a compassionate, devoted and patient-oriented nurse, possessing the qualifications and attributes for provision of safe, efficient and therapeutically effective nursing care. My skills include the systematic collection and communication of patient data and performance of basic actions that maintain patient comfort and attain desired outcomes. In addition, I am multilingual, with language fluency in English, Polish and Russian, further enabling me to communicate effectively with patients.

As a nurse at your facility, I would want nothing more than to contribute to the efficiency of a professional care team and be regarded by my coworkers and patients as someone who is always there for them whenever needed. It would give me great pride to earn the respect of those I work with.

I hope you will find my qualifications desirable for a staff position at your facility. I will be glad to discuss in a personal interview how I may be able to benefit your organization, and I eagerly await hearing from you.

Sincerely,

Zofia Majewski

115

Orthopedic Nurse. *Melanie A. Noonan, West Paterson, New Jersey*
The first paragraph introduces the person, and the second shows that she is up-to-date in orthopedic techniques. The third indicates her skills; and the fourth, her desire to work.

BRYAN ENEA

Home: 811 66th Avenue N. ▪ Herkimer, NY 00000 ▪ (555) 555-5555
School: 123 Sunny Avenue ▪ Boston, MA 00000 ▪ (555) 555-5555

August 19, xxxx

Ms. Jane Smith
123 Street
Poughkeepsie, NY 12603

Dear Ms. Smith:

I am a pediatric physical therapy major at Northeastern University who would like to explore employment opportunities within your practice. Northeastern's program is based on a cooperative educational approach which requires students to pursue paid employment opportunities within their field of study. Therefore, I would accept any position where my skills and abilities would benefit your practice while enabling me to gain an insight into the office environment as well as a realistic understanding of the role of a physical therapist.

If given the opportunity, I will work hard to make positive contributions to your practice. As a sophomore, I realize that I cannot offer you an abundance of experience. However, I would bring with me an exceptional work ethic, an eagerness to learn, and a commitment to my chosen profession. I would also bring general clerical skills--data entry, word processing, and the Internet--and personal qualities which include organized and disciplined work habits, an ability to relate well with people, a high energy level and problem-solving aptitude.

Enclosed is my resume for your review. Should you have any questions regarding my abilities, please contact me at the above number. Thank you for your time and attention in reviewing my qualifications. I look forward to hearing from you.

Sincerely,

Bryan Enea

Enclosure

116

Pediatric Physical Therapy Major. *Kristin Mroz Coleman, Poughkeepsie, New York*
This university sophomore was seeking a co-op position in order to fulfill graduation requirements. The person is up-front about little experience but offers energy and commitment.

500 Scenic Drive, Midwestern Town, MN 55555 • (555) 555-5555

Date

Name
Title
Company
Address

Position of Interest—Personal Trainer / Health and Wellness Specialist

Dear   :

I am exploring companies which specialize in the field of fitness and training, and would like the opportunity to interview with you to discuss your hiring needs and company goals.

My experience interning at the Mayo Clinic as a Health and Wellness Specialist has been invaluable, serving to reinforce my enthusiasm and interest in the field. I have been fortunate to work in positions that forced me to take a very proactive approach with clients. One of my key strengths is the ability to develop relationships which set clients at ease and encourage them to ask questions concerning their program, progress and goals.

The NSCA certifications I hold in strength and conditioning, as well as in personal training, are of special pride. And the Mayo seminars on ergogenic aids, as well as an **August** conference emphasizing fitness programs and performance enhancements, provide important additional training beyond my degree in Exercise Science—Corporate Wellness. As we transition into the next century, I am especially committed to ongoing knowledge and learning.

Since 1996 I have been directly involved in the field, providing leadership in the areas of coaching, training, supervision and management. I have conducted research, designed and developed programs, performed testing, and accomplished much—which the resume further details. You will note that my background is fairly broad-based, and I have the ability to train athletes, deal with corporate wellness, and tailor personal training programs. Work ethic, dependability and integrity are high priorities, and I am very outgoing and professional in relationships with others. Additionally, I am self-motivated, enthusiastic, energetic and entrepreneurial—with an eye toward profitability, growth and sales and marketing issues.

I have already made arrangements for a Spanish tutor to refresh my language skills. I am excited about relocating to Texas and look forward to touching base with you to discuss company hiring needs. If you need additional information, please let me know.

Sincerely,

John Doe

Enclosure

117

Personal Trainer/Health and Wellness Specialist. *Beverley Drake, Rochester, Minnesota*
A rare letter in which interest in an interview is expressed first. The next several paragraphs become increasingly more informative. The fourth paragraph is rich with information.

CYNTHIA PATRICK
5 North Street • Staten Island, New York • 55555
(555) 555-0000

March 6, XXXX

Craig Lawrence
Director
Action Day Treatment Center
5 Arlene Street
Rego Park, NY 55555

Dear Mr. Lawrence:

Thank you for an enjoyable interview today. I enjoyed the tour of the facility and meeting the staff. I was immediately impressed by the professionalism and dedication that you and the staff exhibited. I remain very interested and enthusiastic about the Program Coordinator position and believe that my professional experience, leadership competencies, and strong work ethic will greatly benefit your program.

I am most impressed by the amount that you have accomplished in such a short time. Your philosophy about the importance of client opportunity, age-appropriate programming, and community involvement is one that I share. I also believe in the importance of maintaining an attractive and stimulating physical environment.

Based on our discussion, it seems that you are seeking an administrator who shares your vision and is open to implementing creative and cutting-edge changes. I share your vision and am currently in search of such a professional opportunity—one that allows me to implement policies and procedures that maximize the consumers' functioning and enable them to reach their potential.

I have extensive administrative experience in day treatment programs. In my current position as Director of the Spartan Day Treatment Program, I expect and achieve high standards for services. My thorough knowledge of local, NYS, and federal regulations enables the program to consistently attain positive audits. One of my greatest strengths is my ability to motivate staff to strive for excellence and to work together to achieve common goals. Most significant has been my success in turning new programs into highly effective operations.

Thanks again for your time and consideration. If you need additional information, please do not hesitate to contact me at (555) 555-0000. I look forward to speaking with you again.

Sincerely,

Cynthia Patrick

118

Program Coordinator. *Kim Isaacs, Jackson Heights, New York*
This letter is a follow-up to an interview earlier in the day. More than just a thank-you note, the letter expresses enthusiasm, shared vision, and *a focused restatement of qualifications.*

MARY LOUISE STUART
35 Sherwood Street • Borough, PA 00000
(111) 111-1111

October 15, XXXX

Mr. Philip J. Russell
Senior Residential Services
P. O. Box 154
Borough, PA 00000

Dear Mr. Russell:

In response to your **advertisement** for the position of **Program Director**, I have enclosed my résumé for your review and consideration. I feel my experience in the areas of program development and fund-raising, along with my interpersonal skills and ability to manage multiple tasks, qualifies me for this position.

You will learn from my résumé that I have a solid record of success with 16 years of experience in volunteer services at Memorial Hospital. In addition to processing and placing an average of more than 200 volunteers per year (in-house services and auxiliary fund-raising), I was directly involved in raising three quarters of a million dollars during my career at the hospital. The programs and networks I established continue to benefit the hospital and community in many ways.

Supervisors and customers describe me as a "planning and coordinating leader" with "dedication, loyalty, and cooperation" on the job. I was a "motivating force" in putting together programs in need of "last minute details," promotion, and several hundred tasks completed simultaneously. I was consistently judged to have an "outstanding attitude" and "excellent relationships with other personnel."

In my previous position, my salary compensation was in the upper 20s; however, I would like to know more regarding the responsibilities and expectations of this particular position to be better able to discuss **salary** issues.

I would welcome the opportunity to discuss my qualifications and how my experiences will make a strong contribution to Senior Residential Services. Please call me at the above telephone number to arrange a personal interview. Thank you for your consideration.

Sincerely yours,

Mary Louise Stuart

Enclosure

119

Program Director, fund-raising. *Deborah S. Edwards, Wellsboro, Pennsylvania*
The individual had been downsized, was over 50, and lacked technical skills. The writer included quotations from the person's work evaluations and showed her networking skills.

Melissa Brown Cheever

10 Empire Place, New York 55555   200 • 555 • 5555 Home
                                                200 • 666 • 6666 Work

August 1, XXXX

Pan American Health Organization
World Health Organization
525 Twenty-Third Street, N.W.
Washington, D.C. 20037

In response to your Vacancy Notice 00/PAHO/000, enclosed find my résumé applying for the position of Public Health Nutritionist with a Duty Station in Kingston, Jamaica.

As a high-energy, results-oriented professional, I am able to handle multiple challenges and detail. My background includes a twelve-year position as Food, Nutrition and Cookery Instructor with the Ministry of Education in Jamaica, West Indies.

I believe my professional experience and standards would make me a valuable asset to the Caribbean Food and Nutrition Institute. My knowledge enables me to further their programs while enhancing the health and welfare of the people.

I would be pleased to further discuss my qualifications in greater detail during an interview. I look forward to hearing from you shortly and thank you for your consideration.

Sincerely,

Melissa Brown Cheever

120

Public Health Nutritionist. *Anne G. Kramer, Virginia Beach, Virginia*
The writer chose an attractive font to make the name stand out. The short paragraphs indicate in turn the person's purpose, background, experience, and interest in an interview.

47 Plimpton Drive, Litchfield, Connecticut 55555

(555) 555-5555

Date

Name
Title
Company
Address

Dear   :

My student work experience at Mayo Clinic and St. Mary's Hospital has been rewarding, serving to reinforce enthusiasm and interest in continuing my career as a **Radiology Technologist**. The work has been very diversified, and I have handled patients from pediatrics to geriatrics, and from many cultures and languages.

The enclosed resume details my background and training. Some of the strengths I bring to the workplace include the following:

- Diplomacy, listening and communication skills
- Flexibility and ability to reprioritize on short notice
- Self-motivation and discipline
- Organizational skills and attention to detail
- Strong sense of confidentiality and professionalism

You will find me compassionate and caring, assertive and very much a team player. I function well both with and without supervision and am able to make decisions and exercise sound judgment. My style is productive, accurate and responsible, and I believe that the work ethic, dependability and maturity I offer are traits employers find valuable in today's labor force.

An interview would provide a better assessment of my potential and background. I look forward to hearing from you and having the opportunity to discuss your goals and staffing plans. If you need additional information, please let me know.

Sincerely,

Sheri Klausen

Enclosure: Resume

121

Radiology Technologist. *Beverley Drake, Rochester, Minnesota*
The letter begins with a recap of the student's work experience. Bullets point to strengths, and the third paragraph is a profile. The fourth paragraph gives reasons for an interview.

Michael Van Dyne

9 Quigley Place ▪ Pittsburgh, PA 00000 ▪ (555) 555-5555

July 2, 19XX

The Prudential Insurance Company
PruCare Regional Office
1000 New Century Road
Pittsburgh, PA 00000

Dear Hiring Manager:

If your staffing requirements include someone with a background in financial analysis for a market-driven organization, please consider me an interested candidate.

For the past two years, I have been employed as a rate analyst for General Healthcare, supporting their field sales force and underwriting department in strategic planning initiatives as well as the accurate handling of all account services. During this time, I progressed significantly in responsibility to be entrusted with analytical work on complex applications representing high face values. I am involved daily with the upkeep of major accounts, adjustments in billing and settlement of problems, while maintaining excellent working relationships with our internal departments.

As we were recently notified that General Healthcare is being acquired by Plymouth Rock, given these circumstances, it is doubtful that I will be able to advance on my career path into underwriting.

I am enclosing my resume that will provide you with details of my effectiveness and some indication of how I can contribute to your organization. Please let me know if you have or anticipate an opportunity that may fit my qualifications. I will be happy to schedule an interview to discuss this further.

Sincerely,

Michael Van Dyne

Enclosure: Resume

122

Rate Analyst, health insurance. *Melanie A. Noonan, West Paterson, New Jersey*
The four paragraphs express in turn the individual's purpose in writing Prudential, his current duties and the quality of his work, the reason for a change, and his interest in an interview.

Alisha B. Cory
P.O. Box 1111
Fremont, CA 99999
(555) 333-5555

October xx, xxxx

A. J. Nolte
VP Human Resources
ABC Company, Inc.
7777 Linus Drive - Suite #44
San Jose, CA 99999

Dear A. J. Nolte:

REGISTERED NURSE (*San Jose Mercury News* ad, October xx)

Your advertisement for the above position and the position description provided seem to be a good match with my background. You may wish to consider a candidate with a significant mix of acute care and public health nursing experience. In addition, I have in-depth expertise with industrial, health care services.

You may find some of my successes of interest. For example:

- Provide acute care at 4 different hospitals, working in Mother/Baby, L & D, medical-surgical, acute rehab, and even a subacute care facility.

- Organized a health care team for creating a unique, new, 20-page *Community Resource Prospectus*.

- Administer health and developmental screenings, including DDSTs, then coordinate with doctors and medical facilities, plus several county and state agencies.

Regarding your request for salary information, I would require a salary of $46,000 to $56,000, depending on the range of personal (and family) benefits offered, such as medical, dental, and vision care; commissions; bonuses; profit sharing; 401Ks; stock options; and/or other perks.

Enclosed is a copy of my résumé for your evaluation. I have a serious interest to be considered for the position and am confident that a personal interview would be both interesting and mutually profitable. I look forward to hearing from you.

Sincerely,

Alisha B. Cory

Enclosures

P.S. For your convenience, a special scannable résumé is enclosed, in addition to the standard résumé.

123

Registered Nurse. *Carl L. Bascom, Fremont, California*
A letter with a subject line after the salutation. Arrow bullets point to successes that illustrate the individual's mix of acute care and public health nursing experience.

Sharon A. Cure, RN
1234 Medical Avenue • Anywhere, Michigan 55555
(000) 000-0000 • Pager (000) 000-0000

January 1, XXXX

Ms. Carla Sims, Director of Personnel
Any Medical Hospital
123 Health Court
Anywhere, Michigan 55555

Dear Ms. Sims:

I am interested in obtaining a nursing position with your organization. My current position has helped me develop self-confidence, excellent communication and leadership skills and exposure to many facets of the health care field. My qualifications and key strengths include:

- Bachelor of Science Degree – Nursing
- Strong clinical background
- Excellent communication and interpersonal skills
- Work effectively with individuals at all levels
- Work well under pressure
- Self-motivated, innovative and organized

The enclosed résumé will provide a more complete summation of my background. I believe my professional experience and education would make me a valuable asset to your organization.

To ensure receipt of my correspondence, I will call you in the coming week to answer any questions you might have. I would welcome the opportunity for a personal interview to further discuss my qualifications in more detail.

Sincerely,

Sharon Cure, RN

Enclosure

124

Registered Nurse. *Maria E. Hebda, Trenton, Michigan*
A general letter for a nursing position. In the bulleted list, qualifications mean degree and clinical background; strengths mean communication and people skills, plus worker traits.

Yolanda Ellen Forbest, D.P.M.

100 28th Street
Heights, New York 55555
111 • 555 • 7890/555 • 5678

February 7, XXXX

The Hillview Foot Health Center
Attention, Dr. Richard Newton • Associate Application
1234 Medical Plaza Drive, Suite 199
Hillview, TX 55555

Dear Dr. Newton,

It has come to my attention that your practice is interested in adding a residency graduate specializing in Primary Care Podiatric Medicine to your staff. I believe my background and expertise in general Diabetic and Geriatric Foot Health Care, Sports Medicine, Biomechanics and Podiapediatrics can provide the skills your practice requires.

I am a mature and personable adult with a sincere desire to be of help to those needing care and attention. As the enclosed résumé indicates, I have an in-depth knowledge of podiatric medicine. I am a team player, full of energy and enthusiasm. The number of awards I have received during podiatric training denotes my high motivation.

The residency training program is demanding, and every other month I have rotated through various specialty departments gaining knowledge and experience in general medicine, general surgery, radiology, anesthesiology, emergency room, pathology, podiatric surgery, pediatrics, geriatrics, rehabilitation medicine, rheumatology, neurology, dermatology and psychiatry.

Following the conclusion of the residency program in July, I am interested in obtaining a position in Podiatric Medicine. I look forward to hearing from you in the near future to schedule an interview at your convenience to learn more about The Hillview Foot Health Center, its plans and goals, and how I might contribute to the success of its staff.

Sincerely yours,

Yolanda Ellen Forbest, D.P.M.

125

Residency Graduate. *Anne G. Kramer, Virginia Beach, Virginia*
The four paragraphs indicate in turn the individual's purpose in writing, a profile of the person, her training program, and her interest in an interview to learn the company's plans.

DIANA M. JONES, RN

44 Columbia Street • Arlington, NY 00000 • (555) 555-5555

June 3, XXXX

Dear Ms. Smith:

I read with great interest Local Hospital's plan for a new cancer center. For the past 7 years, I have worked in the Oncology/Bone Marrow Transplant Unit of Regional Medical Center. I sincerely enjoy my profession and would love the opportunity to utilize my skills and experience right here in Arlington!

In addition to extensive oncology experience, I would bring with me a strong work ethic, an energetic nature, and high ethical standards. In my present position, I care for some of the most difficult and acute cancer cases, requiring extensive interaction with patients, families and cross-functional staff. The multidisciplinary care and highly individualized care plans required for these cases have sharpened my assessment and planning skills as well as my ability to make sound time-critical decisions. Each day, my nursing skills are heightened. I willingly accept change and shifting priorities and function successfully in counseling, educating, and addressing the psychosocial needs of the families.

My strength lies in my ability to build partnerships within and outside the hospital environment. In turn, these partnerships have played a key role in improving morale, instilling a sense of community and ultimately improving the overall delivery of health care services. My team-centered approach and professional attitude enable me to effectively project the image required, and throughout the years, I have repeatedly demonstrated my ability to provide vision, effect positive change, and access new ideas.

Enclosed is my resume for your review. I would welcome the opportunity of a personal appointment, during which I can learn more about your requirements and you can assess first-hand the qualities I would bring to Local Hospital. Thank you for your time and consideration. I look forward to hearing from you.

Sincerely,

Diana M. Jones

Enclosure

126

Staff Nurse. *Kristin Mroz Coleman, Poughkeepsie, New York*
The person's goal and reason for a change appear first. The second paragraph shows her special sensitivities; and the third, her people skills. Interview interest is last. See Resume 13.

Cathy Smith, R.N.

2616 Smith Street • Jackson, Michigan 49203 • (517) 555-5555

October 9, XXXX

Pam Cruiser, Head Nurse
ICU / CCU
Elizabeth Hospital
255 Jackson Avenue
Chicago, IL 55555

Dear Ms. Cruiser:

Enclosed is my résumé in response to the available position of Unit Educator. This is an excellent opportunity to utilize my leadership qualities and a love for teaching.

As my résumé indicates, I have a strong background in the education of new orientees, patients/families, and staff. My dedication in this role truly enhances positive communication and interaction with my audience. I maintain a professional attitude at all times, offering a positive role model, especially for new orientees.

My strong organizational abilities would be instrumental in the successful coordination of orientation and in-service training. In addition, I am extremely self-motivated with the ability to think and respond quickly. I am also conscious of the importance of continual personal and professional development.

My career has included involvement in several health care committees, designed to monitor cost efficiencies and/or quality patient care. I am confident that my strong clinical and human relations skills make me a good candidate for the position of Unit Educator.

Thank you for your time and consideration. I look forward to hearing from you soon.

Sincerely,

Cathy Smith, R.N.

Enclosure

127

Unit Educator. *Jan Passmore, Jackson, Michigan*
The writer emphasized the individual's love for teaching by mentioning it at the end of the first paragraph. Recurrent themes show also that she is a strong, positive professional.

STEVEN P. JONES
9002 Wesley Drive
Baltimore, Maryland 00000
(555) 555-5555

Dear _____:

Your ad for an Account Manager with experience in the food and beverage industry captured my interest as it reflects the qualifications that I can offer your company.

I have been successful in:

- *Building and managing account relationships ranging from medium to major customers.*
- *Focusing on customer needs and delivering consistently superior service to ensure repeat business.*
- *Developing, growing and managing all aspects of a successful distributor operation.*
- *Exceeding sales and profit goals while enhancing company and product awareness in the marketplace.*

Specifically, I turned around and managed a nonperforming distributor operation, growing accounts from 50 to 110 and achieving average annual sales of $10M. My success lies in my ability to build strong customer relationships by responding to their business requirements and following through with consistent, quality service. I am recognized by management for my ability to cultivate relationships that lead to new business opportunities and sales growth.

If your company could benefit from a professional with my strengths, I would welcome an interview to discuss the contributions I could make to your team. Thank you for your consideration.

Very truly yours,

Steven P. Jones

Enclosure

128

Account Manager, food and beverage. *Louise Garver, Enfield, Connecticut*
One way to emphasize a theme is to repeat it. Recurrent themes stress that the individual is a successful builder and manager of accounts, offering quality service to repeat customers.

AMY PHILLIPS
15 55th Street
Staten Island, NY 55555
Voice Mail: (555) 555-5050

June 10, XXXX

The Gucci Hotel
55 West 555 Street
New York, NY 55555

Dear Hiring Manager:

I am writing to express interest in the Bartender position advertised in <u>The New York</u> Times. I have more than eleven years of bartending experience in business-oriented hotels. Highlights of my qualifications are the following:

- Thorough knowledge of drink recipes, wines, and spirits

- Computer literacy and proficiency in Micros

- Superior recollection for people served and type of drink

As Service Bartender at the Omni Club from XXXX to XXXX, I was recognized for my excellent customer service skills. After nine months, I was promoted to Front Bartender—the first woman to advance to that position. As Front Bartender for more than seven years, I developed a strong client following, serviced all guests at the bar by myself, and handled approximately $2,500 in daily bar sales. I became skilled at upselling, serving food at the bar, filling orders for cocktail waitresses and waiters, and ordering bar supplies.

In addition to my bartending experience, I also worked for three years as a Food and Cocktail Server at Scooter's Bar at The Golden Palace. Throughout my career, I have earned a reputation for going beyond my job description to ensure the guests are satisfied. I work well in a fast-paced environment and thoroughly enjoy serving the public.

My credentials and work ethic would make me a valuable asset to The Gucci Hotel. If you are searching for a dedicated and competent Bartender, please call me at (555) 555-5050 to arrange an interview. Thank you for your time and consideration.

Sincerely yours,

Amy Phillips

129

Bartender, hotel. *Kim Isaacs, Jackson Heights, New York*
An example of a resume alternative, or letter submitted without a resume. The letter has the equivalent of resume Objective, Qualifications, Work Experience, and Profile sections.

Jane J. Betts
6908 College Avenue
Boulder, CO 00000
(000) 000-0000

May 18, XXXX

James R. Brown, Director
Human Resource Service
000 Main Avenue
University of Colorado, CO 00000

Re: Concierge position

Dear Mr. Brown:

When I returned to Boulder yesterday and heard about the concierge opening, I immediately knew that I would apply for it. Thank you for allowing me the opportunity to apply for the position after the May 15 deadline. I have loved the University of Colorado since my first day there as a student; the prospect of working in the Alumni Center and being part of the University's staff is very exciting to me.

Enclosed is my résumé. As you will notice, the last few years have been devoted to raising my children, volunteer work, and part-time work as an aerobics instructor. I am now ready to resume working and have decided to change my focus from counseling and job placement positions to other areas. The administrative, organizational, and communication skills I have developed over the years will easily transfer to the concierge position.

Please give me a call if you have any questions. I look forward to hearing from you.

Sincerely,

Jane J. Betts

130

Concierge, university alumni center. *Betty H. Williams, Richmond, Virginia*
The letter is "tailored to the specific job opening." The second paragraph indicates that the person wants to "resume her career after a time devoted to parenting." See Resume 16.

DAVID PERRY
1 Main Street • Poughkeepsie, NY 00000 • (555) 555-5555

March 20, XXXX

Chef Grayson Hughes
Great Restaurant
123 West Street
Poughkeepsie, NY 00000

Dear Chef Hughes:

I would like to explore employment opportunities within your restaurant. I have earned an AOS degree in culinary arts from the renowned Culinary Institute of America in Hyde Park, NY. After graduation I secured a position in the Fancy Hotel, and have been quickly promoted and assigned increasing responsibilities.

At a young age I was drawn to a career in culinary arts. My work experience throughout high school and college reflects this clear focus, while my personal qualities and strong work ethic greatly enhance my abilities. In the short time I have been with the Fancy Hotel, I have been consistently praised for my communications skills and ease in dealing with the waitstaff, patrons, and management. I was also instrumental in helping the restaurant attain a 4-star rating. The review was based on a meal that I personally designed and created.

My contributions to your establishment will be immediate and significant, and my commitment will show through daily in my work. I want to learn and to grow so that I may someday fulfill my goal and become an executive chef/owner--a title that I want to earn. I understand that it takes hard work, long hours, and years of practice to hone my craft. I believe in myself and am prepared to do this.

Enclosed is my resume for your review. I would welcome the opportunity for a personal appointment to discuss with you how I may contribute to your restaurant. Thank you for your time and consideration. I look forward to hearing from you.

Sincerely,

David Perry

Enclosure

131

Executive Chef/Owner. *Kristin Mroz Coleman, Poughkeepsie, New York*
The position of Executive Chef/Owner is a long-term goal mentioned to encourage a hotel to hire this person now as its chef. The second paragraph shows what the hotel may expect.

111 Winter Street
Minneapolis, MN 00000

March 1, XXXX

ABC Management, Inc.
P.O. Box 000
Anytown, MN 00000

Dear Hiring Manager:

Please consider this an application for the ABC Hotel Manager position which was advertised in the *Gazette Times*. Because my qualifications so nicely match your job description, I am confident I would be an excellent candidate for this position.

As my enclosed résumé indicates, I am a highly motivated professional with over 10 years' experience in the hotel industry. As manager of the XYZ Hotel, I continually meet revenue per available room, occupancy, and budget goals. I am proactive and consistently practice yield management to further increase sales and profitability. My strong accounting skills enable me to effectively manage all accounts receivables and financial reports. In addition, I directly manage up to 20 employees and consistently maintain open channels of communication. Furthermore, I am an active participant of a Chamber of Commerce networking group—a valuable tool in the hospitality industry.

I am very interested in meeting with you to further discuss my qualifications and background. You may reach me at (555) 555-5555 and may leave a message if I'm not available. Your consideration is appreciated. I look forward to hearing from you.

Sincerely,

John Doe

Enclosure

132

Hotel Manager. *Connie Hauer, Sartell, Minnesota*
The middle paragraph is the selling paragraph. It shows that the applicant has the motivation, experience, management skills, accounting skills, and people skills to excel.

Veronica A. Smithson

5804 - 196th Ave. S.E., Carnation, WA 98000   •   (206) 555-5555

September 21, XXXX

Resort Owner
Westbeach Resort
Route 1
East Sound, WA 98245

Dear Resort Owner:

In response to your September 16th ad seeking applicants for a housekeeper/front desk clerk, I have enclosed my resume for your review.

I am a versatile, hard working person with considerable experience working in the hospitality industry, and exceptional abilities in a customer service environment.

Having spent the last eight years working in the frantic greater Seattle metropolitan area, I would be *very* interested in escaping to a quiet, reasonable life on Orcas Island. My experience includes all of the areas mentioned in your statement of requirements, and I am, in addition, a cheerful, thoughtful, detail-oriented person. I believe that I could add something extra to your resort that would be appreciated by your guests as well as yourself.

I would like to meet with you at your convenience to further discuss my qualifications for the position and to learn more about your expectations.

Sincerely,

Veronica A. Smithson

133

Housekeeper/Front Desk Clerk, resort. *Kathryn Vargo, Issaquah, Washington*
After indicating the job target, giving a profile, stating experience, and expressing interest, the writer presents the selling point: the extra benefits the person would bring to the resort.

ROGER P. BARNES
196 East Goldwater Road
Tempe, Arizona 85858
(555) 555-5555

June 2, 19xx

Mr. Sam S. Smith
General Manager
Rattlesnake Ranch Resort
1234 Rattlesnake Ridge
Tempe, Arizona 89898

Dear Mr. Smith:

As a hospitality professional with a ten-year track record of increasing responsibility, I am seeking a new career opportunity with a resort property in the Greater Phoenix area. I am in the process of permanently relocating to Scottsdale, where I previously worked at the Mesa Mountain Ranch. Enclosed for your consideration is a résumé that briefly outlines my background.

Some of the important experiences that I can bring to a position with your property include:

- **Developing a new club theme from concept through to operation, including hiring and training staff and booking entertainment.**

- **Increasing revenues by enhancing lounge/club atmosphere, developing corporate contacts leading to repeat business, and up-selling patrons on food items.**

- **Setting up Room Service operations at a golf resort, including hiring and training staff and establishing operating procedures.**

- **Full profit/loss accountability for lounge/club operations. This has included fulfilling all administrative, human resource, and purchasing duties, as well as basic accounting functions.**

- **Consistently saving costs through negotiating with suppliers and implementing efficient inventory control procedures.**

I am confident that my knowledge and expertise would allow me to contribute to your property's continuing success in a role as a Lounge/Club Manager, or other appropriate managerial/supervisory position. I would enjoy speaking with you in person about the opportunities that exist with your resort and how my skills can best serve your needs. Please call me at (555) 555-5555 to arrange a convenient time to meet. I look forward to talking with you soon.

Thank you.

Sincerely,

Roger P. Barnes

Enclosure

134

Lounge/Club Manager, resort. *Arnold G. Boldt, Rochester, New York*
The individual's relocation to Arizona is the occasion for the job change and letter. Bullets and boldface highlight relevant experiences. The last two relate directly to the bottom line.

Jennifer Mansen
*11111 — 2ⁿᵈ Avenue NW
Anytown, WA 99999
(555) 555-5555*

An Experienced, Professional PM Server

Available to provide top-quality, efficient, and knowledgeable service to your customers

★ More than 7 years of experience in fine dining establishments

★ Expertise in anticipating and responding to customer needs

★ Sophisticated knowledge of domestic, French, and Australian wines

★ Pride in providing excellent, "five star" customer service

★ Able to comfortably handle 8 to 9 tables at once

★ Sincere appreciation of gourmet foods and attractive presentation

★ Highly regarded by peers and restaurant management

★ 60 hours of service training; 20 hours of wine seminars

Work History includes the following:

Chez Maestro (formerly the Queen's Room), Triumph Hotel, Anytown

XXXX to Present

Henri's Relais de Lyon, Anytown

XXXX to XXXX

Julian's at Seaside Bay, Anytown

XXXX to XXXX

★★★★★

I look forward to discussing in person with you how my expertise, knowledge, and commitment to service can provide your guests with a dining experience they will want to repeat again and again.

135

Professional PM Server, fine dining. *Carole S. Barns, Woodinville, Washington*
A cover letter "flyer" as a resume alternative for a waitress to hand out in personal visits to upscale restaurants. She got a call for an interview from every restaurant she visited.

JOSE ORTIZ

PO Box 1234 • Albany, New York 12345
• (123) 456-7890
• E-Mail: Cycling @abc.com

October 1, XXXX

Mr. Miles Lichtel
Beautiful Resort
High Peaks Drive
Aloha, Hawaii 99999
(555) 111-2222

Dear Mr. Lichtel:

Please accept the enclosed resume, as you requested during our telephone conversation yesterday, as application for cycling-related positions with Beautiful Resort. Specifically, I am seeking to put my passion for cycling to use for Beautiful Resort in the capacity of Mountain Bike Guide, Riding and Operations Instructor or Trail Maintenance. According to Traveler's Magazine, Beautiful Resort is "…the premiere destination for travelers wanting to experience supreme trail accommodations, breathtaking views, and attentive personal riding instructors.…"

As you will note from the enclosed resume, my dedication to the cycling sport began nine years ago with self-study and competition through the American Freestyle Association. To be a successful guide or instructor, I believe one must possess a combination of technical cycling knowledge, leadership ability, and a hospitality service orientation.

For the past nine years, I have been preparing professionally and athletically to teach others the techniques, safety and enjoyment of cycling: mountain bike trail riding, street touring, and freestyle competition. While at Carras Cyclery, I assisted shoppers with purchase decisions, taught beginner's lessons on gear operations and bike maintenance, and offered safety advice on bike and helmet fittings, hydration systems, clipless pedal procedures and proper apparel. Through the National Off Road Bicycling Association, I mastered the technical riding skills necessary to compete in regional and national competitions following the International Mountain Biking Association rules. In order to devote 20-30 hours of group and solo training each week, I have learned the importance of prioritizing responsibilities and effective time management which has had positive effects on all areas of my life.

Naturally, I tend to emerge as a team or project leader. I enjoy sharing knowledge with others and supporting their growing interest in subjects. During college, I was a Teaching Assistant for a 300-student class on multiculturalism. Two days a week, I would assist the professor in presenting class material, and one day a week, I would facilitate a smaller group discussion of the chosen topic. After graduation, I became the advisor of a university fraternity, leading the members in organizational administration, community involvement and personal growth. Additionally, I was a substitute teacher for a class of 2-year-old preschoolers. This wide range of student ages has made me aware of tailoring my communication style for the appropriate audience and assessing nonverbal cues from the class members.

Finally, I believe in becoming a well-rounded professional offering excellent hospitality service to all my customers. I am fluent in both English and Spanish, have worked in the service industry both in the United States and England, and easily adapt to diverse cultural environments. I have found great success in providing guest service before it is asked for. This proactive approach to meeting customers' needs exceeds their expectations and builds strong positive relationships.

Now I am seeking the opportunity to put my love of cycling, leadership ability and service experience to work for Beautiful Resort. I will contact you next week to schedule a time during your New York visit to further discuss employment opportunities with your resort. I look forward to presenting my qualifications in person and learning more of your organization.

Sincerely,

Jose Ortiz

136

Riding and Operations Instructor, resort. *Elizabeth M. Daugherty, East Greenbush, New York*
The individual had only two months of work experience at a bike shop. The writer, therefore, emphasized the person's cycling skills, leadership ability, and service experience.

Julie A. Russell

1900 River Oaks Drive
Canton, Texas 55555

(555) 222-0502 Home
(555) 222-5055 Fax

October 28, XXXX

Ms. Stephanie Jones
Prestigious Concepts, Inc.
4500 Piedmont
Dallas, TX 75555

Dear Ms. Jones:

As a competent professional who has enjoyed a successful career in the educational field the past twenty-two years, I am now exploring opportunities to take my skills and expertise into the business sector. Your advertisement for a Director of Employee Development greatly interested me, and I am submitting my resume for your review and consideration.

I am a positive, high-energy, results-oriented individual who responds well to a challenge and can get the job done. My years as an educator have enhanced my ability to communicate clearly and concisely, handle multiple projects efficiently, and work effectively with people of all ages and from diverse social and economic backgrounds. I have broad-based experience in personnel management and development, problem resolution, and program planning. As someone who is dedicated and hardworking, I am confident that I can meet and exceed your expectations.

Since a brief summary cannot fully convey the benefits I feel I can provide, I would welcome an opportunity to personally discuss your needs and goals and how my experience could benefit your organization. To arrange a meeting at your convenience, I may be reached at (555) 222-0502. I look forward to your positive response.

Sincerely,

Julie A. Russell

Enclosure

137

Director of Employee Development. *Dorothy E. Smith, Denton, Texas*
The individual was making a transition from many years in the educational field to the business sector. The writer therefore stressed in the second paragraph transferable skills.

BENJAMIN STARR

101 Able Way
San Francisco, California 55555
(000) 000-0000

August 31, XXXX

Department of Social Services
Division of Human Resource Management
Theater Row Building
555 East Broad Street
San Francisco, California 55555

This letter is submitted in application for the position of Hearing Manager, Social Services, Position W1111, Control #33333. Enclosed is State Form 10-100, as well as a copy of my résumé, which will acquaint you with my experience, background, and capabilities.

A career attorney in the military, I have extensive litigation experience. As a sitting judge, I presided over approximately 350 criminal cases, both bench and jury, felony and misdemeanor. A significant number of these cases involved issues of a sensitive nature, such as sexual assault and child sexual abuse, similar to those typically handled by Child Protection Services. My duties involved daily interpretation and application of Federal statutes and regulations, court decisions, and Department of Defense policies and procedures. For example, following the 1990 Supreme Court case of **Maryland vs Craig**, involving the use of closed-circuit television to protect a vulnerable child witness in a sexual assault case, I presided over one of the first military cases applying the newly enacted Federal regulations.

From the inception of my legal career, I have been involved in the supervision and mentoring of attorneys and others in providing legal services covering criminal and domestic law. I have extensive experience working harmoniously with those of diverse cultural and socioeconomic backgrounds. I am computer literate and have used the Navy's internally developed automated management information system for case tracking and reporting.

I look forward to the opportunity to personally discuss this position with you.

Sincerely,

Benjamin Starr

Enclosure: Virginia State Form 10-100

138

Hearing Manager. *Anne G. Kramer, Virginia Beach, Virginia*
A letter for a career attorney in the military who was returning to civilian life. The second and third paragraphs summarize the person's experience, duties, skills, and interest.

Mary Cross
8 River Bend Lane
City, State 99999
(555) 555-5555

October 8, XXXX

Ms. Jane J. Jones
Director of Human Resources
Mega Manufacturing Company
4321 Industrial Parkway
City, State 88888

Dear Ms. Jones:

After a rewarding career as a School Counselor, I am seeking a part-time or consulting position that will utilize my extensive experience interviewing and counseling groups and individuals. I believe that my knowledge and expertise could benefit your HR Department in a succession planning, employee development, or personal counseling role.

Some of the relevant experiences I have gained during my career include:

- **Participating in the launch of a staff development program for Honey Hills School District. This district-wide program afforded staff members the opportunity to enhance their skills and grow professionally. I also coordinated in-service training days for faculty members.**

- **Evaluating students' potential and advising them on various educational and vocational paths. I also assisted students in selecting colleges appropriate to their goals and wrote letters of recommendation for college applicants.**

- **Counseling individuals on a wide array of personal, academic, and career issues, including substance abuse, interpersonal conflicts, and career goals. This also encompassed referring students to community services when such action was appropriate.**

- **Participating in the launch of a School-to-Work program for high school students, which encompassed job shadowing, co-op assignments, and internships with local employers.**

- **Delivering presentations to the Board of Education, faculty, parents, and students on topics related to college placement, financial aid, and other career planning issues.**

Enclosed for your reference is a résumé outlining my background. I am confident that my skills would be transferable to your business environment and that I can contribute to your success. I would enjoy meeting with you to explore the potential opportunities and discuss how I can best serve your needs. Please call me at (555) 555-5555 to arrange a convenient date and time for us to begin a dialogue. I look forward to speaking with you soon.

Thank you.

Sincerely,

Mary Cross

Enclosure

139

Human Resources Counselor, part-time or consulting. *Arnold G. Boldt, Rochester, New York*
The first of two letters by the same writer for the same person seeking two different positions.
The person used this letter for a Human Resources position in a business setting.

Mary Cross
8 River Bend Lane
City, State 99999
(555) 555-5555

October 8, XXXX

Mr. Ed U. Cator
Director of Admissions
University of Suburban
1234 College Drive
Suburban, State 54545

Dear Mr. Cator:

After a rewarding career as a School Counselor, I am seeking a part-time or consulting position that will utilize my extensive experience advising students applying to college. I believe that my knowledge and expertise could benefit your university in an admissions interviewing or admissions counseling role.

Some of the relevant experiences I have gained during my 26-year career include:

- **Assisting high school seniors in selecting colleges that are appropriate to their academic and professional goals. In addition, I have written letters of recommendation for college applicants and provided advice on completing college applications.**

- **Delivering presentations to parents and students on topics related to college placement, financial aid, and other career planning issues.**

- **Coordinating "Open House" events allowing student attendees to interface with representatives from various local colleges.**

- **Participating in the launch of a School-to-Work program for high school students, which encompassed job shadowing, co-op assignments, and internships with local employers.**

- **Counseling individuals on a wide array of personal, academic, career, and college issues, including substance abuse, interpersonal conflicts, and career goals.**

Enclosed for your reference is a résumé outlining my background. I am confident that my skills are transferable to a college admissions environment and that I can assist you in fulfilling your mission. I would enjoy meeting with you to explore the potential opportunities and discuss how I can best serve the needs of your office. Please call me at (555) 555-5555 to arrange a convenient date and time for us to begin a dialogue. I look forward to speaking with you soon.

Thank you.

Sincerely,

Mary Cross

Enclosure

140

College Admissions Counselor, part-time or consulting. *Arnold G. Boldt, Rochester, New York*
This letter, an adaptation of the preceding letter, was for a college admissions counseling position.
Compare the bulleted items in the two letters. The order is changed in this letter.

MARK MANAGER
420 Main Street
Newton, MA 02159

(617) 555-1234 (h)   (508) 555-5678 (w)

August 26, xxxx

Jonathan Hertz
Vice President, Human Resources
BioTech Corporation
500 Meadowlark Lane
Waltham, MA 02154

Dear Mr. Hertz:

After reading your advertisement in the August 24th *Boston Globe* for a Human Resources Manager and visiting your Web site for further information, I am very interested in being part of the team you are putting together to manage your HR needs during BTC's anticipated expansion. My résumé is enclosed for your consideration.

As you can see, my background closely matches the requirements in your ad. I am a human resources professional with an MBA and over 15 years' experience in the high-tech industry at Digital Equipment Corporation and Eastman Kodak. My work history clearly demonstrates an action-oriented and innovative approach to employee development and training and employee reward systems. I have instituted a wide variety of original programs that have contributed to improved employee relations as well as to the success of the business.

In addition to my human resources experience, I am a certified mediator, experienced in building a positive work environment characterized by cooperation and constructive problem solving. These skills can benefit BTC as it seeks to build alliances between work groups and across organizational boundaries.

I am eager to meet with you to discuss the contribution I can make to BTC. I will call next week to follow up, or you can reach me at the numbers above.

Sincerely,

Mark Manager

141

Human Resources Manager. *Wendy Gelbery, Needham, Massachusetts*
The challenge was to distinguish this candidate from the many others likely to respond to the same ad. The writer used information the person got from the company's Web site.

Frank Orlando
55 South Highland Avenue · Waterbury, Maryland 00000 · (555) 555-5555

Dear _____:

If you have a search assignment requiring a proactive, innovative management professional experienced in human resources, employee relations and training, my background will interest you. My strength lies in my ability to evaluate organizational needs and deliver programs linked with business objectives.

Highlights of my career include:

- Designed and/or delivered training programs to St. Frances Hospital employees and management staff throughout 38 departments in continuous quality improvement, problem solving, team building, group dynamics, and related techniques.

- Conducted sales training programs for new staff members at a financial services consulting firm which resulted in a 20% increase in sales and client base.

- Created and managed a successful bilingual adult education program offered in 16 different communities, including recruitment and training of instructors.

Additionally, as an administrator, I developed extensive experience in recruitment, selection, mentoring, employee relations, and ensuring legal compliance in staffing several organizations within the Archdiocese of Newark. I am well versed in employment laws including ADA and EEO. Along with management, budgeting and program development expertise, I have the ability to create a motivating environment that empowers others and leads to peak performance.

If it appears that my qualifications meet the needs of one of your clients, I would welcome an interview to discuss my background in greater detail. I am open to relocation, and my current compensation package is $70K per year. Thank you for your consideration.

Very truly yours,

Frank Orlando

Enclosure

142

Human Resources Manager. *Louise Garver, Enfield, Connecticut*
A letter to an executive search firm. The bulleted items show the individual's interest in training employees, and the last paragraph indicates the person's recruiting skills.

TRUDY A. MORALES

114 14th Street South #11
Green River, ND 00000

Home: (701) 000-0000
Work: (701) 000-000

April 1, 1999

Mr. Darryl Parmesan
Senior Vice President
Human Resource Director
Northstar Bank
400 Main Avenue
Green River, ND 00000

Dear Mr. Parmesan:

Please accept this letter as an expression of my interest in the position of **Senior Human Resources Generalist** as outlined in *The Bugle*. Enclosed is my resume, which indicates the great degree to which my qualifications correspond to your needs.

As a professional with 12 years of human resources and managerial experience, I have acquired and exercised effectively the knowledge and skills your position requires. Let me highlight some of the resources and abilities that have enabled me to compile a consistent record of improved workplace environments and increased productivity:

- Strong communications and interpersonal skills
- Interviewing, recruiting, and training experience
- Training in issues of Diversity and Sexual Harassment
- Experience in employee relations and conflict resolution
- Ability to work well independently and as a team member
- Public speaking background
- Bachelor of Arts degree in Business Administration

I believe that these qualifications and my experience with every aspect of human resources will allow me to perform as a valuable and versatile asset to your organization.

I would be happy to meet with you anytime for a more detailed discussion of the many ways in which I can contribute to Northstar. Thank you for your consideration.

Sincerely yours,

Trudy A. Morales

Enclosure

143

Senior Human Resources Generalist. *Jeffrey Thompson, Fargo, North Dakota*
The first of a pair of letters by the same writer for the same person. The first letter is the job search letter. Dash bullets point mainly to skills and experience. See Resume 15.

TRUDY A. MORALES

114 14th Street South #11
Green River, ND 00000

Home: (701) 000-0000
Work: (701) 000-000

April 23, 1999

Mr. Darryl Parmesan
Senior Vice President
Human Resource Director
Northstar Bank
400 Main Avenue
Green River, ND 00000

Dear Mr. Parmesan:

I would like to take this opportunity to thank you enthusiastically for the interview this morning and to confirm my strong interest in the **Senior Human Resources Generalist** position. I left the meeting feeling truly excited about the possibility of working for Northstar.

After our conversation I am even more confident in my ability to reach and exceed your expectations. Let me emphasize again my positive attitude and strong track record in the field. I genuinely enjoy working in Human Resources and have found myself very comfortable in Northstar's environment. Your interviewing techniques are very much like my own; I am certain we would work well together.

I look forward to meeting with you again in the near future.

Sincerely yours,

Trudy A. Morales

144

Senior Human Resources Generalist. *Jeffrey Thompson, Fargo, North Dakota*
The second letter is a thank-you note as a follow-up to a positive interview. The person indicates strong interest in the position, excitement, and a wide range of positive feelings.

Barbara Patterson
74 Hometown Lane
Town, State 33333
(555) 555-5555
e-mail: barpat1@aol.com

September 14, xxxx

Mr. George C. Shipman
President and CEO
Yellow Box Company
111 State Street
City, State 22222

Dear Mr. Shipman:

After a rewarding and successful career as an educator, I am seeking to transfer my talents and expertise into an appropriate position with a private sector firm. I believe that my teaching and interpersonal skills could benefit Yellow Box Company in a training and/or human resource role and have enclosed for your consideration a résumé that details my qualifications.

Some of the key capabilities that I can bring to a position with Yellow Box Company include:

- *Developing curricula that address various learning styles and the individual needs of each student.*

- *Evaluating individual students to identify strengths and areas needing improvement. This leads to educational plans that help each pupil to achieve his or her highest potential.*

- *Providing training to parents, colleagues, and students in basic computer skills.*

- *Writing technology plans and managing projects to implement such plans for public school districts.*

I am confident that my skills and experience are transferable to your business environment. I believe that I can serve your organization in either succession planning or employee development programs. I would enjoy meeting with you to discuss the possibilities that exist and how I can best contribute to your success. Please contact me by phone or e-mail at the above number/address. I look forward to beginning a dialogue with you soon.

Thank you.

Sincerely,

Barbara Patterson

Enclosure

145

Succession Planner/Employee Developer. *Arnold G. Boldt, Rochester, New York*
This experienced schoolteacher "was seeking to move into private industry." Bullets point to key educational skills that are "relevant to a business setting." See Resume 35.

Request Number **97-1558**

Richard Locke
132 Amberly Court
Montgomery, Alabama 36100
✆ [334] 555-5555 (Home)

May 27, XXXX

Mr. James L. Wembly
Vice President
Orion Information Systems, Inc.
8260 Lackly Drive
Suite 400
McLean, Virginia 22100

Dear Mr. Wembly:

I am looking – confidentially – for more challenging ways to put my expertise in system administration to work for a growing company. Naturally, when I saw your posting, I made writing this letter my first priority. Specifically, I would like to join the Orion team as your newest Communications Specialist.

My résumé gives examples of the kinds of results you should expect from me. Because our field changes so quickly, most of the half dozen examples you will see there are recent ones. However, a résumé format cannot show how I approach my work. I never vary from these guidelines:

- 💻 I must transform theory into practical, competitive results. Learning from the past isn't enough to keep my company number one.
- 💻 I must be tenacious in solving problems. There's no "magic" in data systems, only undiscovered information and techniques.
- 💻 I must provide capability to the *users'* standards. The most powerful systems are crippled unless the user can operate them well.

If Orion can use my combination of capability and professional standards, perhaps the next step is to hear about your needs firsthand. May I call in a few days to set up an interview?

Sincerely,

Richard Locke

One enclosure: Résumé

146

Communications Specialist/Network Admin. *Donald Orlando, Montgomery, Alabama*
Keeping a company growing with significant results in a rapidly changing field is the challenge for this individual, who is aware of standards and fixed guidelines. See Resume 14.

MARY SMART

111 Decker Lane
Smithtown, NY 55555
555-555-5555
masmart@bol.net

Dear Hiring Executive:

Technological excellence and success. They lie in the ability to merge the strategic with the practical, to understand needs and expectations, and to deliver and support the technologies and applications appropriate to each functional organization.

As **Director of Applications Development** at Century Technology Sciences, I have provided the technological and organizational leadership that has delivered such success. During the past sixteen years I have been promoted to progressively responsible positions and, under my direction, Century Technology Sciences has undergone an evolution and is now operating as a technologically advanced information/data operations system. Some of my more recent achievements include:

- Project management of a French contract and publishing data conversion (30 million records) for the foreign implementation of a full range of mainframe and PC based products;
- Project oversight in the graphics publishing, information and financial services, automotive and other data intensive industries; and
- Pioneering cross-functional technology solutions across diverse platforms including Y2K and legacy system reengineering and data warehousing.

My success thus far is the result of attention to detail as well as the ability to see the "big picture." If you are interested in quality performance, dependable action and innovative solutions, my proven track record demonstrates what I can do for you. Although my position is secure, I feel it is time for a change to a position that offers greater responsibility, as well as the authority to make decisions in the best interest of the company.

In order to explore your prospective needs, I will call your office next week to arrange a mutually convenient appointment to discuss employment possibilities and job leads. I would appreciate your keeping this inquiry confidential. Thank you in advance for your consideration.

Best regards,

Mary Smart
Enclosure

147

Director of Applications Development. *Susan Guarneri, Lawrenceville, New Jersey*
A confidential, exploratory letter for an individual who had been successful in applications development and wanted more responsibility. The letter explains the reasons for success.

CARL C. JOHNSON
6645 North Oliphant Avenue
Chicago, IL 60631
(773) 774-4420

July 15, XXXX

Mr. Henry Biggins
Partner
XYZ Executive Search
111 East Shore Drive
Chicago, IL, 60600

Dear Mr. Biggins:

Companies today require decisive, goal-driven management professionals who can offer fresh insights, practical business solutions and a creative vision for the future. With this in mind, I would like to introduce my background and qualifications.

I am a solid business leader and hands-on manager with a strong passion for success. My work history encompasses more than 15 years of retail management experience, where I made a significant impact on high-volume, multiunit retail operations. Key strengths include the ability to:

- Formulate financial plans that ensure profitability.
- Develop and navigate strategies that win customers and sustain revenue growth.
- Maintain the highest levels in sales results, customer satisfaction, employee performance, store presentation, inventory and cost controls.

In 1996 I successfully transitioned these skills to a new industry environment, building account sales for an information technology company. I aggressively developed and implemented high-impact, customer-driven strategies that captured new account business in a very competitive marketplace.

A common characteristic throughout all of these endeavors has been my strong people skills. Consistently, I have been able to recruit, train and develop talented management teams and staff motivated to succeed. Of equal importance has been my ability to procure long-standing customer relationships. I achieve win-win situations based on trust.

It is my goal to secure a challenging position in executive management or consulting. I am confident that the rich mixture of real-life work experiences, along with my well-honed people skills and urgency to make business happen, would benefit one of your client companies. For your review, I have enclosed my résumé and salary history. Please be advised that my desired annual compensation is $110,000. Relocation would be considered for the right opportunity.

I look forward to meeting with you. Thank you.

Sincerely,

Carl C. Johnson

enclosures

148

Executive Consultant. *Cathleen M. Hunt, Chicago, Illinois*
A letter to an executive search firm for an individual looking for an executive management or consulting position. His ideas and strategies are always directed to winning results.

PAUL ADAMS

241 Vozy Ln., Planfield, IL 00000 • 857/321-6544 • Email: paul@netscape.com

September 8, xxxx

Mr. John Bailey
President
Wiring Incorporated
Portland, OR 99999

Dear Mr. Bailey:

Strong technological leadership can have a tremendous impact on corporate and organizational value. By building an effective technological infrastructure, providing strategic leadership and controlling escalating compensation and benefit costs, you can immediately improve the financial performance, productivity and viability of your organization.

This is the value I deliver.

As an accomplished Information Systems Executive with a proven track record, I have been instrumental in:

- Building strong and sustainable profit gains.
  Increased profits from $23 million to $600 million in 2 years.

- Driving productivity gains while meeting budgetary constraints.
  Increased revenues from $35 million to $88 million.

- Pioneering Technologies.
  Effectively redefined staffing levels, reducing payroll expenditures.

Although secure in my current position, I am confidentially exploring new professional challenges and opportunities in Information Technology Management.

I appreciate your time and consideration and look forward to speaking with you in the next few days.

Sincerely,

Paul Adams

Enclosure: Résumé

149

Information Systems Executive. *Rosa St. Julian, Houston, Texas*
The first paragraph expresses the view that technology leaders can produce positive results. Bullets point to this person's results in increased profits and productivity and reduced costs.

Stephen F. Douglas

55555 Systems Drive
San Romano, CA 99999

Home (510) 555-5555
Pager (510) 999-9999

Dear Hiring Manager:

I am an IS Operations Manager who consistently maintains a 98% systems uptime rate for an international Fortune 500 company.

My 20+ years of experience include building an IS Operations group from the ground floor up, expanding from a one-person operation to 12 IBM mid-range systems in multiple facilities.

The high level of systems uptime is complemented by an equivalently low employee turnover (two operators have stayed with me for 10 years each), which enables the group to maintain a 7-by-24 schedule, 363 days a year, with limited headcount.

If you are interested in an IS Operations Manager with my proven ability to keep systems up and running, you can depend on me to do an excellent job for your organization.

I look forward to meeting you and will call you next week to see if we can arrange an appointment.

Sincerely,

Stephen F. Douglas

enclosure: résumé

150

IS Operations Manager. *Ms. Sydney J. Reuben, Menlo Park, California*
The writer stresses "two of the most important qualifications for an IS manager: system uptime and the ability to expand the system and staff with a company's growth."

SALLI HARRIS

26 Alena Drive Toms River, New Jersey 08753   (732) 288-1502   Fax (732) 288-1504 salli@adelphia.net

Dear Prospective Employer:

I would like to explore the opportunity for an IT Management position within your organization. I have a career history that spans 17+ years, and a proven track record in enhancing corporate productivity and profitability. My resume is enclosed for your review and consideration of my qualifications.

With an extensive background in computer systems, programming, personal computers and local area networks, I am an ideal candidate for the position. My experience encompasses both technical and managerial accomplishments.

Throughout my career, I have demonstrated an outstanding work ethic. Extremely conscientious, I work as long as it takes to complete a project. Excellent in the diagnosis of problems, I am able to propose successful solutions. I concisely explain processes and issues in an intelligent, nontechnical manner. A problem solver, I am also flexible in adapting to end-user requirements.

Since my resume is an overview of my background, I look forward to the opportunity to provide you with further insight into my professional value. Until then, thank you for your consideration.

Yours truly,

Salli Harris
Enclosure

151

IT Manager. *Nina K. Ebert, Toms River, New Jersey*
A short and clear letter. Topics dealt with quickly are the person's career history, background, experience, problem-solving skills, oral communication skills, and flexibility.

BARBARA ANNE BLACK
1234 Western Avenue, #D-17 ◆ Anytown, WA 98000 ◆ (555) 123-1212

Date

Human Resources
Company
Street Address
City, State ZIP

RE: (Name of Position) advertised in the (Date) edition of (Name of Publication)

As a highly proficient computer information professional with a passion for technology, PC and UNIX knowledge, and the unique ability to translate the technical to nontechnicals, I am particularly qualified to fill the (Name of Position) currently open at (Name of Company).

Currently a LAN Administrator with The Airplane Company, I have a solid background in technical support and project management with other Fortune 500 companies (Federal Express and Big Software Co.), smaller firms, and the public sector. I earned a B.S. in Computer Information Systems and am completing coursework for my Certified Microsoft Professional rating (scheduled for completion in July).

In my present role, I serve as technical focal, consultant, and trainer on development tools and processes for 100 engineers and professionals. More than 50% of my job is devoted to planning, coordinating, implementing, testing, and writing documentation for new computer-based processes. An excellent problem solver, I am able to quickly get to the root of a issue and design a solution. I am skilled in empowering team members while maintaining mutual respect among my peers, subordinates, and other technical experts. One of the secrets to my success is treating each customer — internal and external — as a million-dollar account that deserves and receives excellent service and response. Let me highlight some of my successes with The Airplane Company and past employers:

- Managed successful implementation of a proprietary The Airplane Company inventory tool, including design of an e-mail-based solution when all 1,200 related PCs crashed during testing. The solution fixed the problem, and the tool was implemented without any repair tickets.

- Received a Certificate of Achievement for efforts in implementing a Software Standard Server program. Trained more than 1,200 users with varying degrees of professionalism and technical understanding and created a Web page with tips, information, and hot links to assist in its acceptance.

- Took computer technology for the City of Anytown (located south of Anycity) from an unconnected mixture of systems for 120 users to a unified NT system. . Completed the project within the stringent budget and policy requirements of the City.

- Quickly moved from managing technical support for small accounts (up to 20 employees) at International Computers to a 5-member Beta team and responsibility for several premier accounts, including AT&T, PacBell, and US West.

I look forward to discussing in greater detail with you the ways in which I can use my knowledge and skills to further enhance (Name of Company). I will call you (Time Frame) to schedule a conversation.

Sincerely,

Barbara Anna Black
Enclosure: Résumé

152

LAN Administrator. *Carole S. Barns, Woodinville, Washington*
A generic letter that allows the person to tweak it each time she sends it. Because she often replies to ads without a person's name, she omits the salutation and varies the subject line.

John Staunton
1411 Northridge Drive
Montgomery, Alabama 36100
✆ [334] 555-5555 (Home) 🖥 [334] 416-5555 (Office)

February 7, XXXX

Mr. Shane Gramling
President
Techmasters
2430 Fairlane Drive
Suite C-7
Montgomery, Alabama 36116

Dear Mr. Gramling:

If you think your LAN Project Managers should be full partners in boosting profits, I would like to speak with you about joining the Techmasters team.

Right from the start, I want to give you confidence that you are interviewing the right person. That's why my résumé may not look like others. I went beyond just reciting job titles and training to show results. I also wanted you to have a complete picture of my expertise in each of the software and hardware tools I use every day. Still, there is important information résumés cannot show well.

Even before we meet, I want to indicate *how* I get results. In all I do, I apply these personal standards:

- 🖥 I am responsible for my own, systematic, efficient professional development. While I do this on my own time, it's always focused on improving the mission.

- 🖥 It's up to me to serve users, programmers, supervisors, and vendors *in words they understand and with products they value.*

- 🖥 Controlling costs and doing the mission very well are long-term commitments. I must back up my advice with rock solid logic and numbers.

My employer, the center for computer development for the United States Air Force, has always been pleased with my work. Now, I want to put my skill, energy, and top-notch training to work for a leading company.

As a first step, I'd like to set up an appointment soon to hear about your needs in person.

Sincerely,

John Staunton

One enclosure: Résumé

153

LAN Project Manager. *Donald Orlando, Montgomery, Alabama*
The individual, in showing with bullets *how* he gets results, gives the impression of confiding in the reader. That rapport makes interest in an interview seem more natural at the end.

Paul Plentiful
0000 Sunnydale Road • Money, MO 00000
(555) 555-5555

Dear Human Resources Director:

I am an experienced MIS Manager ready, willing, and able to join your organization.

I offer extensive knowledge of computer programming, design, and purchasing. My technical and management experience has ranged from Computer Programmer to MIS Manager. I have played a key role in the development and implementation of products in a volatile environment of changing technology and have been responsible for budget planning and management. I especially enjoy training and would like to incorporate more of that in my next position to maximize employee performance.

The enclosed resume summarizes my background and experience. I would appreciate the opportunity to further discuss your requirements and mutual objectives. Thank you for your consideration.

Sincerely,

Paul Plentiful

enc.

154

MIS Manager. *Peggy Weeks, Battle Creek, Michigan*
A simple letter with straight talk. The letter says only so much because the individual wants to learn more about the target company. That would be the purpose of an interview.

Nils Bergman

9999 Churchill Street
Seacliff, WA 95555
(444) 444-4444

Dear Hiring Manager:

I was writing code when only 8 years old.

I was not exactly a child prodigy—but someone with a strong mechanical aptitude and a dad who was a systems analyst for Lockheed.

I grew up to be not exactly a computer nerd, either—but someone with endless ideas for networking and utilizing computers.

Today, what I am, exactly, is a highly motivated professional who has built and used computers his whole life *and* has the communication skills to effectively articulate his ideas *and* has the business know-how to implement them.

If this is exactly what you are looking for, I would enjoy working for your organization.

Sincerely,

Nils Bergman

enclosure: résumé

155

Network Specialist. *Ms. Sydney J. Reuben, Menlo Park, California*
A letter for a person with only a GED but who was working on his MSCE! The writer begins the letter with an eye-catching sentence and uses the word *exactly* four times for emphasis.

DOUGLAS L. MORGANSTERN

128 Coral Reef Drive ❖ Clearwater, Florida 33000 ❖ (727) 000-0000

August 3, XXXX

Mr. Martin Stevens
H. R. Recruiter
Microsoft Corporation
One Microsoft Way
Redmund, WA 98000-0000

Dear Mr. Stevens:

Although I have established a successful career as a General Manager with a hotel industry leader, my goal now is to transition my general management experience and technical skills into new, professional roles within the IT arena. To that end, I am confidentially investigating employment opportunities with progressive technology companies and have enclosed my resume, which will provide you with a summation of my credentials.

As a General Manager, I am routinely faced with challenges involving the need to evaluate, upgrade, and implement technologies that will improve our level of operations and provide greater efficiency. This is where I have excelled. My technical proficiency led to expanding my managerial responsibilities to include serving as an *"on-site IT application specialist."* In this capacity, I have gained significant experience in areas such as systems integration, hardware/software analysis, network modeling, reengineering service applications, and systems life cycle management. My success in developing and delivering cost-effective solutions for performance-driven operations yielded notable results in enhancing P&L efficiency and annexing corporate goals.

Besides my unique blend of technical and general management experience, I offer your company an excellent record of peak performance, significant achievements, and decisive leadership, in addition to a strong academic and management training background. As a proactive thinker with a vision toward future challenges, the unprecedented rate of change in Information Technology serves as a catalyst in my pursuit of greater opportunities within this environment.

I appreciate your time and consideration. I will contact your office next week to follow up on scheduling a time for us to meet.

Sincerely,

Douglas Morganstern

Enclosure

156

On-Site IT Application Specialist. *Diane McGoldrick, Tampa, Florida*
A letter for an individual who wanted to move from general business management to an "IT arena." The main paragraph shows knowledge areas in a blend of technology and business.

Jerry O. Berry
3333 Castlemont Trail
Menlo Park, CA 55555
(555) 333-5555

October xx, xxxx

Anne Trimblee
Executive Account Manager
Professional Placement, Inc.
33333 Cherry Avenue
Santa Clara, CA 55555

Dear Anne Trimblee:

<u>SOFTWARE DEVELOPMENT - PROJECT LEADER</u>

Thank you for sharing valuable time to interview me for the above position. Also, please express thanks to your colleagues Tara Mason, Phillip Dawkins, and Stanford Kent for sharing their time. Your candid observations were appreciated.

Your comment about the team approach to production was especially interesting. I have strong experience with this approach and find it a management style that is particularly motivating.

From my perspective, I have a serious interest in the position and look forward to hearing from you.

Sincerely,

Jerry O. Berry

157

Project Leader, software development. *Carl L. Bascom, Fremont, California*
A thank-you note with a subject line below the salutation. After a successful interview, a note such as this lets company personnel know what the candidate is thinking and feeling.

EDWARD EMORY
444 Eagleton Avenue
Riverdale, NY 55555
(555) 555-5555

August 15, XXXX

Dear Hiring Manager,

Does your organization anticipate the need for a Senior Systems Programmer or a Project Leader who can design and implement large-scale database and client/server systems? With over 10 years' experience in both large-scale systems and program design and implementation, perhaps I can be of service.

My resume is enclosed for your review. Some of the qualifications and professional knowledge I can offer your organization are:

- Experienced Senior Programmer / Analyst with over 10 years in the data processing field

- Solid expertise in systems and program design, development and implementation; expert troubleshooter and systems / programming problem solver

- Demonstrated success in producing high-quality work; attention to simplicity of structure, leading to highly reliable and maintainable systems and programs

- Excellent interpersonal and communication skills including public speaking, writing and establishing cooperative relationships with team members

Accustomed to a fast-paced environment where deadlines are priority and handling multiple jobs simultaneously is the norm, I enjoy a challenge and work hard to attain my goals. If you are seeking a well-qualified and productive individual who looks on problems as opportunities to grow and learn, then I believe I am the right person for your team.

I would appreciate a personal interview to discuss the ways in which my areas of expertise could bring immediate results and assist you in accomplishing your goals. I will call your office next week concerning any questions you may have and to arrange a meeting if that seems appropriate to you. Of course, you may contact me directly at any time. Thank you for your consideration.

Sincerely,

Edward Emory

Enc.

158

Senior Systems Programmer/Project Leader. *Susan Guarneri, Lawrenceville, New Jersey*
Qualifications include experience, expertise, high-quality work, and communication skills. In the last paragraph, the person keeps control over phoning, but the tone is not at all pushy.

JAMES JONES
XXX-XXX-XXXX
ALAWYER@wannabe.com

3221 Litigation Drive, Sue Me, USA

February 4, XXXX

David Smith, Esquire
Smith & Associates
2832 Lying Down Road
Your Town, FL 33131

Dear Mr. Smith:

Every now and then in life a unique opportunity presents itself. For me, it was the invitation to submit my résumé and writing samples to a company with the prestigious reputation of Smith & Associates. The prospect of working and learning from the caliber of lawyers in a law firm ranked by the *National Law Journal* is both exciting and fulfilling.

For the past 7 years, I have held positions which have allowed me to direct day-to-day operations in two separate businesses in Florida. I believe my hands-on experience, together with my fluency in Spanish, provides a benefit to both Broad & Cassel and its clients. My reputation is that of a solid, strategic thinker who can analyze complex information and develop creative solutions to get the job done. I am a "deal maker" with the ability to understand and negotiate contracts to consummation.

I am very excited about meeting with you and your partners to learn more about your law firm's needs and how I might help meet them. I would bring flexibility, adaptability, and excellent interpersonal skills to an associate attorney position. Thank you again for your consideration.

Very truly yours,

James Jones

Enclosure

159

Associate Attorney. *Cynthia Kraft, Valrico, Florida*
The first paragraph expresses the extent of the individual's interest in the law firm; and the second, his experience and skills. The third indicates the target position. See Resume 17.

GEORGE J. BULLARO
ATTORNEY AT LAW

HOME: (XXX) XXX-XXXX

44-33 WAY STREET
ASTORIA, NEW YORK **11103**
TEL. (XXX) XXX-XXXX
FAX. (XXX) XXX-XXXX

MEMBER OF:
NEW YORK BAR
NEW JERSEY BAR
U.S. TAX COURT

497 MAIN STREET
HACKENSACK, NEW JERSEY **07452**
TEL. (XXX) XXX-XXXX
FAX. (XXX) XXX-XXXX

(date)

Mr. James King
RRR Enterprises
128 Main Street
Holly, New Jersey xxxxx

Dear Mr. King

In recognition that many foreign companies are establishing operations in the United States, I have enclosed a summary of my career for your consideration in representing your company within the USA. As you can see, I have accumulated a broad range of experience, with emphasis in international law, commercial law, corporate law, real estate matters, immigration and litigation. I am experienced in both domestic and international marketplaces, and I am confident that my ability to advise you on legal/business matters and assist you in establishing US operations in compliance with the tax regulations will prove advantageous to your organization. Additionally, I am knowledgeable of the factors involved under the projected tariff-free treaties and Free Trade Agreement.

Having been born in Italy and developed a successful law practice in the United States, I am well versed in interfacing with professionals from various cultures. I still travel extensively--often to Mexico to pursue the study of the Mayan Indians. Additionally, I am trilingual in English, Spanish and Italian. My strengths also include a thorough knowledge of real estate matters, and I presently own and manage a comprehensive real estate portfolio.

In summary, my goal is to integrate my business management skills and legal experience to enable you to meet your corporate goals and objectives. I would appreciate the opportunity to speak with you concerning the above information and to explore this matter in further detail.

I look forward to speaking with you soon and thank you for your consideration.

Very truly yours,

GEORGE J. BULLARO

Enclosure

160

Attorney at Law. *Alesia Benedict, Rochelle Park, New Jersey*
A letter whose tempo increases as paragraphs get shorter. The first paragraph includes experience, areas of expertise, and skills. The third paragraph indicates additional skills.

Thomas L. Hume, Esq.   2798 Conklin Street • Suite 452 • Patchogue, NY 11772

(516) 555-5555 • fax (516) 000-0000 • tlhEsq@sprintmail.com

June 14, xxxx

Granger & Corbin, LLP
92 West Main Street
Patchogue, NY 11772

Dear Mr. Granger:

Are you overworked? Do you need assistance? Wouldn't it be wonderful to hire a competent and focused per diem lawyer when you need help in emergencies?

Lighten your load and de-stress with my expert services!

You will benefit from my intensive experience in legal research and writing. You will receive expert help without the cost of a full-time salary. You will gain flexibility in your scheduling. You will enjoy relief from pressures and deadlines. You will acquire a cooperative, dependable, and interested colleague.

Professional qualifications are represented on the attached resume. You will find that I offer a unique combination of practical experience acquired from a dual career as an attorney and as an international in-flight administrator for American Airlines.

Here's why my unusual background should interest you….

I understand deadlines and pressure! I attended law school — graduating fifth in my class — while working as a legal writer and researcher for a prominent Chicago law firm. I also worked my way through law school while fulfilling full-time obligations with American. I've passed three bars on the first try.

In addition, my highly demanding work for American taught me the people skills, leadership qualities, tenacity and coolheadedness needed when I was in control of a cabin of 300+ passengers and crew in daily and emergency situations. These same abilities have made me an effective attorney with an exceptional work ethic.

If offered the opportunity to help with your overflow or special projects, I will *exceed* your expectations. I know I can be an asset to Granger & Corbin, making immediate and beneficial contributions to the firm and to your stress level. Call me. I am available to help you now!

Sincerely,

Thomas L. Hume, Esq.

161

Attorney/Legal Researcher and Writer. *Deborah Wile Dib, Medford, New York*
A letter in which the individual aggressively markets himself. In effect, he says, "Contract my services, and I can lower your stress by reducing the amount of writing you must do."

BENJAMIN STARR

101 Able Way
San Francisco, California 55555
(000) 000-0000

August 31, XXXX

The Honorable Nathan J. Sun, Chief Judge
Court of Appeals of California
P.O. Box 555
San Francisco, California 55555

Dear Judge Sun,

The announcement in the *California Law Weekly* for the position of Clerk of the Court of Appeals presents an opportunity in keeping with my legal background. I have enclosed a résumé detailing my knowledge, skills, and abilities for your review and consideration.

Commissioned a naval officer in 1969, I received a Juris Doctorate and was admitted to the California Bar in 1976. I served as a judge advocate and culminated my military career as one of four judges in the Navy's second busiest judicial circuit. Through these duties I became fully acquainted with the daily operation and management of a complex judicial system. Processing 500-600 cases per year, the Southwest Judicial Circuit utilized the Navy's automated trial management information system to docket, track, and report court-martial cases.

My career equipped me with the ability to deal decisively, effectively and simultaneously with multiple situations. It also imbued me with a high degree of organizational and management skills. In addition, I counseled and mentored numerous less-experienced attorneys in the preparation and trial of hundreds of criminal cases.

I would welcome a personal interview to discuss my qualifications to serve as a Clerk of the Court of Appeals. I am available at your convenience.

Sincerely yours,

Benjamin Starr

Enclosure: Résumé

162

Clerk of the Court of Appeals. *Anne G. Kramer, Virginia Beach, Virginia*
This individual was returning from the Navy to civilian life. The challenge was to make his military experience as a Judge Advocate and special skills relevant to civilian legal work.

MIRANDA SMITH

141 Oak, Aloha, Oregon 97008

Phone ■ 503-590-6328
Pager ■ 503-654-9088

January 1, 1999

Nancy Hernandez
State of California
Department of Justice
2720 Taylors St. #300
San Francisco, California 94133

Dear Ms. Hernandez:

I spoke with you last week about your search for an entry-level CRIMINALIST. As you requested, I have enclosed my resume, application and references.

In addition to a Bachelor of Science degree in Biological Science, I offer practical experience in laboratory operations, specimen analysis, testing processes and lab photography. I am highly motivated to pursue this career path and believe that my analytical abilities and multitasking skills are a good match for your requirements. I enjoy challenges and can successfully handle diverse technical and support tasks.

I am confident that I can make a positive contribution to the State of California's Justice Department. I look forward to describing my capabilities in more detail and am available for a personal interview at your earliest convenience.

Thank you for your time and consideration.

Sincerely,

Miranda Smith

Enclosures: 2

Criminalist. *Pat Kendall, Aloha, Oregon*
A short, clear letter with a goal-profile-interview-thanks pattern. The main (second) paragraph indicates the person's practical experience, motivation, skills, and flexibility.

Joan B. Rogers

1515 Main Street ▸ Ft. Lauderdale, FL ▸ 55555
(555) 555-5555 ▸ joanrogers@yahoo.com

May 15, XXXX

Martin McLeod
Director
New York Legal Action
1212 5th Ave.
New York, NY 55555

Dear Mr. McLeod:

This letter is to thank you for taking the time today to discuss employment opportunities with your firm. As you requested, I am faxing my résumé and transcripts for your review. The strength of my education, training, and positive work ethic will be of significant value to New York Legal Action. Highlights of my credentials include:

- J.D. Candidate - Florida University, College of Law.

- Advanced computerized research capabilities; proficient in Westlaw and Lexis Legal Researching.

- Participant in first-year moot court competition.

- Exposure to global legal systems through international travel and study.

In addition, I am motivated by a strong interest in environmental, constitutional, and international law. Most recently, I participated in a British and Comparative Law program in London while volunteering at the British Environmental Law Association. Previously, I served as Legal Intern with National Counsel Assistance. In this role, I performed a variety of research assignments. Most notably, I wrote an article that serves as a reference guide on whether National Counsel Assistance personnel should conduct investigations. I also conducted research for the EEOC Advisor, involving issues such as how and when administrators should deliver public presentations.

I work efficiently in fast-paced environments, effectively manage time, and prioritize projects. I believe that the combination of my energy, enthusiasm, professional experience, and training will add value to your team. If you are seeking a highly motivated candidate with strong credentials, it would be beneficial for us to meet. You may reach me at (555) 555-5555. Thank you for considering my qualifications, and I look forward to speaking with you.

Sincerely yours,

Joan B. Rogers

Enclosures

164

J.D. candidate. *Kim Isaacs, Jackson Heights, New York*
A cold-call networking contact led to this letter. Education, training, and work ethic are illustrated in turn by bulleted credentials, activities after graduation, and work style.

BENTON SHERMAN

101 Able Way
San Francisco, California 55555
(000) 000-0000

October 12, XXXX

Mr. Peter Foote
California Lawyers Weekly
100 South 18th Street
San Francisco, California 94000-1234

Dear Mr. Foote,

I am forwarding, under separate cover, a résumé outlining my background, experience, and capabilities in response to your ad in the *California Law Weekly* for a part-time Legal Reporter.

You will note from the résumé that I have many of the attributes you are seeking for this position. A retired military career attorney and member of the California Bar, I am now perfectly positioned to provide the services you require.

As an undergraduate English major, I was able to hone my writing skills through years of experience as a writer of legal briefs and memoranda of law. While serving as an instructor at the Naval Justice School—a position comparable to an associate professor of law—I directed and edited a complete revision of the school's evidence curriculum.

I would welcome the opportunity to discuss this position with you during a personal interview. I feel that I can make a strong contribution to the *California Lawyers Weekly*. Thank you for your consideration.

Sincerely,

Benton Sherman

Enclosure
Résumé

165

Legal Reporter, part-time. *Anne G. Kramer, Virginia Beach, Virginia*
The resume was sent under a separate cover, so the letter is not really a cover letter; yet it is, because it calls attention to the resume. The letter itself shows clear reporting style.

BORIS STAPLETON

101 Able Way
San Francisco, California 55555
(000) 000-0000

November 13, XXXX

John Smith
Magistrates' Office
Municipal Center
San Francisco, California 55555-5555

Dear Mr. Smith:

In response to the November 10, 1998, announcement in the *San Francisco Star*, enclosed is a completed application in support of the position as Magistrate for the Second Judicial District of San Francisco. A copy of my résumé detailing background, experience, and abilities is also included.

I retired from the Navy with a career as military attorney and judge. I have extensive litigation experience and a comprehensive knowledge of criminal law, the justice system, and judicial procedures. My past duties have given me analytic abilities in the use of computerized management information systems for case tracking.

With good interpersonal and communication skills, I would welcome the opportunity to develop a career as a judicial officer for the City of San Franciso. As a permanent resident, I am very familiar with the area.

I am enthusiastic about the possibility of serving as a Magistrate and will call you next week to see if a meeting can be arranged to discuss my qualifications and the contributions I can make.

Sincerely,

BORIS STAPLETON

Enclosure: VA Form 10-012 w/supplement
           Résumé

166

Magistrate. *Anne G. Kramer, Virginia Beach, Virginia*
Another letter for a military attorney and judge retiring from the Navy and returning to civilian life. The last three paragraphs say, in effect, "I can do the work. I would like to. I want to."

BERNARD SUGARMAN

101 Able Way
San Francisco, California 55555
(000) 000-0000

October 12, XXXX

Charles Jackson, Executive Director
Bay Area Legal Aid Society
6 Main Street, Suite 203
San Francisco, California 55555-5555

Dear Mr. Jackson,

Enclosed is my résumé in response to your ad for the position of Managing Attorney with the Bay Area Legal Aid Society. As a member of the California Bar, I have qualifications that appear to meet this position.

My most direct experience in the area of Legal Aid came as Head of the Legal Assistance Department of the Naval Legal Service Office. Assuming leadership of a division low in morale with a poor reputation for servicing the Bay Area military community, I spearheaded a complete reorganization and relocation into refurbished offices. Service to the eligible population was increased from 4,000 to 12,000 clients annually, enhancing the morale and reputation of the department.

Every military attorney, whatever his primary assignment, is considered the "resident expert" in legal affairs. Thus, throughout my 20-year career, legal assistance was provided to countless clients on a variety of topics such as domestic relations, consumer credit, and the drafting of simple wills. While serving as a ship's attorney, I was able to provide legal assistance to hundreds of sailors. I have also mentored and supervised junior attorneys as they provided representation to military clients.

I would appreciate an appointment to meet with you and discuss how I may contribute to The Bay Area Legal Aid Society.

Thank you for your consideration, and I look forward to hearing from you.

Sincerely,

Bernard Sugarman

Enclosure: Résumé

Managing Attorney, Legal Aid Society. *Anne G. Kramer, Virginia Beach, Virginia*
The strategy for this letter (and for any interview) was to show how this person with twenty years of military legal experience had skills that could transfer to Bay Area legal aid work.

LINDSAY JUDGE
XXXX Curving Drive
Anytown, Southern State 55555
555-555-5555

October 27, XXXX

Ms. Elizabeth Nicholas
Post Office Box 198
Anytown, Southern State 55555

Dear Ms. Nicholas:

In response to your advertisement in the October 27, XXXX, *Anytown Daily News,* please consider my résumé in your search for a paralegal for your law firm.

I have more than 12 years' experience in various office environments, including eight years in law offices. That experience includes work for solo general practice attorneys as well as for partners in a large firm working on complex business and environmental issues. I have provided the entire range of support for my attorneys, including correspondence; client billing on both manual and automated systems; tape transcription; file setup and maintenance; document preparation and filing of motions, notices, orders, and briefs; and abstracts of statements and depositions.

My packages include DOS, Windows 3.1 and Windows 95 and 98 operating systems, and all of the Word and WordPerfect packages up to and including Word 97 and WordPerfect 8. I also have experience in several timekeeping and billing programs as well as calendaring systems.

I would like very much to discuss with you how I could contribute to your firm, and I look forward to hearing from you soon to set up an appointment.

Sincerely,

Lindsay Judge

168

Paralegal. *Lynda Lowry, Knoxville, Tennessee*
The second paragraph is longest with content about the person's experience and skill areas. Of interest in the third paragraph will be the person's proficiency with billing programs.

CHRIS ROBINSON

55 Police Way	Gainesville, Georgia 30000	(404) 000-0000

October 9, 1994

Sheriff Thomas Jones
DeKalb County Sheriff's Department
1 Law Enforcement Way
Decatur, Georgia 30030

Dear Sheriff Jones:

In response to your recent opening in the DeKalb County Sheriff's Department, please find my résumé enclosed for your review.

As you will see, I perform effectively in work environments which require the ability to make quick, reliable decisions and execute multiple responsibilities simultaneously. I have a sincere desire to contribute to law enforcement efforts and have been preparing for an opportunity to demonstrate my capabilities. I run, using the standards established by local agencies; frequently practice shooting and maintain a high level of accuracy at the firing range; and participate in the DeKalb County DUI Task Force Civilian Ride-Along Program. I am a Georgia native with an excellent knowledge of streets, landmarks, and major highways. Additionally, I have just completed a Conversational Spanish course at DeKalb College.

Many of my accomplishments and abilities are documented in the enclosed letters of recommendation from individuals in local law enforcement agencies. You will find that I am honest and exhibit excellent interpersonal, communication, and organizational skills. Further, rotating shifts, holidays, and weekends pose no problems with scheduling for me; my current activities and work history illustrate my flexibility.

I would appreciate an opportunity to meet with you to discuss your specific needs and my potential to contribute as a member of your team. Thank you for your consideration; I look forward to your response.

Sincerely,

Chris Robinson

169

Deputy Sheriff. *Carol Lawrence, Savannah, Georgia*
The person had little law enforcement experience and was working as a security guard of a large department store. He got a call from the Sheriff even before he reviewed the resume!

Lucas G. Bryan

1234 Orange Street
Anaheim, CA 55555
(000) 000-0000

ABC Recruiting Services
Los Angeles, CA 55555
ATTN: Mr. Johnson

Dear Mr. Johnson:

A diversified management career has provided me with exposure to a vast array of personnel and multicultural issues. I am adept at speaking before congressional committees and community groups and conducting discussions with dignitaries from the United States and other countries. My expertise as a law enforcement executive includes both urban ad suburban environments. I have enclosed my résumé with brief highlights of my experience for your consideration. My expertise is recognized through continuous professional development, meeting or exceeding your requirements:

- Highly effective decision maker
- Demonstrated commitment to community policing
- Innovative crime prevention programs
- Successive quality improvements
- Respected/recognized executive law enforcement advisor
- Strict enforcer of laws with an effort to deter future crime
- Genuine care and concern for citizens

The above expertise qualifies me to fulfill the role of law enforcement official for a city, community, university or major corporation.

I am an outstanding speaker, briefer, trainer/instructor, and advisor. My energy level is high, and I seek to complete a mission with top-notch efficiency. Officials from all types of business and law enforcement agencies, as well as from the U.S. government, seek my advice and guidance.

You may contact me at the above address or phone number. I would enjoy discussing with you my qualifications in greater detail and how I could best serve your requirements for placement.

Thank you for taking the time to review my resume. I look forward to receiving a response from you very soon.

Sincerely,

Lucas G. Bryan

Enclosure

170

Law Enforcement Officer. *Diane Burns, Columbia, Maryland*
This individual with a management background and good oral communication skills emphasizes bulleted areas of expertise as qualifications for a law enforcement position.

GERALIN CHARLES

518 Boxcar Drive   Jersey City, New Jersey 08530   (201) 961-2333

Dear Prospective Employer:

Throughout my career at the State of New Jersey Superior Court, Family Court Division, I have been recognized and applauded for my demonstrated skill at managing a fast-paced environment within a demanding office. As a goal-oriented professional, I have employed clear thinking, organizational technique, and the ability to prioritize a daily barrage of matters.

Evaluated by supervisors as an "invaluable asset" to both the Domestic Violence and Crisis Intervention Units, I have played a key role in streamlining workflow throughout my ten-year State employment.

Cited as the "backbone" of the counseling component of the Crisis Intervention Unit, I consistently provided training to newly hired counselors. As Senior Probation Officer within the Domestic Violence Unit, I have enhanced the quality of information provided to the court by aiding it in making the most informed decisions concerning cases, specifically in the areas of risk assessment, custody and visitation.

I have performed public speaking on various occasions and am equally successful in communicating on a one-to-one basis. As liaison and public relations professional, I have met with success when dealing with members of the media.

Since my resume is an overview of my background, I look forward to the opportunity to provide you with further insight into my professional value during a personal interview.

Thank you for your consideration.

Yours truly,

Geralin Charles
Enclosure

171

Senior Provisional Probation Officer. *Nina K. Ebert, Toms River, New Jersey*
Conspicuous compliment words (*applauded, invaluable asset, backbone, successful, success,* and *value*) make the reader feel positive about the person throughout the letter.

Mark M. Allen

401 Lane Allen Road #432 ● Lexington, KY 40505 ● (606) 555-1234 ● mallen@sprynet.com

August 12, XXXX

Mr. George Pankow
Director of Recruitment
Louisville Free Public Library   **RE**: Position of Library
301 York Street   Automation Coordinator
Louisville, KY 40220

Dear Mr. Pankow:

I am pleased to submit my résumé for this position. As you can see, my education, training, and experience uniquely qualify me to meet and surpass your specifications.

Your requirements:	**My qualifications**:
Knowledge of information systems in a client/server environment.	Broad experience working with and troubleshooting WAN and LAN systems.
Facility in various desktop applications.	Extensive familiarity with most major, and many minor, desktop applications.
Knowledge of *SCO, UNIX, Redhat Linux*, and *Netscape Collabra*.	Working, to expert, competence with these programs and environments.
Four-year degree.	Three degrees (B.A., M.A., M.S.L.S.).
Ability to work well with and train end users and other county employees.	Exceptional skills in working with others. Teaching is my greatest joy.
Ability to communicate effectively orally and in writing.	Former English teacher. Adept at business, technical, or expository writing.

I believe I am exceptionally qualified to help your library continue fully to automate its most needed functions while keeping your costs to an absolute minimum. As I'm sure you'll agree, automation doesn't cost money, it saves money. I will contact your office early next week in order to schedule an interview where we can discuss my candidacy more fully.

Sincerely,

Mark M. Allen

172

Automation Coordinator. *David Adler, Lexington, Kentucky*
Two-column, "Your requirements . . . My qualifications" format helps to illustrate convincingly this person's suitability in experience, education, and skills for the position.

Karen A. Librarian

000 Any Street • Anywhere, Michigan 00000 • (000) 000-0000

January 1, XXXX

Ms. Lisa Smith, Department Director
Any County Administration Center
0000 Any Street
Anywhere, Florida 00000

> **RE:** **Position Number 0000**
> **Requisition Number 00000**

Dear Ms. Smith:

I am very interested in securing a position with your organization and am responding to your recent advertisement for a Head Librarian. My current position provides me with the qualifications and experience necessary to successfully fulfill this position. Please allow me to highlight my strengths:

- Over 10 years of Librarian experience with 8 years at the supervisory level
- Strong interpersonal and communication skills
- Excellent analytical and organizational skills
- Solid computer skills, including Internet support
- Master's and Bachelor's degrees in Library Science

A résumé is enclosed covering my experience and qualifications in greater detail. I would appreciate the opportunity to discuss my credentials with you. To ensure your receipt of my material, I will follow up by calling you in the coming week to answer any questions you might have. If you need additional information, please do not hesitate to contact me. I look forward to talking with you soon.

Sincerely,

Karen Librarian

Enclosure

173

Head Librarian. *Maria E. Hebda, Trenton, Michigan*
The bulleted strengths are experience at the supervisory level, skills, and degrees. Indention, boldfacing, and a second line make the subject line stand out before the salutation.

Jane Hillson
555 W. Alter St.
Chicago, IL 55555
(555) 555-5555

October 30, XXXX

Mr. Juan Perez
Director, Information Services
XYZ Corporation
555 Canal St.
Chicago, IL 55555

Dear Mr. Perez:

In response to the advertisement you placed in the *Chicago Tribune*, Sunday, October 28, XXXX, for Information Services Manager, I have enclosed my resume for your review.

My MLIS degree from Holden College is combined with successful experience in managing people and information in different environments, using computer technology, database and research skills for a variety of projects. I feel that my experience in developing and achieving very specific goals for service-oriented groups, expanding user levels and organizing effective operations is a good match for this position, and I would appreciate the opportunity to talk with you further.

I can be reached at the phone number above and will arrange to meet with you at your earliest convenience. Thank you for your time and attention.

Sincerely,

Enc.

174

Information Services Manager. *Christine L. Dennison, Lincolnshire, Illinois*
After completing her MLIS degree, this person wanted to leave years of leadership roles for volunteer organizations and return to the corporate world. The letter is brief and clear-cut.

Linda L. Torricelli
793 Ocean Road
City, State 33333
555-555-5555

May 19, xxxx

Ms. Betty Bookman
Chief Librarian
Dewey, Cheatham, & Howe, LLP
1234 Main Street
City, State 99999

Dear Ms. Bookman:

As a professional librarian with significant experience in both legal and university settings, I am seeking a new professional opportunity. Your advertised opening for a Research Librarian has caught my interest, and I have enclosed for your consideration a résumé that outlines my credentials.

My professional experience has given me knowledge in several key areas that relate to the position you are seeking to fill. These include:

- **Utilizing various CD-based resource materials, including Lexis/Nexis and Westlaw.**

- **Training professional and administrative staff in the use of electronic and conventional library materials.**

- **Developing and implementing an on-line catalog for a collection of 3,000+ volumes.**

- **Conducting research projects for attorneys that include use of the Internet and collections at various community libraries.**

- **Managing a $250,000 operating budget and making recommendations regarding acquisitions, space allocations, and staffing levels.**

I am confident that my education, experience, and professional diligence would allow me to meet the challenges of this Research Librarian role. I would enjoy meeting with you to discuss the mutual benefits of my joining your staff. Please call me at (555) 555-5555 to arrange a convenient time for us to meet. I look forward to opening a dialogue with you soon.

Thank you.

Sincerely,

Linda L. Torricelli

Enclosure

175

Research Librarian. *Arnold G. Boldt, Rochester, New York*
Bullets and boldfacing ensure that the individual's knowledge in key areas will be seen. Grammatically parallel, they all begin with a participle or with compound participles.

Olivia Sanchez

555 Vera Street
Grove, IL 55555
(555) 555-5555

October 15, XXXX

Ms. Jeannine Barrett
ABC School District #34
Grove, IL 55555

Dear Ms. Barrett:

I am interested in pursuing career opportunities with ABC School District #34 and have enclosed my resume for your review. With my previous experience in library administration and my strong academic background, I can offer a wide range of information science skills to your district. Having devoted the last eight years to raising my family, five years ago I resumed the other type of work I enjoy, with a part-time position at the Grove Area Public Library. I would appreciate the opportunity to talk with you about any appropriate full-time positions you are trying to fill.

I can be reached at the phone number listed above. Please leave a message if I'm not there, and I will return your call promptly. Thank you for your time and attention.

Sincerely,

Enc.

176

School Librarian. *Christine L. Dennison, Lincolnshire, Illinois*
After spending some years at home raising children and working part-time, this person wanted to return to full-time employment. This letter is the first inquiry in the process.

STEFAN OGNENOVIC
75 Jersey Street
Hawthorne, State 11111
(555) 555-5555
E-mail: stefano@university.edu

July 22, XXXX

Ms. Francis Nevins
Manager of Human Resources
The City Museum of Art
5510 East Boulevard
City, State 44555

Dear Ms. Nevins:

After reading your recent posting for a Systems Librarian at your Ingraham Library and discussing the position with Alice Adams over the phone, I am most interested in this opportunity. As a library information systems professional with a ten-year track record of both hands-on and managerial experience, I believe that my talents and expertise would benefit your organization in this role. Enclosed for your review is a résumé outlining my credentials, along with supporting documentation as requested in your advertisement.

Some of the key capabilities that I can bring to this position include:

- **Managing implementation projects for new systems. This has included developing specifications, evaluating vendors, supervising installation and setup, and interfacing with vendors to resolve any post-installation operational issues.**

- **Training staff in the use of new systems. Over the course of my career this has encompassed transitioning from manual to automated circulation systems, migrating from DOS-based applications to a Windows environment, and the movement from mainframe architecture to a client/server, PC-based system. In each case, I have developed and delivered relevant training and Help Desk programs to meet specific user needs.**

- **Hands-on experience operating various systems in public and university library facilities. In my current position, we serve five libraries, including a music library and an art library in remote locations.**

I am confident that my professional experience and dedication to staying on the leading edge of library automation technologies would allow me to contribute to furthering The City Museum of Art's mission in this Systems Librarian role. I would enjoy speaking with you in person about the position and how I could serve your needs. Please contact me by phone or e-mail at the number or address noted above. I look forward to opening a dialogue with you soon.

Thank you.

Sincerely,

Stefan Ognenovic

Enclosure

Systems Librarian. *Arnold G. Boldt, Rochester, New York*
This IT professional wanted to move into a leadership position. His entire career had been in a library environment—his preference. Bulleted key capabilities with boldfacing stand out.

JOHN FINANCE
111 Insurance Avenue
Glenview, Illinois 99999
000/000-0000

March 26, XXXX

Mr. John Brown, Senior Vice President
University of the Mountains
100 Mountain Road
Denver, Colorado 00000

Dear Mr. Brown:

This is in response to your ad which appeared in the *Chronicle of Higher Education* for Associate Vice President for University Facilities. My experience and knowledge, as described in the enclosed résumé, are an exact match with your stated qualifications. I have extensive experience in real estate and property management, strategic planning, and all areas of investments.

In property management I handled all final decisions on space planning and design, engineering and electrical, maintenance and repair, safety and security, custodial, and the environment. I have worked closely with architects and engineers on multimillion-dollar new buildings and major renovations of older structures. I was responsible for having all properties in compliance with federal, state, and local regulations.

An analyst by nature, I believe in accuracy and prepare my work in a logical sequence. I possess a high degree of perseverance in carrying out all activities to reach a common goal. In a crisis, I am cool, calm, and collected. Dedication, teamwork, leadership, and creativity are essential to my work ethic. As a decision maker, I evaluate every situation carefully and consider the consequences of all alternative actions.

With my credentials and achievements, which are a matter of record, I know I can contribute to your organization, and welcome the opportunity to discuss this with you. When may we meet?

Sincerely,

John Finance

Enclosure

178

Associate Vice President, university facility. *Sally McIntosh, Jacksonville, Illinois*
In looking at this letter, you would never guess that the individual's original resume was five pages of 8-point type. The improved resume and this letter for it "hit only the high points."

JAMES HANOVER
4 Baywood Boulevard
Brick, New Jersey 05555
Home: (555) 555-5000 • Fax: (555) 555-5005

Dear Prospective Employer:

I am extremely interested in your advertised position and believe my 16+ years' experience in building maintenance and supervision, coupled with an additional 8 years' experience in industrial welding, would make me a strong match for your requirements. I can bring to your organization:

- Extensive experience working with electrical, plumbing, and HVAC systems, along with a proficiency in carpentry and welding.

- The ability to work independently and carry projects through all phases from diagnosis and planning to purchasing supplies and completing the task in a cost-effective and timely manner.

- Knowledge of electrical code and the competence to read blueprints and schematic diagrams.

- Hard-working dedication coupled with excellent interpersonal skills.

I believe these highlights along with those detailed in my enclosed résumé would enable me to contribute to the success of your organization

My current employer has been bought out by a new company, and because of restructuring, my department is being eliminated. I am currently seeking new opportunities, and would appreciate the chance to discuss in person how my skills can meet the needs of your firm. If you don't mind, I will take the liberty of phoning next week to verify receipt of these documents, and if possible, to arrange an interview for a mutually agreeable time.

Thank you for your consideration.

Best regards,

James Hanover

Enclosure: Résumé

179

Building Maintenance Supervisor. *Carol Rossi, Brick, New Jersey*
No job title is mentioned because the person wanted any building maintenance or repair position. He also wanted a dateless generic letter to respond quickly to ads. See Resume 20.

MONTE J. MARTIN, CGCS

000 Paradise Drive   Home: (555) 555-5555
Golf Landing, CA 00000   Work: (555) 555-5555

August 18, XXXX

The Golf Club
Attn: Maintenance Recruiter
0000 Waterway Blvd.
Valley, CA 00000

Dear Sir:

I am interested in the Golf Course Superintendent position at The Golf Club. I learned of this opening from
Golf Course Superintendents Association of America's Employment Referral Service and have enclosed my
résumé for your review and consideration.

Over twelve years of superintendent experience in a private club environment have provided a broad
knowledge base from which to draw and benefit an organization. I majored in Turfgrass Management at
California State University and have GCSAA Certification. My present position as Superintendent with the
Hill Top Country Club requires management, finance, and technical expertise. Although I am secure in my
position, acquiring the Superintendent job at The Golf Club would be the culmination of many of my
professional and personal goals. I am confident that the combination of my education, skills, experience, and
vision would enable me to make a positive contribution to the continued success of your club.

Since a résumé can't fully detail my background or predict my potential to your organization, I respectfully
request an interview to further explore employment opportunities. I look forward to hearing from you soon
and thank you for your time and consideration.

Sincerely,

Monte Martin, CGCS

enclosure

180

Golf Course Superintendent. *Peggy Weeks, Battle Creek, Michigan*
The middle paragraph indicates that the individual doesn't need a different job but would like a
position with the target club to fulfill personal goals. The ending is notably courteous.

SCOTT A. HOUGH
11111 NW 11th Avenue, Anytown, CA 99999

555/555-5555 *(Home)*   555/555-5556 *(Fax)*   555/555-5557 *(Office)*

April 16, XXXX

Mr. John Jones
2222 – 2nd Boulevard
Anytown, CA 99999

Dear Mr. Jones:

As the much-anticipated Golf Club at Sunrise River nears completion, I find my excitement for a golf course in the neighborhood taking a new pathway. A successful and entrepreneurial-focused businessman with a particularly strong bent toward customer service and satisfaction, event planning, and operations, I'd like to use those skills to help grow your newest enterprise.

For the past 23 years I've managed and owned Anytown's premiere garage and auto detailing operation, Prestige Detailing & Parking. Several months ago I decided the time had come to make a change, to step down, sell the business, and move into a new phase of life. I've monitored development of the golf course from the beginning: the initial notice via postcard soliciting local area input and interest six years ago; occasional news articles in the Anytown newspaper; an invitation and attendance to the groundbreaking ceremony; and, most recently, a tour of the grounds and facilities under construction.

Each contact, as well as each information piece, has impressed me with the commitment to quality being built into the project. Operating what's known as "The Nordstrom of garages and auto servicing and detailing," I understand the value of quality and superb customer service. I am confident I can transfer my current expertise and fulfill a customer service role at the Golf Club at Sunrise River.

Let me highlight some of my successes:

- Voted one of the "Best" by readers of several publications — including *L.A. Times Magazine, Vistas Magazine, The California Weekly,* and *The San Francisco Times* — Prestige has grown from a facility with parking and oil and lubrication maintenance to a full-service operation providing detailing and all other auto services except gasoline.

- I'm proud that my clientele — which ranges from retirees to professionals to white-, pink-, and blue-collar downtown Anytown workers — is loyal, long-term, and consistently eager to recommend Prestige to friends, family, and strangers. Many clients have used Prestige for 25 years or more. Many choose to remain clients despite opportunities of free parking through their employers. Repeatedly the reason given is excellent service, a caring attitude, and outstanding work.

- Skilled in event planning, three times a year I present free, three-hour workshops for up to 50 members of area car clubs. I also organize and coordinate annual golf tournaments for the Rock 'n' Roll Golf Association. Additionally, I've managed two fund drives for an Anytown church that generated the highest number of pledges in the church's history.

Well-versed in business operations, problem solving, marketing and promotions, I'm extremely detail-oriented and highly adept at project management. While I haven't worked in the golfing industry professionally, I'm an avid (although not "great") golfer who thrives in a team-oriented environment. I believe I can be an outstanding member of your Sunrise River team and look forward to discussing in greater detail with you or a representative additional ways in which I can contribute. I've enclosed a résumé plus a sample of the many hundreds of comments from customers on the kind of service I consider "normal and appropriate."

Sincerely,

Scott A. Hough

Enclosures: Résumé and Customer Comments

181

Manager, auto detailing and parking. *Carole S. Barns, Woodinville, Washington*
A detailed letter for an individual whose specialty was detailing. He brought to his resume and letter the same care and commitment that he had shown in his work. See Resume 19.

CHARLES SMITH
23 Pine Street
Binghamton, New York 05555
(555) 555-5000

Dear Prospective Employer:

After reading your advertisement for a position in buildings and grounds maintenance, I believe my skills and experience would provide a strong match for your requirements. Highlights of my background include:

- 20 years' combined experience in management and maintenance of professional buildings and grounds.
- Skills in carpentry, masonry, plumbing, and light electrical systems.
- Proficiency in troubleshooting, diagnosis, and repair.
- Excellent relationship-building skills with people of all levels.

I have been successfully self-employed for the last several years operating an office maintenance and groundskeeping company. I have now decided to pursue the security and stability of working for someone else, and wish to relocate to the northern New Jersey or New York area.

My experience and abilities would, I believe, provide a valuable contribution to your organization. I have enclosed my résumé for your review and would appreciate the opportunity for an interview to discuss in greater detail how my skills can meet your needs.

Thank you for your consideration, and I hope to hear from you in the near future.

Best regards,

Charles Smith

Enclosure: Résumé

182

Manager, buildings and grounds maintenance. *Carol Rossi, Brick, New Jersey*
This self-employed person "wanted to be a full-time employee with a regular work week and benefits." Without a computer, this individual wanted a dateless generic letter.

George R. Block

88 Brick Lane ◆ Charlotte, North Carolina 00000 ◆ (000) 000-0000

January 1, XXXX

William E. Jones, President
Jones and Jones, Inc.
15 Jones Avenue
Charlotte, North Carolina 00000

Dear Mr. Jones:

Steve Smith suggested that I contact you regarding possible managerial openings you might have. I am particularly interested in a general manager, purchasing manager, or credit manager position. He thinks that you would be interested in someone with my qualifications. I have enclosed my résumé which will give you an overview of my skills and achievements.

My experience is in the block and brick industry. My track record is one of increasing responsibility. I have a wide range of experience from purchasing and credit management to my most recent position as general manager of eight manufacturing plants and two distribution facilities. This business was recently bought by a company based in Britain; it is in the process of reorganization, and I have decided to explore other career possibilities. I am particularly proud of the fact that I have consistently been able to keep the operations profitable and safe and the production facilities up-to-speed in terms of personnel, equipment, and maintenance. My management style is hands-on, and my staff has always been able to rely on me for the support they need. I am extremely competitive by nature and have worked hard to keep my company in a competitive marketplace position.

I am very interested in exploring opportunities with Jones and Jones, Inc., and look forward to meeting with you. Please expect a call from me at the end of this week.

Sincerely,

George R. Block

183

Executive Vice President/General Manager. *Betty H. Williams, Richmond, Virginia*
A letter for a reliable worker who was being forced to look for another job because of reorganization from a foreign takeover. The middle paragraph explains everything.

ADAM R. APPLETREE
12 Rising Sun Drive
Phoenix, AZ 00000
(555) 555-5555

January 1, XXXX

The Pits Fruit Company
Attn: Joe Smith
Business Unit Manager, Quality Assurance
0000 Apple Tree Lane
Tucson, AZ 00000

Dear Mr. Smith:

With the upcoming closing of the Fruit and Canning Operation, I would like to thank you for the opportunity to be part of the ABC Foods organization over the last year and a half. My experience has been most rewarding, and I remain appreciative of the opportunities you provided.

My association with ABC Foods is both satisfying and challenging in many ways. As Carton Finishing Department Production Supervisor, I am directly responsible for production efficiencies, product quality, employee safety and support of QCD initiatives within all corporate policy and contractual guidelines.

I have a B.S. in Biology, more than four years of experience with The Pits Fruit Company, and over sixteen months of experience within the ABC Foods organization. I am extremely interested in continuing my association with ABC in a suitable position relative to my Production or Quality Assurance Supervisory background.

Naturally, permanent employment is my goal, but another temporary assignment within ABC Foods or another ABC Division would be acceptable. I am flexible regarding hours, shifts, weekends, and location.

Enclosed is my resume for your review and consideration. If you have any thoughts or suggestions or require additional information, please contact me at your earliest convenience.

Sincerely,

Adam R. Appletree

enc.

184

Production Supervisor. *Peggy Weeks, Battle Creek, Michigan*
With the closing of an operation, this individual wanted to continue working in some new way—even temporary—with the current company. The letter shows his strong interest.

RONALD SMITH

79 Melrose Park Road, Dayton, Ohio 00000
(555) 555-5555

Dear _____ :

Is your company struggling with core issues affecting operation, revenues and profitability? Are you in the midst of a start-up or emerging growth? Are you spearheading initiatives to redesign processes or revitalize programs? If so, perhaps I can help.

With more than 20 years of top-flight senior management experience with multinational manufacturing organizations in the electronics industry, I have consistently delivered strong performance results. My contributions led to the successful turnaround of manufacturing and worldwide customer service operations, increased operating gross margins and saved millions of dollars through continuous process improvement initiatives.

My expertise and proven track record include the development and implementation of programs in cost avoidance, enhancements to gross margins, operating cost-of-ownership, energy efficiency and retrofit, as well as spearheading the design/build of specialty environments (clean rooms and associated facilities), and project management.

For the past several years as an executive with ABC Corporation, I have acted as an internal consultant to the company's entire international manufacturing division with three plants. Recruited to design and institute cost/scrap reduction programs at a failing manufacturing organization, I effectively reduced manufacturing scrap from a high of 7.5% of material throughput down to 1% in just two years. Additionally, I have trained and led continuous improvement teams that realized $86 million in cost savings through design and implementation of JIT and other programs.

May we meet to explore the challenges you are facing and your need for decisive and effective project leadership? I am available at your request for a consultation.

Sincerely,

Ronald Smith

Enclosure

185

Senior Manager. *Louise Garver, Enfield, Connecticut*
The first questions show that the letter is target-oriented. The remaining paragraphs express in turn the person's track record, expertise, achievements, and interest in an interview.

THOMAS C. CRANDALL

55 Warsaw Road ▪ Smalltown PA 55555 ▪ 555/555-5555

June 17, XXXX

Charter Manufacturing Inc.
PO Box 555
Midsizecity PA 50505

ATTN: Human Resources

My resume is enclosed in response to your advertisement in the *County Pennysaver* for a Warehouse Supervisor.

In addition to my transportation education through BIT, as Shipping/Receiving Supervisor for an area manufacturer, I have seven years' experience successfully managing and scheduling the daily activities of that department, with more than fourteen years' cumulative background in shipping and receiving. With only 5% of finished product being customer routed, I am responsible for the accurate distribution of the balance of outgoing shipments utilizing truckload, LTL, air and small parcel carriers. In my position, I negotiate contracts and favorable discounts with all carriers, including nationwide shippers. I manage the intra/interstate outbound shipping schedule, adjusting it as necessary to meet customers' needs. In these capacities, our department utilizes ABF, Pennsylvania Motor Freight and UPS Maxiship software, as well as FedEx's most recent version of their proprietary software. I possess working knowledge of these systems and have had exposure to Clippership software in a trial situation. Additionally, I coordinate incoming deliveries, which includes finishing and production materials, company supplies and returned product. Committed to excellent customer service and effective, efficient operations, I constantly review the shipping and receiving functions for improvements and interact successfully with all internal departments.

In addition to excellent organizational abilities, my skills in the areas of communication, leadership, attention to detail and problem solving are strong. My computer capabilities include Mac experience for word processing and some exposure to PCs.

I am confident that my unique combination of training and experience would be an asset to your organization. As a resident of Mountain County, I would be happy to make positive contributions to a firm based in my home county. I would appreciate the opportunity to interview for your Shipping/Receiving Manager position. Please feel free to contact me at the above number.

Thank you for your consideration.

Sincerely,

Thomas C. Crandall

Enclosure

186

Shipping and Receiving Supervisor. *Salome Randall Tripi, Mt. Morris, New York*
The company was having difficulties, and this person wanted to work for another firm. This letter got him an interview. Modified for another firm, the letter yielded another interview.

Kenneth L. James
1005 South Country Road
East Patchogue, NY 11772

voice ■ 516-555-5555
fax ■ 516-000-0000
e-mail ■ kljame@aol.com

June 14, xxxx

Mr. John Cusano
President
Digital Press Imaging
25 West John Street
Hicksville, NY 11801

Dear Mr. Cusano:

Do you have a need for a senior-level custom manufacturing professional with a track record of achievement in expense reduction, revenue enhancement, modular manufacturing, and creative partnership agreements?

My current responsibilities as Vice President and Director of Manufacturing include the hands-on direction of all manufacturing, facilities management and environmental safety functions for one of the largest U.S. manufacturers of custom wallcoverings, decorative laminates, large-scale graphics and point-of-purchase specialties. I have been instrumental in the production of a peak sales volume of $2.2 million that has placed the company as number three in a specialized industry of sixteen contract wallcovering printers.

Career highlights include:

■ The doubling of accounts, increasing of unit sales per employee, reduction of turnaround time, and the creation / implementation of profitable value-added services.

■ The establishment of a profitable and innovative in-house service bureau—the only one of its kind in the industry—that produced new revenue streams representing 12.5% of sales.

■ The design of resourceful programs, manufacturing processes and strategic partnerships that prevented major losses from 40% erosion of customer base during the late '80s recession.

■ The assumption of immediate and productive control of all manufacturing operations in crisis response to partners' mismanagement and subsequent departure.

If you require a results-oriented senior manager who can create and direct profitable programs, control a sizable budget, and reduce expenses without reducing services, then we should discuss the ways that I can help Digital Press Imaging achieve project and company goals. I have enclosed my resume for your review (in both traditional and computer scannable versions). If my qualifications are of interest to you, let's set up a meeting to discuss the possibility of a mutually beneficial association.

Sincerely,

Kenneth L. James

187

Vice President and Director of Manufacturing. *Deborah Wile Dib, Medford, New York*
The company was having difficulties, and this person wanted to move to sales or management in this or another field. The letter shows duties and achievements after a profile.

Charles S. Stoner
1111 Parsons Place
Montgomery, Alabama 36111
℗ [334] 555-5555

March 21, XXXX

Mr. Charles W. Morgan
Vice President
The Comstock Corporation
1200 Argent Circle
Montgomery, Alabama 36111

Dear Mr. Morgan:

Your customers should never be concerned about how I build sales for you. Your sales staff should take for granted all my efforts. But if your company relies on getting the right items to the right place at the right time, I would like to be your next Inventory Control Manager.

Early in my career, I decided that meeting urgent customer needs *today* was not good enough. I wasn't happy until the systems I ran met the needs my customers would have *tomorrow.*

My résumé shows just a small sample of the results I have achieved. What it cannot show is how I can get similar payoffs for The Comstock Corporation team. I think my success rests on the standards I keep:

❑ It is my responsibility to build teams that *want* to do well,

❑ I must understand my customers' mission as well as my own, and

❑ My senior management should always know what it takes to keep our systems best—in time to beat our competitors.

My company has recognized me as an outstanding manager. I love what I do. However, now that I have turned around the operation I inherited, I want more challenging work. As a first step in that direction, I would like to hear about your needs in face-to-face conversation. May I call in a few days to set up an appointment?

Sincerely,

Charles S. Stoner

One enclosure: Résumé

188

Inventory Control Manager. *Donald Orlando, Montgomery, Alabama*
The writer wanted to show that the person was not "a low-level 'bean counter'" but someone who freed others to do their jobs well. Bullets emphasize standards. See Resume 18.

BARBARA J. JOHNS
23658 Meadow Circle
Moreno Valley, California 00000

Home (909) 555-5555   Office (310) 555-5555

December 1, xxxx

Mr. John Jones
ABC Company
123 Main Street
Anytown, New York 14610

Dear Mr. Jones:

Please consider this letter of introduction an expression of my interest in exploring employment opportunities with your organization. The enclosed resume outlines my qualifications.

After a successful 19-year career with XYZ, Incorporated, I am faced with the reality of company reorganization, as well as the challenge of pursuing new opportunities. In addition to my personal qualities of well-developed interpersonal skills, excellent communication abilities, integrity and an exceptional work ethic, I also offer:

- Outstanding knowledge of Project Materials and Inventory Control
- Proven management skills, cost analysis and appropriate procurement actions
- Full understanding of critical production operations and scheduling
- Commitment to quality and customer service

As my resume merely summarizes a successful career history, I believe only a personal interview will afford you the opportunity to fully realize my potential. I look forward to discussing the possibilities with you soon.

Thank you for your consideration.

Sincerely,

Barbara J. Johns

Enclosure

189

Materials Manager and Inventory Controller. *Kim Little, Victor, New York*
Because of an upcoming company reorganization, this person needed a new position. With bullets pointing to knowledge, skills, and commitment, he sought a "personal" interview.

L. BURTON FISHER

0000 Hickory Drive • Hendersonville, Tennessee 00000   (000) 000-0000

March 11, XXXX

Frito-Lay, Inc.
Attn: Human Resources
0000 Perimeter Park, Suite 000
Atlanta, GA 00000

Good morning:

As an industry leader in the manufacture and wholesale distribution of premium quality snack foods, Frito-Lay has continually impressed me with its commitment to quality and service. With this in mind, I am looking to build my career with such an industry leader and would like to be considered for suitable openings within the Frito-Lay company.

As you can see from the enclosed resume, I hold a B.B.A. in Marketing/Transportation and Logistics from Georgia Southern University. In my current position as Purchasing and Inventory Control Manager for a Fortune 500 automotive replacement parts company, I have acquired valuable experience in inventory management with a special focus on purchasing, staff management, and customer service in a high-volume, fast-paced distribution environment. In addition to my technical skills, I am considered to have strong interpersonal, communications, and leadership abilities. All of these characteristics were necessary to obtain my current position and have been critical qualifications needed for effective performance.

I feel I have much to bring to Frito-Lay as a candidate and would welcome the opportunity to meet with you and other appropriate company representatives regarding possible employment. Since my current employer is unaware of my decision to seek other employment, I would appreciate your treating this inquiry with discretion. Thank you for your serious consideration of my credentials, and I look forward to hearing from you soon.

Sincerely,

L. Burton Fisher

Enclosure

190

Purchasing and Inventory Control Manager. *Carolyn Braden, Hendersonville, Tennessee*
The person was relocating to his native Georgia, and he had researched the company he wanted to join. The middle paragraph indicates his experience, skills, and qualifications.

ROBERT J. THOMAS
964 Leaf Circle * San Diego, CA 55555
Tel: (555) 555-5555

Mr. Charles Scoff
Jones Management Services, Inc.
6354 Park North Drive
Chicago, IL 55555

April 24, xxxx

Dear Mr. Scoff:

Without a doubt, I meet or exceed your qualifications for your open positions as business consultant and support services operation manager for military worldwide posts. My expertise and well-respected reputation as a consultant/adviser would certainly enhance your operations, as you could place me anywhere in the world in any community, having full confidence that I could independently provide support services, manage contracts, and reap profits for a military community/base operation. Please review the enclosed résumé for highlights of my career history.

- *Worked and lived with the military for over 20 years*
- *Managed business operations in Saudi Arabia, Spain, France, Germany, and Korea*
- *Highly qualified contract/finance/business manager*
- *Able to relocate immediately*

A highly distinguished career in business and community operations managing multinational work forces in various countries, coupled with expertise in contract negotiations, qualifies me for placement through your services.

How may I further contact you to discuss how my qualifications can best serve your requirements? Please reach me at the above address or phone number.

Thank you for taking the time to review my résumé. I very much look forward to hearing from you soon.

Sincerely,

Robert J. Thomas

Enclosure

191

Business Operations Manager. *Diane Burns, Columbia, Maryland*
A response to a specific announcement for military posts. Bullets point to career history highlights in bold italic. An open-ended question ("How may I . . . ?") calls for an answer.

Richard S. Eberhart

56 N. Penn Street • Indianapolis, Indiana 46220
(317) 555-5555 (office) • (317) 555-5556 (home)

Your position in executive placement puts you in contact with multinational companies looking to maximize their organizational effectiveness and gain unique competitive advantages. My expertise in this area, described briefly in the enclosed résumé, might be of interest to one of your clients. Specifically, I am interested in a senior-level position requiring the ability to:

1) successfully orchestrate and lead large-scale corporate transformations, and
2) build highly competitive organizations based on the principles of continuous improvement.

Over the last decade, I have played an integral part in the strategic realignment of two global Fortune 200 companies:

- **For Eli Lilly and Company**, I directed the planning and implementation of major process changes that completely redefined the way that company thinks about and conducts business on a global scale. As Director of Organizational Effectiveness, I built and managed a world-class internal consulting group that strategically partnered with all business functions to improve their bottom-line contributions. RESULTS: Successfully reduced operating costs by more than $100 million and revolutionized the product development process.

- **For the Amoco Corporation**, I spent seven years orchestrating a major culture change and building a learning organization from the ground floor. It was during this time that I earned several promotions, each time gaining greater responsibility and working more closely with senior management as a consultant for full-scale organizational effectiveness. RESULTS: Directed strategic growth of a major exploration and production division, reducing costs by $250 million, increasing exploration success, and drastically improving its standing as a world class operation.

My preference for relocation is the Midwest, East Coast, or an international assignment. Please call me for further details that will allow you to better present my qualifications to one of your clients. I appreciate your assistance and look forward to speaking with you about your needs, my background, and mutual opportunities.

Sincerely,

Richard S. Eberhart
enc.

192

Director of Organizational Effectiveness. *John A. Suarez, Troy, Illinois*
A letter to an executive search firm to find a new company for this high-level consultant for corporate transformations that reduce costs and revolutionize productivity. See Resume 21.

CATHERINE N. STACK

110 Angel Hill ▪ Poughkeepsie, NY 00000 ▪ (555) 555-5555

June 18, XXXX

Mr. John Smith
ABC Company
123 Street
Poughkeepsie, NY 12603

Dear Mr. Smith:

I am a graduate of SUNY-Albany with a BS degree in Business Administration who would like to explore entry-level opportunities within your company. Like most new graduates, I can't offer you practical work experience. However, I would bring with me an exceptional work ethic, an eagerness to learn, and a commitment to doing a job right.

SUNY-Albany provided an in-depth program designed for future managers to effectively meet the diverse demands of the highly competitive and rapidly changing business environment. The specialized coursework provided the skills necessary to successfully address day-to-day business activities, and I was constantly challenged to expand my knowledge base and prove my adaptability to various situations. Throughout, I was consistently commended on my initiative, cooperative nature, and well-thought-out projects.

I am confident that I would be a successful addition to your company. My organized and disciplined work habits, ability to work well with people, problem solving aptitude, and high integrity will enable me to make positive contributions toward your company's goals and objectives. More importantly, I am determined and enthusiastic about my career and will work extremely hard to achieve results.

Enclosed is my resume for your review. I would enjoy the opportunity to discuss the ways my background and skills might be of benefit to your company, and will make myself available to interview at any time. Should you have any questions regarding my abilities, please feel free to call. Thank you.

Sincerely,

Catherine N. Stack

Enclosure

193

Entry-level management position. *Kristin Mroz Coleman, Poughkeepsie, New York*
This graduate admits up front that she lacks experience; then the writer builds a convincing case for interviewing her. She seems to have all of the right stuff for a successful manager.

38 Fishkill Avenue ■ Stewart Manor, Iowa 55555 ■ (555) 555-5555

June 26, XXXX

John Doe
Allsen Co-op
777 James Road
Nicetown, Kansas 55555

Re: **General Manager / Operations Manager**

Dear Mr. Doe:

I would like to express interest in the above position, which would be a promotion from my current position as Manager of the Agronomy Department at Allsen Co-op.

Employed with the company since 1985, I have grown much professionally—from a position in sales, to a leadership position in custom applications, to my current position. Now I am ready to focus my energies and talents by taking on responsibility at a higher management level. My decision-making and troubleshooting skills are sound, and I enjoy the planning aspects, as well as dealing with manufacturing reps and marketing issues.

With extensive experience in agribusiness, I am qualified to provide this kind of leadership. In addition to in-depth knowledge of the industry, I have hands-on expertise in pricing, purchasing, management, sales, feasibility and payback studies, research concepts, troubleshooting, planning and implementation. I would like to point out the following as well:

◆ coordination / oversight of multiple locations ◆ superior communication skills ◆ agronomy background, with C.C.A. credentials ◆ solid record of increasing production and sales

While working at Allsen Co-op, I successfully built from scratch a sales staff, seed division and lime-spreading operation, as well as greatly increased the custom applications segment. A sense of great pride and accomplishment was gained through codirection of the design and setup of the corporation's bulk pesticide and liquid fertilizer plant.

I look forward to the opportunity to explore company plans and to discuss in greater detail how my background can align with the goals and objectives of the merger plan.

Sincerely,

Gary Little

Enclosure: resume and references

194

General Manager. *Beverley Drake, Rochester, Minnesota*
This letter was for internal promotion in an agribusiness company in which new ownership was pending. Note the unique use of diamond bullets to draw attention to key points.

BARRY D. SMITH
1140 Old Tappan Road
Old Tappan, New Jersey xxxxx
(xxx) xxx-xxxx

(Date)

Ms. Mary Janer
XYZ Company
555 Maple Avenue
Hills, Colorado xxxxx

Dear Ms. Janer:

Why would a person from New Jersey write to a company located in Colorado for the purpose of obtaining a position? My reason is quite simple: after much thought and consideration, my wife and I have made the decision to leave New Jersey and relocate to the Colorado area. Our reason has to do with the quality of life and the type of environment in which we would like to live.

My background includes over 15 years of management, including training staff, business analyzation, and general profit-and-loss responsibility. Additionally, my strengths include the following: excellent communication skills with the ability to interact with individuals at all levels to ensure smooth operations; superb financial evaluations, including the management of cash flow; and solid motivational techniques to inspire staff personnel to work with a team spirit for maximum productivity, and increased morale.

It is my intent that this letter serve merely to begin dialogue. I am planning to come to Colorado soon, and would appreciate the opportunity to meet with you so that I may learn of your needs, discuss my background in detail, and determine the best possible course of action.

I thank you in advance for your consideration and time, and I look forward to speaking with you in the near future. I can be reached at the telephone number listed above to answer any immediate questions you may have and to arrange a mutually convenient conference date.

Very truly yours,

BARRY D. SMITH

Enclosure

195

Manager. *Alesia Benedict, Rochelle Park, New Jersey*
An example of a favorite style of this writer: italic text within a page border. The opening paragraph gives the reason for the letter (relocation) and the real reason (quality of life).

JOHN SUTTON

55555 Paris Avenue ■ Valley Glen, California 55555 ■ (555) 555-5555

Could your company benefit from a seasoned management professional who enjoys the challenge of "putting out fires," identifying cost-saving measures and making a positive contribution to bottom-line results? Then my enclosed resume may be of interest to you.

With over 30 years of progressive experience in a fast-paced, ever-changing environment, I have developed the skills required to streamline and increase operating efficiency while interacting effectively with all levels of co-workers, vendors and the public to establish and maintain positive working relationships and enhance productivity. Among my strengths are:

- Team-building and leadership skills

- Sourcing quality vendors and negotiating favorable contracts

- Troubleshooting strengths

- Well-developed interpersonal skills

I am seeking a General or Operations Management position where experience and a strong work ethic can contribute to company success. My compensation requirements are flexible.

If my background and experience fit your present or future requirements, then we should talk! I appreciate your time and consideration and look forward to speaking with you.

Very truly yours,

John Sutton

196

Operations Manager. *Vivian Van Lier, Valley Glen (Los Angeles), California*
This individual in his 50s wanted "to capitalize on his maturity rather than try to hide it."
Following his wishes, the writer emphasizes the person's fast-paced work environment.

George T. Vans

555 Liberty Lane * Columbus, OH 55555
(555) 555-5555

Dear Sir or Madam:

I have professionally served the United States military for the past 20 years at the executive level in both the United States and Europe. I will retire next year and plan to return to the United States to seek civilian employment. My expertise in fiscal programming, budgeting, logistics, and executive administration would greatly enhance your operations.

During the years I served in senior-level management for the U.S. military, I was personally commended for outstanding creativity, exceptional and efficient operations and programs, superb liaison and communications skills with all levels of the military and Congress, and for providing expert logistical program analysis. Please refer to the enclosed résumé for a brief look at a few professional accomplishments.

I would be delighted to further discuss with you my professional skills and abilities, which would provide your operations with streamlined efficiency, exact logistical requirements, detailed fiscal planning, and top-notch procurement capabilities.

Please contact me at the above address or phone number for additional information. I will be available for employment in Fall xxxx, and I will relocate for an appropriate offer.

Thank you for taking the time to review my qualifications.

Sincerely,

George T. Vans

Enclosure

197

Senior Operations Manager. *Diane Burns, Columbia, Maryland*
A letter for an Executive Officer (Colonel) who was planning his return to civilian life. The writer portrays his fiscal and logistics experience as a great background for operations.

John S. Martin

1604 NE 68th Street ◇ Marlstone, Missouri 00000 ◇ ℘ [406] 555-5555

October 29, XXXX

Mr. William Hargrove
Vice President for Operations
Magnus Corporation
1400 Platte Circle
Suite 1200
Wichita, Kansas 64000

Dear Mr. Hargrove:

Which item in your "I-really-should-do-this" box would you most like to complete? If it concerns increasing productivity and competitiveness, I think I can help.

For the past several years I have been making organizations more productive and more efficient by leading their Total Quality Management Programs. And I have learned – the hard way – two important things. First, TQM really *does* make firms better at what they do. Second, TQM is guided best by someone who isn't afraid to get his hands dirty doing what he thinks of as a calling, not a job.

Now I would like to put my drive, energy and experience to work for you and the Magnus Corporation team. To help you learn a little about who I am and what I have done, I have enclosed a brief résumé. As you read it, I hope a central point stands out: I do best when I am accountable for results decision makers can see.

But words on paper cannot replace face-to-face conversation. May I call in a few days to see when your schedule might permit an interview?

Sincerely,

John S. Martin

One enclosure: Résumé

198

Total Quality Manager. *Donald Orlando, Montgomery, Alabama*
This Air Force officer was returning to civilian life. The writer wanted to overcome stereotypes about military people and succeeded in avoiding a stereotypical letter.

Mary Marketer
58 Village Park Way
Anywhere, CA 55555
(555) 555-5555

February 21, XXXX

Mr. John P. Gentleman
Director, Financial Services
Personal Services Corporation
5555 West Big Street
Anywhere, CA 55555

Dear Mr. Gentleman:

With over fifteen years of accounting, marketing and operations management experience, and a proven record of improving bottom-line profitability, I am well prepared to work with Personal Services Corporation in your efforts to design and implement future growth strategies.

My résumé is enclosed in response to your advertisement in the *Wall Street Journal* for a Vice President of Operations with the ability to operate in a "performance-driven atmosphere."

Creating financial, marketing and operational performance improvement in established businesses and orchestrating the launch and multilocation expansion of a fledgling advertising agency have been accomplishments I have been proud to consider trademarks of my career. I am now poised to explore new directions for growth.

If you are seeking a responsible, proactive problem solver with a proven track record of success, I look forward to speaking to you about the benefits my experience, energy and creativity can bring to Personal Services Corporation. I will contact you next week, or you may reach me or leave a message at the above number.

Sincerely

Mary Marketer

199

Vice President of Operations. *Sonja A. Wittich, Santa Monica, California*
Known for having turned a fledgling agency into a multisite operation, this person with impressive achievements was ready to move on. The letter conveys the person's energy.

Robert S. Morton
100 Emerald Drive
Jordan, Alabama 36081
☎ [334] 555-5551 (Office); [334] 666-5552 (Residence)

October 8, XXXX

Mr. Charles W. Morgan
Chief Executive Officer
Vanity Fair Mills, Inc.
624 South Alabama Avenue
Monroeville, Alabama 36462-0002

Dear Mr. Morgan:

When you look at your organization chart, where would you find the person responsible for peace of mind? Peace of mind that you'll meet demanding customers' requirements. Peace of mind that costs will stay under control. Peace of mind that employees *want* to be part of your team. In short, peace of mind that frees your senior decision makers to do what they do best.

I would hope you'd look to me. I want to serve the Vanity Fair Mills' team as your next Vice-President of Operations.

My résumé concentrates on my contributions to two of America's leading companies, samples of what I might do for you. However, a résumé cannot show *how* I get results. I follow these unwavering professional standards:

- ⟡ I reach my goals when I help your people reach theirs.
- ⟡ I must never forget my service at lower-level jobs. It helps build trust in everyone from stock clerks to senior vice presidents.
- ⟡ When I give people the authority and resources to do the job, the good ones amaze me; the "deadwood" clears out fast.

My company values me. However, I can make even greater contributions. So I am "testing the waters" with this confidential application. As a next step, may I call in a few days to hear about your needs in your own words?

Sincerely,

Robert S. Morton

Enclosure: Résumé

200

Vice President of Operations. *Donald Orlando, Montgomery, Alabama*
The writer chose the "peace of mind" idea because the reader would be a CEO—"the person with the greatest number of worries." The "standards" are advice for CEOs.

GRACE COLEMAN
11 Walker Street ▪ New York, NY 00000 ▪ (555) 555-5555

March 25, XXXX

Mr. Smith
ABC Company
123 Street
Poughkeepsie, NY 12603

Dear Manager:

I am a Commercial Photographer with extensive industry experience, expert technical knowledge, and natural creative talent. I started in this business at a very young age, and at this point in my career, I am exploring new professional challenges and opportunities.

As you will see, I have diverse experience in both the international and domestic arenas. I have worked with fashion models for many years and believe my photographs to be unique and evoke interest from the viewer. An unfaltering commitment to quality has contributed to the publication of much of my work in a variety of books, magazines, ad campaigns, and posters.

Staying current is a primary focus. Anticipating trends, redefining strategies, and consistently approaching projects with an open mind are keys to my success. I take pride in producing quality images, and my output is reflective of my exceptional interpersonal and communication skills, strong attention to detail, and sincere dedication to my career. Combining these characteristics with solid technical skills and true creative abilities enables me to maintain a constant presence in this ever-changing industry.

Enclosed is my resume for your review. I am confident that my experience, qualities, and skills will enable me to make positive contributions to your organization. Should you have any questions or wish to view my portfolio, please feel free to call. Thank you for your time and consideration.

Sincerely,

Grace Coleman

Enclosure

201

Commercial Photographer. *Kristin Mroz Coleman, Poughkeepsie, New York*
The person's work history made him seem older than he was, so the writer asserts that he started when he was very young. Experience, quality, and skills are the three main themes.

JENNIFER A. MARTIN
555 South Main Street
Anytown, USA 00000
Voice Mail/Pager: (555) 000-XXXX

September 14, XXXX

Mr. John B. Smith, Agency Manager
Worldwide Talent Agency
554 Anystreet
Anytown, USA XXXXX

Dear Mr. Smith:

I would like to introduce myself to you. My name is Jennifer Martin, and I am very interested in expanding my career as a Hand Model. Your agency has been highly recommended to me, and I have enclosed my current composite for your consideration.

My most recent hand modeling assignment was for XYZ Laboratories, May 1997. My "regular" work experience has included positions where I have worked extensively with the public. I have been employed by National Airlines since August 1986, currently as a Station Operations Representative. Prior to that, I was employed by the Flamingo Hilton (Las Vegas, Nevada) for two years and promoted from entry-level to management. Among my academic credentials are an A.A.S. degree in Hotel Management, and I have accumulated some credits toward a B.A.

I would welcome the opportunity to further discuss my qualifications in relation to your agency's needs. Please feel free to contact me at the above telephone number, and I will promptly return your call. I do have a flexible work schedule—this affords me the opportunity to be available for you, as long as I have adequate lead time.

Thank you very much your consideration, and I'll look forward to hearing from you.

Sincerely,

Jennifer A. Martin

enclosure

202

Hand Model. *Joellyn Wittenstein, Arlington Heights, Illinois*
This was not a resume cover letter but a marketing letter that included a photo for agencies.
There was no resume, for the person had worked little and was just starting a career.

GEORGE NORRIS
4118 Carmichael Place
Sacramento, California 91000
☎ [916] 555-5555

May 13, XXXX

Mr. Michael G. Flint
President
The Flint Group
4415 Placer Boulevard
Suite 1600
Sacramento, California 91001

Dear Mr. Flint:

Let me put the bottom line right at the top: I want to serve The Flint Group as your political consultant.

My résumé may not look like others you have seen. I went beyond just listing positions and responsibilities. You deserve to see how well I can set and reach goals and the kind of results I produce. As I got my degrees, I sought the most experienced professors and took assignments that required critical thinking. To gain "real world" experience, I found the most challenging, politically oriented jobs I could.

While the résumé can show a little of *what* I've done, it cannot show *how* I've served my employers. I always follow these personal standards:

- I serve you best when I look beyond any question asked of me. I must provide all the information needed to help move your agenda forward.
- When it comes to analyses, I understand the balance between time and quality.
- I must do "bulletproof" work. Competing constituencies should never find embarrassing errors.

Hearing about The Flint Group's special needs might be an excellent first step in exploring how I can serve you. Please tell your secretary to expect my call in a few days to see when your schedule can accommodate a meeting.

Sincerely,

George Norris

One enclosure: Résumé

203

Political Consultant. *Donald Orlando, Montgomery, Alabama*
The writer wanted to cast the person as an aggressive player whom decision makers could count on. Putting the bottom line at the top is the first aggressive act. See Resume 22.

555 22nd Street ▸ Rochester, Minnesota 55555
(555) 555-5555

April 17, XXXX

Association of Internal Medicine
555 Smith Boulevard
Chicago, Illinois 55555

RE: Communications Manager Position

I am looking for a career position which would combine my interests in Internet research, writing, communication and marketing, and have enclosed a resume for the above opening.

The main areas of strength which I offer include:

- ▸ Writing, design, computerized typesetting and research skills
  - ▸ business policies and procedures, reports, proposals, training materials
  - ▸ marketing materials and presentations
  - ▸ press releases and articles for professional newsletters
  - ▸ ad copy for newspapers and radio
- ▸ Hands-on familiarity and experience with variety of software and technical issues
  - ▸ Corel's WordPerfect 8.0 Professional Suite, WIN95 / 3.1 and Office 97 (MS Word, MS Excel, MS PowerPoint), MS Works, MS Photo Editor
  - ▸ troubleshooting of own software and hardware problems
  - ▸ Internet expertise (university and ISP Internet connections, email, gopher, listservs, message boards and chat rooms, instant messaging)
  - ▸ knowledge of medical, legal and technical terminology
  - ▸ ability to self-teach new software, as well as train others
- ▸ Communication, marketing and general business skills
  - ▸ marketing and public relations, as well as internal business policy
  - ▸ Chamber of Commerce committee member (input and examination of local labor, technology and educational issues)
  - ▸ customer service, client relations and quality issues
  - ▸ office oversight and management
  - ▸ experience networking nationwide with business professionals via Internet

My past employment and volunteer work indicate a strong and positive record of commitment to clients, employers and the community ... team spirit ... enthusiasm ... attention to confidentiality ... creativity ... verbal and listening skills ... high motivation and "can do" attitude ... strong work ethic ... decision making and problem solving ... time management and organizational skills ... and multitasking.

A resume can tell only so much. I'd really appreciate the opportunity to meet with you in person to discuss your needs. I believe that you will find my salary requirements in line with the demands of the position you have available and the experience I bring to the workplace. If you need additional information prior to setting up interviews, please let me know.

Sincerely,

Jane Doe

204

Communications Manager. *Beverley Drake, Rochester, Minnesota*
Areas of strength are clustered according to three categories: writing skills, computer skills, and business (marketing) skills. The paragraph with ellipses (. . .) serves as a Profile section.

Justin Fiddelynn
333 Argonaught Way
Sunnyvale, CA 99999
(888) 555-4444

October xx, xxxx

Tracy Agnew
City of Sunnyvale
777 Hamblyn Street
Sunnyvale, CA 99999

Dear Tracy Agnew:

Subject: <u>ELECTRICAL SYSTEMS DISPATCHER</u>

According to the City of Sunnyvale, Job Hotline, you are searching for a qualified professional to fill the above position in your organization. I am a serious candidate with more than 6 years of hands-on experience as a dispatcher and supervise up to 32 employees. In addition, I have more than 12 years' experience in hazardous materials handling.

Dispatching is communication and is basically the same for products or services. Understanding needs, scheduling, good listening skills, and attention to detail is critical. Timing is very important as well, and in my experience all of these factors apply in every type of dispatching.

My dispatching experience includes:

• Scheduling and routing	• Written communication	• Telecommunications
• Computer skills	• Document handling	• Records and reports

Enclosed is a copy of my résumé for your evaluation. I would welcome an opportunity to discuss my qualifications with you. I will call you in a few days to discuss this further.

Sincerely,

Justin Fiddelynn

Enclosure

205

Electrical Systems Dispatcher. *Carl L. Bascom, Fremont, California*
The challenge was to show that the person's dispatching experience was relevant to electrical systems dispatching. That is the concern of the second paragraph and the bulleted list.

Tina Nestavez

4019 W. Inman Ave   Tampa, FL 33609   (813) 289-0919   t.nestavez@juno.com

November 20, XXXX

We hope Tina joins our team!

Mr. Gary Frank
Director of Marketing
Nike, Inc.
One Nike Drive
Seattle, Washington 98744

Dear Mr. Frank:

"Just Do It." That is what I said to myself after hanging up the phone with my friend Jim Hald. He had just described his conversation with you—about needing a new public relations person in Brazil. I had to write after hearing your requirements! Jim said they are:

YOUR NEEDS	MY EXPERIENCE
Communicate in Portuguese and Spanish	✔ Fluent in reading, speaking and writing Portuguese, Spanish and English ✔ Translated an entire book from Portuguese to English ✔ Lived, worked and studied in Brazil
International Experience	✔ B.A. in International Relations ✔ Currently have 100% travel job with extensive foreign travel ✔ U.S. citizen who has lived in Brazil, Japan, Australia, and Africa
Public Relations/Liaison/ Communications/Sports Experience	✔ Completed Sporting Goods Analysis on Brazil's economy for U.S. Department of Commerce ✔ Effective multiorganizational liaison as a relief worker in Africa ✔ Resolve ongoing public relations and communications challenges as the "flight attendant in charge," American Airlines

My enclosed résumé provides further details of my accomplishments and experience. I look forward to reviewing them with you. I will call you in a few days to see if we can meet next week and discuss how I can help you meet the goals for "Brasil futebol." I'm ready to go!

Sincerely,

Tina Nestavez

Enclosure

206

International Publicist. *Gail Frank, Tampa, Florida*
A dynamic letter with a cartoon for a subject line, two-column format (Your Needs . . . My Experience), and strong opening and closing statements. A take-charge tone throughout.

PETER E. MUSID
83 Wall Street • Ridgewood, New York xxxxx • (xxx) xxx-xxxx

July 3, xxxx

Ms. Janice Worth
ABC Company
1 Main Street
New York, NY xxxxx

Dear Ms. Worth:

With so many individuals applying for a position within your organization, how can you decide who is the best candidate?

If you're seeking an individual who merely performs the work assigned to him, without any innovative leadership on his own, then surely, I am <u>not</u> the person to call!

However, if you seek a capable, creative, team-oriented person with a dynamic outlook on life and a strong desire to succeed within the industry, then you should

<u>STOP</u>

examining the other resumes and call me to discuss positions within your organization.

As you will note, I have a B.S. degree in Speech Communication from Syracuse University and solid interpersonal skills with the ability to interface with individuals at all levels. Finally, my organizational skills have allowed me to prioritize schedules and complete projects within time and budget guidelines.

I am impressed with the high quality of service and the standards of excellence that your company has come to represent, and I would be very interested in becoming a contributing member of your team. I am confident that you will find my skills and experience to be valuable assets to your company, and I look forward to the opportunity for a personal interview in order to discuss in greater detail how I may be of service.

In terms of salary requirements, I realize that flexibility is essential in this market and am willing to discuss your company's salary range for an individual with my qualifications.

Thank you for your time and consideration in this matter. I look forward to hearing from you in the near future.

Very truly yours,

PETER E. MUSID

Enclosure

207

Public relations/Communications position. *Alesia Benedict, Rochelle Park, New Jersey*
The first half of the letter is proof that the person is innovative, creative, and dynamic in his outlook on life. Centering ***STOP*** and using all-italic text are ploys that capture attention.

WAYNE M. JOHNSON
555 Main Street
Anytown, USA 00000
(555) 000-0000

September 14, XXXX

Mr. George Allen, President
FBG Printing Company
555 Any Street
Anytown, USA XXXX

Dear Mr. Allen:

As an experienced specialty printing professional, I am writing to express my interest in career opportunities with your firm. For the past fifteen years, I have been employed by Acme Corporation, a commercial printer of pressure-sensitive, foil-embossed labels for a variety of consumer products. Our client base has included small businesses and Fortune 500 companies, as well as federal and local government agencies. This past year, company sales have exceeded $10 million.

After serving three years in the United States Navy, I began my career at Acme in an entry-level position and was steadily promoted. As Team Leader, I have managed all operations for four presses in the first shift, from make ready to finished product. I am proficient on a number of web presses (Skiki, Superior 3-4 CS, Superior Superspeed, Jore's 8000), paper cutters and slitters; and I am also quite skilled in PMS color matching.

Besides my skills and expertise, I consider myself to be a self-directed, industrious and personable individual who is committed to detail and outstanding quality. Throughout my career, I have been continually rated "Above Average" by my superiors and am known for completing all jobs within time and budget constraints, according to customer specifications. I have always worked well with my peers and they have always been able to depend on me to assist them with particularly difficult or challenging jobs. Because of these efforts, I have been twice-named "Employee of the Month."

I would welcome the opportunity of a personal interview to further discuss my background in relation to your needs. Please feel free to contact me or leave a message at the above telephone number so that we can schedule a mutually convenient day and time.

Thank you for your time and consideration. I look forward to hearing from you.

Sincerely,

Wayne M. Johnson

208

Specialty Printing Professional. *Joellyn Wittenstein, Arlington Heights, Illinois*
A "'letter of intention' in lieu of a resume." The five paragraphs express in turn the person's work history, skills, profile with achievements, interest in an interview, and thanks.

Alex Duart
P. O. Box 125
Prattville, Alabama 36000
℘ [334] 555-5555

April 29, XXXX

Mr. Charles W. Morgan
Senior Editor
Variety Press International
1224 Peachtree Street, NW
Atlanta, Georgia 31000

Dear Mr. Morgan:

Long before it became popular to talk about "continuous quality improvement," I used that idea to measure my success as a writer and editor. I thrive launching new ventures, turning around acquisitions, and maintaining solid, qualified circulation. Finally, as a business owner, I understand exactly how cost control, productivity, and promotion build profits. If those capabilities appeal to Variety Press International, I would like to join your team.

My résumé and selected samples of my work can help you learn more about me. The résumé does more than recite a dry job history. I wanted you to see how I contributed to publishers' profitability. Behind those words are my unchanging professional standards:

❖ My responsibility goes far beyond researching and writing articles your readers can use. I must find the right stories while they are still fresh.

❖ I must help you build productivity by expanding the size of your readership and watching for failing ventures I can help turn around.

❖ My success depends upon my credibility – with my sources, with my coworkers, with your readers.

I am employed now, but I want to return to the joy of reaching readers with ideas they value. The first step is hearing how I can serve your needs in your own words. May I call in a few days to arrange an appointment?

Sincerely,

Alex Duart

Two enclosures:
    Résumé
    Samples of my work

209

Writer/Editor/Owner. *Donald Orlando, Montgomery, Alabama*
This individual had dual goals of becoming a Technical Writer and a Turn Around Specialist—someone who thrives on acquiring a failing project, turning it around, and making it thrive.

Charles W. Broadway

6600 Carmichael Way #901-B   ❖   Montgomery, Alabama 36100   ❖   ℰ [334] 555-5555

July 14, XXXX

Mr. Allen M. Woodall, Jr.
President
Solar Broadcasting
1236 Broadway
Columbus, Georgia 31904

Dear Mr. Woodall:

I much enjoyed our meeting yesterday. I think I can bring to Solar Broadcasting a philosophy that has been successful for many years. Specifically, as a manager I must serve these three "clients":

- ❖ *Those who pay the bills* know my success rests upon getting them top value for every advertising dollar they spend;
- ❖ *Those who buy the products or service we advertise* must think of my accounts first and often;
- ❖ *Those who pay my salary* must see the number of the first two increase.

Because that approach seems to appeal to you, I would like to continue exploring joining your team as a general manager.

I have enclosed a condensed résumé that focuses on the capabilities that might benefit you. I hope it may expand your view of my track record and experience.

Sincerely,

Charles W. Broadway

One enclosure: Résumé

210

General Manager. *Donald Orlando, Montgomery, Alabama*
Bullets point to this person's "philosophy" that he serves three "clients": sponsors; consumers; and his boss, who is happy when the other two clients are happy and increasing.

Edward J. York

10 Lucerne Avenue
Memphis, TN 00000

Phone: (555) 555-5555
Beeper: (555) 555-5555

November 15, XXXX

Jason Farrell
Vice President of Marketing
Electronic Photography Division
AVM America, Inc.
P.O. Box 174
Denver, CO 00000

Dear Mr. Farrell:

During the past nine years I have owned and operated a video production company targeting the fast-growing special events marketplace. In this capacity, I had many opportunities to use and evaluate cameras and editing equipment that would produce the high quality results demanded by my clientele. There was never any question in my mind that AVM products were far above the competition for their innovative features and ease of use.

Having sold my business at a peak growth stage, I am now seeking to represent AVM at the other end of the spectrum. In addition to increasing your sales and market share, I can contribute valuable insights from a user's point of view that could be incorporated in AVM's product line to maintain your technological cutting edge in the field. Some of my interests include:

❖ providing input into the technical development of new products through interface with dealers and videographers in the special events market

❖ demonstrating AVM products at trade shows/showroom environments

❖ post-sale service, including setup of equipment and training clients at their business sites to maximize the value of their investment

My resume is enclosed, which further details my background, skills and accomplishments. Should you have an appropriate opening that I might fit, I would appreciate learning more about it in a personal interview. Since I am free to travel and relocate, I will not be limited as to geographic territory.

Thank you in advance for any consideration, and I look forward to our meeting.

Sincerely,

Edward J. York

Encl. Resume

211

President/Owner. *Melanie A. Noonan, West Paterson, New Jersey*
A straightforward letter. After indicating the person's background and the occasion for a change, the writer mentions the benefits the person would bring to the new company.

VICTORIA SAVONE

55555 Elm Terrace ■ Hollywood, California 55555 ■ (555) 555-5555 ■ xxxxxx@xxx.com

If ever there was a Soap Fan, I am it!

Add to that a degree in journalism, professional experience in writing and an "insider's" perspective, and what you have is a talented professional who is able to put a very special spin on the who's, what's, where's, and why's of the world of soap.

Being a "Soap Insider," I offer a unique perspective into the industry. As the wife of the Supervising Producer of "Sunrise Place," I have the good fortune of attending industry events and interfacing on an ongoing basis with the on-camera and behind-the-scenes players in the industry.

Of course, I am familiar with the storylines — past and present — from Port Charles to Salem ... Bay City to Springfield. I share the trials and travails of Luke, Laura, Bobbie, Erica, Bo, Hope, Jake, Viki, Victor, Nikki, Cole, Caitlin et al. For years I have experienced their joys and sorrows, successes and setbacks. I have been deeply involved with the intricacies of their romances and family relationships.

My resume, briefly outlining my professional background, is enclosed for your review. If you could benefit from the skills of a talented journalist/writer with a high level of enthusiasm and a unique perspective into the industry, then we should talk! I look forward to a personal meeting in which we can discuss the possibilities of a mutually beneficial professional relationship.

Sincerely,

Victoria Savone

212

Soap Opera Script Writer. *Vivian Van Lier, Valley Glen (Los Angeles), California*
This letter helped this "quintessential 'soap' fan" receive more writing tasks than she can do.
(The writer concocted the fictional name *Savone* from *savon*, the French word for soap.)

Lisa Reynolds 333 Daffodil Lane ★ Central Park ★ New York 00000 ★ (555) 555-5555

Date

Contact name
Title
Name of organization
Street address
City, state, Zip code

Dear Program Manager:

As a recent graduate of Pennypack College with a B.A. in Communication, I am eager to begin my career in television production. Please accept this letter and attached resume as an expression of my interest in working for your organization in any capacity that will allow me to develop the skills necessary to advance in this field.

My activities for the past fifteen years have been geared toward the avid pursuit of a television career. As you read my resume, you will see that I have training and experience both in front of the camera and behind the scenes. While I was still a child, my dance instructor recognized my talent and encouraged me to try out for commercial work. This resulted in my appearance in a spot for a household cleaning product and subsequent admission to SAG. My other past successes have included numerous trophies for dance competitions and bit parts as an actress in community theatre productions.

I am accustomed to the hectic pace of a studio environment and comfortable around directors, newsmakers and celebrities. In addition, my educational preparation included exposure to the technical aspects of TV production and program scheduling. I realize, however, that beginning positions often involve clerical work or other menial tasks, which I will have no objection to. I am confident that within a very short time I can prove my value as a contributor to your production team.

Thank you for your time and consideration. I would be very happy to meet with you personally at your earliest convenience if you have an interest in my potential.

Sincerely,

Lisa Reynolds

213

Television Producer. *Melanie A. Noonan, West Paterson, New Jersey*
The contact information running vertically makes both the resume and the cover letter for this experienced graduate stand out from other such documents. See Resume 23.

JAMES DONOVAN

90 Baron Drive • Stone Mountain, Georgia 30000 • (404) 985-0000

August 10, 0000

Mr. Robert Adams, Director
Fulton County Personnel Department
1000 Peachtree Street, Suite 2
Atlanta, Georgia 30000

Dear Mr. Adams:

During a recent conversation with George Adams, I learned the **Chief Appraiser - Administrator** in the Fulton County Tax Assessor's Department will be leaving soon. I would like to be considered for this position and have taken the liberty of enclosing my credentials for your review. As you will see, my qualifications closely parallel your requirements:

- 16 years of comprehensive real estate appraisal experience encompassing land, residential, and commercial properties. Progression to the level of Appraiser IV in the DeKalb County Tax Assessor's Department demonstrates a history of success, increased levels of responsibility, and my commitment to this profession.

- Degree in Business Administration with a major in Personnel Management and a minor in Accounting. Additionally I regularly participate in Continuing Professional Education classes to ensure that I maintain a solid and relevant knowledge base.

- Licensed real estate appraiser and broker in the State of Georgia. I have also fulfilled all qualifications of a Senior Residential Appraiser (SRA) as specified by the Society of Real Estate Appraisers and serve as an Expert Witness for County Superior Court.

Throughout my career, I have participated in numerous professional organizations and have performed well in leadership roles. I am a team player with a strong commitment to my co-workers and to the organization for which I work. My communication and interpersonal skills are excellent, and I enjoy training and sharing knowledge to further the performance of others in the Department. I believe that I possess the education, knowledge, experience, and management abilities to successfully administer the Chief Appraiser's position.

I look forward to speaking with you personally so that we may discuss your specific needs and my ability to meet them. In the interim, thank you for your consideration, attention, and forthcoming response.

Sincerely,

James Donovan

214

Chief Appraiser/Administrator, County Tax Assessor's office. *Carol Lawrence, Savannah, GA*
The letter expresses in turn the person's purpose, experience, education, licensing, management abilities, and interest in an interview. The bulleted info is doubly indented.

Jeanne Shannon

44 Cambridge Street
Watertown, MA 02072
(555) 555-5555

Dear Hiring Manager:

If you are looking for an accurate and conscientious lease administrator for your organization, please consider the enclosed résumé.

My background includes two years' administering leases and several years in restaurant management. I have demonstrated the ability to produce significant cost savings for my employers through a combination of keen analytical abilities and excellent interpersonal skills. In particular, I offer your company:

> ➤ a track record of producing expense savings of $90,000 in less than a year, administering leases for 225 stores nationwide for Hallmark;
> ➤ an ability to conduct accurate and timely research, resulting in rapid resolution of disputes and reduced costs;
> ➤ a high rate of productivity resulting in completion of tasks accurately and ahead of schedule in a high-pressure environment.

In sum, I am a diligent and motivated employee with a solid background of skills and accomplishments. Given the opportunity, I believe that I would be a valuable asset to your organization.

Thank you for taking the time to review my résumé. I enthusiastically await the opportunity to discuss my qualifications with you in an interview.

Sincerely,

Jeanne Shannon

215

Lease Administrator. *Wendy Gelberg, Needham, Massachusetts*
Three accomplishment sentences, introduced by arrow bullets and doubly indented for white space, "draw the eye immediately to this candidate's high level of performance."

CHRISTINA P. CHALMERS

000 Gateway Drive, Apt. 1C
Phoenix, AZ 00000
(555) 555-5555

Dear Human Resources Director:

Please consider the enclosed resume as application for a Store Manager/Planner position offering advancement opportunities.

I am a skilled professional with extensive experience in management, merchandising, and store operations. Although my current position has been challenging and has provided a real sense of achievement, I feel it is time for a change offering more advancement opportunities. My strengths include experience, related education, drive and motivation, team motivational skills, and adapting easily to change. I am used to working in a fast-paced environment under pressure and have great problem identification/resolution abilities. Salary is negotiable.

The enclosed resume is an overview of my experience. Since a resume can neither fully detail my background nor predict my potential, I would appreciate the opportunity for a personal interview to further explore employment opportunities with your company. I look forward to speaking with you soon and thank you for your time and consideration.

Sincerely,

Christina P. Chalmers

enc.

216

Assistant Store Manager. *Peggy Weeks, Battle Creek, Michigan*
The middle paragraph carries the main message: this individual is ready for a change to a higher career level. Experience, related education, motivation, and team skills are strengths.

JANET DOWNEY

000 Money Maker Lane
Fall Leaves, MN

(555) 555-5555

Dear Human Resources Director:

I am interested in working in upper management with a large retail store with multiple departments, in a general manager position.

My experience and training with The Company have provided me with strong and diverse management, marketing, buying, advertising, and merchandising skills. I enjoy working with people and eagerly rise to the challenge of learning new things. I love merchandising and have tremendous contacts as a buyer, especially in the New York market. You will find that I have strong office skills and the ability to look at a multitude of things objectively.

My successes in all aspects of operations further underscore the valuable contribution I could make to an innovative firm such as yours. I will consider relocation for an enterprising company that views experience and capabilities essential to achieving their goals.

I look forward to a personal interview to further discuss employment opportunities and my potential. Thank you for your valuable time and consideration.

Sincerely,

Janet Downey

enc.

217

General Manager, large retail store. *Peggy Weeks, Battle Creek, Michigan*
A four-paragraph letter that expresses in turn the individual's goal, skills, successes, and interest in an interview. Reading tempo increases from the second paragraph to the end.

ELIZABETH MAJOR
XXXX Avenue Drive
Center City, Mountain State 55555
555-555-5555

February 4, XXXX

Ms. Louise Roman
Post Office Box 999
Center City, Mountain State 55555

Dear Ms. Roman:

I am responding to your announcement in the February 3, XXXX, edition of *The Center City News Beacon* in which you sought applications for the position of retail manager for a Books & Discs retail outlet. Please consider this letter and the accompanying résumé to be my application for that position.

As indicated in my résumé, I have several years of successful retail store management experience in corporate-owned Major Oil Company retail outlets. As store manager for the Anytown, Southern State, retail outlet, I successfully remerchandised the store, resulting in an increase in inside sales (non-gasoline) of more than 15%. I also trained my employees in suggestive selling techniques and motivated them to increase car wash sales surpassing previous store records.

In my position as Recruiter/Trainer, I implemented a three-day retail training program to train cashiers to be fully ready to begin working in the stores. This program covered necessary safety issues and equipment as well as selling techniques, EEO issues, sexual harassment and hostile workplace policies, and drug testing policies and procedures.

My tenure at Major Oil Company has been very positive, and my goal in seeking this change is to achieve professional growth, which is not available in this market area. I would welcome the opportunity to discuss a position as retail manager with Books & Discs. Please feel free to contact me at the above number if you need more information or if you wish to schedule a personal interview.

Sincerely,

Elizabeth Major

218

Retail Manager. *Lynda Lowry, Knoxville, Tennessee*
In this four-paragraph letter, the two middle paragraphs express in turn experience with achievements and a major achievement. The final paragraph tells the reason for a change.

G. Michael Davidson

000 Cherokee Drive
Hendersonville, TN 00000

Home: (000) 000-0000
Office: (000) 000-0000

April 29, XXXX

Bayer Corporation
Pharmaceutical Division
000 Landers Lane
Franklin, TN 00000

Dear Sirs:

I am responding with a great deal of interest to your recent ad in *The Tennessean* for an **Account Executive - Biological Sales**. My qualifications, as outlined in the enclosed resume, appear to be an excellent match with the requirements listed for this position.

Detailed on my resume is a solid, successful background in pharmaceutical sales with Reputable Pharmaceuticals spanning more than 10 years. During this time I have established professional relationships with hospitals, retailers, wholesalers, and retail buying groups throughout the Southeast. This enables me to offer Bayer an in-depth knowledge of the pharmaceutical market in Tennessee, as well as providing key contacts throughout the region, particularly in Nashville, Memphis, and Jackson.

In addition, the fact that Bayer is looking for someone to promote its product line to such a diverse customer base is very appealing to me. Among my strengths is the ability to communicate effectively and maintain positive relationships with customers, plus additional success in launching new products, territory management, and customer service.

I feel particularly well qualified to provide the leadership and experience you envision for this position. The opportunity to meet with you to explore the contributions I can make will be most welcome. I look forward to hearing from you soon.

Sincerely,

G. Michael Davidson

Enclosure

219

Account Executive, biological sales. *Carolyn Braden, Hendersonville, Tennessee*
This person sensed that his position was going to be eliminated, so he sought employment with a new company. The writer plays up his regional knowledge of pharmaceutical buyers.

JEFFREY M. HANSON

Current:	June 'XX:
3333 Granada Lane ● Prairie Village, Kansas 66666	33333 Butler Bend ● San Antonio, Texas 77777
Home: (913) 555-5555 ● Mobile: (816) 555-5555	Home: (210) 555-5555

May 30, XXXX

Mr. Tom Jones
Vice President of Sales
International Business Company
5555 Hawkins Lane
Suite 333
San Antonio, TX 77777-5555

Dear Mr. Jones:

Are you looking for an *energetic*, *self-motivated*, and *career-minded sales professional?* If so, then you and I should certainly meet. I have enclosed a copy of my résumé for your review. I am confident that my broad-based experience in sales, marketing, and public relations would be an asset to your organization.

My qualifications <u>include</u>:

- *Proven sales ability as demonstrated by seven years of successful sales experience.*
- *Self-starter: driven by the challenge of competitive sales and new responsibilities.*
- *A sincere desire to provide the highest level of customer service possible while attaining individual and company profitability goals.*

Although presently in Kansas, <u>I plan to relocate to San Antonio in June</u>. Since my résumé is only a brief overview of my qualifications, I would appreciate the opportunity to speak with you personally to discuss how I could meet the needs of your organization. Please feel free to contact me at either of the above telephone numbers or addresses. I look forward to meeting with you in the near future.

Your consideration of my qualifications is greatly appreciated!

Sincerely,

Jeffrey M. Hanson

Enclosure: résumé

220

Account Executive, credit card sales. *Karen D. Wrigley, Round Rock, Texas*
An easy-to-read letter with bullets, boldfacing, bold italic, and even some underlining for additional emphasis. Energy, experience, qualifications, and relocation are the selling points.

LISA ANN DONOVAN
2222 Eggplant Boulevard ■ Anytown, Florida 33615
(813) 555 5555

In the interest of investigating Pharmaceutical Sales opportunities within your organization, enclosed is my resume for your review and consideration. I hope, after reviewing my experience and accomplishments, that you feel the need to look no further. Recent sales accomplishments include "Triple Crown" winner and "Account Executive of the Month" for achieving monthly quotas in excess of 150%, new business development and account retention. I also ranked 9th place internationally for revenue and market share growth.

I am a proactive professional networker within the Hillsborough and Pinellas County Medical Associations. Niche markets include medical and professional services, manufacturers and real estate associations. I offer a broad range of knowledge in new product rollout through market infiltration. Additional experience includes marketing program design, sales presentation development and in-service and customer training.

I know that, given the opportunity, I would be able to bring similar accomplishments into your organization and assist you in exceeding your sales and marketing objectives. I would like to meet with you, at your convenience, to further discuss your sales objectives, as well as my career goals. Thank you for your time. I look forward to meeting with you soon.

Sincerely,

Lisa Donovan

Enclosure

221

Account Executive, pharmaceutical sales. *Anne-Marie Carroll, Tampa, Florida*
A three-paragraph letter that indicates in turn sales experience and accomplishments, areas of knowledge and expertise, and interest in meeting the reader to discuss mutual goals.

MICHAEL BAIR
0000 Money Lane
Dollarsville, GA
(000) 000-0000

Dear Human Resources Director:

The marketplace is becoming increasingly competitive. New companies with new products, old companies with better products, and still more companies with aggressive sales forces are contributing to the struggle.

If you are concerned with sales performance, I invite you to take a close look at my resume. You may discover some qualities you like. I offer over six years of increasingly responsible sales experience in a very competitive environment. During my first year as Account Manager with Martin Industrial Supply Company I increased sales 40%, and sales are steadily climbing.

My professionalism, work ethics, organization, and customer relations have contributed to a successful sales career. I am looking for a sales position with a well-established and progressive organization where I can continue to learn and contribute to overall company success.

To request additional information or to arrange a convenient interview, please contact me at the above number. Thank you for your consideration.

Sincerely,

Michael Bair

enc.

222

Account Manager, sales. *Peggy Weeks, Battle Creek, Michigan*
The two middle paragraphs convey the substance of this letter. The first refers to the person's track record, and the second shows his desire for a change. See Resume 24.

LINDA JANE NATOLI
63 Chestnut Drive
Bellevue, NJ 00000
(555) 555-5555

August 10, XXXX

Barbara Evans
Office Manager
Qualicraft Office Products
4000 Commerce Way
Newark, NJ 00000

Dear Ms. Evans:

I am writing and sending you my resume at the suggestion of Kathy Gallagher, one of your sales reps, who informed me that sales positions may be available with Qualicraft Office Products in the New York/New Jersey metropolitan area.

I met Kathy recently while waiting to be interviewed for a position at one of her accounts, Pickwick Associates in Manhattan. It was an extremely hot day, and the air conditioning in the building was not working properly. I noticed that she was enjoying a bottle of seltzer water prior to her sales call, and being overcome with an intense thirst myself, inquired where she purchased it. She directed me to a vending machine, but having only a $5.00 bill, I asked her to change it for me. Realizing she didn't have enough single bills to equal $5.00, she just gave me a dollar to buy the much-needed refreshment. When I requested that she write down her name and address so I could return the dollar, she simply said there was no need to and that she was glad to be able to help.

Still, I considered Kathy's kind gesture an enormous favor that I was truly grateful for, so I found out her name and company affiliation from the Pickwick receptionist. Shortly after receiving my brief thank you note, Kathy wrote back to me. In her note she gave me some background about Qualicraft Office products and also mentioned possible position openings in sales.

I've shared this story with you just to let you know that I have met very few people in my life who showed me such generosity. I am most interested in working for a company that employs people such as Kathy.

So far in my career, my sales experience has been limited to administrative support of sales and marketing functions, as reflected on the enclosed resume, and concurrent employment in catering assistance. However, I can learn quickly and always perform beyond expectations. As you may have inferred from this letter, I am basically a people person who places a great deal of emphasis on networking and relationship building as my keys to success.

I would appreciate an interview to learn more about the Qualicraft organization and how I may be able to contribute to your goals. Given the opportunity and training, I am sure I could be one of your top producers.

Sincerely,

Linda Jane Natoli

223

Administrative Support of Sales and Marketing. *Melanie A. Noonan, West Paterson, New Jersey*
This letter with an anecdote accompanied a weak resume but created a win-win situation. The person was hired, and "Kathy" received an "Employee of the Month" award.

JENNIFER JAMES
4 Baywood Boulevard
Brick, New Jersey 05555
Phone: (555) 555-5000 • E-Mail: jjames@aol.com

Month xx, year

Faxed to (555) 555-0505: Mailed hard copy to follow.

Mary Emberly, Regional Manager
Ralph Lauren Inc.
55 West 55th Street
New York, New York 55555

Dear Ms. Emberly:

Tara Johnson spoke with you recently on my behalf regarding employment opportunities within Ralph Lauren Inc. I found my recent holiday employment with Ralph Lauren Inc. to be both rewarding and challenging, and I would welcome the opportunity to contribute to the success of your organization on a permanent basis. I offer:

- Over six years' experience within the fashion industry, encompassing merchandising, management, and retail/wholesale sales.

- Excellent communication and interpersonal skills with people of all levels.

- Strong leadership and motivational skills with the ability to prioritize multiple tasks.

- A self-motivated, highly organized, and dependable team player.

- Knowledge of WordPerfect and e-mail software programs.

Based upon these highlights and those detailed in my enclosed résumé, I am certain I would be a strong match for your requirements. I would enjoy meeting with you to learn more about career opportunities with Ralph Lauren Inc. and to discuss how my qualifications can meet the needs of your organization. I look forward to hearing from you soon.

Thank you for your consideration.

Best regards,

Jennifer James

Enclosure: Résumé

224

Assistant Merchandising Coordinator. *Carol Rossi, Brick, New Jersey*
The faxed letter and the mailed letter were identical except, instead of "Mailed hard copy to follow," the mailed copy had "Follow-up hard copy to faxed letter." See Resume 25.

Montgomery Christopher Herman

363 Torino Drive   (650) 555 5555
San Carlos, CA 94070   cmtherman@aol.com

Dear Hiring Manager:

How many sales professionals do you know who are the first to arrive in the morning and the last to leave at night—every day?

In addition to being highly motivated and self-directed, I also have a very strong work ethic and make efficient use of my time. My gift of gab and intuitive understanding of people enable me to quickly establish rapport and make persuasive presentations.

I believe I could sell almost anything. However, I have a particular penchant for financial products and services, with strong mathematical and analytical abilities.

You might be wondering about my customer satisfaction? I figure that if an auto sales customer can say (and he did), "You made it a good experience," I must be doing it right.

If you could use someone on your sales team with my dedication and natural sales ability, I would do an excellent job for your organization. I look forward to meeting you.

Sincerely,

Montgomery "Chris" Herman

enclosure: résumé

225

Auto Consultant. *Ms. Sydney J. Reuben, Menlo Park, California*
This individual wanted to move into a different area of sales. The sentence in italic in the middle paragraph says that he could do so easily. The quotation in the fourth shows finesse.

BRANDON S. DUNN

1789 Homestead Way
San Antonio, Texas 78716
Phone: (555) 555-5555   E-mail: bdunn@earthgroup.com

DATE

NAME
TITLE
COMPANY
ADDRESS
CITY, STATE ZIP

Dear :

Building corporate value for high-tech companies is my specialty. Whether creating a complete finance function, reengineering existing business operations or providing solid leadership to support fast-track growth, I have delivered strong and sustainable results.

Highlights of my background that may be of particular interest include:

- Integration of diverse business practices, systems and infrastructures to create top-performing organizations.

- Success in leveraging advanced technologies with core business operations.

- Cross-functional expertise in sales, new business development and general management.

- Innate ability to build positive customer, vendor and third-party relationships.

- Attainment of solid revenue and profit improvement combined with equally impressive cost reductions, quality gains and productivity improvements.

With a record of strong performance within fast-paced, dynamic work environments, I am now seeking new challenges with a sophisticated technology company. If you are seeking a candidate who can make an immediate impact on your current operations, we should meet. I would welcome the opportunity to further explore how we might mutually benefit one another.

Sincerely,

Brandon S. Dunn

Enclosure

226

Business Development Specialist. *Rebecca Stokes, Lynchburg, Virginia*
A notable feature of this person's expertise is his ability to integrate diverse practices and operations. The letter could just as easily have been grouped with operations cover letters.

JACQUELINE L. MASON

6645 North Oliphant Avenue
Chicago, IL 60631
Residence: 312.555.1212 • Business: 773.555.1212

October 10, 1998

Mr. Kevin P. Spillane
Director of Sales
Big Sales Company
4586 Lincoln Drive
Chicago, IL 60600

Dear Mr. Spillane:

Achieving sales and marketing success in today's highly competitive marketplace requires a creative and strategic thinker who has the ability to establish profitable relationships, accelerate revenue growth and maintain value-added service. My background reflects these qualifications. Please take a moment to review my enclosed résumé.

I am a high-caliber business development professional with over five years of outstanding sales and marketing experience. Through a series of increasingly responsible positions, I have eagerly accepted the challenges presented to me with positive results. In brief, I have been successful in:

- Developing and implementing strategic action plans that have stimulated national account growth
- Identifying and capturing new business opportunities, from new and existing clients
- Creating win-win situations by effectively addressing the client's specific needs
- Working cohesively with all levels of the organization to deliver goals and objectives
- Making a measurable difference for both the company and the client

At this point in my career, I am interested in exploring new opportunities where my creative drive and energy can be further utilized, and where I can continue to grow professionally. I welcome a personal interview with you to discuss my background in more detail and how my qualifications can bring value to your organization.

Thank you for your consideration.

Sincerely,

Jacqueline L. Mason

enclosure

227

Business Development Professional. *Cathleen M. Hunt, Chicago, Illinois*
"An upbeat cover letter for a young, dynamic sales professional." The first paragraph is a quick profile, and the second indicates experience. In effect, bullets point to achievements.

MARION L. PEACHTREE

000 Fruit Tree Lane
Fruitville, IN 00000
(000) 000-0000

Dear Human Resources Director:

If you're looking for an energetic, dedicated, and motivated person for your staff, I have the results-oriented background for the job.

My diverse experience includes office work, marketing, and promotions, all involving a great deal of variety. My excellent history in customer service, which I feel is one of my best strengths, along with my creativity in marketing/promoting and ability to coordinate multiple tasks, is a winning combination. I work very well with all types of people, learn quickly, and adapt to new situations very easily. You will find me to be a person with attention to detail and accuracy, who takes great pride in a job well done.

I am confident that my experience and education, coupled with an eagerness to learn and a motivation to succeed, would contribute to a productive association with your company. I would value an opportunity to discuss any positions that may be available and look forward to hearing from you soon.

Sincerely,

Marion L. Peachtree

enc.

228

Client Services Lead, promotions. *Peggy Weeks, Battle Creek, Michigan*
The clues to this letter are the words *diverse* and *variety*. The individual does not have a specific target in mind but mentions customer service and marketing as possibilities.

DOUGLAS T. WINGER

XXX-XXX-XXXX

9685 Whitney Place, Houston, Texas 55555

February 4, XXXX

Mr. Robert Reed
Software Sales Company
1832 Norfolk Drive
Kensington, KY 22333

Dear Mr. Reed:

Thoroughly understanding a product and presenting it effectively to solve a client's challenges are powerful weapons in a salesman's arsenal. If your company could profit through collaboration with such a highly focused, talented sales and marketing professional, then I believe it would be to our mutual benefit to talk.

My career background demonstrates progressive sales and marketing experience in the technology industry. With key project planning and account development expertise, I have extensive experience in cultivating relationships and providing solutions to a wide range of customer challenges. My professional growth reflects my commitment to achieving company goals, delivering outstanding customer service, and effectively cultivating and managing client relationships.

I am enthusiastic about employment opportunities within your organization and exploring how I might best contribute my energy and experience to your company's future bottom-line successes. I will contact you within the week to arrange a convenient time when we might meet to discuss in detail your objectives and challenges.

Very truly yours,

Douglas T. Winger

Enclosure

229

Director, new business development. *Cynthia Kraft, Valrico, Florida*
Reasons for an interview are first expressed in the first paragraph. The middle paragraph mentions background, experience, and commitment. The last shows follow-up plans.

SALLY A. JEFFERSON
1111 China Boulevard North ♦ **Apartment 1414 Southern Tower**
Saigon, Vietnam 000000
1234 / 1111-0000 *(Office)* ♦ 1234 / 1111-0001 *(Home)* ♦ 1234 / 1111-0002 *(Fax)*
sajefferson@internet.sa.vn

November 12, XXXX

Mr. Avery Jones, Vice President-Business Growth
An Excellent Organization
1111 Park Avenue
New York, New York 00000

Dear Mr. Jones:

Living and working in Asia for 10 years, plus an expertise in developing, producing, and promoting corporate imaging, brand development, and entertainment packages for multinational companies in international markets, provide me with the unique abilities to serve as An Excellent Organization's new Director of Business Development.

Since 1990 I have been employed in Vietnam where I manage several large entertainment and marketing venues and produce a variety of theatrical, musical, sports activities, and corporate events at Liberation Entertainment & Conference, a $250 million "city within a city" with luxury apartments, offices, a 5-star hotel, restaurants, and world-class shopping. I also spent two years planning and managing exhibits and conferences in Japan and China for Select Marketers, a New York-based company.

Inherent in my current responsibilities as Director of Theatre and Exhibitions is the negotiation of complex strategic alliances between international business partners — including Pepsi Cola, Ford Motor Co., GTE, American Express, and Miller Brewing Co. Frequently required, as well, is coordination with various government agencies. My strengths in building financially rewarding ventures and facilitating cooperation among diverse business cultures are a significant contributor to my employer's success, continued expansion, and profitability.

Developing television, theatre, and promotional activities in other countries requires a sound knowledge of joint venture and international business techniques; an understanding of the culture, economy, and market; plus skill in working with diverse populations. I can bring to your organization a strong record of performance in these areas, as well as my skills in human resource administration, financial control, and top-flight cross-cultural communication. Among my promotion, production, and management successes are:

♦ Management of over 750 hours of original programming for Vietnamese television, including idea inception, preproduction planning, on-site shooting supervision, advertising, media buys, and all postproduction activities.

♦ Development and production of a wide range of special events and entertainment properties from Broadway shows to world-renowned performers.

♦ A more than 50% increase in gross operating profits of Liberation's exhibition and theatre divisions each year under my direction.

I welcome the opportunity to discuss my thoughts and ideas and explore ways in which I can significantly benefit An Excellent Organization. I will be back in the United State for 30 days later this month and will contact you to schedule a meeting.

Sincerely,

Sally A. Jefferson
Enclosure: Résumé

230

Director of Business Development. *Carole S. Barns, Woodinville, Washington*
A cover letter for an individual who wasn't a salesperson as such but who made deals and arranged promotions multinationally that would involve advertising and sales at lower levels.

GEORGE B. TURNER

5555 Westchase Drive ❖ Tampa, Florida 33600
Home: (813) 000-0000 ❖ Office: (813) 555-0000

August 25, XXXX

Mr. Oliver Holmes, Vice President
Human Resources
TPC Tour
10100 Fairway Boulevard
Vero Beach, FL 33000

Dear Oliver:

One of the essential keys to success in today's business environment is to attract quality people with proven experience and a successful track record of delivering sustainable results.

I was recently made aware of an internal posting for the position of Director/Vice President of Business Development by Jim Smith, Senior Vice President, Competition. Jim and I have shared both a business and personal relationship since 1985. Jim, Harold Thomas, Bob Paine, and I have had discussions over the past three years pertaining to my business expertise and possibilities for transitioning those skill sets into career opportunities within the TPC Tour.

Whether challenged to lead an aggressive market expansion into new domestic market sectors, launch the start-up of a new product/service, or introduce innovative market programs, I have achieved measurable results. In accordance with my recent promotion to Focused Account Manager, I was charged with leading Copy Corporation's efforts to implement an emerging business initiative (within a strategic, vertical market) and produce a new profit center at the executive selling level. The result of this benchmarking endeavor has championed $2,000,000 in additional revenue growth to date.

Oliver, I realize your search for this position is presently internal. However, I did want you to be aware that I am confidentially investigating new professional roles and offer qualifications that match the directorship position in areas such as:

1. Generating new business revenue.
2. Retaining current revenue streams and alliances.
3. Providing effective partnership building, communications, and interpersonal skills.
4. Executive-level selling experience.
5. Comprehensive knowledge of market assessments, niche markets, and research and development.

The TPC Tour is a premier, promotional sports operation, with competent leadership and a proven formula for success. I would welcome the opportunity to join your organization and play an active role in driving forward the future prosperity of this organization. I will contact you on Tuesday, September 1, at 8:45 a.m., to further discuss this position or other staff positions where your needs and my credentials coincide.

Sincerely,

George Turner

Enclosure
bcc: Jim Smith

231

Director/Vice President of Business Development. *Diane McGoldrick, Tampa, Florida*
A confidential probe from an outsider for an internal job posting. The third paragraph ends with an impressive achievement. As an outsider, the person treads softly. See Resume 26.

Derek A. Good

1705 Heat Road, #103
Fort Collins, CO 80526

(970) 400-9000

August 18, xxxx

Mr. John B. Wilcox
Human Resources Director
American Orange Company
804 Diner Street
Fort Collins, CO 80526

Dear Mr. Wilcox:

I am a recent graduate from the College of Business Administration, University of Northern Colorado. UNC was ranked the *Best Undergraduate Business Program by* Colorado Business Magazine's, "Best of Colorado Business" in the February 1995 issue. My career objective is to advance professionally and personally in a highly competitive industry.

To introduce myself, let me highlight some of my qualifications:

- Strong work ethic developed in North Dakota.
- Steady employment in a variety of jobs since the age of 16.
- Direct sales, merchandising, and marketing experience.
- Professional appearance and mature character.
- Excellent communication skills.

Please review my enclosed résumé and match it to any entry-level sales position available. I am confident that I can make a positive contribution to American Orange Company. A job application and any further information on your company would be appreciated. I look forward to hearing from you.

Sincerely,

Derek A. Good

Enclosure

232

Entry-level sales position, recent graduate. *Mary Laske, Fargo, North Dakota*
A letter that introduces a recent graduate to the target firm. The writer presented bulleted qualifications to sell the person. A follow-up letter got the person a position.

Gerald Levitan

32 Osage Drive • Garden City, NY 11530 • 516-555-5555

June 14, xxxx

Mr. Harold Blumenthal
Director, International Sales
Data Technology, Inc.
Melville, NY 11747

Dear Mr. Blumenthal:

Richard Sorenson of Computer Associates suggested that I contact you in regard to an entry-level position in your international sales department.

Richard is a family friend and knows that I have training in economics, an intense interest in global business, and a background of demanding work experiences that have fully prepared me to make an immediate contribution.

At New York University, I recently earned a B.S. in Business with a concentration in International Business, Marketing, Economics, and History. This past Spring, I studied British and Western European life and culture at the University of London where I acquired a valuable knowledge of past and current European economics, business practices, political climates, and cultural mores. Travel throughout Europe matured my interest in global events and historical perspectives—interests that will enhance my international business abilities as the world's communities continue to merge.

Five years of experience working in a variety of positions have sharpened my business-related supervisory, organizational, and administrative skills. I've worked as an administrative assistant and trainer for the NYU Arts' Department. I've worked various summer jobs including fulfilling highly sensitive and pressured administrative tasks with the Red Cross after the Flight 800 disaster. Summer experience with the International division of UPS gave me basic import/export exposure.

Taking initiative has always been my academic and career focus. I certainly understand responsibility, hold an intense work ethic, and strive to do my best in any situation. I'd like to meet and discuss the ways in which I can contribute my experience and energy to Data Technology's success.

Sincerely,

Gerald Levitan

enclosure: resume in traditional and computer scannable versions

 Recent NYU Graduate ● International Business Focus

233

Entry-level sales position, recent graduate. *Deborah Wile Dib, Medford, New York*
The writer referred to this person's work ethic and determination to dispel any "GenX" bias. He received offers from five states and relocated to the Southeast. See Resume 27.

GRANT L. KEMPER

Home: (913) 555-5555
Office: (913) 555-5555

5555 East Elm Terrace
Olathe, Kansas 66666

September 25, XXXX

Mr. Tom Jones
Senior Vice President of Administration and Operations
Southwest Irrigated Growers
P.O. Box 5555
Dallas, TX 73333

Dear Mr. Jones:

Per our telephone conversation this week, I am forwarding my résumé for your review. I am excited about the possibility of joining Southwest Growers as a Hay and Cottonseed Sales Representative!

I have been involved in the hay business since my foot could reach the tractor pedal on the family farm. At the age of fourteen, I started my own hay crew and hauled hay for neighboring farmers.

My sales experience began with selling my grandfather's hay, then buying neighbors' hay and reselling it. I expanded by renting ground to produce my own hay to sell. By the time I was ready to concentrate on sales alone, I was putting up about 30,000 small square bales and up to 600 round bales.

Over the past ten years, I have developed strong industry contacts, knowledge, and experience in hay sales that would allow me to "hit the ground running" and make an immediate contribution to Southwest Irrigated Growers.

As my résumé will indicate, my strengths *include*:

- **A demonstrated ability in developing loyal relationships with growers, buyers, and trucking companies.**
- **A talent for creating new and effective ways of selling hay and other commodities.**
- **A thorough understanding and knowledge of the hay sales process and products.**
- **Over ten years' demonstrated ability in hay sales.**

Since my résumé is only a brief overview of my qualifications, I would appreciate the opportunity to meet with you personally so that we can discuss how I can meet the particular needs of Southwest Irrigated Growers. I will contact you the first of next week to verify your receipt of this information and to see when an interview can be arranged.

Your consideration is greatly appreciated!

Sincerely,

Grant L. Kemper

Enclosure: résumé

234

Hay and Cottonseed Sales Representative. *Karen D. Wrigley, Round Rock, Texas*
The writer needed to show that this individual had a strong background of related and practical experience and could build contacts with all involved—from farmers to truckers.

Miosho Nigushi

5555 Orange Lane, Belmont, CA 99999, (666) 666-6666

Dear Marketing Director:

How important is the Japanese market to your business?

Do you know what fonts and graphics appeal to Japanese users? Or what terminology they are familiar with?

I am completely bilingual and understand both the American and Japanese cultures. My experience in marketing and sales support within the U.S. has included considerable translating of technical and cultural information.

Working closely with VPs and directors, I have played an important role in implementing the corporate vision and am ready to play a bigger part in researching opportunities and mapping out marketing strategies.

If your marketing plan includes breaking into or expanding your business in the Japanese market, I believe I can help you to realize that plan.

I look forward to meeting you.

Sincerely,

Miosho Nigushi

enclosure: résumé

235

Marketing Coordinator. *Ms. Sydney J. Reuben, Menlo Park, California*
The letter was for a marketing position. The writer started the letter with a question in boldface that would interest any company wanting to expand to Japan. See Resume 28.

EMILY WINTER
2832 Vineland Road
Tampa, FL 33602
813/555-5555

winter@gator.net
University Dorms, #222
Gainesville, FL 32612
352/555-5555

January 3, XXXX

Jennifer Smith
Human Resources Manager
Theme Park Corporation
P.O. Box 2222
Tampa, FL 33602

Dear Ms. Smith:

As promised, enclosed is my updated résumé. Please accept this as confirmation that I am very interested and enthusiastic about the possibility of a marketing internship with your company for the summer of 1999.

I will be finished with spring semester on April 30, 1999, and would be available to start work anytime after that date.

Thank you very much for your consideration and your help. I will call you on Thursday, January 7, to make sure you received my résumé, answer any questions you may have, and get further direction from you on anything I need to do to pursue a marketing internship position with your company.

Very truly yours,

Emily Winter

Enclosure

236

Marketing Intern. *Cynthia Kraft, Valrico, Florida*
A letter for a student looking not for a job but for a marketing internship for the upcoming summer. The opening implies that the student has already talked with the reader.

ROBERT SILVER

13245 Fidel Avenue
Seattle, Washington 90789

(302) 453-0087
robertsilver@mci.com

December 28, 1998

Tom Lim, Marketing Director
SportShoes, Inc.
9605 S.W. First Avenue
Issaquah, Oregon 97008

Dear Mr. Lim:

Competing in the U.S. sporting goods industry requires expert market intelligence. Sixteen years in the industry—and 10 years in market research with Avia Corporation—have made me uniquely qualified to join your marketing team.

Due to my broad experience and knowledge of the athletic footwear market, I have the ability to:

- Conduct research that will allow you to identify retail purchasing behavior and trends

- Help category managers understand their specific markets, consumer behavior, and competitor brand positions

- Contribute key insights that will allow you to fine-tune your marketing efforts and increase sales

I am confident that I can make an immediate impact to your bottom line by actively participating in SportShoes' marketing and planning efforts. I would appreciate an opportunity to describe my potential contributions in more detail and will contact you in the next few days to see when you are available for a brief meeting.

Thank you for your time.

Sincerely,

Robert Silver

Enclosure

237

Marketing Manager. *Pat Kendall, Aloha, Oregon*
Statements bulleted with en dashes claim that this person can make the target company's market more understandable through his knowledge and further research. See Resume 29.

LEAH M. WESTBROOK
5555 GulfviewLane
New Port Richey, FL 34600
(813) 000-0000

May 12, XXXX

FAX: (813) 000-0000

Ms. Marjorie Miller, NHA
5555 Park Boulevard
Pinellas Park, FL 33000

Dear Ms. Miller:

I am writing to express my interest in your advertisement published in the *St. Petersburg Times,* May 10, XXXX, for a professional **Medical Sales Management Coordinator**. Enclosed is my resume for your review.

Qualifications I offer your company include:

- Bachelor of Arts degree from the University of South Florida.

- Twelve years of progressive sales experience encompassing extensive interfacing with manufacturers such as Schering-Plough, Johnson & Johnson, Novartis, and Unilever.

- Ability to identify and capitalize on market opportunities to build revenues and strengthen customer relations.

- Team-oriented attitude with demonstrated expertise in training, developing and motivating sales staff; providing proactive leadership; and generating productivity.

- Well-developed project management, public relations and presentation skills.

Supplementing my ability to produce sales dollars are equally strong qualifications in strategic and tactical planning, executing action plans, implementing innovative marketing and merchandising techniques, and responding to constantly changing demands of the market. I lead by example and provide competent decision-making and problem-solving skills.

Although I have established a successful career in the sales/marketing of non-food items such as over-the-counter pharmaceuticals and other health-care-related products, I have decided to pursue new opportunities. Utilizing my solid experience and accomplished track record as a catalyst, my goal now is to transition my qualifications into other corporate sales arenas.

I would welcome the opportunity to further discuss this medical sales position and how my credentials parallel your needs. To contact me, please call the telephone number above and leave a message in my voice mail. Thank you.

Sincerely,

Leah Westbrook

Enclosure

238

Medical Sales Management Coordinator. *Diane McGoldrick, Tampa, Florida*
In preparing this cover letter, the writer mirrored the language of the ad, used bullets to emphasize the person's qualifications, and then mentioned additional qualifications.

SHANNON R. STANFORD

17 Hillside Avenue • Smithfield, Rhode Island 12345 • (555) 555-5555

October 19, XXXX

Bruce Newcomb
Great Clothing Company
1234 Bracken Street
San Francisco, California 12345

Dear Mr. Newcomb:

Please accept the enclosed résumé as an indication of my interest in applying for the Merchandise Coordinator position for northern California. I am extremely interested in this position since my qualifications so closely match your requirements.

Along with a BS in Business Management from Boston University, my experience and capabilities include:

- a strong background in retail,
- excellent interpersonal, presentation and communications skills, and
- the self-starting qualities that you require.

Also, having worked in the airline industry for the past four years, I am quite used to travel and am willing to relocate.

I noticed on your Web site that you are looking for people who are risk-averse, entrepreneurial in spirit, innovative and energized. I believe when you review my résumé and read of my past accomplishments, you'll find me to be a good fit to your corporate culture.

I would welcome the opportunity of meeting with you personally to discuss my qualifications and how my background might benefit Great Clothing Company.

Thanks you for your time. I look forward to your response.

Sincerely,

Shannon R. Stanford

Enclosure

239

Merchandise Coordinator. *Mary Sward Hurley, Smithfield, Rhode Island*
A personalized letter for a specific position. The writer wanted to show that this person was right for the job. The Web site reference shows she's done her homework. See Resume 30.

CHARLES MITTON
291 Oak Drive • Maplewood, New York xxxxx
Tel: (555) 555-5555 • Email: xxxxx@xxxxxx.net

(date)

Ms. Jane Folk
Roberts & Winkler
329 Third Avenue
New York, New York xxxxx

Dear Ms. Folk:

As an experienced Divisional Sales Manager, I possess extensive knowledge in developing new accounts and driving business, turning around sluggish sales and significantly impacting growth and profits. I have enclosed a résumé outlining my contributions for your review regarding the position of National Sales Manager.

My strengths include developing my region ($46 million) to peak levels of productivity through effective management and sales strategies. In addition to expanding a client base, my accomplishments include:

♦ **Achieving 115% of quota**
♦ **Piercing previously closed markets**
♦ **Personally generating over $6.9 million in sales within the past year**
♦ **Penetrating accounts to the U.S. government, generating more than $2 million**

As an aggressive, tenacious and true team player, I am enthusiastic about continuing my career, and I look forward to discussing the position in greater detail.

Very truly yours,

CHARLES MITTON

Enclosure

240

National Sales Manager. *Alesia Benedict, Rochelle Park, New Jersey*
A short, persuasive letter for an aggressive individual. Letters don't need to be long to be convincing. In fewer words, this letter makes an interview with the person seem inevitable.

ALBERTA O. GILBERT, B.S., J.D., R.N.

| 0000 Barker Road | Goodlettsville, TN 00000 | (000) 000-0000 |

June 10, XXXX

Adam O. Miller
Territory Manager
Parke-Davis
Diabetes Division
000 Lancaster Highway
Lancaster, TN 00000-0000

Dear Mr. Miller,

It was a pleasure speaking with you at the May meeting of AADE held at Arthur's in the Union Station hotel. During our conversation you mentioned that Parke-Davis might be expanding and that I could contact you if I was interested in pursuing a career in pharmaceutical sales. Enclosed is a resume summarizing my qualifications, education, and experience.

In my current position as a Field Nurse R.N. with Sunshine Home Health Services, I make home visits to check my patients' status and provide needed education and counseling to these patients and their family members. A large number of these patients are diabetic, and I have gained valuable experience and understanding in addressing the unique health problems of diabetic patients.

Although I thoroughly enjoy the daily contact and influence I have on my patients' lives, I would like to direct my skills, experience, and education toward a new position in the field of pharmaceutical or medical sales. As you know, I am an active member of the American Association of Diabetes Educators and will become certified as a Diabetes Educator in October of this year.

I would welcome the opportunity to speak with you again, Mr. Miller, to discuss my qualifications and opportunities that may be available with Parke-Davis. I will check with you in a few days to confirm your receipt of my resume and answer any questions you may have. Thank you for your time and your interest.

Sincerely,

Alberta O. Gilbert

Enclosure

241

Pharmaceutical Sales. *Carolyn Braden, Hendersonville, Tennessee*
This person wanted to combine her nursing background and marketing experience in a sales job with a pharmaceutical company. The letter was sent to a person she had already met.

Margaret B. Higgins

100 Midway Road
Verona, Virginia 55555
800 • 555•1000

September 9, XXXX

Kathryn Collins
100 Kings Court
Midway, N.C. 55555

Dear Kathryn,

I would like to thank you for taking the time to speak with me about a sales position in the pharmaceutical field. At your request, I am including a copy of my résumé for *Nicotina*. A résumé has already been sent to Ellen Talbot.

Although I enjoy my present teaching position, I am eager to pursue new challenges and opportunities in the pharmaceutical field. My personal strengths include the ability to quickly apply sales techniques to meet and beat the competition. I have strong communication skills and the ability to prepare and make presentations to decision makers on all levels.

My added experience in W. Africa and England, combined with an intense will to succeed, a strong work ethic, and team orientation, will allow me to make positive and valuable contributions to *Nicotina*.

I welcome the opportunity to discuss my qualifications with you in a personal interview. I am ready to make a change and could start producing on short notice. I enjoyed talking with you and look forward to meeting with you in the near future.

Sincerely yours,

Margaret B. Higgins

242

Pharmaceutical Sales. *Anne G. Kramer, Virginia Beach, Virginia*
A resume for a teacher who wanted to make a change to a new field for new challenges. She believed that her Peace Corps Volunteer work in West Africa would be useful in sales.

Adam A. Jamieson

305 18th Avenue South
Lincoln, ND 58000
701-222-2222

April 5, xxxx

Ms. Michelle Piercy
Pacific Pharmacy
600 Wayne Place
Oakland, CA 94600

Dear Ms. Piercy:

As a high-energy, award-winning Women's Cross Country/Track and Field coach at the college level, I feel very confident applying for the **Pharmaceutical Sales** position with Pacific Pharmacy, as advertised in *The Lincoln Press*. In the last 20 National Championships, our team placed in the *top ten* 15 times, which shows my consistency in performance. The qualifications that led me to success in the coaching field would also lead me to success in the sales field. Enclosed is my résumé that outlines these qualifications.

I developed one of the most respected and premiere programs in NCAA Division II athletics. In relating this accomplishment to your company, I feel confident I could expand a territory to the same level of excellence. Recruitment of athletes and sales of products are one in the same, in that they require the same qualifications—interpersonal/communication skills, relationship building, persuasion, and belief in the product or program being promoted. Just as I developed many athletes to exceed their potential, I would use the same skills to develop a territory to that level.

It is with this same enthusiasm that I apply for the Pharmaceutical Sales position with Pacific Pharmacy. I look forward to meeting with you to discuss this transition and how I can contribute to the continued success of your company in greater detail.

Sincerely,

Adam A. Jamieson

Enclosure

243

Pharmaceutical Sales. *Mary Laske, Fargo, North Dakota*
This Track and Field Coach believed that her coaching performance was a good indication of how she could be successful in pharmaceutical sales. The letter indicates her enthusiasm.

TONI TAYLOR WYNDHAM

4812 Old Laurens Road ✦ Camden, SC 00000   (000) 000-0000

September 30, XXXX

Mr. Bob Landley
PFIZER PHARMACEUTICALS
P.O. Box 2958
Tallahassee, FL 00000

RE: Pharmaceutical Sales position

It was a pleasure talking with you on the phone Sunday night, and I greatly appreciate your time. My resume is enclosed for your perusal. As stated, my career goal is to secure a position in pharmaceutical sales.

Please recall that I have a degree in Health Care Management and love working with people. My current position as Physician Recruitment Coordinator at Camden Memorial Hospital allows me to communicate with physicians and their staff on a daily basis. Specifically, I have learned how to approach the unique challenges and time constraints they continually face.

You'll find me to be dedicated, goal-oriented, driven and hardworking. I intend to study this craft and learn quickly. I don't complain about pressure, long hours or any of the other tough situations that may arise. I will learn the pharmaceutical industry from the bottom up, happily starting at the entry level. For the right opportunity, I am certainly willing to relocate. Given the combination of these factors and the fact that I am eager to break into this field, I am confident that I will eventually achieve my goal of becoming a truly successful pharmaceutical sales representative. To work for Pfizer Pharmaceuticals would be a dream come true!

I look forward to hearing from you again, once you have reviewed my resume. Please feel free to call me at (000) 000-0000 to arrange for an interview. As I mentioned before, I will be glad to meet you at your convenience. I can pledge in advance, you'll be adding an effective, **enthusiastic** member to a team that I know is going to continue accomplishing wonderful things. I truly believe, if you'll give me the opportunity, I can become one of the best hiring decisions you've ever made!

Sincerely,

Toni Taylor Wyndham

Enclosure

244

Pharmaceutical Sales. *Gwen P. Noffz, Greenwood, South Carolina*
An enthusiastic letter for a recent graduate who became excited about pharmaceutical sales.
She sent four resumes, had four interviews, and received three job offers.

TONI TAYLOR WYNDHAM

4812 Old Lexington Road ✦ Camden, SC 00000   (000) 000-0000

October 20, XXXX

Mr. David Howell
109 Cherokee Drive
Atlanta, GA 00000

Dear Mr. Howell,

I found your presentation of *The Personal Touch* to be very informative and useful. The information you gave us will no doubt serve to improve our relations with others.

Also, I want to thank you for allowing me to mention my interest in the pharmaceutical industry to you. After doing some additional research, I find that a position in pharmaceutical sales sounds very appealing to me. I have a degree in Health Care Management and love working with people. As Physician Recruitment Coordinator at Camden Memorial Hospital, I interact with physicians and others within the health care field daily. These contacts would certainly be of benefit to me in such an endeavor.

Please keep me in mind if you hear of a position for someone with my potential. I would certainly be willing to relocate for the right opportunity. My resume is enclosed for your review or for passing along to someone else you think may be interested.

Thank you for your time and consideration. If you would like any further information, please feel free to call me at home (000) 000-0000 or work (000) 000-0000.

Sincerely,

Toni Taylor Wyndham

Enclosure

245

Pharmaceutical Sales. *Gwen P. Noffz, Greenwood, South Carolina*
A letter by the same writer for the same individual but for networking with a different reader. No position was currently available, so the reader is asked to pass on the resume.

Karen S. Gillington
222 Garrett Street   Residence (517) 555-5555
Smalltown, Michigan 45555   Voice Mail (517) 555-5551

August 23, XXXX

Valerie Coats
Caldwin Pharmaceuticals
555 Smith Avenue
Chicago, IL 44444

Dear Ms. Coats:

ATTENTION: Human Resource Director

RE: Potential Employment Opportunities

I am extremely interested in the position of Pharmaceutical Sales Representative with Caldwin Pharmaceuticals. Enclosed is my résumé detailing my background and qualifications.

My experience has enhanced excellent interpersonal and communication skills, both written and verbal. I exercise an ambitious approach to development of new business and am quickly able to establish rapport with potential clients. I come from a long line of successful sales professionals and realize the importance of customer satisfaction and top-quality service.

In addition, I have considerable public speaking experience, excelling in persuasive and informative types of communication. Forensic competition taught me to be precise and personable. College and work demanded self-motivation, organization, and the ability to successfully complete several projects simultaneously. Because of these experiences, I am able to quickly adapt to various situations and personality types. I am also skilled in effective listening and rhetorical sensitivity – attributes that are essential in sales.

If you would like to discuss how my qualifications relate to your needs, I will be happy to meet with you at your convenience. Thank you for your consideration.

Sincerely,

Karen S. Gillington

Enclosures

246

Pharmaceutical Sales Representative. *Jan Passmore, Jackson, Michigan*
This individual had no experience in pharmaceutical sales, so the writer highlighted traits necessary for success in that field. The two main paragraphs mention those traits and skills.

CONFIDENTIAL

Christine A. Turner
3210 Normand Road
San Diego, California 92100
✆ [619] 555-5555 (Home) – [619] 555-6666 (Direct office line)

January 13, XXXX

Charles W. Morgan
Southeast Region Recruiter
Merck & Company
5 Concourse Parkway
Suite 2430
Atlanta, Georgia 30328

Dear Mr. Morgan:

If you wanted the best pharmaceutical sales representative, would the following be a tough enough test to get you the prime candidate?

- Must have numbers to reflect **solid success selling the nearly unsellable: an intangible, expensive concept** for a new **company with no name recognition,**
- And **build such confidence** in the customers (including churches) that they **entrust children to your company – for overnight parties,**
- And attract repeat **buyers from 5-year-olds to grandfathers,**
- And **do it all with hourly associates** in a 10,000 square foot facility that stays open **every day until midnight.**

You have just read the 72-word version of my résumé. Now consider this: I put that track record together starting with no experience in sales.

I work for a company that is obviously pleased with my results. However, now that my outlet leads our district in sales, I want more challenges. And so I am "testing the waters" with this confidential application.

My résumé will help you learn more about me. However, when it comes to exploring ways to serve Merck's needs, words on paper are no substitute for conversations. May I call in a few days to arrange a meeting?

Sincerely,

Christine A. Turner

Enclosure: Résumé

CONFIDENTIAL

247

Pharmaceutical Sales Representative. *Donald Orlando, Montgomery, Alabama*
The person had two obstacles to overcome: little time in sales, and experience with a company without name recognition. The writer pushed valued sales skills and her record.

Ms. Terry J. Branson   000 Langley Drive • Antioch, Tennessee 00000 • (000) 000-0000

October 2, XXXX

Charles Hooper
Human Resources Department
The Baptist Sunday School Board
000 Ninth Avenue North
Nashville, TN 00000

Dear Mr. Hooper,

As an industry leader in the publishing and distribution of Christian literature, resources, and supplies, The Baptist Sunday School Board has continually impressed me with its commitment to quality and service. With this in mind, I am looking to build on my background in sales, marketing, advertising, and promotions with an industry leader such as the Sunday School Board and would like to be considered for suitable openings within the Baptist Publishing family.

As a Promotions Specialist with The United Fellowship Publishing House, I was active on teams chartered to improve market share and customer service. My enthusiasm for conducting research and writing reports and proposals was valued highly by fellow team members, team leaders, and executive management. The proposal I wrote for a customer loyalty campaign was distributed throughout UFPH and served as a performance model for future campaigns.

This position also required extensive interaction with 70 Christian bookstore managers. As their key support person, I wrote newsletters and other communications to keep the managers up to date on current and future store events. In addition, I coordinated their annual sales and marketing plans, requiring a great deal of organization and cooperation with in-house product managers, as well as coordinating advertising campaigns for the Christian retail bookstores. This experience, combined with my creative professional abilities, would certainly be of value to your upcoming marketing and promotions projects.

Mr. Hooper, I would welcome the opportunity to speak with you to discuss my qualifications in light of opportunities that may be available with The Baptist Sunday School Board. I will check with you in a few days to confirm your receipt of my resume and answer any questions you may have. Thank you for your time and consideration.

Sincerely,

Terry Branson

Enclosure

248

Promotions Specialist. *Carolyn Braden, Hendersonville, Tennessee*
The writer focused on this person's writing and research abilities as well as her creativity in contributing to market strategies. The company contacted the individual for an interview.

Your Address
Town, State, Zip
Date

Name
Title
Company
Address
Town, State, Zip

Re: TITLE OF POSITION

Dear Company Representative:

As an achiever with a solid background in merchandising and account management, I can assist your company's sales growth.

In my current position, I have advanced to Regional Manager and proudly brought in the highest sales revenue of any other region nationwide. My successful record is a result of many factors, including my ability to motivate my staff, build relationships with store management and above all get the job done well and on time. As a result of my performance, I was selected to roll out an account of 2,500 stores on the west coast, which to date represents the company's largest account.

Presently, I am seeking an opportunity in which I can utilize my well-honed territory management and business development skills and be further challenged to achieve. Although I am well versed with the northern New Jersey/metropolitan area and eastern seaboard regions, I am open to considering other locations. I welcome the opportunity to meet with you to explore areas of mutual benefit. Enclosed is my resume for your review.

I will follow up with you to answer any questions you may have. Thank you for your consideration.

Very truly yours,

Nancy Morgan

249

Regional Manager. *Vivian Belen, Fair Lawn, New Jersey*
The writer emphasizes this person's achievements by calling her "an achiever" and then citing an achievement not included in the resume. Openness to other locations is key also.

JANET R. SALES

33333 Woodmere Avenune ● Kansas City, Kansas 66666
HM: (913) 555-5555 ● Email: JSales@aol.com

Confidential Communication

October 30, XXXX

Ms. Veronica Smith
Mid-West Telecommunications
333 College Parkway
Kansas City, Kansas 66666

Dear Ms. Smith:

Are you in need of an executive-level sales and management professional with a verifiable track record of accomplishments? A candidate with proven abilities who can "hit the ground running" and make an immediate contribution? If so, you and I should certainly meet! I have enclosed a copy of my confidential résumé for your review and consideration.

Please allow me to point out a few strengths I can offer Mid-West Telecommunications.

- In a tight job market when quality employees are hopping from one company to the next, the assurance of stability as demonstrated by my long commitment and successful history with Fisher Price, Inc.

- A solid background of consistent success driving sales and developing sales organizations in a highly competitive marketplace.

- Extensive and broad-based knowledge of all areas relating to account development, marketing, and management.

Although I am pleased with my career progress with Fisher Price, Inc., I am now seeking new challenges to conquer. Mid-West Telecommunications is a well-known, established and progressive organization and just the type of company to which I would like to commit the next phase of my career.

Since my résumé is only a brief overview of my qualifications, I would appreciate the opportunity to meet with you personally so that we may discuss how I can meet the particular needs of Mid-West Telecommunications. I will contact you the week of November 2nd to verify your receipt of this information and to arrange for an interview.

Your consideration is greatly appreciated!

Sincerely,

Janet R. Sales

PS: Please keep this information confidential. I would not like to compromise my position with Fisher Price, Inc.

250

Regional Operations Manager, sales. *Karen D. Wrigley, Round Rock, Texas*
The person had been with one company for a long time. To make certain that this was seen as positive, the writer used terms like *stability* and *long commitment*. See Resume 31.

LESLIE BAKER
1022 Robina Lane ♦ San Jose CA 95100
(408) 555-5555

November 12, XXXX

Ms. Patricia Lewis
Employment Manager
Dawson Distributing
111 Porter Street
San Jose CA 95000

Dear Ms. Lewis:

Could you use an employee with a record of consistent sales growth and long-term, productive customer relationships...one who thrives on challenge and refuses to accept "getting by" as good enough? If so, I believe the enclosed résumé will interest you.

Throughout my career in inside sales, I have demonstrated the ability to establish strong rapport with customers and maintain ongoing relationships that generate both significant repeat business and new-business referrals. Overall, I have consistently met sales targets and improved sales over the previous year. On a personal note, I have been able to capitalize on my interest in vintage cars during communications with men in the construction industry, which is the focus of my current position.

Although I enjoy making decisions and acting independently, I also understand the importance of teamwork and can work cooperatively with diverse individuals and groups, both within and outside the company. I frequently contribute ideas at sales meetings and offer suggestions regarding promotional pieces being developed by the advertising department.

My current employer has recently been acquired by another organization and is undergoing numerous changes that do not fit my career focus. Consequently, I have decided to seek other employment, where I can apply my sales and interpersonal strengths effectively in addressing new challenges.

If my qualifications interest you, I would welcome a personal meeting to discuss your specific needs and the value I can add to your company. Feel free to contact me at the number shown above. I look forward to speaking with you.

Sincerely,

Leslie Baker

Encl.

251

Regional Sales Manager. *Georgia Adamson, Campbell, California*
This person was unhappy with changes that were taking place in her company. To avoid the appearance of running from a negative situation, the writer put a positive spin on that fact.

CORY O'HARA

123 Kings Highway • Ocean City, New Jersey 05555
Home: (555) 555-5000

Date

Name, Title
Company
Street Address
City, State Zip

Dear Mr./Ms. _____:

After reading your advertisement for a sales / account management position, I believe my skills and experience would provide a strong match for your requirements. Highlights of my background include:

- Four years' experience in sales strategies, penetrating new markets, managing existing accounts, and building client relationships.

- Proficiency in problem solving, cold calling, negotiating, and time management.

- A verifiable record of achievement including a consistent increase in total revenues from year to year.

- B.A. degree in Economics and additional outside courses to hone sales skills.

Although secure in my current position, I am confidentially seeking new challenges and opportunities for advancement. I have enclosed my resume and would appreciate the opportunity for an interview to discuss in greater detail how my skills can meet the needs of your organization and contribute to its profitability.

Thank you in advance for your consideration, and I hope to hear from you in the near future.

Best regards,

Cory O'Hara

Enclosure: Résumé

252

Sales/Account Manager. *Carol Rossi, Brick, New Jersey*
The individual was successful in his position but wanted more compensation than his employer was willing to pay. The writer supplied this traditionally formatted letter.

CORY O'HARA
123 Kings Highway
Ocean City, New Jersey 05555
Home: (555) 555-5000
E-mail: ohara@aol.com

Date

Name, Title
Company
Street Address
City, State Zip

Dear Mr/Ms. _____:

After reading your advertisement for a sales / account management position, I believe my skills and experience would provide a strong match for your requirements. Highlights of my background include:

OR

I am currently searching for a sales / account management position. If you are looking for someone to fill this type of position, I believe my skills and experience would provide a strong match for your requirements. Highlights of my background include:

* Four years' experience in sales strategies, penetrating new markets, managing existing accounts, and building client relationships.

* Proficiency in problem solving, cold calling, negotiating, and time management.

* A verifiable record of achievement including a consistent increase in total revenues from year to year.

* B.A. degree in Economics and additional outside courses to hone sales skills

Although secure in my current position, I am confidentially seeking new challenges and opportunities for advancement. I have enclosed my resume and would appreciate the opportunity for an interview to discuss in greater detail how my skills can meet the needs of your organization and contribute to its profitability.

Thank you in advance for your consideration, and I hope to hear from you in the near future.

Best regards,

Cory O'Hara

Enclosure: Resume

253

Sales/Account Manager [ASCII]. *Carol Rossi, Brick, New Jersey*
The same individual wanted this ASCII version of the letter to customize himself as needed. He could then e-mail his ASCII cover letter and ASCII resume to online ads or databases.

ANDREA SCHOENFELD

5 Plank Road • Staten Island, NY • 55555
(555) 555-5555 • andreascho@aol.com

<Date>

Dear —

In the interest of exploring opportunities for a Sales and Development (SD) Configurator, I am forwarding my confidential résumé for your review. The strength of my professional training, experience, and results-oriented work philosophy will be of significant value to your consulting operation. Areas of expertise include the following:

- SAP R/3 Release 3.X SD Certification
- SAP background in FI/CO, MM, and PP
- System configuration
- Leadership in SAP software implementation
- Diverse background in SAP training and development

My goal is to use my technical expertise to implement high-quality integrated business systems solutions. Presently, I am employed as a Consultant in International Consulting's SAP Practice. In my current role as Team Lead for an SAP integration project, I am responsible for developing and executing project strategies. This project is setting the framework for the Fortune 500 client's future testing strategies. I have previously served as Trainer for the R/3 SD Certification Course, in which I developed course materials and provided instruction to internal consultants.

I also played a key role in monitoring and facilitating activities between the Technology Based Training group and an alliance partner, which facilitated the development of 100 SAP courses geared toward executives, managers, technical teams, project teams, and end users. I have also written CBT storyboards, devised training manuals, created automated spreadsheets and databases, and written proposals. In all of these roles, I have closely collaborated with clients, project management, and team members from all modules to ensure delivery of high-quality services that were within contractual specifications. This is the value I offer your company.

If you are interested in a highly motivated SD Configurator with a proven track record of success, please call me to arrange an interview. I look forward to speaking with you.

Sincerely,

Andrea Schoenfeld

Enclosure

254

Sales and Development Configurator. *Kim Isaacs, Jackson Heights, New York*
A confidential exploration of a possible change. Recurrent themes indicate areas of importance.
For the individual, these are his technical expertise and high-quality work.

AARON MITCHELL
3739 Nebraska Circle
Lexington, Kentucky 55555
Phone: (555) 555-5555   E-mail: AMitchell@crm.net

DATE

NAME
TITLE
COMPANY
ADDRESS
CITY, STATE ZIP

Dear :

Building market value is my expertise. Throughout my Sales and Marketing Management career, I have designed and implemented the strategies, plans and actions that have consistently delivered strong and sustainable revenue and profit growth. Notable achievements include:

- **Start-up Operations.** Recruited and developed a top-performing multichannel sales network, implemented advanced order processing technologies and led a series of strategic sales and client relationship programs for a start-up retail sales operation. **RESULTS:** Grew revenues to $110 million within four years.

- **Internal Reorganization.** Orchestrated a complete change in corporate culture, organizational structure and account management to transition a $100 million national sales organization from distributor to direct sales. **RESULTS:** Positioned small industry player into the #1 market leader.

- **Sales & Marketing Leadership.** Identified and capitalized on emerging opportunities to outperform competition and win market share. Led cross-functional teams of product development, marketing and sales professionals. **RESULTS:** Spearheaded the market launch of more than 40 new products and opened three new channels of business.

- **Client Relationship Management.** Developed key account relationships with major retailers throughout the U.S. Implemented improved quality, productivity and service standards throughout the organization to address the constantly changing demands of the marketplace. **RESULTS:** Consistently improved sales volume within existing accounts and acquired new business despite intense competition.

These competencies have been the foundation for a successful sales management career. Despite the challenge – a start-up, turnaround or rapid growth in both public and private companies – I have developed the teams, built the relationships and delivered strong revenue performance. Now, I am looking for another challenge.

My goal is to secure a senior management position with an organization in need of strong and decisive sales and operating leadership. As such, I would welcome a personal interview to explore potential assignments with your company. Thank you.

Sincerely,

Aaron Mitchell

Enclosure

255

Sales and Marketing Manager. *Rebecca Stokes, Lynchburg, Virginia*
A strong letter for a highly productive individual who is looking for a new challenge. The Results statements are especially effective in calling attention to the person's achievements.

Gina A. Osborn
3800 Some Pretty Road
Anytown, NY 00000
Tele: (000) 000-0000
Office: (555) 555-5555
VMS 000-5555

November 23, XXXX

John Doe
Search Firm Consultants
Street Address
City, State zip

Dear Mr. Doe:

A professional associate, Joel Geller, suggested I contact you regarding my interest in advancing my career in management. I have an outstanding track record of top performance in the areas of sales, marketing, and manufacturing management for Company Incorporated, one of the country's leading Fortune 500 companies. A complete résumé is enclosed for your review.

As you examine my résumé, I would appreciate your input as to areas in which my experience, skills, and training would be particularly valued. During my 15 years with Company Incorporated, I have established myself as a top producer in both domestic and international markets and have successfully worked within all levels of the organization, from customer relations to personnel management. I am most interested in an opportunity which would carry me into the heart of company operations, complete with my own sales staff with Profit and Loss responsibilities. I realize that you are in a position to see possibilities I may not be aware of, and I am eager to tap your expertise in targeting my efforts.

Because of the economic and internal political climate now in evidence at Company Incorporated, I feel it is in my best professional interests to expand my search for advancement opportunities. I want to emphasize that I am not merely "testing the waters" in this regard; on the contrary, I believe I have reached a plateau in my career with Company Incorporated, and a change at this time is imperative if I am to continue moving toward the personal and professional goals I have set for myself. I am willing to relocate, preferably within the Mid-Atlantic region, should the right opportunity present itself.

I look forward to discussing my career goals and potential in more detail in a personal interview. I appreciate your time and consideration, and I hope to hear from you soon.

Sincerely,

Gina A. Osborn

Enclosure: resume

256

Sales and Marketing Manager. *Betty Geller, Elmira, New York*
The individual makes it clear that he is not just testing the waters but is ready to move on and upward. His approach in the second paragraph is that of networking.

JAMES BARRINGTON
6889 Monroe Avenue
Cleveland, Ohio 00000
(555) 555-5555

Dear _____:

Could I help you as a sales management executive or general manager?

I have created strong sales and marketing organizations, driving forward consistent revenue growth through the following areas of expertise:

strategic sales planning and management
team building, training and development
identifying and capitalizing on market opportunities
building and managing multichannel distribution networks
developing and managing key account relationships
consultative selling, negotiating and closing skills

At Harmon Company, I designed and implemented sales strategies **generating a pipeline of over $45 million** in the first 5 months of hire. At Technology Systems, I rebuilt a new sales team in just 4 months and **grew sales from $2.5 million to $7.5 million** in the first year. At the Benton Company, I delivered **38% cumulative sales growth** over a 3-year period and developed an effective multidistribution network producing more than 40% of overall revenue.

If you have the need, I am confident that I can accomplish profitable results for your company. Regarding salary requirements, I understand that flexibility is important in this market and am willing to discuss your organization's target salary range for an executive with my experience.

May we talk?

Sincerely,

James Barrington

Enclosure

257

Sales Management Executive/General Manager. *Louise Garver, Enfield, Connecticut*
Center-justification of the areas of expertise helps them stand out. Boldfacing is used for quantified achievements to make certain the reader sees the important figures.

Colette DuBois

45 Heron Drive, Long Beach, NY 11561   516-555-5555   colettedub@aol.com

June 14, xxxx

Mr. Thomas Rightmire
Executive Vice President of Sales
Ernst & Young, LLP
100 Park Avenue
New York, NY 10010

Dear Mr. Rightmire:

Nancy Randazzo, one of your senior tax accountants, suggested I send you my résumé as I would like to discuss the possibility of bringing my expertise to Ernst & Young. Nancy knows that I specialize in sales management, branch start-ups, and business turnarounds and feels that my sixteen-year record of successfully generating multimillion-dollar revenue streams would be of value to your new outside sales initiative.

As Regional Manager, Sales Executive, and Sales Manager for ADP, I have been instrumental in the origination of business representing a career total of $19 million. Here's a short representation of my accomplishments:

- Obtained executive approval to plan, open, and manage Metro New York area branch that has generated $9.4 million within three years of its creation.

- Assumed crisis leadership of Manhattan branch and doubled sales performance to $8.5 million.

- Managed acquisition, sale, and conversion of 4,400 Chemical Bank clients to ADP system.

- Developed 47 associates to key sales and management positions.

- Received 14 awards for excellence in sales and management.

Broad leadership experience, vision, tenacity, and boundless energy have been essential components in my generation of these bottom-line results. The aggressive origination of new business has required strong client relations skills and proactive development of cross-industry expertise.

My résumé is enclosed for your review. If my qualifications are of interest to you, I'd like to meet and discuss the ways in which I can contribute my experience and energy to a management position guiding the Ernst & Young outside sales team. I look forward to the possibility of a mutually beneficial association.

Sincerely,

Collette DuBois

258

Sales Manager. *Deborah Wile Dib, Medford, New York*
The four paragraphs express in turn this aggressive person's areas of expertise, bulleted and quantified accomplishments, profile, and interest in an interview. A persuasive letter.

CHARLES COPA

55 50th Street, Apt. 5-D • Far Rockaway, New York • 55555
(555) 555-0000

September 2, XXXX

Doris Weakman
Human Resources Department
American Bank
550 Canton Road
Poughkeepsie, NY 55555

Dear Ms. Weakman:

One of your Sales Associates, Anthony Walsh, suggested that I contact your office regarding employment opportunities with American Bank. Mr. Walsh is familiar with my background and feels that I would be an excellent candidate for a sales management position. I am forwarding my confidential résumé for your review. Consider the following credentials:

- 11+ years of experience in sales and customer service. Dynamic leader with the ability to teach employees effective sales and customer service techniques.

- Proven ability to generate sales and attract repeat business. Background is marked by sales achievements.

- Bilingual English-Spanish, written and verbal.

- Excellent manner in dealing with customers in person and over the phone.

- Computer literate; knowledge of spreadsheet programs, including Excel and Lotus 1-2-3.

In addition, I am motivated by a strong interest in working with team members to achieve corporate goals. In my current position as Client Associate at New York Savings Bank, I sell financial/banking services and deliver outstanding customer service. In this capacity, I have been recognized for consistently meeting and surpassing sales expectations and commended for consistently providing quality services. By ensuring customer satisfaction, I have developed an extensive and loyal customer base.

I believe that the combination of my positive work ethic, experience, and sales/customer service capabilities will help boost your bottom line. If you are seeking a highly motivated Sales Manager with strong credentials, please call me at (555) 555-0000. I would welcome an opportunity to meet with you to discuss this opening.

Thank you for considering my qualifications.

Sincerely yours,

Charles Copa

enclosure

259

Sales Manager, banking. *Kim Isaacs, Jackson Heights, New York*
This job seeker was using a networking contact to get his foot in the door. The bulleted credentials are experience and skills. The next-to-last paragraph shows achievements.

JOHN Q. LANE

1300 7th Street South
Fargo, ND 58000

Home: (701) 000-0000

April 2, xxxx

Mr. Bill Hoff
Furniture Plus
505 5th Avenue South
Snow, ND 58000

Dear Mr. Hoff:

Please consider this letter as an expression of my interest in obtaining a position with Furniture Plus. The lease on our store has expired, and after 20 years in the furniture industry, new adventures beckon. I would welcome an exciting opportunity where I would be able to utilize my sales abilities and experience to the fullest with a reputable company. I have enclosed my résumé for your review.

I would like to highlight my top qualifications:

❖ My experience, sales ability, and personality would make me productive immediately.

❖ I take pride in selling "the best" and have an award-winning sales performance history. (Received 1995 Softquilt Sales Growth Award and was selected as "Dealer of the Year" by Sure Rest, 1992)

❖ I am customer-service driven. I am not satisfied until the customers are satisfied.

❖ You will not find a more loyal and dedicated employee. My desire is to succeed to my fullest personally and professionally.

I would appreciate the opportunity to discuss my past achievements and the ways in which I can excel in a position with your company. Thank you.

Sincerely,

John Q. Lane

Enclosure

260

Sales position. *Mary Laske, Fargo, North Dakota*
The writer highlights the person's qualifications because they are strong. It's easy to think that the reader would interview this experienced professional who could sell immediately.

GINA BASKIN-CARTER

000 Wartrace Road
Madison, Tennessee 00000

Home. (000) 000-0000
Voicemail: 000-0000 Box 000

July 17, XXXX

Mr. Mark Hamilton
Region Operation Manager
National Tobacco Company
000 Concordia Drive
St. Louis, Missouri

Dear Mr. Hamilton:

At the suggestion of Steve Sullivan, NTC's Retail Manager in the Nashville/Paducah area, I am writing to express my interest in the Sales Representative position that may be available in the Nashville territory. Enclosed is a resume outlining my qualifications and experience.

Through my current position as a Retail Representative I have developed effective time and territory management skills that are crucial in such a diverse geographic territory with a large retail base. Also, I have established strong relationships with the retailers in this area by consistently delivering on promises and responding to their needs. These qualities, combined with my previous sales experience, should enable me to successfully meet and exceed the sales goals set for this territory.

During my four years with National Tobacco, I feel that I have succeeded in making a positive contribution to the company's impact on tobacco consumers. The position of Sales Representative would offer me the opportunity to extend that contribution, and I feel well prepared to handle its challenges and responsibilities.

I look forward to speaking with you to discuss my interest in this position. Thank you for your time and consideration.

Sincerely,

Gina Baskin-Carter

Enclosure

261

Sales Representative. *Carolyn Braden, Hendersonville, Tennessee*
This letter was written to let management know that the individual was interested and qualified for an opening that would soon be available within the same company.

28 Lugar Street
Portsmouth, New Hampshire 55555
(555) 555-5555

July 7, XXXX

Name
Title
Address
City, State zip

Position of Interest – Sales Representative

Dear   :

For the past thirteen years I have worked extensively with the general public, marketing and selling supplies and services for the funeral industry, as well as coordinating all the details associated with a very intensive and delicate field.

I am interested in transferring these valuable skills to another industry, and in using my management and leadership skills to an even greater degree. I bring outstanding skills in customer service and human relations, in additional to the following strengths:

- motivation
- close rein on expenditures
- sound decision making
- integrity and work ethic
- dependability
- excellent presentation skills
- self-direction and self-motivation

I would welcome the opportunity to join a management or sales team concerned with productivity, quality customer service and managed growth patterns. You will find my salary requirements to be in line with my experience and level of responsibility. I will be contacting your office to set up an appointment to review my excellent record of performance in greater detail. I look forward to our conversation.

Sincerely,

Jerry Smythe

Enclosure

262

Sales Representative. *Beverley Drake, Rochester, Minnesota*
The individual wanted to change careers and become a sales representative. The challenge for the writer was to downplay the mortician image and display relevant skills.

Britain Jesse Walker

P.O. Box 555 □ Blue River, Wisconsin 55555 □ (555) 555-5555

Current Date

Lloyd T. Schmitt
Murphy Manufacturing
5555 Peaceful Way
Blue River, WI 55555

Dear Mr. Schmitt:

If there has been a theme to my life, it would have to be: "Once she sets her mind to something, she gets what she wants." Of course, my mother didn't see this as an asset, but it has certainly served me well in the world of sales.

For me, success in sales boils down to three elements:

✓ Thorough knowledge of the product, the customer, and current trends

✓ Selling solutions to customer problems and then backing up those sales with top-quality service

✓ Creating a master plan of action and going the extra mile to achieve success

As you'll see from my enclosed résumé, this strategy has served me well over the last ten years, and I'd like to put it to work for you. As a self-starting, focused professional, I believe I can make a substantial, immediate contribution that will translate into increased sales for Murphy Manufacturing. Selling is the work that I love, and my enthusiasm is apparent to all who know me, particularly to my customers.

Thank you for your consideration of my qualifications. I'll follow up with a phone call in the next few days to see if we might be able to arrange an interview. In the meantime, if you have questions or need additional information, please feel free to call me at the number listed above. I look forward to exploring career opportunities with Murphy Manufacturing.

Respectfully,

Britain J. Walker

Enclosure

263

Sales Representative. *Barbie Dallmann, Charleston, West Virginia*
This person's reputation for getting what she wants is made a part of the first paragraph and with humor. Bullets "check" her three key elements for sales success. See Resume 33.

Claudia T. James

12 Orange Tree Lane
Port Washington, NY 11050
(516) 000-0000

June 14, xxxx

Mr. Donald Jameson
Vice President of Information Technology
TRW
96 Park Avenue
New York, NY 11010

Dear Mr. Jameson:

Do you have a need for an experienced business or credit analyst? As a senior information consultant and team leader with over ten years of financial analysis and sales background with Dun & Bradstreet, my credentials may meet your requirements.

You will find me to be a take-charge, self-motivated team player. I am equally efficient in analysis, sales and marketing functions, and I have helped to build businesses through resourceful data compilation techniques. You can speak to any number of industry professionals who will tell you that my commitment to quality has gained me a reputation of excellence. I regard the following as representative accomplishments:

• Consistently surpass objectives in all categories including direct and indirect sales.

• Currently running highest percentage in D&B nationwide for financial statement information timeliness.

• Maintain a very high, 85% success rate for obtaining executive-level interviews to access and compile valuable corporate financial information.

If you require a candidate with outstanding analysis, sales, and supervisory abilities combined with a motivation to excel, then we should meet to discuss the ways that I can help achieve your division and company goals. My analytical acuity, sales skills, ingenuity and passion for excellence would absolutely make me an asset to TRW. I thank you for your time and await your reply.

Sincerely,

Claudia T. James

264

Senior Information Consultant/Analyst. *Deborah Wile Dib, Medford, New York*
The person wanted to move "to another industry leader in the credit information field." This letter is a direct inquiry rather than a response to an ad. Strong achievements are bulleted.

ERIK J. DEMARCO

45 Denver Avenue
Alexandria, Virginia 55555

Phone   (555) 555-5555
Fax   (555) 555-5555

DATE

NAME
TITLE
RECRUITER
ADDRESS
CITY, STATE ZIP

Dear :

I have had a successful career as President, COO and Vice President of Sales & Marketing for several major corporations. Most recently, I played a key role in the start-up of an advertising promotional firm, rapid growth of an emerging Internet venture, and aggressive market expansion of a specialized global manufacturer.

To each, I have provided the strategic and tactical leadership, addressing unique challenges and delivering solid financial gains. In fact, in all instances, I was asked to join the senior management team in a permanent role. Unfortunately, none of these positions was the "right" opportunity.

My goal is a senior-level position where I can provide corporate development, marketing and/or operating leadership. The breadth of my experience is extensive and includes:

- Full P&L and operating management responsibility at the corporate and divisional levels for major consumer packaged goods, durable goods and housewares/hardgoods businesses.
- Oversight of countless product development, commercialization, global manufacturing and market launch programs.
- Expertise in new business development, strategic marketing, and leadership of multichannel sales and distribution networks.
- Aggressive control of accelerating operation, marketing and overhead costs with consistent improvements in net profit contributions.

I would welcome the chance to explore any current search assignments you feel appropriate for a candidate with my qualifications. Please note that I wish to remain in the Washington/Baltimore region. Thank you.

Sincerely,

Erik J. DeMarco

Enclosure

265

Senior-level position in sales and marketing. *Rebecca Stokes, Lynchburg, Virginia*
This person wanted a long-term corporate assignment after having held interim executive positions with five different companies. Bulleted items show the breadth of his experience.

FRANK FOSTER

151 Kingsley Road
South Beach, NY 55555
555-555-5555

May 20, XXXX

Dear Hiring Executive:

Building market value is my expertise. Throughout my 14-year Sales and Marketing career, I have designed and implemented the strategies, plans and actions that have consistently delivered strong and sustainable revenues and profit growth. Some achievements of particular note are:

- Launching a start-up fuel oil venture to $1.7 million in annual revenues, managing operations, sales and operations as President and CEO;
- Facilitating revenue growth within an established business market (Western Estate Wines) against stiff competition, delivering 24% growth in revenues and profits within one year; and
- Revitalizing the Eastern Region of Western Wines of New York, guiding the region through a period of accelerated growth and expanded distributions.

Through my efforts in growing and nurturing customer relationships, spearheading new market / new product development and effectively managing regional sales and marketing, I have delivered impressive results and outperformed the competition. In addition, I have created top-flight sales training programs to train field sales teams in strategic selling, client relationship management and contract negotiations.

My goal is a senior-level sales and marketing position within an organization poised for growth. I guarantee that the strength of my market experience, leadership skills and personal selling and negotiating talents will be of significant value. If you are interested in quality performance, dependable action and innovative sales and marketing solutions, my proven track record demonstrates what I can do for you.

The enclosed resume describes my qualifications for the position advertised. I would welcome the opportunity to personally discuss my qualifications with you at your convenience. Thank you in advance for your consideration.

Sincerely,

Frank Foster

Enclosure

266

Senior-level position in sales and marketing. *Susan Guarneri, Lawrenceville, New Jersey*
The opening paragraph displays this person's chief area of expertise and track record. Bulleted achievements appear relatively early because they are clearly impressive.

RICHARD F. VITNER, JR.
6001 West 6ᵗʰ Avenue
North City, IL 60000
(773) 555-1212

January 12, 1998

Mr. Dean L. Jonas
Executive Recruiter Firm
4000 East Avenue
City, IL 60000

Dear Mr. Jonas:

My wife and I will be relocating to Phoenix, Arizona, prompted by her recent acceptance of a senior management position with Major Conglomerate. As a result, I am exploring new, challenging job opportunities in the Phoenix area where my work experience, leadership skills and educational background would make a positive impact, and where I can continue in my professional growth. Perhaps you have a client company that would be interested in my qualifications.

Over the past 10+ years, I have had a successful career in the strategic planning, development and launch of creative sales and marketing plans for industry-leading companies. Through a series of increasingly responsible roles, I have built a solid track record of exceeding assigned objectives and boosting revenue and profit growth within aggressive markets, on regional and national levels.

Note the following specific achievements:

- Attained rapid advancement at Food Company to final post as Area Manager; held full P&L accountability for a $17 million territory; developed and implemented key strategies that increased account food sales as much as 33% and all brand sales up to 18%.

- Cultivated productive relationships with major customers to generate 125% of national account sales while as Regional Sales Representative for Paper Products, Inc.

- Presently as Marketing Manager with Products Enterprises, played an integral part in company achieving an outstanding 135% increase in sales and 48% growth in gross profit within three years.

- Introduced new products, services, technologies and cost controls to favorably affect bottom line.

If you are working with a client who seeks a strong, high-energy professional to join their sales and marketing team, I would welcome a personal interview. Enclosed is my résumé for your review. My goal is to secure a senior-level position (e.g., Director of Sales and Marketing, National Accounts Manager, Regional Sales Manager) with a growth-oriented company. I am willing to travel. My current annual compensation is $89,000 plus bonus.

Sincerely,

Richard F. Vitner, Jr.

enclosure

267

Senior Marketing Manager. *Cathleen M. Hunt, Chicago, Illinois*
A letter to an Executive Recruiter for help in finding a position in another part of the country. Bullets point to quantified achievements. The original was on decorative paper.

Carl Whitmore

10 Larkfield Avenue ■ Greenwich, CT 06830 ■ (203) 555-5555

June 14, xxxx

Mr. Donald Jameson
Vice President of Information Resources
TRW Corporation
96 Park Avenue
New York, NY 10010

Dear Mr. Jameson:

You have advertised for a senior business analyst. As a technically oriented strategic business analyst with a track record of achievement in Fortune 500 analysis and process consulting with Dun & Bradstreet, my credentials meet your requirements.

You will find me to be a take-charge team builder, win-win negotiator and accomplished presenter. I do not accept failure, and "It cannot be done" is not in my vocabulary. My commitment to excellence and proactive customer management has gained me a reputation that speaks for itself. My skills are transferable to any industry that requires cutting-edge analytical capability coupled with exceptional customer service.

Current responsibilities include performance of highly consultative analysis as well as the design and implementation of strategic programs and processes for key D&B clients. I interview CEOs, presidents and VPs to obtain, compile and analyze corporate financial data. Much of my job entails learning high-technology data and software product and services, and training customers and D&B sales teams in the use of these services. In addition, I function as a troubleshooter for customers' data quality concerns and act as intermediary between D&B technical support and strategic accounts' MIS departments.

My analytical skills, technological abilities, ingenuity and passion for excellence would absolutely make me an asset to TRW. I have enclosed my resume for your review (in both traditional and computer scannable versions). If you require a results-oriented analyst who can consult with high-level customers, understand and implement cutting-edge software programs, identify sales opportunities and train staff and customers, then we should meet to discuss the ways that I can help you achieve your project and company goals.

Sincerely,

Carl Whitmore

268

Strategic Business Analyst. *Deborah Wile Dib, Medford, New York*
In this response to an ad, the writer presents a quick profile of the individual, mentions his skills, indicates his responsibilities in more detail, and then refers to a possible interview.

DOUGLAS C. ALLEN

000 Montrose Avenue
Chicago, Illinois 00000
(000) 000-0000 or (000) 000-0000

Dear Sir/Madam:

I am interested in exploring employment opportunities within your organization.

Are you in need of a professional with a proven track record of top sales and effective management? I have been with Hillside Ford of Chicago for the past seven years in increasingly responsible positions. Although the work has been challenging and rewarding, I am seeking a new association as a Used Car Manager or in a related position.

My expertise is in developing, motivating, and managing a top-production sales team in a highly competitive market. I am an effective communicator with skills designed to generate results when dealing with management, personnel, and the general public. I have established and continually maintain a record of achievement for generated sales and margin of profits, with a closing ratio well over 50%.

The enclosed resume summarizes my background. Since it can't fully detail my experience or predict my potential to your organization, I would request a personal interview to further explore employment opportunities and my ability to meet your requirements. I look forward to hearing from you and thank you for your time and consideration.

Sincerely,

Douglas C. Allen

enclosure

269

Used Car Manager, sales. *Peggy Weeks, Battle Creek, Michigan*
A clear, well-written letter. It shows first the general purpose and then indicates a specific job goal. Expertise, skills, and achievements are mentioned before the interview request.

Erik Merritt

4448 Main Avenue South, Seattle, WA 98000 • (000) 555-5555

September 22, xxxx

Weatherdata, Inc.
5 Triad Center, Suite 315
Chicago, Illinois 84180

Attention: Jamie

Dear Jamie:

In response to your recent ad seeking applicants for a *Climatologist* vacancy, I have enclosed my resume for your review/consideration.

I am an atmospheric scientist with a Bachelor of Science in the field and seven years' experience collecting, compiling, and analyzing climatological data for private and public clients. My experience includes the verification of climatological data as well as specialized, tightly focused research projects.

My strengths include a strong climatological background, excellent forecasting skills, and the ability to effectively communicate information to clients and the general public. Having a naturally outgoing personality, I am doubly pleased by the opportunity to practice my science, and still maintain an active, two-way exchange of information with the client/public.

Thank you for your time, and I look forward to meeting with you soon to further discuss my qualifications and your expectations.

Sincerely,

Erik Merritt

270

Climatologist. *Kathryn Vargo, Issaquah, Washington*
This letter shows clearly that the individual is not a weatherman but a weather scientist who does scientific research for clients. The letter shows also that he has communication skills.

Angel Wings

0000 Cloudy Avenue
Heaven, NE 00000
(555) 555-5555

June 19, XXXX

Medical Labs, Inc.
MT
P.O. Box 5555
Heavensent, NE 55555

Dear Human Resources Director:

I am interested in the first shift Microbiology position or the second shift Generalist position advertised in the Sunday, June 14th, *Marion Newspaper.*

My attached resume outlines my professional and educational background, which includes more than seventeen years of diverse laboratory experience and four years as supervisor. You will find I work well with others and effectively handle the pressures of a fast-paced working environment. I am investigating new opportunities where I can continue to develop my skills and apply my knowledge toward broader responsibilities and advancement. I am interested in furthering my education and would like to find a working environment where continuing education is encouraged.

Since a resume can neither fully detail all my skills and accomplishments nor predict my potential to your organization, I would appreciate a personal interview to further explore employment possibilities and mutual benefits. I look forward to your reply and thank you for your time and consideration.

Excellent references will be furnished upon request.

Sincerely,

Angel Wings

enc.

271

Microbiologist. *Peggy Weeks, Battle Creek, Michigan*
A letter used for two different positions for the same company. The middle paragraph succinctly indicates the person's background, experience, work style, and career goals.

Victoria Iverson

26 Green Avenue, Apt. 2B
Jackson, NJ 00000

Residence: (555) 555-5555
Pager: (555) 555-5555

March 6, XXXX

Major Pharmaceutical Company
Antibiotics Division
P.O. Box 0000
West Park, NJ 00000

To those concerned:

I am attracted to Major Pharmaceutical Company as a progressive leader in the biotechnology field, and one that can provide the challenge and diversification I am seeking. For the past 16 years, I have worked as a microbiologist in hospital and laboratory environments, and now desire to redirect my career to research and development within the pharmaceutical industry.

As you review my enclosed resume, you will find that my background at the other end of the spectrum closely parallels the mechanics involved in the production of antibiotic drugs. Much of my emphasis has been on microbial isolation, aseptic techniques, efficacy testing, and recording/ review of lab data. My experience has included the assessment of infectious disease states following treatment with the various antimicrobials, including tetracyclines, sulfa drugs, cephalosporins, and pipercillin.

I am a dedicated, resourceful and articulate individual with an intense sensitivity to the perceptual aspects of microbiological investigation. Within the course of my work, I have been extensively involved with technical problem solving and the handling of multiple priorities, effectively communicating my findings to management and inter- disciplinary professionals. I am eager to utilize my knowledge and skills in team projects where I can provide input to help bring online your organization's plans, strategies and objectives.

Should my qualifications fit your current or anticipated staffing requirements, please contact me through my above address or phone number to arrange an interview. Thank you for your attention, and I look forward to your positive response.

Sincerely,

Victoria Iverson

Enclosure

272

Microbiologist. *Melanie A. Noonan, West Paterson, New Jersey*
The first paragraph shows the person's career redirection; the second, her background and experience; the third, her skills and motivation; and the fourth, her interview interest.

CARLOS J. MONDE

Phone: (555) 555-5555
Beeper: (555) 555-0000

55-55 555th Street
Forest Hills, New York 55555

July 8, XXXX

Helaine Martinez
Vice President
Advanced Public Relations
55 First Avenue
New York, NY 55555

Dear Ms. Martinez:

It was a pleasure speaking with you today and meeting you at the January 26 post premier party for *Wind In the Willows*. At this event, I was assigned to serve as personal security for Tom Starr and Meghan Starlette. As I mentioned, I am currently exploring new opportunities in the security/protection services field and realize that you may be able to help.

My specialty is in providing high-level, personal, and discreet services to high-profile celebrities. In all of my experiences, my emphasis has been delivering exceptional services and security leadership. In fact, at the post-premier party, Margot Moon commented that I was doing such a great job—she and her guests were watching me all night! At the party, I realized that Tom Starr and Meghan Starlette would benefit from personal security services. Since you work with them, you may have a better idea of their needs in this area, or be able to advise me on where to direct an inquiry.

Several copies of my résumé and business card are enclosed—please feel free to share them with any of your associates who may be interested.

Any assistance or advice that you can give me would be greatly appreciated! I know that you are very busy and I appreciate your help. I look forward to speaking with you again.

Best regards,

Carlos J. Monde
Close Protection Specialist/
Private Security Professional

Enclosures

273

Close Protection Specialist/Private Security Professional. *Kim Isaacs, Jackson Heights, NY*
A networking letter that was sent with multiple resumes and business cards. The individual not only networks for advice but also mentions the reader's clients as possible candidates.

Judith Thompson
P. O. Box 10045
Fall City, Washington 90000
(000) 000-0000

October 30, XXXX

Carl Bennett, Director
Oceanside Recovery Center
10722 S. E. 216th
Seattle, WA 90000

Dear Mr. Bennet:

I am seeking a position as a *Chemical Dependency Counselor*, and I believe my education, experience, and personal qualities make me an ideal candidate for a career in this environment.

As you will see from my resume (attached), I have recently earned a Master's of Education in Guidance and Counseling. In addition, I have completed two internships, one with the Somewhere School District, and one with the Cedar Branch Treatment Center. These experiences have prepared me to deal with the complex issues faced by youth (and parents) today.

The personal qualities that I believe to be of particular importance are my ability to empathize and to approach clients with a gentle, open, nonjudgmental attitude. It is important to state here that I thoroughly understand the problems surrounding at-risk youth--to a great extent because of my own experiences. I have been in recovery for 13 years.

Perhaps partially because of this very fundamental understanding, I am seen by my youthful clients as nonthreatening, approachable, and easy to talk to. It's my belief that everyone in counseling has a "story" to tell, and that healing can begin only after this very basic communication takes place and is dealt with.

I would be happy to meet with you to further discuss my qualifications and how they might meet the needs of your at-risk youth. Thank you for your consideration.

Sincerely,

Judith Thompson

Attachment: Resume

274

Chemical Dependency Counselor. *Kathryn Vargo, Issaquah, Washington*
This person had recently earned an M.A. in counseling but was unsuccessful in finding a job. This letter calls attention to her own experience as a basis for empathy. See Resume 32.

CONNIE CARELOTS

111 Devine Road
Endurance, MO 55555
(555) 555-5555

October 30, XXXX

Mr. John Little, Dean
Endurance State Hospital
P. O. Box B
Endurance, MO 55555

Dear Mr. Little,

"Far and away the best prize that life offers is the chance to work hard at work worth doing." – Theodore Roosevelt, former President of the United States.

This quote is particularly meaningful to me; it's the foundation of my desire to help others through counseling. Certainly, I have seen and counseled clients with what seem to be insurmountable problems. Yet, we both know of "success" stories – cases where clients have turned their lives around. I want to be a part of the team effort in just such "success" stories.

With a recent master's degree in Counseling and experience in substance abuse and food addiction counseling at The Treatment Center - Outpatient Services in Kimberly, I have demonstrated an intuitive assessment ability and the high-energy and communication skills necessary to achieve positive results. A copy of my resume is enclosed. My particular qualifications include:

- M.A. Counseling and Personnel Services, The College of Missouri 1996
  National Honor Society Member and GPA 3.8
- National Certified Counselor, National Board for Certified Counselors, Inc.
- Over one year of direct experience in substance abuse/addiction counseling and general counseling in life skills, employment and family issues

In order to explore your prospective needs, I will call your office next week to arrange a mutually convenient appointment, if that seems advisable to you, to discuss employment possibilities and job leads. I would appreciate your keeping this inquiry confidential. Thank you in advance for your consideration.

Best regards,

Connie Carelots

Enclosure

275

General counseling position. *Susan Guarneri, Lawrenceville, New Jersey*
The opening quotation is effective because it helps the reader understand the person's attitude toward meaningful work and dedication to it. Bullets point to strong qualifications.

ARTHUR C. BARRY

220 Newbrand Store Road
Athens, Georgia 30000
(222) 222-2222

June 17, 0000

Mr. Adam Smith, Director
Economic Housing Leadership Partners
100 Broadest Street, Suite 101
Macon, Georgia 33333

Dear Mr Smith:

In response to your recent ad in the *Macon Herald* for a **Housing Counselor**, please find my résumé enclosed for your review.

As my performance demonstrates, I am a committed, task-oriented individual who determines and implements appropriate resources to achieve a better quality of life for individuals with diverse socioeconomic backgrounds. I have always been involved with community activities and have held various volunteer positions with organizations such as Goodwill and Clarke County Correctional Institution. Additionally, I have substantial counseling experience with the Community Treatment Center in Athens and ten years' experience in general residential construction. After building my own home and assisting numerous friends and family members with their building endeavors, I have gained extensive knowledge of:

- Practical home design
- Energy-efficient construction
- Routine maintenance and repair and
- Reading and drawing blueprints

With this combination of skills, and my ability to work with and care about individuals in all walks of life, I know I would be an asset to your organization.

To contact me, please call (222) 222-2222. I look forward to hearing from you and discussing a mutually beneficial endeavor. Thank you for your time and consideration.

Sincerely,

Arthur C. Barry

276

Housing Counselor. *Carol Lawrence, Savannah, Georgia*
The individual was limited in his work with older persons and in professional construction work. The writer plays up the person's related personal and voluntary work. See Resume 34.

MAVIS HAWKINS

39 Barkley Road
Selma, AL 00000

(555) 555-5555

March 12, XXXX

Reginald Carter, Director
Clayton Department of Health
461 Ninth Street
Clayton, Alabama 00000

Dear Mr. Carter:

As an official primarily concerned with the well-being of the fine citizens of Clayton, I thought you might be interested in employing a young woman with my qualifications and experience in health education, substance abuse/crisis counseling, community outreach youth work and child care work.

As you review my resume, you will note that I received my B.S. degree in Community Health with a minor in Psychology from Alabama State University and have worked in the field of public health for over three years. Currently, I am a Senior Health/Sexuality Educator at the Montgomery chapter of Planned Parenthood, where I supervise the educational staff of the Healthy Mothers/Healthy Babies Coalition. I also conduct workshops and seminars on substance abuse, dating violence, sexuality, HIV/AIDS, STDs, contraceptives, self-esteem, teen pregnancy, and effective parenting. In addition, I have taught family life education for grades K-12, as well as in colleges, and have addressed members of various community-based organizations.

My employment has exposed me to the various facets of public health, in work and in planning activities with the youth and adult groups in my community. This exposure has provided me with a sharpened perception and the opportunity to truly understand the fundamentals of the public health field. As a result, I have come to recognize that there is a need for caring, skilled individuals who can work with people of different cultural backgrounds. The wide variety of groups and populations that I have dealt with has increased my insight and depth relating to the ethnic diversity that exists in this area.

Flexibility and a high energy level, combined with effective planning, organizing and problem solving ability, are my decided strengths. With these abilities, my professional goal in life is to assist young people and adults in their development as mentally and physically healthy individuals. I perform at my best in a moderate-paced office environment that fosters mutual respect and support among all coworkers. Believing in a team approach as the most effective means to accomplish objectives, I strive to maintain open lines of communication at all times.

If there is a need on your staff for someone with my capabilities, I would appreciate the opportunity for an interview to discuss in detail some of my accomplishments and, hopefully, convince you that I can be an asset to your organization.

Sincerely,

Mavis Hawkins

277

Senior Health/Sexuality Educator, Planned Parenthood. *Melanie A. Noonan, West Paterson, NJ*
One can infer from the letter that "Senior" refers neither to the individual's age nor to the age of her clients but to the level of her responsibilities. She is "Senior" also in her maturity

JANE JUNGLE, MSW

123 West Tree Limb
Green Leaf, Illinois 00000

(XXX) 000-0000 Home
(XXX) 000-0000 Work

September 2, XXXX

Ms. Sally Jones
9874 Rio Lane
Westridge, LA 00000

Dear Ms. Jones:

I am writing to express interest in the position of Social Worker/Mental Health Counselor. My résumé is enclosed for your review.

I have a Master's in Social Work and am a licensed Social Worker. Recently I completed a CADC program with certification anticipated October 1, 0000. My professional experience has complemented my educational training and enhanced my ability to implement individualized treatment plans. I have counseled others on a variety of human issues and emotions, including alcohol and substance abuse, domestic violence, depression, anxiety, and child/family issues. In additional, I have developed effective behavioral modification strategies in working with troubled individuals.

As I developed my skills and expertise over the years, I realized the importance for continuing my education. My objective is to find a program that possesses an atmosphere of learning and affords me the ability to increase my knowledge through continuing education seminars and programs.

The position that would fit my needs would be one in which I would have an LCSW as my direct supervisor. This would help me to achieve my goals towards more in-depth counseling and obtaining my LCSW.

I am experienced at using a variety of assessment tests and profiles to assist in diagnosing psychological difficulties, as well as personality traits. I feel, however, that my best asset is my ability to listen well, communicate well, and be compassionate with individuals, thus helping them emotionally to recover more quickly.

I am a highly dedicated and motivated individual with an enthusiastic and energetic style and the ability to learn new skills and concepts. In addition, I possess strong communication skills and the ability to work effectively with individuals at all levels. I am confident of my ability to make a significant contribution to your program in the capacity of Social Worker/Mental Health Counselor and look forward to discussing this opportunity with you in a personal interview.

Thank you for your consideration.

Sincerely,

Jane Jungle

Enclosure: Résumé

278

Social Worker/Mental Health Counselor. *Christine Edick, Orange, California*
A letter for an individual who prizes lifelong learning not as an end in itself but as a means to be of better help to others. She can learn well, but she is best at listening and helping.

JANE JUNGLE, MSW

123 West Tree Limb   (XXX) 000-0000 Home
Green Leaf, Illinois 00000   (XXX) 000-0000 Work

September 2, XXXX

Ms. Sally Jones
9874 Rio Lane
Westridge, LA 00000

Dear Ms. Jones:

I would like to take this opportunity to thank you for the interview and to confirm my strong interest in a position with your organization. In addition to experiencing a very enjoyable and informative interview, I came away very enthusiastic about the position you are seeking to fill.

As we discussed, I feel that my education and background have provided me with an understanding, strengths, and abilities that would prove to be an asset to your organization, specifically in the therapeutic aspects of making a difference.

Please keep me in mind when considering candidates for your position. I look forward to meeting with you again in the hope that our discussion will precede a long-term working relationship.

Sincerely,

Jane Jungle

Enclosure: Résumé

279

Social Worker/Mental Health Counselor, follow-up letter. *Christine Edick, Orange, California*
A thank-you letter for the preceding person. It confirms her interest in the job and makes it clear that she really wants it. The letter calls further attention to her strengths.

KATHLEEN M. DAWHLEN
500 Oakley Avenue ◆ Anytown, CO 33333 ◆ (333) 333-3333

October 17, XXXX

Lisa Collett
County Department of Social Services
555 Allen Avenue
Anytown, CO 33333

Dear Ms. Collett:

As discussed on an earlier occasion, I am enclosing a copy of my resume for your information. If any appropriate opportunities come to your attention, I would appreciate it if you would keep me in mind.

I am looking for a social-related position, preferably working with children and/or families placed in special enrichment programs. My strong desire would be to facilitate instructional programs on a contractual basis, but I am open to most anything my qualifications would fit.

I recently completed a Bachelor of Arts degree in Family Life Education and am looking forward to utilizing my educational credentials. My clinical experience included facilitation of programs required by parents accused of child abuse and neglect. In addition, I supervised visits between non-custodial parents and their children and monitored their interaction. Experience gained at the Child and Parent Center exposed me to all aspects of the process necessary for parents to regain custody of their children.

If any situations come to mind where you think my skills would fit or if you have any suggestions as to others with whom it might be beneficial for me to speak, please contact me. I can be reached at the telephone number listed above.

Thank you, and I look forward to hearing from you.

Sincerely,

Kathleen M. Dawhlen

Enclosure

280

Social Worker. *Jan Passmore, Jackson, Michigan*
A combination job search/networking letter: the person wants a job or job leads. Her goal is not simply to educate others but to mend families with a history of abuse or neglect.

Tom Mathews, MCSE

1345 Tiffany Street
Littleton, FL 35641
(904) 555-5555
e-mail tmathew@cybermax.net

Dear Hiring Manager,

Please accept this letter as an expression of my interest as a computer technician with your company. Enclosed is a copy of my résumé and a scannable version for your review and consideration.

I am personally familiar with the requirements for success as a computer technician, and I believe that I possess the education and the initiative to accomplish any task assigned. As you will note from my résumé, I have just received my MCSE certification. I also have computer skills in Windows NT, Windows 95, WordPerfect, Microsoft Word 97, Netscape and Internet Explorer 4.01. In addition to these skills, I

- assisted in the successful integration of 80 workstations and two servers.

- understand the importance of providing strong customer support.

- enjoy solving problems and have proven leadership skills.

In all of my work, I take great pride in maintaining a high level of professionalism. As my background has included a wide variety of responsibilities, the résumé can only begin to describe the contribution I can provide to your organization.

Thank you for your time and consideration. I would appreciate an interview at your earliest convenience at which time we could discuss my qualifications. Please telephone me at (904) 555-5555 to arrange a time for an interview. I look forward to hearing from you soon.

Sincerely,

Tom Mathews

Enclosure: Confidential Résumé

281

Computer Technician. *Valerie Roberts, Middleburg, Florida*
This letter was difficult to write because the individual had with his MCSE only 20 hours of on-the-the job training through a temp agency. The writer plays up initiative and skills.

BRIAN DOUGLAS
1393 Bayshore Drive
Sandy Hook, NJ 00000
(555) 555-5555

April 17, XXXX

Tim Gibson, Business Manager
Local 123 Operating Engineers
700 State Highway 84
Asbury Park, NJ 00000

Dear Mr. Gibson:

I have worked as an automotive and diesel engine technician for the past 11 years. Many of the skills I developed can easily transfer to boiler operations. My qualifications include an excellent ability to diagnose malfunctions and a mechanical aptitude to make the proper adjustments in valve pressure on engine systems. I am self-motivated and equally comfortable working independently or in a team with others.

For eight years I have been a vested member of Teamsters Local 480 but have taken a withdrawal to pursue a different career direction in high pressure boiler maintenance. Recently I received my Black Seal certification, which qualifies me for an in-charge position in this field.

I wish to get back into a union atmosphere and once again contribute to a strong brotherhood as well as share in its benefits. My uncle Bernard Douglas, who is a member in good standing of Local 123, recommended that I submit to you my resume and this letter of interest. If included in the union, I can assure you that I will be a dedicated and responsible member. I would also like to continue my training so that I may be eligible for more advanced responsibilities. Being a quick study, I am eager to apply my knowledge and increase my value to the organization.

Your consideration of me will be greatly appreciated.

Sincerely,

Brian Douglas

282

Diesel Engine Technician. *Melanie A. Noonan, West Paterson, New Jersey*
The letter begins by introducing the individual's skills, qualifications, and motivation. The second paragraph indicates new certification, and the third expresses his goals.

MICHAEL S. SHZECECH (say chee)
2437 Quail Run Road
El Paso, TX 79925
(915) 581-1234
michael1 @ alpha.net

November 10, XXXX

Human Resources Manager
Darby Electronics, Inc.
345 Stanhope Avenue
Lexington, Texas 23493
Fax: (798) 456-3456

Dear Human Resources Manager:

While I was researching career opportunities on America's Job Bank, my attention was caught by your ad (# 549876) for the position of electronic technician. I will soon be completing a successful career with the U.S. Army and have been looking for a position that will make full use of the skills which I have acquired while in the military.

I have extensive experience as an electromechanical technician, operating and repairing complex radar systems, computers, instrumentation, and communications equipment. I am proficient in diagnostic procedures and electronic theory. In addition, I am qualified with a variety of test equipment as well as experienced in soldering techniques and able to isolate malfunctions to the component level.

Throughout my career I have handled a full range of responsibilities and taken advantage of every opportunity to develop my management and supervisory skills while at the same time increasing my technical capabilities. I am convinced that my background would be an asset to Darby Electronics, Inc.

I will take the liberty of contacting you the last week of November to see if we can arrange a mutually convenient time to meet to discuss career opportunities with your company. If you would like to contact me before that time, I can be reached at _____.

Thank you for you consideration.

Sincerely,

Michael Shzecech

283

Electronic Technician. *Shari Favela, El Paso, Texas*
A letter for a person leaving the U.S. Army and returning to civilian life. The writer indicates a range of technical expertise so that his skills will be seen as relevant to an employer.

PAUL J. ARMOUR
2369 Jennifer Drive
Killeen, Texas 76542
(254) 526-3321

Dear Sir/Madam:

I am seeking a position with your organization and have enclosed my resume for your review in light of your current or future need for an Electronics Technician. I have excellent qualifications for this position and would appreciate your careful consideration.

My background is diverse and covers a variety of experiences that would be directly transferable to a position you may have open. Highlights include:

- Over 5 years' electronics experience, plus an Associate of Science degree.

- Successful supervision and management experience.

- Ability to solve problems and maximize resources.

- Thorough knowledge of electronics, both in theory and in practice.

- Good eye for detail, well organized, and skilled in setting priorities.

My employment availability date is December 1, 1998, and I am currently seeking interviews for the near future. If my qualifications match your needs, I would welcome the opportunity to meet with you.

Thank you for your time, and I look forward to talking with you shortly.

Sincerely,

Paul J. Armour

Enclosure(s)

284

Electronics Technician. *Jackie Sexton, Fort Hood, Texas*
A letter for a person leaving the service and returning to civilian life. Bullets point to transferable experiences, knowledge, and skills. On disk, the letter was customizable.

FERNANDO VELEZ

377 MacArthur Turnpike
Oakwood Park, New Jersey 00000

Home Phone: (555) 555-5555   Cell Phone: (555) 555-5555

October 10, XXXX

Managed Care Prescription Plan
P.O. Box 000
Any Town, USA 00000

To those concerned:

I was attracted to your advertisement for Pharmacy Technicians and believe I have
the qualifications you are seeking for an auditor position.

In my ten years of progressively responsible experience with retail pharmacies, I
have an extensive knowledge of third-party programs and online billing procedures.
This work required that I continually verify correct dispensing of dosages as well as
adhere to the pricing and billing regulations established by each of the prescription
management companies whose plans we accepted. By carefully analyzing
information, I was able to detect inconsistencies and prevent them from later
becoming problems.

From a pharmacy standpoint, I realize how important it is to provide accurate
information to the third-party payor in order to receive prompt reimbursement. Also,
because I have dealt daily with different types of people regarding their plan
coverage, I have developed my interpersonal communication and diplomacy skills to
a high level to preserve good customer relations.

My resume is enclosed which further details my background and effectiveness. I am
confident that I could make a significant contribution to your organization and look
forward to hearing from you soon.

Sincerely,

Fernando Velez

Enclosure: Resume

285

Pharmacy Technician. *Melanie A. Noonan, West Paterson, New Jersey*
The first of the two key paragraphs shows the person's experience, knowledge, and duties; the
second, two payoffs for hiring him: quick reimbursement and good customer relations.

Tom Wolcott

389 Comstock Avenue ◆ Smalltown, Michigan 44444 ◆ (517) 555-5555

October 8, XXXX

Mr. James Olding
Smith Production
333 Outing Avenue
Smalltown, MI 55555

Dear Mr. Olding:

I am responding to your advertisement in the *Patriot* for a Service Technician. My resume is enclosed for your review and consideration.

My background includes extensive experience in the manufacturing environment, including welding, machine operation, preventative maintenance and problem resolution. I am a very detail-oriented person with excellent troubleshooting abilities. My assignments have provided hands-on experience in both mechanical and electrical maintenance. I enjoy new challenges and am often approached for advice concerning methods of improved efficiency. I am also committed to continual development of current skills and knowledge.

In addition, my experience has enhanced strong communication skills and leadership qualities. I am extremely organized and able to prioritize multiple responsibilities. These qualities would certainly prove beneficial when coordinating travel to and from various service locations.

I am confident that my qualifications make me an excellent candidate for the position of Service Technician. I would welcome the opportunity to discuss my background in further detail.

Thank you for your consideration, and I look forward to hearing from you shortly.

Sincerely,

Tom Wolcott

Enclosure

286

Service Technician. *Jan Passmore, Jackson, Michigan*
The first main paragraph in this letter starts with a background statement and ends with a profile. The second begins with an experience statement and continues with a profile.

Dannie Lee Walker

P.O. Box 555 • Crabville, Maryland 55555 • (555) 555-5555

Current Date

Evelyn King
XYZ and More, Inc.
555 North Ridge
Crabville, MD 55555

Dear Ms. King:

When it comes to the world of instrumentation control system repair and maintenance, the three most important characteristics of any technician are:

✓ A broad base of knowledge and experience with multiple systems
✓ Outstanding troubleshooting, analytical problem-solving, and repair skills
✓ Absolute dependability and dedication to providing excellent customer service

As you'll see from my enclosed résumé, I can provide your company with "the top three" and more. As a self-starting, focused professional, I believe I can make a substantial, immediate contribution that will translate into greater profits for XYZ. When system downtime and errors are reduced, profits inevitably increase. It's the work at which I excel and the work I have loved for nearly 20 years.

Thank you for your consideration of my qualifications. I'll follow up with a phone call in the next few days to see if we might be able to arrange an interview. In the meantime, if you have questions or need additional information, please feel free to call me at the number listed above. I look forward to exploring career opportunities with XYZ.

Respectfully,

Dannie Lee Walker

Enclosure

287

Specialist, instrumentation control systems. *Barbie Dallmann, Charleston, West Virginia*
Check marks call attention to this individual's knowledge and experience, skills, and worker traits. The next paragraph tells of more profile information and the payoff: greater profits.

Susan Techno
58 Village Park Way
Anywhere, CA 55555
(555)555-5555

October 28, XXXX

Mr. Charles Information
Manager, Information Systems
Computer Services of America
555 Office Way
Anywhere, CA 55555

Dear Mr. Information:

As an enthusiastic student of computer systems, I am well aware of the challenges involved in training and motivating others in the use of new technology. Configuring and installing new computer systems, as well as achieving client satisfaction in understanding and utilizing their customized workstations, provide some of my greatest satisfaction.

You will see from my enclosed résumé that I am not only pursuing a degree in Computer Information Services while working full time, but also have been recognized as a leader and teacher in the computer lab. This facility to simplify complex concepts has led to intern work in the business world.

While continuing with my professional education programs, I am anxious to move into a full-time paid position where my skills in installation, training and support can be more fully applied. Please consider me for your advertised position as Technical Support Training Specialist.

I look forward to hearing from you as to how I might contribute resourceful, motivated, problem-solving abilities to the growth of your company. You may call me at the above number. Or I will call next week for your response to my résumé.

Sincerely,

Susan Techno

Technical Support Training Specialist. *Sonja A. Wittich, Santa Monica, California*
This cover letter shows that the individual "has the motivation to learn and take on extra tasks even while working full-time." The closing handwritten note personalizes the letter.

Andrew Demetrios
555 Flint Street
Nyack, NY 00000
(555) 555-5555

January 14, XXXX

Eagle Lines
Personnel Offices
999 13th Avenue
New York, NY 00000

Dear Hiring Manager:

After a 25-year career as a Sea Captain, I am about to retire at a fairly young age (44). I am writing you because I would like to become part of your organization in an administrative capacity that could utilize my:

— extensive experience in all phases of the maritime industry,
— broad knowledge of most countries of the world, and
— talent for directing people.

I have achieved notable success as:

— Captain of a luxury cruise ship, sailing the Caribbean
— Captain of various freighters and container ships for major American and foreign steamship companies
— Port Captain for a large merchant marine fleet docked in San Francisco
— Chief Petty Officer in the U.S. Navy

My expertise covers:

— Ship operation and scheduling
— High tech navigational and communications systems
— Cargo handling and storage
— Marine claims
— Passenger relations
— Safety programs
— Accident investigation
— Labor relations
— Personnel management

I am fluent in Greek, Italian and Spanish and have a working knowledge of the Russian language.

In addition, I am a recognized authority on maritime current events and over the years have written many published articles on maritime subjects.

Should you have an interest in my varied background, I will be glad to provide you with further details in a personal meeting.

Very truly yours,

Andrew Demetrios

289

Administrator/Luxury Cruise Ship Captain. *Melanie A. Noonan, West Paterson, New Jersey*
Three "bulleted" lists make this letter visually different from all the others in this book. Because the dash bullets point mostly to short phrases, the lists create much white space.

MICHAEL MOORE

000 Waterfront Drive
Hendersonville, TN 00000

Home: (000) 000-0000
Cellular: (000) 000-0000

May 4, XXXX

Charles Bradford
Federal Express Corporation

Via Fax: (000) 000-0000

Dear Mr. Bradford:

I am responding to your current online job posting for a **Manager of Trucking Operations** at your Nashville facility. In today's tight labor market, finding the right person to do the job and do it well can be time-consuming, but a strong background in delivery operations and traffic management is a key element in qualifying me for consideration as part of the FedEx team.

As Inbound Coordinator/Quality Assurance Coordinator for Retail, Inc.'s national distribution center (Old Army Clothing Company division), I was in charge of high-volume unloading operations, handling up to 25,000 cartons per shift during peak times, as well as closely monitoring the quality of the merchandise sent by our vendors. These duties required well-developed skills in team leadership, time management, and communication plus the ability to "wear many hats" in order to maintain a harmonious and productive work environment.

Along with experience, I can offer FedEx a bachelor's degree from Colorado State University with an emphasis on Organizational Psychology and Business, as well as the necessary training and ability to operate a tractor/trailer.

I feel particularly well qualified to provide the leadership and experience you require for this position. The opportunity to speak with you by phone or in person to explore the contributions I can make will be most welcome. Thank you for your time, and I look forward to hearing from you soon.

Sincerely,

Michael Moore

Enclosure

290

Manager of Trucking Operations. *Carolyn Braden, Hendersonville, Tennessee*
All four paragraphs indicate that the individual was well qualified for the posted position. He found this posting while doing online research and faxed the letter as requested.

HARRIET ROBERTS

611 Bogus Lane
Edukashion, NY 11000
(212) 998-7766

I am seriously interested in enrolling in your special education program. Considering my solid background of working with children, coupled with a record of past scholastic achievements, I think I make a perfect candidate to pursue a career in the field of special education.

During my years as a student, I achieved many top honors. In eighth grade, I was nominated business manager of the annual yearbook, a high-ranking, noteworthy, much-sought-after position which is occupied with great pride. My task was overseeing the soliciting and payment of ads, which I executed with meticulous care, producing positive results. Furthermore, in high school, I was awarded certificates for academic achievement each year. As a Sunday School counselor, I delivered Bible lessons to a crowd of rapt children regularly. I made thorough preparations to compile interesting lessons to stimulate their attentiveness. The lessons received rave reviews from leading church authorities as well as from casual listeners. In addition, I assisted in coordinating a "wax museum booth" for a school project. This included concept, development, and presentation.

Besides having leadership and communications skills, I am computer proficient. I have studied computer basics and am knowledgeable in WordPerfect. Currently, I am in the midst of completing a course in Microsoft Excel.

In conclusion, I feel that the field of special education is just made for me. I have always had a deep love for children with special needs. My unlimited resources of patience, devotion, and acceptance played a large role in preparing myself to get initiated into the world of special children. As the oldest of a family of seven children, I have accumulated a track record of patience and love for children. Presently, I am involved with a little boy who has behavioral problems and difficulties in eye-hand coordination. Through my intense efforts, this little boy is learning community integration and many basics of daily life. I focus on his developmental daily activities and his social capabilities. My friendly, easygoing, yet determined manner is certainly a help in my quest to enrich the life of this challenged youngster. I am very eager to make a difference in the lives of handicapped, disabled, delayed, or otherwise challenged children. This is a fervent passion of mine. I truly feel that I have an enormous potential which I want to use in a constructive manner. With a deep affinity for special children, I strongly believe that I will succeed in this field. My eagerness, drive, and determination to positively affect the lives of special children will most certainly be an asset in a future career in special education.

Truly yours,

Harriet Roberts

291

Variation of a cover letter. *Rebecca Weissner, Brooklyn, New York*
Cover letter style can be used for other purposes. The goal here was enrollment in a special education program. You can easily detect the goal, achievements, skills, and enthusiasm.

PharmaTech Solutions, Inc.

Dr. Kenneth Wells, President & CEO
99 Eaglesmere
McClintock, NJ 55555

Phone: 555-555-5555
Fax: 000-000-0000
kenwells@worldnet.net

Introducing New Contract Research Laboratory

Are you interested in quality performance, dependable action and innovative solutions in pharmaceutical and health care product research and drug delivery systems?

Are you in the midst of a start-up or emerging organizational growth?

Are you spearheading a revitalization of your products and laboratory research?

Are you looking for fresh perspectives and strategies to expedite product development?

Perhaps I can be of help. With 20 years of research and management experience in major pharmaceutical companies such as Lilliput Laboratories, Wetterly Company, and ABC Laboratories, as well as emerging pharmaceutical technology ventures, I have delivered consistently strong performance results. My expertise spans cross-functional research and business management areas, including achieving cGMP facility approval and consistently bringing products to the marketplace with FDA approval.

Today, I am the principal of a Contract Research Laboratory in New Jersey conducting formulation research in the area of Drug Delivery Systems. Specifically, I will be developing Oral and Transdermal Delivery Systems for several different classes of drug candidates. My resume is enclosed for your review.

Let's take a few minutes to explore the challenges you are facing and your product development needs. I will contact your office next week to discuss our mutual interests and schedule an appointment, if that seems appropriate to you.

Kenneth Wells, Ph.D.
President & CEO

Enc.

292

A marketing letter. *Susan Guarneri, Lawrenceville, New Jersey*
This cover letter is a marketing letter for a contract research laboratory. Having a different purpose, the letter can begin differently—in this example, with a series of four questions.

3
P·A·R·T

Best
Resume Tips

Best Resume Tips
at a Glance

Best Resume Tips

In a passive job search, you rely on your resume to do most of the work for you. An eye-catching resume that stands out above all the others may be your best shot at getting noticed by a prospective employer. If your resume is only average and looks like most of the others in the pile, the chances are great that you won't be noticed and called for an interview. If you want to be singled out because of your resume, it should be somewhere between spectacular and award-winning.

In an active job search, however, your resume complements your efforts at being known to a prospective employer *before* that person receives it. For this reason, you can rely less on your resume for getting someone's attention. Nevertheless, your resume has an important role in an active job search that may include the following activities:

- Talking to relatives, friends, and other acquaintances to meet people who can hire you before a job is available

- Creating phone scripts to speak with the person who is most likely to hire someone with your background and skills

- Using a schedule to keep track of your appointments and callbacks

- Working at least 25 hours a week to search for a job

When you are this active in searching for a job, the quality of your resume confirms the quality of your efforts to get to know the person who might hire you, as well as your worth to the company whose workforce you want to join. An eye-catching resume makes it easier for you to sell yourself directly to a prospective employer. If your resume is mediocre or conspicuously flawed, it will work against you and may undo all of your good efforts in searching for a job.

The following list offers ideas for making resumes visually impressive. Many of the ideas are for making resumes pleasing to the eye; other ideas are for eliminating common writing mistakes and stylistic weaknesses.

Some of these ideas can be used with any equipment, from a manual typewriter to a sophisticated computer with desktop publishing software. Other ideas make sense only if you have a computer system with word processing or desktop publishing. Even if you don't have a computer, take some time to read all of the ideas. Then, if you decide to use the services of a professional resume writer, you will be better informed about what the writer can do for you in producing your resume.

Best Resume-Writing Strategies

1. **Although many resume books say that you should spell out the name of the state in your address at the top of the resume, consider using the postal abbreviation instead.** The reason is simple: it's an address. Anyone wanting to contact you by mail will probably refer to your name and address on the resume. If they appear there as they should on an envelope, the writer or typist can simply copy the information you supply. If you spell out the name of your state in full, the writer will have to "translate" the name of the state to its postal abbreviation.

    Not everyone knows all the postal abbreviations, and some abbreviations are easily confused. For example, those for Alabama (AL), Alaska (AK), American Samoa (AS), Arizona (AZ), and Arkansas (AR) are easy to mix up. You can prevent confusion and delay simply by using the correct postal abbreviation. As resumes become more scannable, the use of postal abbreviations in addresses will become a requirement.

    If you decide to use postal abbreviations in addresses, make certain that you do not add a period after the abbreviations. This applies also to postal abbreviations in the addresses of references, if provided.

    Consider, however, not using the state postal abbreviation when you are indicating only the city and state (not the mailing address) of a school you attended or a business where you worked. In these cases, it makes sense to write out the name of the state in full.

2. **Adopt a sensible form for phone numbers in the contact information and then use that form consistently.** Do this in your resume and in all of the documents you use in your job search. Some forms for phone numbers make more sense than others. Compare the following forms:

123-4567	This form is best for a resume circulated locally, within a region where all the phone numbers have the same area code.
(222) 123-4567	This form is best for a resume circulated in areas with different area codes.
222-123-4567	This form suggests that the area code should be dialed in all cases. But that won't be necessary for prospective employers whose area code is 222. This form should be avoided.
222/123-4567	This form is illogical and should be avoided also. The slash can mean an alternate option, as in ON/ OFF. In a phone number, this meaning of a slash makes little sense.
1 (222) 123-4567	This form is long, and the digit 1 isn't necessary. Almost everyone will know that 1 should be used before the area code to dial a long-distance number.
222.123.4567	This form is becoming more popular.

Note: For resumes directed to prospective employers *outside* the United States, be sure to include the correct international prefixes in all phone numbers so that you and your references can be reached easily by phone.

3. **If your resume has an Objective statement (or a Career Goal), make it focused, developed, or unique so that it grabs the reader's attention.** See the Career Goal in Resume 7. If your Objective statement fails to do this, the reader might discard the resume without reading further. An Objective statement can be your first opportunity to sell yourself.

4. **If you can sell yourself better with some other kind of section, consider omitting an Objective statement and putting a Qualifications Summary, a Profile or Summary, or an Areas of Expertise section just after the contact information.** See Resumes 2, 10, 27, and 35.

5. **Consider replacing an Objective statement with a Profile in which you feature or highlight the target field or intended position.** See Resume 6.

6. **Making a Highlights section long helps to position important information on the first page.** See Resume 6.

7. **Displaying your Qualifications (or Areas of Expertise, Skills, or Strengths) in columns makes them easy to alter if your target job or target industry changes.** See Resumes 17 and 21.

8. **Spend considerable time determining how to present your skills.** You can present them in various ways, such as Competencies (Resume 7), Representative Abilities (Resume 10), Performance Highlights (Resume 6), Areas of Knowledge and Experience (Resume 12), Highlights of Qualifications (Resume 13), Skills (Resume 16), Areas of Core Competency (Resume 26), Computer and Communication Skills (Resume 27), or Career Highlights (Resume 33).

9. **In the Experience section or elsewhere, state achievements, not just duties or responsibilities.** Duties and responsibilities for a given position are often already known by the reader. Achievements, however, can be attention-getting. The reader probably considers life too short to be bored by lists of duties and responsibilities in a stack of resumes. See Resume 30.

10. **In the Experience section and for each position held, consider explaining responsibilities in a brief paragraph and using bullets to point to achievements or contributions.** See Resumes 21, 29, and 31.

11. **When you indicate achievements, consider boldfacing them (Resume 26), quantifying them (Resumes 6, 14, 18, and 21), or providing a separate heading for them (Resume 30).**

12. **When skills, abilities, and qualifications are varied, group them according to categories for easier comprehension.** See Resume 19.

13. **Include information that explains lesser-known companies.** See Resume 19.

14. **Group positions to avoid repetition in a description of duties.** See Resume 21.

Best Resume Design and Layout Tips

15. Use quality paper correctly. If you use quality watermarked paper for your resume, be sure to use the right side of the paper. To know which side is the right side, hold a blank sheet of paper up to a light source. If you can see a watermark and "read" it, the right side of the paper is facing you. This is the surface for typing or printing. If the watermark is unreadable or if any characters look backward, you are looking at the "underside" of a sheet of paper—the side that should be left blank.

16. Use adequate "white space." A sheet of white paper with no words on it is impossible to read. Likewise, a sheet of white paper with words all over it is impossible to read. The goal is to have a comfortable mix of white space and words. If your resume has too many words and not enough white space, the resume looks cluttered. If it has too much white space and too few words, the resume looks skimpy and unimportant. Make certain that adequate white space exists between the main sections. For resumes with a satisfying amount of white space, see Resumes 4, 12, 34, and 35. For resumes with adequate white space even with a small font size, see Resume 26. For white space provided through blank lines, see Resume 10. For white space accomplished through center-alignment, see Resume 30.

17. Margins in resumes for executives, managers, and other administrators tend to be narrower than margins in other resumes. See Resume 21. Narrower margins are often used in connection with smaller type to get more information on a one- or two-page resume.

18. Be consistent in your use of line spacing. How you handle line spacing can tell the reader how good you are at details and how consistent you are in your use of them. If, near the beginning of your resume, you insert two line spaces (two hard returns in a word processing program) between two main sections, be sure to put two line spaces between main sections throughout the resume.

19. Be consistent in your use of horizontal spacing. If you usually put two character spaces after a period at the end of a sentence, make certain that you use two spaces consistently. The same is true for colons. If you put two spaces after colons, do so consistently.

Note that an em dash—a dash the width of the letter *m*—does not require spaces before or after it. No space should go between the *P* and *O* of P.O. Box. Only one space is needed between the postal abbreviation of a state and the ZIP code. You should insert a space between the first and second initials of a person's name, as in I. M. Jobseeker (not I.M. Jobseeker). These conventions have become widely adopted in English and business communications. If, however, you use other conventions, be sure to be consistent. In resumes, as in grammar, consistency is more important than conformity.

20. Make certain that characters, lines, and images contrast well with the paper. The quality of "ink" depends on the device used to type or print your resume. If you use a typewriter or a printer with a carbon tape, make certain that your paper has a texture that allows the characters to adhere permanently. For a test, send yourself a copy of your resume and see how it makes the trip through the mail. If you use an inkjet or laser printer, check that the characters are sharp and clean, without ink smudges or traces of extra toner. Mail yourself

a laser-printed envelope to make sure that it looks good after a trip through the mail. A cover letter with a flaking impression for the address does not make a good impression.

21. **Use vertical alignment in stacked text.** Resumes usually contain tabbed or indented text. Make certain that this "stacked" material is aligned vertically. Misalignment can ruin the appearance of a well-written resume. Try to set tabs or indents that control this text throughout a resume instead of having a mix of tab stops in different sections. If you use a word processor, make certain that you understand the difference between tabbed text and indented text, as in the following examples:

> Tabbed text: This text was tabbed over one tab stop before the writer started to write the sentence.

> Indented text: This text was indented once before the writer started to write the sentence.

Note: In a number of word processing programs, the Indent command is useful for ensuring the correct vertical alignment of proportionally spaced, stacked text. After you use the Indent command, lines of wrapped text are vertically aligned automatically until you terminate the command by pressing Enter.

22. **For the vertical alignment of dates, try left- or right-aligning the dates.** This technique is especially useful in chronological resumes and combination resumes. For an example of left-aligned dates, see Resume 7. For right-aligned dates, look at Resumes 8, 17, and 24.

23. **Use as many pages as you need for portraying yourself adequately to a specific interviewer about a particular job.** Try to limit your resume to one page or two pages, but set the upper limit at four pages. No rule about the number of pages makes sense in all cases. The determining factors are a person's qualifications and experiences, the requirements of the job, and the interests and pet peeves of the interviewer. If you know that an interviewer refuses to look at a resume longer than a page, that says it all. You need to deliver a one-page resume if you want to get past the first gate.

More important than the question of how many pages is the issue of complete pages. A full page sends a better message than a partial page (which says "not enough to fill"). Therefore, one full page is better than 1.25 pages, and two full pages are better than 1.75 pages.

24. **When you have letters of recommendation, use quotations from them as testimonials.** Devoting some space (or even a full column) to the positive opinions of "external authorities" helps make a resume convincing as well as impressive. When placed effectively, such quotations can build respect, add credibility, and personalize a resume. See Resume 32.

25. **Unless you enlist the services of a professional printer or skilled desktop publisher, resist the temptation to use full justification for text.** The price that you pay for a straight right margin is uneven word spacing. Words may appear too close together on some lines and too spread out on others. Although the resume might look like typeset text, you lose readability. Professional resume writers may use full justification effectively for variety.

26. **If you can choose a typeface for your resume, use a serif font for greater readability.** Serif fonts have little lines extending from the top, bottom, and end of a character. These fonts tend to be easier to read than sans serif (without serif) fonts, especially in low-light conditions. Compare the following font examples:

Serif	**Sans Serif**
Baskerville	Avant Garde
Courier	Futura
Times New Roman	Helvetica

Words like *minimum* and *abilities* are more readable in a serif font.

27. **If possible, avoid using monospaced type like this Courier type.** Courier was a standard of business communications during the 1960s and 1970s. Because of its widespread use, it is now considered "common." It also takes up a lot of space, so you can't pack as much information on a page with Courier type as you can with a proportionally spaced type like Times Roman.

28. **Think twice before using all uppercase letters in parts of your resume.** A common misconception is that uppercase letters are easier to read than lowercase letters. Actually, the ascenders and descenders of lowercase letters make them more distinguishable from each other and therefore more recognizable than uppercase letters. For a test, look at a string of uppercase letters and throw them gradually out of focus by squinting. The uppercase letters become a blur sooner than lowercase letters. Professional resume writers, however, may use uppercase letters effectively for emphasis and variety.

29. **Think twice about underlining some words in your resume.** Underlining defeats the purpose of serifs at the bottom of characters by blending with the serifs. In trying to emphasize words, you lose some visual clarity. This is especially true if you use underlining with uppercase letters in centered or side headings.

30. **If you have access to many fonts through word processing or desktop publishing, beware of becoming "font happy" and turning your resume into a font circus.** *Frequent* <u>font changes</u> *can distract* the reader **adversely, AND SO CAN GAUDY DISPLAY TYPE.**

31. **To make your resume stand out, consider using a nonstandard format or an unconventional display font in the contact information or in the headings.** See Resumes 12 and 23. What is usually fitting for resumes for some prospective jobs, however, is not always the most appropriate resume strategy for executive positions. Try to match the style of your resume to the target company's "corporate image" if it has one.

32. **Be aware of the value differences of black type.** Some typefaces are light; others are dark. Notice the following lines:

A quick brown fox jumps over the lazy dog.

A quick brown fox jumps over the lazy dog.

Most typefaces fall somewhere in-between. With the variables of height, width, thickness, serifs, angles, curves, spacing, ink color, ink density, boldfacing, and typewriter double-striking, type offers an infinite range of values from light to dark. Try to make your resume more visually interesting by offering stronger contrasts between light type and dark type. Browse through the Exhibit and notice the differences in light and dark type.

33. **Use italic characters carefully.** Whenever possible, use italic characters instead of underlining when you need to call attention to a word or phrase. You might consider using italic for duties or achievements. Think twice, however, about using italic throughout your resume. The reason is that italic (slanted) characters are less readable than normal (vertical) characters. You might have to hold the resume at an angle to make an all-italic resume more readable. Such a maneuver can irritate a reader. Even so, "all italic" may be just the thing to make a particular resume stand out.

34. **Use boldfacing to make different job titles more evident.** See Resumes 2, 3, 15, 20, and 28.

35. **For getting attention, make headings white on black if you use software that has this capability.** See Resume 33.

36. **If you use word processing or desktop publishing and have a suitable printer, use special characters to enhance the look of your resume.** For example, use enhanced quotations marks (" and ") instead of their typewriter equivalents (" "). Use an em dash (—) instead of two hyphens (--) for a dash. To separate dates, try using an en dash (a dash the width of the letter *n*) instead of a hyphen, as in 1998–1999.

37. **To call attention to an item in a list, use a bullet (•) or a box (■) instead of a hyphen (-).** Browse through the sample resumes and notice how bullets are used effectively as attention getters.

38. **For variety, try using bullets of a different style, such as diamond (◆) bullets, rather than the usual round or square bullets.** Examples with diamonds are Resumes 5, 10, and 19. For other kinds of "bullets," see Resumes 1, 6, and 12 (arrows and arrow tips); 7 (check marks); 14, 15, and 22 (decorative); 11 (filled squares); 2 and 18 (shadowed squares); 33 (unfilled squares); and 23 (stars).

39. **Make a bullet a little smaller than the lowercase letters that appear after it.** Disregard any ascenders or descenders on the letters. Compare the following bullet sizes:

     • Too small   ● Too large   • Better   • Just right

40. **When the amount of information justifies a longer resume, consider repeating a particular graphic to unify the entire resume.** See Resume 14.

41. **If possible, visually coordinate the resume and the cover letter with the same line enhancements or graphic to catch the attention of the reader.** See Resume 10 and Cover Letter 73; Resume 12 and Cover Letter 114; and Resume 27 and Cover Letter 233.

42. **Use a horizontal line or a combination of lines to separate the contact information from the rest of the resume.** See Resumes 5, 14, 25, and others.

43. **Use horizontal lines or bars to separate the different sections of the resume and thus make them visible at a glance.** See Resumes 16, 22, and 24.

44. **For variety in dividing sections of your resume, use partial horizontal lines that extend from the left margin to text, or from text to the right margin.** See Resumes 7 and 26. Note that Resumes 6 and 13 have partial lines that extend from centered occupations to *both* the left and right margins.

45. **To avoid a cramped one-page resume that has small print, narrow margins, and reduced line spacing, consider using a two-page resume instead.** (Those who insist on one-page resumes will not agree with this tip.)

46. **To call attention to resume sections or headings, use horizontal lines to enclose them.** See Resumes 13 and 15.

47. **Use thicker horizontal lines to call attention to a section heading above or below the line.** See Resumes 1 and 2.

48. **Use vertical lines or bars to spice up your resume.** See Resumes 12, 23, and 33.

49. **Use various kinds of boxes (single line, shadowed, or decorative) to make a page visually more interesting.** See Resumes 26 and 32.

50. **Use a page border to make a page visually more interesting.** See Resumes 17 and 31.

51. **Consider using a chart or table to present relevant numerical data.** See Resume 9.

52. **Use centered headings to make them easy to read down a page.** See Resumes 11, 25, and 30.

53. **Consider using hanging indentation of section headings to make them stand out.** See Resumes 16 and 20.

54. **Near the top of the first page but below the contact information, place a list of keywords that can easily be scanned for storage in an online resume database.** See Resumes 6 and 21.

Best Resume-Writing Style Tips

55. **Check that words or phrases in lists are parallel.** For example, notice the bulleted items in the Representative Abilities section of Resume 10. All the entries contain verbs in the present tense. Notice also the consistent use of nouns in the three bulleted items at the top of Resume 18.

56. **Use capital letters correctly.** Resumes usually contain many of the following:

   - Names of people, companies, organizations, government agencies, awards, and prizes
   - Titles of job positions and publications
   - References to academic fields (such as chemistry, English, and mathematics)
   - Geographic regions (such as the Midwest, the East, the state of California, Oregon State, and northern Florida)

   Because of such words, resumes are mine fields for the misuse of uppercase letters. When you don't know whether a word should have an initial capital letter, don't guess. Consult a dictionary, a handbook on style, or some other authoritative source. Often a reference librarian can provide the information you need. If so, you are only a phone call away from an accurate answer.

57. **Check that capital letters and hyphens are used correctly in computer terms.** If you want to show in a Computer Experience section that you have used certain hardware and software, you may give the opposite impression if you don't use uppercase letters and hyphens correctly. Note the correct use of capitals and hyphens in the following names of hardware, software, and computer companies:

LaserJet III	Hewlett-Packard	dBASE
PageMaker	MS-DOS	Microsoft
WordPerfect	PC DOS	Microsoft Word
NetWare	PostScript	

   The reason that many computer product names have an internal uppercase letter is for the sake of a trademark. A word with unusual spelling or capitalization is trademarkable. When you use the correct forms of these words, you are honoring trademarks and registered trademarks.

58. **Use all uppercase letters for most acronyms.** An *acronym* is a pronounceable word usually formed from the initial letters of the words in a compound term, or sometimes from multiple letters in those words. Note the following examples:

BASIC	Beginner's All-purpose Symbolic Instruction Code
COBOL	COmmon Business-Oriented Language
DOS	Disk Operating System
FORTRAN	FORmula TRANslator

   An acronym like *radar* (*radio detecting and ranging*) has become so common that it is no longer all uppercase.

59. **Be aware that you may need to use a period with some abbreviations.** An *abbreviation* is a word shortened by removing the latter part of the word or by deleting some letters within the word. Here are some examples:

adj. for *adjective*	*amt.* for *amount*
adv. for *adverb*	*dept.* for *department*

Usually, you can't pronounce an abbreviation as a word. Sometimes, however, an abbreviation is a set of uppercase letters (without periods) that you can pronounce as letters. AFL-CIO, CBS, NFL, and YMCA are examples.

60. **Be sure to spell every word correctly.** A resume with just one misspelling is not impressive and may undermine all the hours you spent putting it together. Worse than that, one misspelling may be what the reader is looking for to screen you out, particularly if you are applying for a position that requires accuracy with words. If you calculate the salary you don't get *times* the number of years you might have worked for that company, that's an expensive misspelling!

    If you use word processing and have a spelling checker, you may be able to catch any misspellings. Be wary of spelling checkers, however. They can detect a misspelled word but cannot detect when you have inadvertently used a wrong word (*to* for *too*, for example). Be wary also of letting someone else check your resume. If the other person is not a good speller, you may not get any real help. The best authority is a good, *current* dictionary.

61. **For words that have a couple of correct spellings, use the preferred form.** This form is the one that appears first in a dictionary. For example, if you see the entry **trav·el·ing** *or* **trav·el·ling**, the first form (with one *l*) is the preferred spelling. If you make it a practice to use the preferred spelling, you will build consistency in your resumes and cover letters.

62. **Avoid British spellings.** These slip into American usage through books published in Great Britain. Note the following words:

British Spelling	American Spelling
acknowledgement	acknowledgment
centre	center
judgement	judgment
towards	toward

63. **Avoid hyphenating words with such prefixes as** *co-, micro-, mid-, mini-, multi-, non-, pre-, re-,* **and** *sub-.* Many people think that words with these prefixes should have a hyphen after the prefix, but most of these words should not. The following words are spelled correctly:

coauthor	microcomputer	minicomputer
coworker	midpoint	multicultural
cowriter	midway	multilevel
nondisclosure	prearrange	reenter
nonfunctional	prequalify	subdirectory

    Note: If you look in a dictionary for a word with a prefix and can't find the word, look for the prefix itself in the dictionary. You might find there a small-print listing of a number of words that have the prefix.

64. **Be aware that compounds (combinations of words) present special problems for hyphenation.** Writers' handbooks and books on style do not always agree on how compounds should be hyphenated. Many compounds are

evolving from *open* compounds to *hyphenated* compounds to *closed* compounds. In different dictionaries, you can therefore find the words *copy editor, copy-editor,* and *copyeditor.* No wonder the issue is confusing! Most style books do agree, however, that when some compounds appear as an adjective before a noun, the compound should be hyphenated. When the same compound appears after a noun, hyphenation is unnecessary. Compare the following two sentences:

> I scheduled well-attended conferences.
>
> The conferences I scheduled were well attended.

For detailed information about hyphenation, see a recent edition of *The Chicago Manual of Style*. You should be able to find a copy at a local library.

65. **Be sure to hyphenate so-called *permanent* hyphenated compounds.** Usually, you can find these by looking them up in a dictionary. You can spot them easily because they have a "long hyphen" (–) for visibility in the dictionary. Hyphenate these words (with a standard hyphen) wherever they appear, before or after a noun. Here are some examples:

all-important	self-employed
day-to-day	step-by-step
full-blown	time-consuming

66. **Use the correct form for certain verbs and nouns combined with prepositions.** You may need to consult a dictionary for correct spelling and hyphenation. Compare the following examples:

start up	(verb)
start-up	(noun)
start-up	(adj.)
startup	(noun, computer industry)
startup	(adj., computer industry)

67. **Avoid using shortcut words, such as abbreviations like *thru* or foreign words like *via.*** Spell out *through* and use *by* for *via.*

68. **Use the right words.** The issue here is correct *usage*, which often means the choice of the right word or phrase from a group of two or more possibilities. The following words and phrases are often used incorrectly:

alternate (adj.)	Refers to an option used every other time. OFF is the alternate option to ON in an ON/OFF switch.
alternative	Refers to an option that can be used at any time. If cake and pie are alternative desserts for dinner, you can have cake three days in a row if you like. The common mistake is to use *alternate* when the correct word is *alternative.*
center around	A common illogical expression. Draw a circle and then try to draw its center around it. You can't. Use *center in* or *center on* as logical alternatives to *center around.*

For information about the correct *usage* of words, consult a usage dictionary or the usage section of a writer's handbook.

69. **Use numbers consistently.** Numbers are often used inconsistently with text. Should you present a number as a numeral or spell out the number as a word? One approach is to spell out numbers *one* through *nine* but present numbers 10 and above as numerals. Different approaches are taught in different schools, colleges, and universities. Use the approach you have learned, but be consistent.

70. **Use (or don't use) the serial comma consistently.** How should you punctuate a series of three or more items? If, for example, you say in your resume that you increased sales by 100 percent, opened two new territories, and trained four new salespersons, the comma before *and* is called the *serial comma*. It is commonly omitted in newspapers, magazine articles, advertisements, and business documents; but it is often used for precision in technical documents or for stylistic reasons in academic text, particularly in the Humanities.

71. **Use semicolons correctly.** Semicolons are useful because they help to distinguish visually the items in a series when the items themselves contain commas. Suppose that you have the following entry in your resume:

    Increased sales by 100 percent, opened two new territories, which were in the Midwest, trained four new salespersons, who were from Georgia, and increased sales by 250 percent.

    The extra commas (before *which* and *who*) throw the main items of the series out of focus. By separating the main items with semicolons, you can bring them back into focus:

    Increased sales by 100 percent; opened two new territories, which were in the Midwest; trained four new salespersons, who were from Georgia; and increased sales by 250 percent.

    Use this kind of high-rise punctuation even if just one item in the series has an internal comma.

72. **Use dashes correctly.** One of the purposes of a dash (an em dash or two hyphens) is to introduce a comment or afterthought about preceding information. A colon *anticipates* something to follow, but a dash *looks back* to something already said. Two dashes are sometimes used before and after a related but nonessential remark—such as this—within a sentence. In this case, the dashes are like parentheses, but more formal.

Exhibit of Resumes

This part of the book contains an Exhibit of 35 resumes that accompanied cover letters in the first part of the book. Cross-references let you know readily which cover letter accompanied a particular resume so that you can view the two documents as a package.

Resume writers commonly distinguish between chronological resumes and functional (or skills) resumes. A *chronological resume* is a photo—a snapshot history of what you did and when you did it. A *functional resume* is a painting—an interpretive sketch of what you can do for a future employer. A third kind of resume, known as a *combination resume*, is a mix of recalled history and self-assessment. Besides recollecting "the facts," a combination resume contains self-interpretation and is therefore more like dramatic history than news coverage. A chronological resume and a functional resume are not always that different; often, all that is needed for a functional resume to qualify as a combination resume is the inclusion of dates for some of the positions held. All three kinds of resumes are illustrated in the Exhibit. In this Exhibit a functional resume with a work history is labeled a functional resume.

Instead of making 200 copies of a resume and sending the same document to different prospective employers, you should consider tailoring each resume to a specific job target. Creating multiple versions of a resume may seem difficult, but it is easy to do if you have (or have access to) a personal computer and a laser printer or some other kind of printer that can produce quality output. You will also need word processing capability. Remember that most professional resume writers have the hardware and software, and they can make your resume look like those in the Exhibit. A local fast-print shop can make your resume look good, but you will probably not get there the kind of advice and service the professional resume writer provides.

Alicia Lee Combs

888 SOMERSET DRIVE ◁▷ BLOOMFIELD HILLS, MICHIGAN 48331
248.555.2626

CAREER OVERVIEW

Accounting Professional with an excellent background and diverse industry experience.

EXPERIENCE IN AREAS OF:

▷ Accounts Payable/Receivable	▷ Cash Management	▷ General Ledger
▷ Payroll & Property Taxes	▷ Account Reconciliation	▷ Billing & Invoicing
▷ Staff Training & Development	▷ Public Accounting Tax/Audit	▷ Third-Party Billing
▷ Consolidated Financial Statements	▷ Credit & Collection	▷ Financial Analysis

SUMMARY OF QUALIFICATIONS

Management
  ▷ Experienced administrator of time, people, and programs to effectively support corporate objectives.

Finance/Accounting
  ▷ Excellent analytical and problem-solving skills; logical thinker with a mature understanding of processes and procedures.

Project Management
  ▷ Focused commitment to excellence, accuracy, and timing concerns; able to handle multiple ongoing projects.

SELECTED ACHIEVEMENTS

  ▷ Championed a purchase order system that increased work flow and improved time commitments.
  ▷ Designed "flash" financial reporting to support management in timely decision making.
  ▷ Developed a successful cash flow analysis/cash management system.
  ▷ Redesigned new office space including all the logistics to a successful move.
  ▷ Developed accounting department from 2-person/1-computer office to 7 networked employees.
  ▷ Currently working on software applications for the year 2000.

EXPERIENCE

VANNOSTRAND & MANLEY ADVERTISING   West Bloomfield, Michigan
Media advertising specialists with accounts in media, public relations, special events, fast food, and nonprofit organizations.
ACCOUNTING MANAGER, 1992-current
  ▷ Scope of responsibility includes all accounting functions through financial statement.
  ▷ Prepare monthly financial schedules and account analyses.
  ▷ Monitor cash receipts application, A/P functions, client invoicing, and account reconciliations.
  ▷ Responsible for network and computing functions, and research new applications.
  ▷ Administrate employee insurances (health/life/disability), 401(k) programs, and payroll.
  ▷ Manage banking systems including ACH and EFT; taxes (sales/personal/property/payroll).

Previous positions and other companies included **ASSISTANT CONTROLLER, TAX ACCOUNTANT, PARA-PROFESSIONAL,** and **ACCOUNTANT** from 1975-92.

EDUCATION AND PROFESSIONAL DEVELOPMENT

CALIFORNIA STATE UNIVERSITY — **Accounting, Business Systems**
UNIVERSITY OF COLORADO — **Statistics**
UNIVERSITY OF WISCONSIN — **Economics, General Business**
VALPARAISO UNIVERSITY — **Mathematics**

Various classes/workshops on computer applications and current accounting trends.

OTHER INFORMATION

PTA Council — **District Treasurer**
Eisenhower Elementary School — PTA **President**; School Improvement Committee
Founder/President of Women's Softball League
Local Lutheran Church — **Board of Education**

Functional. *Lorie Lehert, Novi, Michigan*
A pair of horizontal lines enclosing each section heading makes the headings easily seen.
Experience areas in lists can be altered quickly for different job targets. See Cover Letter 6.

Maggie Morris, CPA

5555 Actress Boulevard
Dramatic, Montana 55555
(555) 555-5555 - Office • (555) 555-5556 - Home

Qualifications Summary

- ❏ Certified Public Accountant with 20 years' experience
- ❏ Specialties in audits, rate design, actuarial studies, FASB
- ❏ Computer expertise including spreadsheets and word processing
- ❏ Experienced in general bookkeeping and accounting, payroll processing, and quarterly employer tax reports
- ❏ Effective communicator with an ability to foster an atmosphere of cooperation during audits
- ❏ Quick learner of both theory and practice; easily pick up new procedures and computer programs
- ❏ Strong research skills and a reputation for thoroughness and precision in all areas of responsibility

Experience

❏ **Senior Utilities Specialist**   **1980-Present**
Utilities Regulators of America, Dramatic, MT
- Selected by Deputy Director to specialize in actuarial auditing and FASB regulation compliance
- Supervise and participate in corporate utility audits
- Prepare cost of service reports, design utility rates, and submit revenue requirements/tax impact analyses
- Testify at public hearings

❏ **Accountant**   **1977-1980**
Montana Department of Health
- Accounted for municipal bond program, loan and grant program, personal services, and operating expenses
- Prepared all journals and ledgers, monthly funding status reports, and the annual audited financial statements
- Participated in bonding and grant processing for municipal governments and public service districts
- Prepared agency's annual budget

Education

- ❏ Bachelor of Science in Industrial Management, Montana University
- ❏ CPA, 1986-Present; continuing education in a variety of corporate, FASB, actuarial, and tax accounting areas

2

Combination. *Barbie Dallmann, Charleston, West Virginia*
The Qualifications Summary helps a prospective employer know where to put the person's talents to use. Thick lines make the name and headings stand out. See Cover Letter 15.

Lori D. Harris

152-1 Safi Rd – Fort Hood, TX 76544   (000) 000-0000

SUMMARY

Good cooperator, hardworking, productive, conscientious, and loyal. Well organized, able to remember and use facts, and perform routine tasks with unerring accuracy. Enjoy hands-on application of practical skills and customer and client contact. Able to gather, organize and analyze factual information, plus excellent technical and mechanical abilities. Performance areas include:

Administrative Support/Reception

• Customer Service	• Daily Cash Mgmt	• Data/Order Entry
• Filing/Typing	• Nonsufficient Funds	• Nature of Inquires
• Wire Transfer of Funds	• Insurance Claims	• Trial Balance
• Inquires/Services Information	• Appointment Scheduling	• Clerical Duties
• Collect/Distribute Mail/Msgs	• Forms/Applications/Tests	• Greet/Direct Callers
• Records Maintenance	• PBX Telephone System	• Received Payments

Cashier/Teller

• 10-Key by Touch	• Cash Drawer Balancing	• Cash/Check/Charge/Refunds
• Customer Service/New Accounts	• Daily Transaction Reports	• Electronic Register/Scanner
• Ticket Dispensing Machine	• Verification/Refunds	• Opening/Closing
• Receipt/Ticket Issuance	• Stocking/ATM	• Pricing/Price Marketing

COMPUTER/OFFICE

Hardware: IBM, Panasonic; *Software:* MS Windows 95, MS Word,
Other: encoder, fax, microfiche, PBX, photocopier, Pitney Bowes postage meter, shredder.

EDUCATION

Principles of Banking Course (xxxx)

EMPLOYMENT

SCOTT & WHITE HOSPITAL - Temple, TX   xxxx
     • **File Record Clerk**

TOTAL PLACEMENT (Personnel Services) – Temple, TX   xxxx
     Assignment: • **Provider Relations (Insurance)** – Consolidated Association of Railroad Employees

KELLY TEMPORARY SERVICES – Temple, TX   xxxx
     Assignments: • **Purchase Order Clerk** – McLane Corporate Division (Temple)
                  • **Receptionist** – Central Texas Youth Services Bureau (Belton)
                  • **Receptionist** – Total Program Management (Temple)
                  • **File Clerk** – Scott & White (Temple)

KELLY TEMPORARY SERVICES – Tyler, TX   xxxx-xxxx
     Assignments: • **Data Entry Clerk** – Aetna U.S. Healthcare
                  • **Lobby/Drive-Thru Teller** – Southside Bank

FIRST SAVINGS BANK – Manhattan, KS   xxxx-xxxx
     • **First Accredited Teller/Vault Teller/Teller**

GEARY COMMUNITY HOSPITAL – Junction City, KS   xxxx-xxxx
     • **PBX Operator/Registrar**

Additional Information Available upon Request

3

Combination. *Jackie Sexton, Fort Hood, Texas*
Performance areas are grouped by side headings. The original resume and cover letter were tastefully in two colors. Under Employment, jobs are bulleted and bold. See Cover Letter 28.

Dianne T. Meyers

7 Larkspur Lane • Needham, MA 02492 • (555) 555-5555

Qualifications

Dedicated, hardworking secretary with broad range of experience including more than 25 years at Wellesley College. Solid background overseeing and maintaining smooth operation of busy office. Outstanding organizational skills, creativity, and attention to detail. Proficient in word processing using MS Word. Ability to work independently and as part of a team. Excellent interpersonal and communication skills.

Skills

- 60-70 wpm typing speed
- shorthand
- transcription
- telephone reception
- MS Word for Windows
- research
- scheduling
- customer service
- filing

Achievements

- As hospital receptionist, handle all calls, including locating and contacting physicians, social workers, or other necessary staff.
- Composed, edited, and typed correspondence and reports in various office settings.
- Handled hospital admissions, taking medical histories over the phone; processed paperwork; signed patients in at residences.
- Interacted successfully with all levels of management and employees.
- Researched information for legal cases and wrote reports.
- Set up and maintained filing systems.
- Scheduled appointments and events.
- Greeted and directed visitors.
- Assembled and processed large mailings.
- Answered up to 9 telephone lines.
- Ordered supplies and maintained inventory.

Work History

Secretary	Wellesley College Science Department, Wellesley, MA (1965–1990)

Additional Experience

Receptionist/Admissions Coordinator	Auburn Hospital, Jamaica Plain, MA (per diem, xxxx–present/xxxx–xxxx)
Secretary/Receptionist	New England Contractors, Inc., Natick, MA (xxxx–xxxx)
Secretary/Receptionist	Secure Horizons, Dedham, MA (xxxx–xxxx)
Secretary/Clerk	Rivers and Sons, Wellesley, MA (xxxx–xxxx)
Secretary/Receptionist	Jones Engineering, Newton, MA (xxxx–xxxx)
Freelance Secretary	Self-Employed, Dedham, MA (xxxx)
Legal Secretary	Connors & Connors, Wellesley, MA (xxxx)

Education

Associate degree	Lasell Junior College, Newton, MA, in Medical Secretarial Science

4

Functional. *Wendy Gelberg, Needham, Massachusetts*
The jobs under Additional Experience are cast as incidental, compared to her long-term Wellesley position, and thus appear as a strength rather than a liability. See Cover Letter 29.

Morton N. Downer

214 Waltham Trace
Prattville, Alabama 36000

[334] 555-5555 (Home)
[334] 555-6666 (Office)

VALUE TO ARTISAN PRODUCTS, INC.

As your **corporate pilot**, provide safe, reliable air transportation and make the impression you would want your important clients to remember.

RATINGS AND CERTIFICATES

- Commercial Pilot, Airplane, Multi Engine, Land, Instrument
- Current Flight Engineer Written Exam
- Military Flight Examiner and Instructor Pilot – F-16
- Medical Certificate: FAA Class I – No Restrictions, Jul 95

TOTAL FLIGHT TIME: 4410

Pilot-in-command	2944	Total Instrument	483
Instructor/Evaluator	1466	Simulator	220
Combat	32	Night	85
Multi Engine	1585	Types flown:	F-4E, AT-38B, F-16
Single Engine	1552		

FLIGHT EXPERIENCE

- F-16A/C Flight Examiner/Instructor Pilot, Air Force Advisor, Alabama Air National Guard, Creighton Field, Alabama, Aug 92 – Present
- Chief, Rated Officer Assignments, Arcon AFB, Virginia, Nov 89 – Aug 92
- F-16 Assistant Operations Officer/Instructor Pilot, Skrydstrup AB, Denmark, Oct 88 – Nov 89
- Assistant Operations Officer, Instructor Pilot, MacDill AFB, Florida, Nov 85 – Oct 88
- Flight Commander, Flight Examiner, Instructor Pilot, Nellis AFB, Nevada, Jul 83 – Nov 85
- F-16 Upgrade, Luke AFB, Arizona, May 83 – Jul 83
- Four years of increasing pilot responsibilities from student pilot to flight examiner, Apr 76 – May 83

REPRESENTING CORPORATE INTERESTS

- Chosen by senior decision maker from among 20 eligible mid-level managers (half with more seniority) to escort key, civilian supporter of our operations.

SPECIAL RECOGNITION

- Top Gun, F-16, Jun 85
- #1 Officer in the Wing, Jan 83

EDUCATION

- Pursuing MBA, Lorton University, Montgomery, Alabama, GPA to date: 3.7
- BBA, Juniper University, Juniper, Alabama, AFROTC Scholarship, 1975

Functional. *Donald Orlando, Montgomery, Alabama*
The writer wrote the cover letter for executives who want a pilot to be an ambassador to VIPs. The resume with numerical data was written for the Chief Pilot. See Cover Letter 37.

Bradley R. Kemmer

101 Square Boulevard — Monroe, Michigan 46623
313.555.8998

PROFESSIONAL PROFILE

Senior Finance Executive

Corporate Finance Executive and troubleshooting specialist with a command of operations, organization, and general management. Expert competence in financial planning and analysis, cost reduction, and performance/profit improvement.

Excellent qualifications in managing large-scale projects, from concept through planning, design, development, and task management. Detail-oriented and analytical.

Experience in the areas of:

· Economic Analysis	· Team Building and Leadership
· Forecasting and Budgeting	· Customer Development
· Staffing and Management	· Project Management
· Quality and Finance Control	· Strategic Planning
· Sales and Marketing Programs	· Competitive Pricing Analysis
· Revenue Management	· Diversity Strategies

PERFORMANCE HIGHLIGHTS

> Orchestrated a winning partnership between Service Parts Operations and Monroe divisions. Supported $1.3 billion in annual sales business; reviewed all finance issues, provided profit & loss analysis, collaborated with six divisions to consummate alliance.

> Developed a $2 billion five-year integrated business plan for partnership retention that included projected volume, sales, and business performance initiatives with the objective to establish profitable targets.

> Facilitated the business plan portion of "Troubled Products" initiative (unfavorable operating profit). Generated support to make the product lines more profitable ($57 million in favorable profits) in areas of manufacturing, distribution, pricing, and other customer-driven incentives.

> Secured approval on numerous sales and marketing proposals/programs on behalf of corporate aftermarket sales staff. Made presentations on significant programs (exceeding $500K in operating profit impact) to the Price & Policy Review Group.

> Managed a zero-based budget as Staff Assistant to the Regional Personnel Director. Project included a $30 million operating budget (400+ security personnel, doctors, nurses, and personnel benefits administration) in 11 divisions. Created budgets and forecasts for the area Personnel Directors in the city of Monroe, Michigan.

> Managed various functional financial departments (Budgets, Forecasts, Payroll, Cost Accounting, Accounts Receivable, Audit, and Accounts Payable).

> Currently coordinating project to achieve market-based competitive prices (excess of $70 million) on aftermarket parts from suppliers.

> Experienced international traveler.

> Knowledge of conversational French; learning Swahili.

EDUCATION

EASTERN MICHIGAN UNIVERSITY   1982
MASTER OF SCIENCE degree — Business Management *(Cum Laude Honors Graduate)*

MICHIGAN STATE UNIVERSITY   1979
BACHELOR OF SCIENCE degree — Business Administration *(Magna cum Laude Honors Graduate)*

6

Combination. *Lorie Lebert, Novi, Michigan*
The resume opens with an unlabeled profile that mentions qualifications. Areas of Experience are presented in a two-column list. These can be altered to tailor a resume to a different job

EXPERIENCE

FORD MOTOR CORPORATION   1979-current

FINANCE MANAGER — *Service Products Operations (1991-current)*
Manage the Pricing and Product Programs Group; review, analyze, and report on proposals; support the sales & marketing staff; supervise and develop employees; ensure that profitability goals are met in the aftermarket channel; ensure that people development is consistent with diversity strategy; serve as financial liaison to other staffs/divisions.

Provide financial analysis and impact on the corporation and customers; supply distribution analysis and make corporate decisions on value-added proposals.

Currently working on introducing expanded product lines at a national retailer/installer. Proposed package would impact 'Hot Shot Delivery,' with a projected annual sales of $15 million in the first year and $80 million in the third year, with a margin of 10-15%. Process includes P&L analysis, customer/distributor partner interface, implementation using cross-functional workgroups, and 12-15 new product launches.

Pricing/Product Programs and Market Support initiatives/objectives include:

> Improve staff efficiency/manage head count (41 employees); implement synchronous improvements.

> Skills enhancement/employee development; apply cross-training initiatives.

> Strategic/action-oriented analysis; administer channel/product line/customer profitability reporting processes; utilize common processes.

> Enhance partnership reporting; interact with divisions to establish integrated business plan and establish profitability targets for product lines.

> Conduct competitive price analyses, family pricing, life-cycle model strategies, elasticity analyses, profitability analysis to identify opportunities.

STAFF ASSISTANT — *Regional Personnel Center (1989-91)*
Developed budget and forecasts. Monitored and recorded expenses. Presented statistical data on costs, head counts, and initiatives to 11 area Personnel Directors. Coordinated billing of actual costs. Performed actual vs. forecast analysis.

GENERAL SUPERVISOR — *Engine Plant & Metal Fabricating Plant (1985-89)*
Responsibilities encompassed operations analysis, payroll, receivables, and disbursement analysis; supervised 14 direct-report personnel.

Developed annual budgets and monthly plant reports; performed ad hoc analyses; reported on actual vs. budget performance. Managed all payroll, receivables and disbursement analysis liaison activities.

Supervised and monitored annual $30 million inventory at engine facility. Chief financial person who ensured accurate physical inventory count (worked with outside accounting firm of Deloitte & Touche).

SUPERVISOR/GENERAL ACCOUNTANT/SENIOR CLERK — *Manufacturing (1979-85)*
Managed supplier disbursement payments and the audit department. Developed plant operating budget for the Toledo Plastics Plant. Group leader for 40 employees in accounts payable.

Generated production material cost forecasts; managed capital expenditures; recorded and audited special inventories; reconciled general ledger accounts, developed inventory forecast; journalized sales and cost of sales entries.

BRADLEY R. KEMMER
101 Square Boulevard — Monroe, Michigan 46623 — 313.555.8998

target. Performance Highlights contain mostly quantified achievements. In the Experience section, paragraphs present mostly responsibilities. Another feature is the use of small caps in the side section headings, in the names of universities and degrees under Education, and in job titles. See Cover Letter 100.

SHARON M. HOFFMANN

391 North 18th Avenue
Redmond, Washington 00000
(555) 555-5555

CAREER GOAL

To provide superior levels of customer service to an organization that empowers their representatives to make decisions and recognizes the value of their contributions.

COMPETENCIES

■ *Over eleven years of experience in customer service within diversified industries.*

■ *Proven effectiveness in the areas of:*
  ✓ *phone and personal customer assistance with inquiries, special orders or complaints*
  ✓ *client billing and credit issues*
  ✓ *support for field and internal sales staffs*
  ✓ *order processing, expediting, research and troubleshooting*
  ✓ *training and motivation of other customer service staff members*
  ✓ *design and implementation of streamlined work systems*
  ✓ *automated office operations (service workstation and ACD Call Center environment)*
  ✓ *database management (Oracle system) and Microsoft Windows word processing (Word; WordPerfect), with desire for further learning in computer applications*

■ *Throughout career, achieved success far beyond employer's expectations through:*
  ✓ *attentive listening to understand customers' problems*
  ✓ *dependability and consistently positive attitude despite ongoing challenges*
  ✓ *friendliness and genuine concern for people, resulting in solid trust relationships*
  ✓ *knowledge of company's products and procedures*
  ✓ *open lines of communication with interrelated departments*
  ✓ *strong detail orientation with thorough documentation and follow-through to satisfactory resolution*
  ✓ *flexibility to assist in any area where needed*
  ✓ *continuous self-development and upgrading of skills through on-the-job training*

EXPERIENCE

20XX – Present
■ *IADPP, Redmond, WA*
  (International Association for Data Processing Professionals)
  Group Leader, Member Services, *promoted from* **Telephone Associate** *after one year.*

  ✓ *Responsible for the integrity of membership records for two regions encompassing the western U.S., Alaska and Hawaii. Ensured nearly 70,000 members in these regions were up-to-date with dues renewals and were receiving publications. Answered their inquiries received by phone and electronic or conventional mail and expedited processing of their requests.*

  ✓ *Routinely went beyond normal means to investigate members' problems and received appreciative correspondence from researchers who depend upon IACP to provide them with information on new developments in their field.*

  ✓ *Extensively utilized Oracle system to enter and verify daily activities of department, then compiled reports for management's review. Trained, motivated and delegated workloads of staff of five.*

Continued ...

7

Combination. *Melanie A. Noonan, West Paterson, New Jersey*
Thick, partial horizontal lines extending to the right margin point to the person's name and the section headings in small caps. Square bullets of the same thickness complement the lines

SHARON M. HOFFMANN

19XX – 20XX
- SWIFTDATA ACCOUNTING SERVICES, Seattle, WA
  Client Account Representative — Payroll Services

  ✓ Managed an account base of 400-450 clients all over the United States and Canada, resolving and preventing recurrences of a variety of problems regarding billing and credit, missing checks or reports, and incorrect earnings/deductions/reports.

  ✓ Provided nontechnical phone assistance to clients encountering difficulty in downloading their payrolls for on-line processing. Received commendations for professional assistance with complex payroll setups involving numerous changes.

  ✓ Contributed to task force to develop uniform departmental operating procedures and filing system improvements.

  ✓ Suggested incentives adopted by company to promote better employee relationships and reduce stress through activities outside the work setting.

19XX – 19XX
- MORGAN WITTER TRUST COMPANY, Seattle, WA
  Customer Service Representative — Mutual Funds

  ✓ Provided a specialized service to shareholders, brokers and outside agents, enabling them to access information concerning their accounts and resolve problems in a timely manner.

  ✓ Handled between 75-120 calls daily involving diversified and complicated matters such as fund transfers, tax reporting, statement discrepancies and research requests.

  ✓ Set up a tickler file to organize inquiries and correspondence which facilitated prompt follow-up. This system was so successful that management depended heavily on it and encouraged its use by others.

  ✓ Of 33 representatives in the department, won monthly incentive awards 14 times during three-year employment, including first place four times.

19XX – 19XX
- MCI INTERNATIONAL, San Francisco, CA
  "Hot Line" Billing Clerk

  ✓ In this newly created position, responded directly to a heavy volume of calls from clients and field sales representatives concerning invoicing problems, equipment malfunctions and new installation orders.

  ✓ Set up a concise and uniform client database to separate equipment charges from service fees, which saved time and facilitated the microfiche process.

19XX - 19XX
- MACY'S WEST, San Francisco, CA
  Sales Consultant — Women's Better Sportswear and Career Fashions

  ✓ Maintained a client book of $.5 million while developing a continuous professional clientele. Trained new sales consultants in department operations. Received numerous awards for exemplifying the highest standards of a personalized selling organization.

EDUCATION

- REDWOOD COLLEGE of BUSINESS, Big Sur, CA
  Associate in Science degree in Business Management, 19XX
  Served on the College Board of Trustees for two years

- Continuous career development seminars in computer applications, interpersonal communications, and supervisory skills, among others.

visually. The whole resume is in italic, which is a bid to make this resume stand out from others. The lines, square bullets, and a second level of bullets—check marks—tie together the two pages visually. Job titles are bold to help them stand out. Liberal use of blank lines ensures white space. See Cover Letter 46.

Mary E. Lamb

Current Address:	Permanent Address:
000 Merriweather Lane	00 Cloudy Avenue
Sunny, OH 00000	Moon, ME 00000
(555) 555-5555	(555) 555-5555

CAREER OBJECTIVE: To actively be involved in and enrich the lives of children with special needs, as an elementary teacher.

EDUCATION: Hop 'n' Skip University, Hartford, ME
Bachelor of Science in Education, May XXXX
Major: Teaching the Emotionally Impaired
Minors: Child Development / English
Certifications:
Emotionally Impaired, K-12
Regular Education, K-5
English, K-12
Child Development, PreK-2
ZA Endorsement

TEACHING EXPERIENCE:

Student Teacher (Special Education) XXXX–XXXX
Leftowitz Middle School, Mandel, OH
- Student teaching included preparing lesson plans and interactive bulletin boards and presenting lessons daily. Whole group lessons were taught in math, reading, language arts, and geography. My responsibilities included creating a safe and comfortable learning environment for students with special needs.

Substitute Teacher (Regular Education)
Victory Elementary Schools XXXX–XXXX
Peace Elementary School, Peace, OH XXXX
- Responsibilities included instructing children and carrying out the school requirements.

Student Teacher (Regular Education) XXXX–XXXX
Berryton Public Schools, Lambkin Elementary
Berryton, OH
- Student teaching included preparing this multiage classroom for the students. Other responsibilities included creating and presenting lesson plans, planning thematic units, and meeting the district outcomes. Whole group and one-on-one lessons were taught in math, social studies, language arts, and science.

Practicum Experience (Special Education) XXXX–XXXX
Peachtree Elementary, Hudsonville, OH
- Responsibilities included preparing and adapting lessons for students with special needs. Taught whole group and one-on-one lessons.

8

Chronological. *Peggy Weeks, Battle Creek, Michigan*
A single, thin horizontal line separates the contact information in balanced format from the rest of the resume. Another line separates the person's name in a header from the rest of

Mary E. Lamb   Page Two

<table>
<tr><td></td><td>**Mid Tier Experience (Regular Education)**</td><td>**XXXX**</td></tr>
</table>

	Mid Tier Experience (Regular Education)	**XXXX**

Mid Tier Experience (Regular Education)   XXXX
Eaton Primary School, Eaton, IN
- Responsibilities included working with students one-on-one, teaching whole group lessons, and observing and assessing the students in a kindergarten classroom.

RELATED   **Student Volunteer**   XXXX
EXPERIENCE: Berryton Adult Education, Berryton, OH
- Cared for children ages three to six. Responsibilities consisted of planning and teaching lessons, reading to the children, and playing with the children.

Field Trip Guide   **Fall XXXX & Fall XXXX**
High Five Elementary, Berryton, OH
- Responsibilities included guiding second grade students on their nature hike and helping them complete their packet.

Camp Teacher   **Summer XXXX**
Apple Dumpling Preschool, Madison, OH
- Taught children ages three to six. Responsibilities included getting them ready for swim class, one-on-one instruction, and group instruction.

OTHER   **Lead Cashier**   **Summer XXXX - Fall XXXX**
EXPERIENCE: Mountain Lumber, Valley, MN
- Responsibilities included providing quality service to customers.

HONORS AND   Dean's List (Fall 1996, Spring 1997)
ACTIVITIES: Columbia University Scholarship
                         Company Excellence in Education Scholarship
                         Omega Phi Alpha (Executive Board Officer)
                         National Honor Society

PROFESSIONAL   National Council of Teachers of English (NCTE)   Fall XXXX
DEVELOPMENT: Presented "Reflective Writing"
                         Maine State "Bright Ideas" Conference   Spring XXXX
                             Presented "Reflective Writing" and "Classroom Issues"
                         The Tri-State Area Teachers of Mathematics, Attendee Fall XXXX
                         Student Council of Exceptional Children Conference
                         Make it Take it Workshop, Columbia University
                         Multiage Training during Student Teaching

REFERENCES / PORTFOLIO /
LETTERS OF RECOMMENDATION
                         Available upon request

the information on page 2. Job titles are in boldface to make them readily seen. For each job position, a single bullet points to a description of responsibilities for the position. Achievements are evident in the Honors and Activities section. Blank lines between sections provide ample white space. See Cover Letter 61.

Helen Ridgeway

21 Spruce Hill Terrace • Belleville, Illinois 62221
(618) 555-5500 Ext. 374 (W) • (618) 555-5555 (H)

Scouting Report

Five years' experience as a successful junior college basketball coach. Inherited a program with only 14 wins in the previous six seasons and created a winning program (.705 winning percentage) ranked nationally in both academics and athletics. Proven athletic administration skills and track record for graduating student-athletes (97%).

- A dynamic motivator, recruiter, and bench strategist who strives to instill a genuine love of the game as the cornerstone for success on and off the court.

- Twice named Great Rivers Athletic Conference Coach of the Year. Currently hold additional duties as Assistant Athletic Director and Part-time Physical Education Instructor.

- Featured Panelist on the topic "Rebuilding a Program" at the WBCA Final Four Conference in Cincinnati, March 1997.

- Member of the National Junior College Athletic Association (NJCAA) Region 24 Basketball Executive Committee *(1992-Present)*. Chair of the NJCAA Region 24 Women's Basketball Committee *(1995-Present)*.

Coaching Highlights

TROY COMMUNITY COLLEGE, Troy, Illinois, 1992 - Present
Head Women's Basketball Coach
Took over a program that accumulated a 14-125 record from 1986-1992. Manage all recruiting, budgeting, and scheduling activities. Help students maintain academic standards. Finished 1996-1997 as the Region 24 Runner-Up with a 23-10 record.

TCC BASKETBALL	1992-1993	1993-1994	1994-1995	1995-1996	1996-1997	Totals
Won/Lost (winning %)	22-4 (.846)	17-15 (.531)	21-11 (.656)	25-5 (.833)	23-10 (.696)	108-45 (.705)
All Region 24	1	1	n/a	3	2	7
All Conference	1	1	2	3	2	9
All American	n/a	n/a	n/a	1	n/a	1
Academic All American	n/a	n/a	n/a	1	1	2
National Ranking				13th	12th	
National Academic Ranking					10th	

Additional duties:

Assistant Athletic Director
Coordinate administrative duties including physicals, insurance bills, and sports budgets. Help oversee student/athlete conduct code, sports advertising, and soliciting funds for athletic programs. Monitor academic progress of female athletes.

9

Functional. *John A. Suarez, Troy, Illinois*
An innovative resume with original section headings and a unique table. The contact information is in "springboard" format. Scouting Report is a Profile section with some achieve-

Academics/Playing Career

BACHELOR OF SCIENCE, Eastern Illinois University, Charleston, Illinois, 1985-1990
- Basketball Team Captain *(1989-1990)*
- Gateway Honor Roll *(1988)*
- Gateway Athlete of Week *(1989)*
- Participant, Division I NCAA Tournament *(1988)*
- Participant/Bronze Medalist, Olympic Festival Games *(1991)*

GRADUATE, Mater Dei High School, Breese, Illinois, 1982-1985
- Basketball Team Captain *(1984 and 1985)*
- Basketball Team MVP *(1984 and 1985)*
- All-State Selection *(1985)*
- Mid-State Conference Selection *(1984 and 1985)*

Free Throws

- Head Coach, Prairie State Women Basketball, Southern Team *(1991-1993)*
- Head Softball Coach, Troy Community College *(1990-1993)*
- Venue Director of Prairie State Games *(1995-Present)*
- Liaison for USA Basketball at Olympic Festival, St. Louis *(1994)*
- Camp Director, Troy Community College Summer Basketball Camps *(1992-1995)*
- Assistant Camp Director, Eastern Illinois University Basketball Camps *(1988-1990)*

Field Goals

Published two articles in JUCO Review: "Preseason Conditioning" (1992) and "How to Build a Successful Program" *(1997)*.

Spoke with students and coaches of local basketball programs on various topics:
- Team Cohesiveness, Okawville High School *(1994)*
- Full Court Defense, Mater Dei High School Basketball Camp (1994)
- Pressure Defense, Freeburg High School Coaching Clinic *(1993)*

Three-Pointers

- Great Rivers Athletic Conference Coach of the Year *(1995-1996)*
- Great Rivers Athletic Conference Coach of the Year *(1992-1993)*
- Inducted into the Mater Dei High School Hall of Fame *(1995)*

References Available on Request

ments. The table progresses chronologically from left to right (less evident because of the "xx'ed" year numbers for this book). Free Throws is a work history, and Field Goals indicates publications and presentations. Three-Pointers lists awards and honors. Blank lines ensure ample white space. See Cover Letter 65.

Lorraine Johnson

23 Larkin Boulevard, Patchogue, NY 11772 ◆ 555-555-5555 ◆ lojo@sprintmail.com

Dedicated to the creation and nurturing of a lifelong passion for health and fitness that will enhance students' well-being and directly impact their academic success.

Permanently Certified Teacher

◆

Physical Education

◆

Adaptive Physical Education

◆

Health and Nutrition

Profile

Convey an enthusiastic attitude that promotes sportsmanship, develops teamwork, and motivates children to welcome physical fitness participation. Encourage young people to make activity and wellness an enjoyable part of daily life.

Create an energized atmosphere while maintaining discipline and safety standards. Utilize specific physical activities to enhance students' classroom curriculum.

Develop and implement districtwide curricula and lesson plans which adjust to students' needs. Skilled in the identification and screening of special-needs children.

Education and Certification

Master of Arts in Education with Special Certificate in Adaptive Physical Education
Dowling College, Oakdale, NY, 1989

Bachelor of Science in Physical Education and Health
Columbia University, New York, NY, 1982

New York State Permanent Certification in Physical Education # 000-0000

Representative Abilities

Teach individual students, small groups, or classes of over thirty students.
Function in single location, or as districtwide teacher.
Construct districtwide curricula geared to specific age groups and ability levels.
Develop screening instruments.
Identify children's gross motor skills and special needs.
Write Individualized Educational Plans.
Screen students throughout school system for program participation.
Coach high school junior varsity – volleyball and basketball.
Coach middle school intramurals – volleyball, basketball, softball, and track.
Coach Special Olympics and prepare students for events.
Create and implement interschool competitions in volleyball, track, basketball, gymnastics, and swimming.

Career Development

Merrick School District	1998 to XXXX
Teacher of Physical Education (K-5), Merrick Student Workshop	
New York City Public Schools	1984 to 1994
Teacher in Adaptive Physical Education	
St. Louis Public Schools	1983 to 1984
Teacher in Adaptive Physical Education Department (three years)	
Teacher of Health and Physical Education, grades 6-8 (four years)	

10

Functional. *Deborah Wile Dib, Medford, New York*
Another original resume. The graphic is in both the resume and the cover letter. Areas of expertise are in the left column. Career Development is a work history. See Cover Letter 73.

John D. Waterman
P.O. Box 555 ▪ Somewhere, USA 55555 ▪ (555) 555-5555

Certifications
- Federal Aviation Administration Inspection Authorization (IA), 1993-Present
- Federal Aviation Administration Aircraft and Powerplants License (A&P), 1987-Present

Experience Overview
- Director of Maintenance
- Inspector/Chief Inspector
- Broad range of maintenance experience on aircraft and equipment, including jets, turbojets, turboprops, and reciprocating aircraft
- Experience in developing training programs as well as training aircraft maintenance personnel
- Machinist/Millwright with experience on lathes, drill presses, milling and grinding machines, setting tanks, steel frames, and motors

Employment History

McDONNELL DOUGLAS TECHNICAL SERVICES   1997-Present
- Working at local Air Center in manufacturing military aircraft

EXECUTIVE AIR TERMINAL, Somewhere, USA   1987-1997
- **Director of Maintenance in General Aviation**
  - Performed routine and scheduled maintenance, operational checks, and troubleshooting. Aircraft maintenance included airframes; engines; engine R&I; HSI; landing gear R&I; flight control R&I; rigging, skin, and rib replacement; wing and tail section R&I.
  - Conducted hands-on maintenance on Beechcraft, Cessna, Lear, and Piper General Aviation Aircraft; USAir 727 and DC-9, Comair and ASA 340; Shorts 330; United Express 146 commercial aircraft.
  - Chief Inspector in general/commercial aviation.

UNITED STATES AIR FORCE   1971-1987
(Retired with honorable discharge as an E8 Senior Master Sergeant)
- **Aircraft Maintenance Specialist/Flight Chief**
  - Responsible for 78 personnel and 12 aircraft, performing scheduled maintenance and completing operational checks on engine run-ups.
  - Conducted airframe and engine troubleshooting and maintenance on jets, turbojets, turboprops, and reciprocating aircraft. Military aircraft included C-130, DC-9, B-52, KC-135, C-141, F-4, F-15, F-16.
  - Heavy maintenance includes aircraft modifications, engine upgrades, fuselage and wing modifications/replacements, landing gear and component changes. Repaired and/or replaced stringers, ribs, and bulkheads.
- **Inspector General Staff, Aircraft Maintenance Inspector**
  - Performed command-directed inspections of aircraft and maintenance activities to determine combat readiness.
- **Superintendent of Standardization and Training Division**
  - Supervised 27 inspectors.
  - Responsible for the quality of maintenance on 30 aircraft and training of 1,000 personnel.

UNION CARBIDE CORPORATION, South Charleston, West Virginia   1966-1971
- **Machinist/Millwright**
  - Worked with heavy equipment and various industrialized machines such as lathes, drill presses, milling and grinding machines, welding and punch presses.

Education
- Graduate of Senior Noncommissioned Officer Academy
- Graduate of Management School for Air Force Supervisors
- High school diploma with 35 semester hours of college credit
- Extensive formal training in aircraft maintenance with the Air Force

11

Combination. *Barbie Dallmann, Charleston, West Virginia*
A resume for an individual whose education after high school has been mainly in the U.S. Air Force and whose career path displays increasing responsibility. See Cover Letter 38.

Maria D. Rodriguez, LPN

22 River Road, Patchogue, NY 11772   516-555-5555

Licensed Practical Nurse

Recent graduate with professional experience in healthcare settings and private duty nursing. Committed to the medical profession and to quality patient care.

Nursing style blends professionalism, capability and compassion to truly integrate patients' medical and emotional care within hospital, facility or private duty environment. Communicate well with doctors, colleagues and patient families, ensuring continuity of patient care.

Dedicated beyond normal expectations. Absolutely reliable and punctual with perfect school and clinical attendance record. Will be at work no matter what the weather or personal circumstances. Own a four-wheel-drive vehicle.

Personal experience with two severely disabled children—who could not interact and who did not live to adulthood—was preparation for dedication to all patients, especially those who are unable to communicate in normal ways.

Education, Licensure, and Certification

Board of Cooperative Services Diploma in Practical Nursing, XXXX
Louis A. Wilson Tech, Western Suffolk BOCES, Northport, NY

Licensed Practical Nurse, New York State License # 000-0000

IV Certification: Central and Peripheral lines, through I.V.E.C.O.N., 1999
Infection Control, through BOCES, 1998
CPR, through The American Heart Association, 1998

Areas of Knowledge and Experience

- ➤ chest, NG, nephrostomy, gastro tubes
- ➤ IV lines, all types
- ➤ renal I&O catheterization
- ➤ urinalysis, culture and sensitivity
- ➤ finger sticks
- ➤ wound and burn care
- ➤ labor and delivery observation
- ➤ postpartum, newborn nursery

- ➤ cast care, pin care, traction care
- ➤ tracheostomy care
- ➤ pediatric and geriatric basic care
- ➤ rehabilitation support functions
- ➤ psychiatric basic care
- ➤ private duty nursing
- ➤ private duty care plan development
- ➤ family, aide, LPN care integration

Undergraduate Clinical Training

Med-Surg	Good Samaritan, St. John's, Brunswick and Huntington Hospitals
Pediatrics	Good Samaritan Hospital
Orthopedics	Brunswick Rehabilitation Center
OB / GYN	Good Samaritan Hospital
Gerontology	St. John's and Our Lady of Consolation Nursing Homes
Psychiatric	Brunswick Psychiatric Hospital

12

Combination. *Deborah Wile Dib, Medford, New York*
A left column filled only by a stethoscope graphic and some extra blank lines between sections help to increase white space for an uncrowded look. The section headings and the individual's

Maria D. Rodriguez, LPN   *2*

Employment in Healthcare

Private Duty Nurse   **1999 to XXXX**

Perform total patient care for end-stage Parkinson's patient (a former RN) including medications, personal hygiene, range of motion, tube feedings, PT and OT for ten hours a day. Determined needs in initial home visit evaluation and initiated beneficial changes including establishment of nursing care plans, a charting system to ensure continuity of care, and development of comprehensive patient history for emergency hospitalizations. Take a compassionate and proactive approach to patient's care—encouraged purchase of high-top sneakers for patient's foot drop, continually provide personal services such as hair care and manicures to stimulate patient, and inform family as to care changes necessary as patient's condition deteriorates.

Medical Office Secretary, Donal's Chiropractic, Coram, NY   **1996 to 1999**

Fulfilled basic patient assistance for 40 to 45 patients per day in this very busy office. Calmed patients' fears, created comfortable atmosphere, and acted as emotional support. Handled full range of medical secretarial duties—scheduling, billing, insurance, collections and heavy phones. Cleared up old accounts and worked out payment arrangements. Renovated office, replacing very old decor and increasing patient satisfaction.

Prior Employment

Trainer and Data-entry Operator, PDQ, Hauppague, NY   **1994 to 1996**

Position required high degree of self-motivation, organization, time-management and accuracy. Worked from home, picked up and delivered daily workload and finished on schedule although job could be given anytime one day and be expected for completion the next day. Compiled information from surveys, reading and translating often illegible documentation and code into computer for next day delivery. Mentored new hires—trained on data entry techniques and policies.

Direct Mail Handler, Midlantic Graphics, Mastic, NY   **1994 to 1994**

Performed bindery, tagging and bagging functions for clients' direct mailings.

Community Service Award

1996 BOCES Toy Drive Chairperson

As student project, independently organized campaign and collected over 2,000 new and gently used toys to relieve toy shortage for the children and adolescents at Brunswick Psychiatric Center and the Stony Brook Hospital Psychiatric Unit.

Project was a huge undertaking that was personally rewarding. Was unexpectedly honored by school principal at graduation and given the BOCES' Annual Community Service Award.

name in the contact information are in Brush Script. The opening section ("Licensed Practical Nurse") is a profile, and the bulleted items in "Areas of Knowledge and Experience" are listed for easy alteration for a different job target. Employment paragraphs indicate mostly duties. See Cover Letter 114.

DIANA M. JONES, RN

44 Columbia Street • Arlington, NY 00000 • (555) 555-5555

───────────────── **ONCOLOGY NURSE** ─────────────────

Offering over 7 years of oncology experience and a clinical expertise in bone marrow transplants.

A dedicated nurse with a record of consistent job performance and belief that continuous professional learning is essential to meet rapidly changing health care needs. A strong patient advocate who readily accepts change and initiates new ideas. Delivered substantial contributions through strengths in direct patient care, patient education, and assessments. Areas of special emphasis include:

Care Plan Development & Implementation	*Hospital / Home Health / Primary Care*
Integrated Healthcare Approach	*Precepting: Graduate Nurses / Students / Floats*
Employee Relations / Motivation	*Team Building & Leadership*

HIGHLIGHTS OF QUALIFICATIONS:

◆ Extremely focused and task-oriented. Provide highly skilled clinical care while recognizing and attending to the full impact of the disease on patients and their families.

◆ Strive to understand the patient's individual personality, family dynamics, culture, coping style and emotional, physical and spiritual needs.

◆ Consistently seek to identify better ways of caregiving and teaching that are both cost-efficient and outcome-based.

◆ Exceptional communication and interpersonal skills. Serve as a positive role model fostering effective employee relations and instilling a sense of team and unity among nursing staff.

PROFESSIONAL EXPERIENCE:

Regional Medical Center, Albany, NY   ***xxxx to Present***

Staff Nurse - Oncology / Bone Marrow Transplant Unit
Work with patients receiving autologous, allogeneic, and matched unrelated transplants in this center of excellency. Maintain thorough understanding of all body systems, the breakdown of each system and its effects from chemotherapy. Counsel families on lifestyle adjustments and psychosocial needs. Strictly adhere to policy/procedures and uphold the integrity and confidentiality of each patient's condition and medical record. Assume Charge Nurse duties.

• Attained Clinical Ladder III.

• Certified to access and maintain SVADs for the entire Medical Center.

• Established a highly functional educational library which enables patients, families, and medical personnel to access and update the most current cancer literature.

• Created a photo history of the Oncology Unit's patients, families, and staff activities.

• Initiated and established a Nurse Sunshine Fund.

• Organized and served as captain for the ACS Breast Cancer Walk-A-Thon which generated over $35,000 and earned several awards including team spirit and creative site design.

• Key contributor to the development of the first RMC Bone Marrow Donor Day.

• Successfully rallied support for improvements to the nurses' lounge which significantly increased morale and improved staff relations.

13

Combination. *Kristin Mroz Coleman, Poughkeepsie, New York*
Horizontal lines enclosed the profile ("Oncology Nurse") and call attention to it. The areas of special emphasis are listed in two columns and can be easily altered for a different job

PROFESSIONAL EXPERIENCE continued:

Home Quality Care, Inc.   ***xxxx to Present***

Registered Nurse - Per Diem

Provide direct home nursing care to a full range of patients/clients with various needs. Encourage active mental and physical involvement of clients, stressing preventive care and providing emotional support to promote an optimal level of well-being. Consistently commended on effective client relations, high energy level, friendly manner, and positive attitude.

- Work closely with agency staff and referring physicians.
- Provide effective patient and family/caregiver education.
- Train patients and families to safely conduct complex therapies within the home setting.

PROFESSIONAL DEVELOPMENT:

Certifications:
CPR
Blood Transfusions
IV Therapy
Venipuncture
Therapeutic Touch
Fundamentals of Cancer Nursing
Preceptor Training
Advanced Medical Surgical
Infection Control

Associations:
Oncology Nursing Society (ONS) - xxxx to Present
New York State Nurses Association   xxxx to Present

Seminars/Workshops:
Omega Institute Healing Conference - New York, NY
ONS Annual Conferences - Philadelphia/Pittsburgh
Supportive Care of the Cancer Patient
ONS - Coping Skills for the Care Giver
ONS - Symptom Management in the Home
ONS - Achieving Personal & Balance Professional Balance
Holism - Art & Spirit of Nursing

EDUCATION:

State University of New York at Albany - Candidate for a Bachelor of Science in Nursing
Herkimer County Community College, Herkimer, NY - AAS in Nursing

target. Small diamond bullets point to qualification highlights. In the Professional Experience section, the paragraph after each job title shows responsibilities, and the bullet items point mostly to achievements—some of them quantified. Professional Development items are grouped by categories. See Cover Letter 126.

CONFIDENTIAL   Request Number **97-1558**

Richard Locke
132 Amberly Court   Montgomery, Alabama 36100   ✆ [334] 555-5555 (Home)

Value to Orion: As your **Communications Specialist**, use my rare, hands-on experience in the newest systems to solve your networking problems right the first time.

Capabilities that can build your profits:

- 🖥 Expert at building maximum value into every project
- 🖥 Critical thinker who finds *all* the bottlenecks efficiently
- 🖥 Dedicated, tenacious worker who masters, often on my own time, the newest techniques to help control costs

Computer skills:

- 🖥 Networking:
Expert: LAN, WAN and MAN Networking, Ethernet 802.3, TCP-IP
Proficient: FDDI protocols
- 🖥 Operating Systems:
   Expert: **MS Certified Product Specialist in Windows NT 4.0**, Windows 95, DOS 6.22
   Working knowledge: UNIX, VMS (DEC VAX)
- 🖥 Database: Proficient in dBASE III
- 🖥 Programming:
   Expert: Pascal, BASIC
   Proficient: COBOL, C, Assembler

Relevant experience with selected examples of success:

- 🖥 NETWORK ADMINISTRATOR, TriStar Corporation (*under contract* to the USAF's Unified Systems Division), Bright Air Force Base, Alabama, Jun XX – Present

  - 🖥 Restored our competitiveness when lack of a network or the money to buy one put us behind. Persuaded a VP to let me get the right equipment at the best price, worked nights on my own time, installed all the hardware and software. *Payoffs:* **Saved $15K in labor and shipping costs alone.** Now 40 of our people get seamless online services and e-mail. **Monthly cost? $97.**

  - 🖥 Inherited network with systems management software that hadn't supported nearly 1,000 applications running on 112 NT workstations and five NT servers for six months. Studied the documentation, then came in on the weekend to fix the problem. *Payoffs:* System working in 10 days. **Hundreds of man-hours saved** installing, inventorying and managing software.

  - 🖥 Stepped in when project manager's workstation wouldn't boot at all – just hours before a major contract milestone review. Usual methods had failed. Months of effort at risk. *Payoffs:* Found new way to fix corrupted vital files. **System restored. Review back on track.** Senior decision makers' time saved.

CONFIDENTIAL

14

Combination. *Donald Orlando, Montgomery, Alabama*
The resume displays a number of attempts by the writer to go beyond conventional resume practices. The word CONFIDENTIAL is placed in diagonally opposite corners on both pages to

CONFIDENTIAL   Request Number **XX-1558**

Richard Locke   Communications Specialist   [334] 555-5555

Work history continued

- NETWORK ADMINISTRATOR, Allen Data Services Corporation, *under contract* to the USAF's Unified Systems Division), Bright Air Force Base, Alabama, Sep XX – May XX

    - Got stand-alone network necessary for new multimillion-dollar venture up and running fast. Found unused hardware. Overcame inaccurate schematics. *Payoffs:* Developers using new network in less than three days without a single glitch. **Implementation cost nearly zero.**

    - Took responsibility for program that found illegal users and cleared bottlenecks on mainframes. With no time to attend usual four-day school, mastered unforgiving, badly documented program in just two days. *Payoffs:* **Applications** totally new to me **now running smoothly**.

    - Sought out by program developer to fix a problem that had stumped her and a seasoned expert for months. *Payoffs:* Fixed the system in hours. **Stalled project back on track.**

- LABORATORY INSTRUCTOR IN COMPUTER SCIENCE, Slapout State University at Montgomery, Montgomery, Alabama, Jan XX – Present

- Part-time jobs as a college student, James State University, Montgomery, Alabama, Mar XX – Sep XX

- COMPUTER SPECIALIST, United States Army, Jan XX – Jul XX

Current security clearance: SECRET

Education:

- B.S., Computer Science, James State University at Montgomery, **Dean's List**, XX
  Earned this degree while working 20 hours a week in two part-time jobs to help pay for college.

Training:

- "System Engineer Process – Executive Training," Unified Systems Division, 80 hours, XX
- "Supporting MS Windows NT Server 3.51," Clark University, Montgomery, Advanced Technology Group, 40 hours, XX
- "Networking Principles," Alabama Training Center, 27 hours, XX
- "Operating in a Rational Environment," J. W. Carlton & Co., 40 hours, XX

CONFIDENTIAL

Page two

keep the reader from contacting the person's current employer for information about the candidate. Instead of an Objective, the resume has a Value. Computer (theme) bullets tie together the two pages. Achievements end with a Payoffs statement to indicate benefits to the company. See Cover Letter 146.

TRUDY A. MORALES

114 14th Street South #11   Home: (701) 000-0000
Green River, ND 00000   Work: (701) 000-000

PROFILE

❖ **Human resources professional** with 12 years' experience and consistent record of success in improving workplace relations and productivity.

❖ Excellent written and verbal **communications skills**, with a working knowledge of Spanish; compassionate and a good listener.

❖ **Interpersonal abilities**; expertise employee relations, guest relations, and conflict resolution.

❖ Extensive **management skills**, training, and experience; efficient and well organized; proactive problem solver.

❖ **Computer literate.**

EMPLOYMENT

MEGALO STORES: Green River, ND
   Guest Service Team Lead   1995–Present
   Responsible for all guest service areas. Handle personnel, conflict management, employee relation, and guest service functions.

- Supervise work center of 80 employees and eight supervisors.
- Interview and train employees; maintain appropriate number of staff; ensure timeliness of performance reviews.
- Maintain all financial records in accordance with company standards.
- Oversee all computer hardware and software updates.
- Represent Megalo Stores as public speaker and in radio and television interviews.

   Human Resources/Team Relations Lead   1992–1995
   Responsible for implementing all personnel policies and decisions for staff of 250 employees.

- Anticipated staff vacancies; advertised position openings; interviewed and hired candidates; conducted new-hire orientations; trained employees and conducted performance reviews.
- Maintained proper paperwork according to company, state and federal regulations, including benefits administration and payroll; aggressively managed Workers Compensation cases.
- Coordinated an served as District trainer and speaker for seminars.
- Received specialized training in Diversity and Sexual Harassment; gained further experience in recruitment and conflict management.

PRAIRIE ART MUSEUM—THREE RING BINGO: Green River, ND
   General Manager   1988–1991
   Responsible for profitable operation of charitable gaming facility.

- Supervised 50-person workforce and six managers.
- Wrote profitable Bingo programs in compliance with all state and federal laws.
- Mentored and developed subordinate to ensure successful transition.
- Gained diversity and customer service skills.

15

Combination. *Jeffrey Thompson, Fargo, North Dakota*
Horizontal lines enclosing section headings make them more visible. Decorative bullets enhance the Profile section. In the Employment section, statements in italic indicate responsibilities for

TRUDY A. MORALES

Personnel Manager   1988–1989
Performed all personnel duties including interviewing, hiring, and training.

- Created and implemented Personnel Manager position; position still exists and is in effect throughout the organization.
- Wrote and implemented training manuals and reviews.

DENNY'S RESTAURANT: Oak Park Terrace, IL
Manager   1985–1987
Responsibilities included personnel recruitment and training, budget management, inventory control, and supervision of daily operations

- Gained expertise in training and diversity.
- Improved Spanish language skills.

EDUCATION AND TRAINING

UNIVERSITY OF PEORIA: Peoria, IL
Bachelor of Arts • *Business Administration*   1984

MEGALO STORES
*Challenge of Change • Diversity • Sexual Harassment • Humor Perspective
Team Building • Planning and Organization • Workers Compensation*

SEMINARS
CGAND (Charitable Gaming Association of North Dakota): 1991
CGAND: 1990
World Gaming Congress: 1989
"In Search of Excellence": 1989
Promoting Marketers Association of America: 1987

BIOGRAPHICAL LISTINGS

International Who's Who of Professional and Business Women (1990)
The Who's Who of Women (1991)
Who's Who in America (1990)
Who's Who in U.S. Executives (1990)
2000 Notable American Women (1990 & 1989)
Who's Who in the Midwest (1988)
Who's Who in Executive and Professional Women (1988)

COMMUNITY INVOLVEMENT

National Association for Female Executives
YWCA Jobs Plus Program, Advisory Board Member

each position listed. Bulleted items specify duties. Some of these items count explicitly as experience for the individual. Under Education, italic enhances topics covered through store training. Small caps enhance key items throughout the resume. Biographical listings as titles are italic. See Cover Letter 143.

Jane J. Betts

6908 College Avenue
Boulder, CO 00000
(000) 000-0000

Summary

Energetic and enthusiastic individual who will project a good public image. Will work well independently or in a team structure. Skills sharpened in counseling and employment agency positions will transfer easily to another sector.

Skills

Interpersonal/Communication

- In pilot program endorsed by Governor Smith, built and promoted effective working relationships between the Denver business community and Denver public high school administration and faculty; result was improved links between high school students and potential local employers.
- As a job placement specialist with a local employment agency, developed contacts with local employers, interviewed job applicants to assess their strengths and skills, and trained applicants in interviewing techniques. Located job openings through telephone and personal visits.
- Facilitated alcohol education classes. Led individual and group counseling sessions.

Administrative/Organizational/Follow-Up

- Maintained detailed records in employment agency and counseling positions.
- Coordinated agency alcohol safety program.
- Conducted extensive follow-up with employers and job applicants.

Experience

Full-Time Parent, Aerobics Instructor, and Volunteer, XXXX-present

Job Placement Liaison, XXXX-XXXX
JOBS FOR COLORADO GRADUATES, Denver, CO

Adolescent Counselor, XXXX-XXXX
DENVER HEALTH CENTER, INC., Denver, CO

Job Placement Specialist, XXXX
WILLIAMS AND WILLIAMS, Denver, CO

Education

Master of Social Work, XXXX
UNIVERSITY OF DENVER, Denver, CO

Bachelor of Arts in Psychology and Sociology, XXXX
UNIVERSITY OF COLORADO, Boulder, CO

16

Functional. *Betty H. Williams, Richmond, Virginia*
A full horizontal line above each section heading makes it easy to see each section at a glance. All-uppercase letters make institution names stand out. See Cover Letter 130.

JAMES JONES
XXX-XXX-XXXX
ALAWYER@wannabe.com

3221 Litigation Drive, Sue Me, USA

Energetic and enthusiastic attorney with a keen interest in transactional law. Admitted to the Florida Bar on January 25, 1999. Seven years' experience in business building and accounting. Fluent in speaking and writing Spanish. Proficient in MS Word, MS Publisher, MS Excel, WordPerfect, Lotus 1-2-3, and Peachtree Accounting.

Strengths:

- Construction Law
- Commercial Development
- Zoning & Permitting
- Residential Closings

- Condominium Law
- Contracts
- Mechanics Liens

EDUCATION

J.D., May, 1997
University of Florida, Gainesville, FL

B.S.B.A., Accounting, May, 1991
B.A., International Studies, May, 1991
The American University, Kogod College of Business Administration, Washington, DC

PROFESSIONAL EXPERIENCE

SATURN INVESTMENT, INC., Somewhere, Florida   1997 to Present
Vice President
Direct day-to-day real estate development operations including rezoning and permitting, lease negotiations, and contracts with design professionals. Successfully managed $1.5 million service station/convenience store project from raw land through final construction; developed the business plan and secured financing.

UNIVERSITY TITLE COMPANY, Somewhere, Florida   1996
Closer
Handled residential closings as part-time employment during law school.

PAWN SHOPS, INC., Somewhere, Florida   1991 to 1994
General Manager and Account Executive
Managed 8 employees for start-up business. Grew business to 6 locations which grossed over $1 million per year. Handled daily bookkeeping and accounting functions and collected debts.

INTERNSHIPS

Accounting Firm, P.A., Somewhere, Florida
Summer Intern - Accounting, 1989 and 1990

Banco Nacionale De Buenos Aires, Buenos Aires, Argentina
Bank Intern for International Division, September - December, 1989

School of International Service, The American University
Assisted with Ford Foundation Grants, January - May, 1988

Physics Department, The American University
Lab Director's Assistant, September - December, 1987

Combination. *Cynthia Kraft, Valrico, Florida*
A full-page border helps to make this resume stand out. The opening paragraph is a profile, and the listed strengths can be adjusted easily for other job targets. See Cover Letter 159.

Charles S. Stoner

1111 Parsons Place   Montgomery, Alabama 36111   ☎ [334] 555-5555

Value to the Comstock Corporation: As your next Inventory Control Manager, get the right materials to the right place at the right time – consistently and profitably.

Skills you can use right now:

- Ability to make systems serve people
- Proven skills to help people get results
- Solid track record of holding costs down while increasing productivity

Recent work history with examples of success:

CONTRACT MANAGER   1991 – Present
Data Monitor Systems, Inc., Midwest City, Oklahoma

(Single manager of $2.8 million contract to provide shipping support to 160,000 students in the world's largest distance education program)

- Guide shipping of 390,000 packages a year – from single sheets to 70-pound boxes. **Supervise 13** people, eight with more than double my experience in this field. Oversee operation of $1.6 million in gathering, wrapping and handling equipment. *Results:* Other senior **managers from across the country seek me out** for ideas.
- Inspected on 16 work performance standards, without warning, each month. *Results:* Error rate in the last 5 years: **0.1%.**
- Use up-to-the-minute, detailed knowledge of every shipper to get the most from my $750,000 shipping budget. *Results:* Key player in introducing **more streamlined, accountable** and **accurate billing** system.
- Introduced major effort that recycles packing. *Results:* **Cut** operating **expenses 25%; overhead** in handling trash **dropped dramatically.**
- Streamlined manning to get all the jobs done faster with fewer people. *Results:* **$13,000 saved each year** in salary costs alone.
- Met with customers to better determine their needs over time. Introduced new stocking system and trained my people to use it fast. *Results:* **Cut** retrieval **time in half. Saved 200 man-hours a month.**
- Moved from three warehouses to one in 30 days **without a single disruption** in shipping. *Results:* Movers **bid $50,000,** budget was $15,000 – **I did it for $5,000.**
- Inherited disorganized, rat-infested, unsafe, 50-year-old building. *Results:* Made the facility clean and safe **without overtime.** Discarded 20 truckloads of outdated material.

18

Combination. *Donald Orlando, Montgomery, Alabama*
Another resume that begins with a Value statement rather than an Objective. Skills in three columns can be altered easily for different job targets. Shadowed square bullets are used

Charles S. Stoner **Inventory Control Manager** [334] 555-5555

Examples of success (continued):

SENIOR ANALYST, SUPPLY REPORTS 1986 – 1991
United States Air Force, Gunter Air Force Base, Alabama

(Supervised nine logistics analysts who design, develop, test and maintain the system used by 124 major installations and 277 satellite activities around the world. Senior supervisor for all line employees.)

- Developed database the Air Force uses to track 128 major supply accounts worldwide **Provided complete audit trail** for everything from high-cost items, to explosives, to security dogs: **over 100,000 line items.** Guided overhaul of software that generates 15 key management reports. *Results:* **Saved 8% processing time** for this huge program.
- Supervised major work on program that generates supply lists needed to move large corporate assets overseas with little notice. Helped define unique requirements of **nearly 300 customers.** *Results:* 90% of all deliverables on time and on spec. **Cut required computer time 70%.**

Awards:

- Outstanding Project Manager, Data Monitor Systems, Inc., 97 - 98
  Chosen over more experienced managers for this performance-based award.

Computer capabilities:

- Working knowledge: Proprietary software to track inventory, create ordering documents and generate activity reports; MOSAIC, DOS, Word for Windows 6.0
- Proficient: Course Development and Student Administration/Registrar System, Excel

Education and training:

- "Total Quality Management for Managers," United States Air Force, 96
- Training in operating, maintaining and handling the following systems:
  - Mechanized Material Handling, 95
  - High Speed, High Volume Disk Duplicating Systems, Advanced Office Products, 94
  - Collating and Packing System, Advanced Engineering, 94
- Community College of the Air Force, Business Management, Maxwell Air Force Base, Alabama, 90
- "Supervising On-The-Job-Training," United States Air Force, 73
- "Inventory Management for Mid-Level Managers," one year, United States Air Force, 68
- "Inventory Management Specialist Course," one year, United States Air Force, 64
- South Hampton College, Suffolk County, New York, attended for two years

Page two

throughout and tie together the two pages visually. In the work history, a statement in italic within parentheses explains each position. Bullets point to "examples of success." The word *Results* highlights outcomes as achievements. Many of these are quantified in dollars or percentages. See Cover Letter 188.

SCOTT A. HOUGH

11111 NW 11th Avenue, Anytown, CA 99999

555/555-5555 *(Home)*   555/555-5556 *(Fax)*   555/555-5557 *(Office)*

CUSTOMER SERVICE – THE GOLF CLUB AT SUNRISE RIVER

Combining outstanding skills in customer service, event planning, and organization with experience in multifaceted business operations

---

High-energy, results-driven professional with an entrepreneurial spirit and extensive experience providing top-quality service in a timely manner. Excellent problem-solving skills with a particularly strong orientation in customer service and satisfaction. Approachable, trustworthy, people-oriented. Proven ability to take an ordinary action and turn it into something special for clients. Particularly skilled in motivating others to generate their best performance. Seek and achieve win-win situations for company, clients, and colleagues. Display confidence and esprit de corps in leadership and team member roles. Highly flexible self-starter who eagerly accepts risk, ownership, responsibility, and decision making. Able to make individuals of all cultures, personalities, ages, and levels comfortable. Skilled in organizing and coordinating special events. Possess a passion for the game, ambiance, and sociability of golf.

Notable proficiencies include:

- Customer Relations
- Policy & Procedure Development
- Productivity Improvement
- Human Resource Management
- Seminar Development & Presentation
- Financial Management & Budgets

- Team Building & Leadership
- Group Dynamics & Motivation
- Quality Assurance
- Resource Utilization
- Project Management
- Documentation & Records

- Communications
- Organization
- Planning
- Event Planning
- Fund-Raising
- Follow-Through

Developed reputation for quality, commitment to customers, and product excellence

---

EXPERIENCE

PRESTIGE DETAILING & PARKING, Anytown, XXXX to Present   *Owner/Manager*
A downtown Anytown garage providing parking, auto detailing, and a wide range of auto/auto body needs.

*Customer
Service*

- Voted by readers of *L.A. Times Magazine, Vistas Magazine, The California Weekly*, and *The San Francisco Times* as the "Best Place to Have Your Car Detailed" and regularly described as the "Nordstrom of garages and auto servicing businesses."
- Grow and maintain a customer base of retirees, doctors, lawyers, office personnel, real estate agents, and other white-, pink-, and blue-collar workers, many for more than 25 years.
- Highlighted in *VunderKar*, the official publication of the Mercedes Automobile Club of America, in an article entitled "Details from Prestige" promoting the company's "exceptional customer service, attention to quality, and level of job knowledge."
- Generate auto-detailing business from most clients from 1 to 4 times/year.
- Lined garage walls with carpet for extra door protection of customers' vehicles.
- Services consistently booked a minimum of 2 weeks in advance.
- Turn new customers into repeat business through quality work; effective follow-up; and clear, concise explanations on how to maintain vehicles between visits.

*Communications
& Presentations*

- Developed and deliver free, 3+-hour detailing seminars for car clubs 3 times/year. Held after-hours in garage for up to 50 attendees and include care and maintenance demonstrations.

Continued

19

Combination. *Carole S. Barns, Woodinville, Washington*
An exceptional resume. Enclosed within shorter, thinner lines at the top of page 1 is first a projected motto for the club with the applicant's services in place, and then a profile of the

- Orchestrate and coordinate annual golf tournaments for the Rock 'n' Roll Golf Association, a group of amateur golfers from the music and video industry who for 20 years have operated a league.
- Volunteered as worker at the XXXX PGA Tournament at Pebble Beach.
- Participate in car club "Concourse to Elegance" events, providing product and car care demonstrations.
- Organized 2 annual fund-raisers for an Anytown church, netting record pledge amounts each year.
- Promoted and coordinated a variety of rock concerts.

Problem
Solving

- Requested by Top Notch Wax & Paint, worldwide manufacturer of auto paint and waxes, to resolve customer complaint when company representative was unavailable. Turned customer threatening Top Notch with a lawsuit into a positive, enthusiastic user of the products.
- Subcontract tune-ups, brake services, windshield replacement, and auto body repairs to meet one-stop service needs of customers.
- Regularly exceed expectations in resolving problems, resulting in loyal following of customers, many who will walk extra blocks to work and refuse free parking from employers to maintain space at Prestige.

Marketing
& Promotions

- Added full-service detailing in XXXX, quickly established a reputation as "the best" through word of mouth, advertising, and active participation in car club activities and shows.
- Selected an auto wax and paint product requiring 2 to 4 times the work for application because of excellent quality, developed strong relationship with manufacturer, and participated in cooperative advertising with the firm.
- Established long-term relationships with auto detailing product representatives who regularly provide products or services for car club fund-raising auctions.

Management

- Grew business a minimum of 10% each of last 3 years.
- Hire, train, and supervise 10 employees, including 8 full-time.
- Managed garage for 3 years prior to purchasing business.
- Manage all payroll, taxes, bookkeeping, and P&L responsibilities.

EDUCATION

B. S., Economics & Business Administration, *University of California, Berkeley*

PROFESSIONAL AFFILIATIONS

Greater Anytown Chamber of Commerce
International Keep Cars Clean Association
Vice President, Rock 'n' Roll Golf Association

individual. Proficiencies can be easily altered for another job target, but the person wants only this position. Items in the Experience section are clustered according to five categories (Customer Service, Communications & Presentations, etc.) for easier reading. What distinguishes this resume is the third page, which contains

SCOTT A. HOUGH

11111 NW 11th Avenue, Anytown, CA 99999

555/555-5555 *(Home)*   555/555-5556 *(Fax)*   555/555-5557 *(Office)*

CUSTOMER COMMENTS

"Best Place (in Anytown) to Have Your Car Detailed — Prestige Detailing & Parking" *Voted by readers of L.A. Times Magazine, Vistas Magazine, The California Weekly, The San Francisco Times*

"As a practitioner and student of business management, it was easy to observe something very special (at Prestige). I am always impressed by positive attitude, exceptional customer service, attention to quality, and level of job knowledge. From the moment I arrived…I was surrounded by people who created a welcoming experience." *Jeff Duggan, Published article in the Mercedes Automobile Club of America magazine, May XXXX*

"You do an excellent job of customer service and job performance. Thank you for *all* of your attention to the details." *Susan Quell*

"You are terrific!" *Wesley Jenson*

"Very professionally managed operation where people obviously take pride in their work." *Brent Yorkel*

"Everything was super. Not only was the job done exceptionally, the staff was extra courteous and Scott spent extra time explaining to me how to maintain my vehicle. Very sincere. Very helpful." *Leslie Misengener*

"How many ways can I say I love your attention to detail, desire to provide quality work, helpful hints, and advice." *Mark Hogen*

"Because we are a retirement home, many of Scott's customers are the frail elderly. Scott has a strong appreciation for these residents and is especially aware of their needs. He has on many occasions assisted residents. When a resident dies, I have always seen Scott at the funeral. There are several residents who like the parking service better than anything else at Graytops. That is saying a lot because there are many nice features and programs in our facility." *Patty Shortter, Administrator, Graytops Retirement Home*

"I wanted to thank you once again for your help with the case. Your effort was definitely appreciated. You went out of your way for us and we will not soon forget it. After you had a talk with (the complainant), he became delightful." *Customer Relations, Top Notch Wax & Paint, Inc.*

"I have been a client for several years. I must confess that I came to Prestige after four false starts. I was extremely disappointed with my prior arrangements. However, at Prestige, I have been totally pleased with the care provided to my car and the personalized care provided to me. You have always provided that 'something extra.' I am nothing short of pleased." *John Rens, M.D., General Hospital*

"I've always felt like your most important customer and, while I don't know any of your other monthly customers, I imagine many of them must feel that way, too. You practice principals that most businesses ignore: Remembering your customers and their needs." *Allan Akers*

"Mr. Hough is an extremely competent, pleasant and dedicated individual who runs an exemplary business. He always has the best interest of his customers at heart." *Rupert T. Nelson, M.D., Head, Colorectal Surgery, Deaconess Hospital*

"I have been parking at the Prestige for 10 years. My employer has offered me parking in my own building several times and I have declined because of the wonderful treatment and service I have received at Prestige. I can't imagine getting better service anywhere or working with a nicer or more trustworthy person." *Todd Nicholson*

"Parking at your garage has undoubtedly been the highlight of my commuting to work. Finding businesses that really care about what they are doing is difficult these days. Those of us that park at Prestige have done just that and are pleased because of it." *Eric Louder*

testimonials from a wide variety of sources: newspapers, magazines, customers, a vendor's rep, and so on. Some of the best testimonials are near the end, so reading momentum is sustained down the page. People like to read about people and their ideas, so this page makes good reading. See Cover Letter 181.

JAMES HANOVER
4 Baywood Boulevard
Brick, New Jersey 05555
Home: (555) 555-5000 • Fax: (555) 555-5005

OBJECTIVE

Seeking Building Maintenance Mechanic, Facility Supervisor, Lighting Maintenance or comparable position.

CAREER SUMMARY

- Over 16 years' experience in building maintenance and supervision for commercial structures with an additional 8 years' experience in industrial welding.
- Proficient in electrical, plumbing, and HVAC systems; carpentry; and welding.
- A conscientious, dependable, self-motivated hard worker.
- Able to get along well with people of all levels and learn new things quickly.
- Possess complete set of hand and power tools, and a valid New Jersey driver's license.

PROFESSIONAL EXPERIENCE

FIRST FIDELITY BANK • Red Bank, New Jersey • 1981 - Present
Facility Supervisor • 1994 - Present
Maintenance Technician • 1981 - 1994
Diagnose, plan, purchase supplies, and implement a variety of building maintenance tasks including electrical, plumbing, HVAC, and carpentry for commercial structures.

Conduct electrical and HVAC renovations/installations, electrical retrofits, and pole lighting installations. Run electrical circuits, trace out shorts, and change breakers. Measure and cut pipe, wire, and conduit. Diagnose electrical problems utilizing voltmeters, continuity testers, amp probes, and circuit tracers.

Familiar with electrical code, read blueprints and schematic diagrams, operate bucket trucks, and maintain a complete personal set of hand and power tools. Repair plumbing fixtures, leaks, and woodwork as needed.

EAST COAST SMELTING & REFINING • Newark, New Jersey • 1973 - 1981
Industrial Mechanic and Class A Welder
Utilized various welding techniques and knowledge of metallurgy for welding pipe fittings and small-medium (1-3 story buildings) structural steel within an international ore mining plant.

Read blueprints, met deadlines, and conformed to standards of pressure. Stepped in as Relief Foreman to cover vacation days and absences of Foreman.

EDUCATION & TRAINING

Residential Electrical Wiring Course • Ocean County Vocational-Technical School • Waretown, New Jersey
Low-Pressure Oil Burner and Heating Course • Ocean Co. Vocational-Technical School • Waretown, New Jersey
Welding & Metallurgy Course • Ocean County Vocational-Technical School • Waretown, New Jersey
Diesel Mechanics Course • Ford Diesel Mechanics School • Detroit, Michigan
Diploma • Dover High School • Vocational-Technical Concentration in Industrial Arts • Dover, New Jersey

MILITARY EXPERIENCE

Honorably discharged from United States Army during Vietnam Era.

20

Combination. *Carol Rossi, Brick, New Jersey*
This person was given three months' notice that his job was being eliminated. He had no goal in mind, so the writer put three possible jobs in the Objective. See Cover Letter 179.

Richard S. Eberhart

56 N. Penn Street • Indianapolis, Indiana 46220
(317) 555-5555 (office) • (317) 555-5556 (home)

Senior Organizational Effectiveness Executive
Multi-Industry Experience...Fortune 200 Companies...International Consulting

Demonstrated expertise managing all aspects of large-scale organizational change. Especially skilled at developing powerful business strategies and aligning organizations, business processes, and HR functions to deliver world-class standards of productivity, efficiency, and quality. Solid record of fast-track advancement, building organizational development and training functions that deliver tangible and measurable business results. Strong knowledge of leading-edge technologies that promote corporate growth, profitability and sustained organizational competitiveness.

Expertise includes conducting and managing:

Strategic Planning	Staff/Management Training	Team Development
Capability Assessment	Process Reengineering	Performance Measurement
Organization Redesign	Total Quality Management	Diversity Awareness

Career Highlights

ELI LILLY AND COMPANY, Indianapolis, Indiana   19xx to Present
(Global research-based pharmaceutical company with 29,000 employees in 156 countries and $7.3 billion in revenue)

Director of Organizational Effectiveness
Recruited to provide global leadership for a comprehensive corporate transformation process, requiring the integration of four different improvement groups into an effective consulting organization focused on strategic bottom-line performance. Manage a 30-person department with a $4 million operating budget. Report to Executive Director of HR.
- Cocreated with the Strategic Planning Group the company's first strategic planning and integrated change process, monitored by balanced scorecard measures.
- Coauthored with CEO the company's first-ever value statement, used as foundation for senior management training and implementation plans to bolster commitment of new value-based culture aligned to strategy.
- Oversaw, coordinated, and evaluated consulting activity for major process redesign projects:
  ⇒ Reduced product development cycle by more than 30%.
  ⇒ Redesigned the largest supply chain to reduce costs by $120 million.
- Lead consultant to initial transition assessment of a $4 billion acquisition. Consultant to new president on complete restructuring, governance system setup, and executive team building that stabilized and redirected critical acquisition.
- Strategically realigned and managed major corporate change efforts in the areas of TQM/Baldridge Assessments, Employee Attitude Surveys, Performance Management Systems, 360-degree Management Assessment, and Diversity.

AMOCO CORPORATION, Chicago, Illinois   19xx to 19xx
(International natural gas and petroleum refining company with 41,000 employees and $33 billion in revenue)

Practice Area Leader for Organizational Capability, Architecture, and Assessment (19xx to 19xx)
Directed the development of a new strategic organizational analysis process. Served as primary partner to the Strategic Planning Group to build a corporate-wide integrated planning system and consulting approach.
- Designed, documented, and trained internal consultants to facilitate the application of a consistent strategy format tied directly to corporate decisions.
- Facilitated multiple organizational capability assessments and action planning sessions with senior management.

21

Combination. *John A. Suarez, Troy, Illinois*
A resume with features commonly found in resumes for high-level executives: narrow margins, wide lines, smaller font size, and enough blank lines to ensure adequate white space. The

AMOCO CORPORATION (cont.)
Manager of Organizational Development and Learning Systems (19xx to 19xx)
Orchestrated the worldwide organizational development and training functions for a 14,000-employee exploration and production division. Managed multiple departments with a budget of $11.8 million. Partnered with Strategic Planning Group to direct full-scale, integrated change efforts in alignment with strategic objectives. Reported to the Vice President of HR. Third promotion in four years.

- Successfully implemented four reengineered business processes that saved $250 million annually.
- Redesigned executive management and committee processes that enhanced strategic thinking and decision making.
- Established processes that translated organization capabilities to competency profiles. Aligned strategic staffing, training, and performance management processes to ensure competency acquisition.
- Achieved "best-in-class" levels of organizational effectiveness survey results through successful implementation of major change efforts. Results increased an average of 25%.
- Created and implemented a learning organization strategy and served as corporate liaison to Peter Senge's Organizational Learning Center at MIT. Instituted company-wide, high-performance, team-building process.

Lead Organization Effectiveness Consultant (19xx to 19xx)
Senior Organization Effectiveness Consultant (19xx to 19xx)
Senior Corporate Training and Development Consultant (19xx to 19xx)

Promoted twice in two years to build start-up organizational effectiveness and training capability. Consulted to senior management by designing and facilitating high-leverage change processes that enhance organizational effectiveness. Designed and implemented first organizational effectiveness survey; an employee involvement process; recognition and reward processes; performance management processes; and a career development process.

THE SIGNATURE GROUP, Schaumburg, Illinois   19xx to 19xx
(Insurance and direct market company with 4,000 employees and profits of $78 million; subsidiary of Montgomery Ward)

Director of Service Quality and Training (19xx to 19xx)
Corporate Training and Organization Development Manager (19xx to 19xx)
Manager of Management Development (19xx to 19xx)

Promoted rapidly to increasingly responsible departmental management positions with emphasis on implementing a comprehensive customer service strategy using improved training and staffing processes, management development, and redesigned business operations.

Additional experience (19xx to 19xx): Directed campus activities and student union operations at three universities (Northwestern University, Mercer University, and University of Iowa). Provided OD consulting and held adjunct faculty positions teaching organizational and leadership development.

Professional Memberships

Organizational Development Network...Strategic Leadership Forum...World Future Society...The Human Resource Planning Society...Organizational Development Institute...American Society for Training and Development

Education

Advanced degree, Organization Development/HR Management, Columbia University, New York, NY (19xx)
Master of Arts degree, College Student Personnel/Business Management, University of Iowa, Iowa City (19xx)
Bachelor of Science degree, Psychology, University of Iowa, Iowa City (19xx)

opening paragraph summarizes the person's expertise, skills, record, and knowledge. Expertise areas can be easily altered for a different job target. Each company name is followed by an explanation in italic. Paragraphs after job titles show duties; bulleted items present achievements. See Cover Letter 192.

GEORGE NORRIS

| 4118 Carmichael Place | Sacramento, California 91000 | [916] 555-5555 |

Value to **The Flint Group**

As a **political consultant**, translate your vision into actions that serve your constituency and your senior leadership well.

Capabilities you can use now

- **Ability** to work calmly in a crisis
- **Dedication** to finish the job despite long hours
- **Intelligence** to produce "bulletproof" analyses

Work history with selected examples of results

- **Instructor in American Government,** Sacramento Junior College, Sacramento, California Mar 97 – Present
- Intern, *promoted to* **Political Policy Coordinator**, Central Valley Farmers' Federation, Sacramento, California, Feb – Nov 96

  - Completed detailed survey that couldn't be handled by computer. Wrote paper that analyzed results, proposed solutions, and made solid recommendations. *Results:* Senior decision makers **approved my paper virtually without change**. Edited proposed **Congressional testimony based on my work.**
  - Found and fixed potential problem with data supporting electoral projections just a week before the deadline. *Results:* Our team called **11 out of 12 outcomes correctly.**
  - Gathered vital financial and organizational material using in-house capabilities that had been overlooked for years. *Results:* **Key information available faster than ever.**
  - Helped handle crisis when bill we supported was about to be ambushed in a House floor fight. Answered pressing questions from legislators and other key players. *Results:* **Bought time my boss needed** to get fully involved.

- **Freelance Political Researcher,** Merced and Stockton, California Jan – May 96

  - Uncovered full details of opponent's media campaign in tough tax issue. *Results:* **My client** able to launch **successful** counter campaign. Issue decided **in our favor two to one.**

Education

- M.A., **Political Science**, GPA 3.69, University of the Sierras, Sacramento, 95 Completed while working up to 30 hours a week
- B.A., **History** (minor in **Political Science**), Dean's List of **High Honors** two semesters, Foot Hills College, Grass Valley, California 93

Computer literacy

- Working knowledge: WordPerfect, StatPac 4.4, Westlaw, Alert **(legislation tracking)**
- Proficient: **Lexis/Nexis**

Professional credentials

- Registered lobbyist with the State of California

22

Combination. *Donald Orlando, Montgomery, Alabama*
Centered, sentence-style headings in shaded bars make this resume different. It begins with a Value statement. Unique bullets unify visually the other sections. See Cover Letter 203.

Lisa Reynolds 333 Daffodil Lane ★ Central Park ★ New York 00000 ★ (555) 555-5555

OBJECTIVE — Entry-level opportunity to become involved in the various phases of television programming and production.

EDUCATION — PENNYPACK COLLEGE, Philadelphia, PA
B.A. Communication with concentration in TV Production, December 19XX. GPA 3.8 in major.

HIGHLIGHTS of BACKGROUND and TRAINING

Studio Production

★ Held rotating responsibilities on student team producing and directing "High School Bowl," a half-hour game show, and "Focus on Pennypack," a political commentary show broadcast from college's facilities through local cable access. Demonstrated exceptional organizational skills in coordinating the different aspects of production and was chosen most frequently for floor manager/director position.

Technical Expertise

★ Developed hands-on ability to operate a broad range of equipment which included television cameras, audio boards, Chyron/character generator, Abeckas/special effects designer, VTR, video switcher, and prompter. Also had brief experience with videotape editing.

Programming

★ Assisted with preliminary interviews and auditions to determine acceptability of guests to appear before camera.
★ Scheduled program lineup for regular and alternative time slots.

Creative Writing

★ Wrote a one-act play that was retained as a model for other students.
★ Organized and developed a 130-page movie script from original idea, receiving grade of "A."
★ Composed public service announcements, slogans and jingles aired on cable TV station.

Administrative Capabilities

★ Used computer for general word processing tasks; ran errands; screened and responded to phone calls; arranged for guest accommodations/transportation; researched material for news stories.

Performing Arts

★ Since age 5, performed before audiences in acting, dancing and singing disciplines. Exposed to behind-the-scenes theatrical environment involving interaction with directors and actors of different temperaments.
★ Acted in commercial for a popular cleaning product in 19XX, gaining admission to Screen Actors Guild.
★ Through association with Mindy's School of Dance, assisted teacher with tap, jazz, ballet and gymnastic performances, and was given lead role in most productions.
★ Won numerous trophies in dance competitions over 15 years. Achieved national finals as participant in duet and trio acts, 19XX-XX.
★ Commended by Drama/Improv instructor at Pennypack College for exemplary student presentations.
★ Performed in following community theatre productions:
  — Played smallest orphan in Annie at Pocono Dinner Theatre, 19XX.
  — Won Best Bit Actress award for dancing and speaking part of angel/showgirl in Anything Goes at Red Barn Theatre, Montrose, PA, 19XX.

OTHER WORK EXPERIENCE

CASHIER/SALES ASSISTANT — THE JEWELRY BOX, PHILADELPHIA, PA — 19XX
CASHIER — SUPER FRESH FOOD MARKET, UPTOWN, PA — 19XX

23

Functional. *Melanie A. Noonan, West Paterson, New Jersey*
Contact information running vertically with a thick vertical bar is the distinctive design feature of this resume. Highlights are grouped by six topics. See Cover Letter 213.

MICHAEL BAIR
0000 Money Lane
Dollarsville, GA
(000) 000-0000

SUMMARY

Results-oriented account manager with solid experience in all aspects of industrial supplies sales . . . Demonstrated ability promoting company goals and image . . . Established record of problem solving and meeting customer needs to consistently generate top sales . . . Research and evaluate competition to develop and implement sales strategies . . . Pursue personal and professional growth through study and application of proven ability to create win-win opportunities for all parties involved . . . Strong communication skills . . . Proven organizational and follow-through skills.

PROFESSIONAL EXPERIENCE

MARTIN INDUSTRIAL SUPPLY COMPANY, Marion, OH   XXXX - Present
    Account Manager, Outside Sales Representative   XXXX - Present
- Responsible for Marion / Bowling Green sales territory.
- Increased sales 40% in first year as account manager.
- Consistently meet and exceed sales goals.
- Develop ongoing customer relationships, enhancing future sales.
- Successfully sell "superb customer service."
- Perform inside sales rep responsibilities.

    Inside Sales Representative   XXXX - XXXX
- Made scheduled calls and cold calls.
- Established customer / company relations.
- Performed sales and invoice activities.
- Trained new employees.
- Pulled / Packaged orders.
- Assisted in Shipping / Receiving / Inventory.

HELMSLEY & WAGNER FUNERAL HOME, Marion, OH   XXXX - XXXX
    Trained in all aspects of the business.

HAMILTON INN, Georgetown, WA   XXXX - XXXX
    Assistant Banquet Manager / Banquet Captain
- Trained and supervised up to twenty employees.

EDUCATION

Associate of Arts Degree, Community College, Georgetown, WA	XXXX
Industry-Specific Seminars and Classes	XXXX - Present
Engineering and Flight Management, Saginaw State University, Ball, MA	XXXX - XXXX
Real Estate Law, Hamilton Community College, Hamilton, MA	XXXX - XXXX

24

Combination. *Peggy Weeks, Battle Creek, Michigan*
A horizontal line above each section heading enables you to size up the shape of the resume at a glance. Ellipses (. . .) separate Summary statements. See Cover Letter 222.

JENNIFER JAMES

4 Baywood Boulevard
Brick, New Jersey 05555
Phone: (555) 555-5000 • E-Mail: jjames@aol.com

CAREER SUMMARY

- Over 6 years' experience in the fashion industry including merchandising, management, and retail/wholesale sales.
- Strong communication and interpersonal skills with coworkers, supervisors, and customers.
- Solid leadership and motivational skills with the ability to prioritize multiple tasks.
- A self-motivated, highly organized, and dependable team player Knowledge of WordPerfect and e-mail software programs.

PROFESSIONAL EXPERIENCE

RALPH LAUREN INC. • USA • November - December XXXX Holiday Season
Assistant Merchandising Coordinator
Assisted coordinator in merchandising men's, denim, and children's sportswear within high-end clothing stores including Macy's, Bloomingdale's, and Lord & Taylor. Merchandised independently utilizing self-originated display ideas. Developed excellent working rapport with staff.

UPSCALE LEATHERS (Sold handbags & accessories) • New York, New York • 1993 - 1995
Sales Associate
Provided individual client consultations and recommendations. Managed daily store operations, calculated daily receipts, and compiled sales reports. Trained staff regarding proper sales techniques and accessorizing fashions. Delegated daily tasks to appropriate personnel.

INSTITUTE FOR FASHION INDUSTRIES • Short Hills, New Jersey • 1991 - 1993
Senior Student Researcher (Full-time internship)
Organized fashion seminars. Attended workshops covering merchandising, marketing, and manufacturing. Conducted research during fashion shows to identify current trends. Organized supervisor's daily agendas. Completed high-volume word processing and general office duties.

MACY'S INC. • Short Hills Mall, Short Hills, New Jersey • 1988 - 1990
Assistant Manager
Created visual merchandising displays for women's clothing. Supervised staff of 10-12 associates. Increased sales volume through shortage/theft elimination and staff training. Completed daily, weekly, and monthly sales reports.

OTHER EXPERIENCE

OCEAN DERMATOLOGISTS • Toms River, New Jersey • 1997 - Present
Receptionist (Part-time: Concurrent with Sand Piper Restaurant)
Organize daily operations of physician's office: schedule patients, pull patient charts, and prepare insurance paperwork for processing. Act as liaison between patients and physician. Answer telephones in a friendly, professional manner.

SAND PIPER RESTAURANT • Belmar, New Jersey • 1995 - Present
Bartender • 1995 - Present (Part-time: concurrent with Ocean Dermatologists)
Train new employees, resolve customer problems, attractively arrange bottles/glasses, and maintain accurate cash drawers.
- Performed assistant manager duties 1995 - 1996 including scheduling of 10-15 staff members.
- Certified bartender through TAM (Techniques of Alcohol Management).

EDUCATION & TRAINING

Accessory Design Studies Program • Fashion Institute of New Jersey • Short Hills, New Jersey • 1990 - 1992, and 1993 - 1994
~ Alumni Affairs Vice President   ~ Student Government Executive Board   ~ Leadership Workshop Attendance
Fashion Coordination Course • Rutgers University • New Brunswick, New Jersey • Spring 1993
AA Degree in Liberal Arts • Georgian Court College • Lakewood, New Jersey • 1990

25

Combination. *Carol Rossi, Brick, New Jersey*
This resume has the look of an executive resume. Centered headings make it possible to read down the center and see quickly the resume's organization. See Cover Letter 224.

GEORGE B. TURNER

5555 Westchase Drive ❖ Tampa, Florida 33600
Home: (813) 000-0000 ❖ Office: (813) 555-0000

SENIOR MARKETING / SALES MANAGEMENT PROFESSIONAL

Top producer with notable success in executive-level selling, building high-profile market presence, customer relationship management, direct response marketing campaigns, and driving revenue growth in highly competitive markets nationwide.

PROFESSIONAL SUMMARY

Dynamic career reflecting a track record of successive advancement and well-defined experience in areas such as sales cycle management, business development, consultative sales, new product launches, and market positioning. Equal talents in strategic and tactical planning, program management, upholding fiscal efficiency, resource administration, contract negotiations, and account management/retention. Steadfast leader with well-honed skills in directing tactical sales training programs, team building, facilitating an efficient infrastructure, and overachieving business objectives. Offer effective written/verbal communications; positive attitude—respond effectively to changing market demands; and demonstrated ability to build, produce and succeed.

AREAS OF CORE COMPETENCY

Sales Management
- **Goal-Directed** - Success defined as year-over-year improvement in revenue growth while delivering customer satisfaction, achieving corporate objectives, and improving internal productivity and efficiency. **Named number one Sales Manager nationally for Supplies Marketing and Sales Organization in 1993. Finished in top five nationally from 1990 to 1995.**

Sales/Market Planning
- **Action-Oriented** - Structure and implement results-driven decisions in a timely and effective manner with a pace dictated by the marketplace. **Served as member of Sales Managers Advisory Council to Senior Management.**

Business Development
- **Market-Connected** - Conversant with dynamics of today's marketplace. Key role in directing competitive market intelligence, with focus on positioning value-added services, launching new products, developing long-term customer relationships, and accelerating revenue performance.

Financial Management
- **Bottom-Line Driven** - Directly accountable for management of $50M+ in business. **Increased revenue growth from $15M to $53M in five years.**

Steadfast Leadership
- **Team Building** - Encourage openness, candor, and honesty. Consistently recognized for assisting in the success of others and minimizing unproductive conflict while encouraging diverse opinions and constructive debate. **Member of National Task Force that designed and developed a District Engagement Process launched nationally in 1992.**

Sales Training/Mentoring
- **Communication Skills** - Initiated and conducted innovative and tactical training and marketing programs. Utilize an empowering management process to establish realistic expectations with proactive processes and objectives for measuring business results. **Recognize and reward performance for improved morale and loyalty.**

EDUCATION

UNIVERSITY OF MIAMI, Florida
Bachelor of Science degree - Biology/Chemistry

KANSAS JUNIOR COLLEGE, Kansas
Associate of Arts degree

26

Combination. *Diane McGoldrick, Tampa, Florida*
The shadowed box with a four-line border is easily spotted at a distance. Partial horizontal lines point to the person's name and headings in small caps. In the Areas of Core Competencies

GEORGE B. TURNER

EMPLOYMENT SUMMARY

COPY CORPORATION, Tampa, Florida   1969 - Present
Outstanding record of peak performance throughout tenure has provided progressive opportunities for career growth.

<u>**Focused Account Manager**</u> - *Copy Business Services Organization* (1/98 - Present)
Spearhead two targeted market segments — Government of State of Florida and Copy Agent Channel. Charged with diverse scope of responsibilities emphasizing the growth of new business and revenue streams.

- **Successfully negotiated, closed, and implemented a unique state consulting services contract that served as a nationwide benchmark for the industry.**

<u>**Manager, Strategic Outsourcing**</u> (4/97 -1/98)
Directed Advanced Business Services and Technological Solutions Team, accountable for generating new account growth and strengthening existing account revenue.

- **Facilitated cross-functional relationships and engaged resources.**

<u>**Supply Sales Manager**</u> - *Supplies Marketing & Sales Organization* (1/88 - 4/97)
Managed a team of 10 Supply Account Managers dedicated to full-time sales of supplies product line. Geographic territory included Florida, Alabama, Mississippi, Virginia, and Washington, D.C.

- **Demonstrated ability to significantly increase sales growth and achieve leadership objectives.**
- **Recipient of President's Club Achievement for nine consecutive years.**

<u>**Manager, Contract Marketing**</u> (1/86 12/87)
Identified, negotiated, closed and implemented corporate ventures into third-party service business.

- **Established strong alliances with NationsBank, Boeing, and Baptist Medical Center.**

<u>**Regional Association Marketing Manager/Special Markets**</u> (1/83 - 1/86)
Negotiated direct mail/market share growth programs with third parties and integrated direct marketing operations with Major Accounts Organization on state and national levels. Specific emphasis focused on net additions, profitability, revenue growth and expense control.

- **Achieved program placement with AT&T Opportunity Calling, Chase, Eastern Airlines, Stouffer's Hotel, USA Today, Century 21, National AFL-CIO, Florida AFL-CIO, Diner's Club, and American Postal Worker's Union.**

<u>**Sales Planning Manager**</u> - *Information System Division* (1/81 - 1/83)
Interviewed, recruited, hired and trained new sales representatives. Initiated introduction of new products, conducted recognition meetings, and taught improvement of skill levels. Managed six customer support representatives and administered college relations program.

<u>**Account Manager**</u> (7/69 - 1/81)
Upheld progressive sales positions involving a full range of major account segments for a broad base of commercial, government, educational, and medical markets.

- **Earned numerous PAR and attained President Club status for exceptional performance.**

PROFESSIONAL DEVELOPMENT

- Managing In Copy Corporation
- Middle Management School
- P.S.S. - Professional Selling Skills
- Leadership Through Quality (LTQ)
- Problem Solving Process (PSP)
- Total Quality Company Diagnosis (TQC)
- Building Support and Coalitions
- Systems Literacy
- Sales Planning Manager Seminar

- Management Effectiveness Studies
- Basic and Advanced Sales Schools
- Spin Selling Skills
- Measures of Quality
- Competitive Benchmarking
- Diversity Training
- Negotiating
- Manager as a Coach
- Vertical Markets Sales Training

section, the areas are doubly focused with side headings in italic and underlined, embedded headings. In the Employment Summary, job titles are bold and underlined. The paragraph after each job title indicates responsibilities, and bullets and boldfacing emphasize achievements. See Cover Letter 231.

Gerald Levitan
516-555-5555

32 Osage Drive
Garden City, NY 11530

 Recent Graduate with International Business Focus

Profile

Academic background in International Business, Marketing, Economics, and History, including a semester of study in Great Britain. Practical foundation of administrative, supervisory, computer, and organizational skills acquired from broad-based part-time work experience.

Enthusiastic, resourceful and trainable. Offer old-fashioned work ethic and excellent prioritization abilities developed through balancing of rigorous academic and employment objectives throughout high school and college. Will do whatever is necessary to get a job done.

Education

Bachelor of Science in Business
New York University. New York, NY   May, xxxx

Concentration: International Business and Economics   Minor: History   Member: Italian Club
Representative courses: Marketing, Economics, Accounting, Business Information Systems, Management, Corporate Finance, International Trade and Investments, Business Law, Statistics, Quantitative Methods, International Relations, History and Culture of Africa.

University of London. London, England   Spring, xxxx

Studied British and Western European life and culture from medieval times to present.
Gained a valuable overview of European economic and social culture through travel throughout Great Britain, Ireland, France, Italy, Germany, Austria, Belgium, and the Netherlands. Observed European and British cultural differences, economic and business practices, currency exchange, Euro Dollar conversion process, and national political environments.

Business Experience

Acquired International import-export exposure with UPS. Learned to work in high-pressure, quick-response disaster environment with Red Cross. Gained supervisory and training knowledge from NYU's Arts' Department. Experienced working in local government with Nassau County.

Visual / Performing Arts' Assistant	New York University, New York, NY	1999 to xxxx
Estée Lauder Assembler / Auditor	Grover Packaging, NY	1998 to 1999
International Audit and Key Entry Clerk	United Parcel Service, NY	1998
Audit and Control Clerk	Nassau County Government, NY	1997
Flight 800 Disaster Administrative Aid	Red Cross, NY	1996

Computer and Communication Skills

Working Knowledge of Microsoft Word, Excel, and Access; WordPerfect; Windows 95/3.1 and DOS. Familiar with Quattro Pro. Accomplished writer and editor.

27

Functional. *Deborah Wile Dib, Medford, New York*
Display type is used for the contact information, a headline, and section headings. Of 200 applicants, five were interviewed. This individual was offered the job. See Cover Letter 233.

Miosho Nigushi

5555 Orange Lane, Belmont, CA 99999, (666) 666-6666

MARKETING COMMUNICATIONS / PRODUCT MARKETING

- Highly motivated Marketing Coordinator experienced with Japanese markets and OEMs.
- Excellent interpersonal and bilingual communication skills. Expert at person-to-person interpreting and translating verbiage for collateral materials.
- Familiar with both American and Japanese cultures, able to coach engineers and sales staff on improving business relationships and marketing strategies.
- Well organized with proven ability to handle multiple projects within budgets and deadlines.

Computer Skills: Word, Excel, PowerPoint, PageMaker, PageMill, Illustrator, Photoshop, HTML. Proficient in both Windows and Macintosh platforms.

MAXISYNC CORPORATION, Santa Clara, CA   XXXX-Present
Marketing Coordinator/Japanese Product Marketing

Facilitate Japanese subsidiary in promoting synchronization software. Report to Director of Product Marketing and work closely with VPs, Engineering, and Sales.

- Create Japanese brochures, data sheets, packaging and other collateral materials, and work with graphics companies in designing advertising.
- Coordinate Japanese-related marketing events: press releases, trade shows, seminars and co-marketing on the Web with OEMs.
- Edit Japanese documentation and on-line help to ensure ease of use and uniformity of terminology. Designed and maintain Maxisync's Japanese Web site.
- Developed Press Kits consisting of company profile, data sheets, statistical information, and trial software for OEMs: Toshiba, Sony, Panasonic, Sharp, Cassio, NEC, Canon.
- > Helped create name recognition and retail presence for American-based company in Japan, triggering interest in feature articles from Japanese *PC Week* and mobile magazines.

NYSHIAMA TECHNOLOGIES, Cupertino, CA   19XX-19XX
Sales Support Representative, Import Division

- Interpreted and translated between U.S. engineers and those at Japanese manufacturers for exchanging critical information on specifications.
- Created sales presentations and provided post-sale assistance in expediting deliveries.
- Coordinated with trade show management and Marketing in creating a triple-unit booth space at Semicon in San Francisco and Diskcon in San Jose.
- > Facilitated good working relationships that resulted in million-dollar sales

Desktop Publisher, FAIRCHILD RESOURCES, INC., Pottstown, PA   19XX-19XX
Produced collateral materials, newsletters, reports, and overhead and slide presentations.

Interpreter/Translator, JAPAN INSTITUTE, Pittsburgh, PA   19XX-19XX
Interpreted for business and legal proceedings; translated documents and computer manuals.

EDUCATION:

B.A., Sociology (Spanish minor), Pennsylvania University
- Volunteer Event Planner, International Student Organization

28

Combination. *Ms. Sydney J. Reuben, Menlo Park, California*
The first section serves as a profile and a summary of skills. Under job titles, bullets point to duties and activities. Greater-than signs (>) point to achievements. See Cover Letter 235.

ROBERT SILVER

13245 Fidel Avenue	(302) 453-9087
Seattle, Washington 90789	robertsilver@mci.com

MARKETING PLANNING & RESEARCH
Research Project Management ▪ Strategic Planning ▪ Brand Management

Professional Profile

Goal-driven professional with 16+ years' proven performance with Avia Corporation, including nine years of experience conducting market research, tracking athletic footwear markets and developing business strategies. Thoroughly familiar with the global market, including key regional and country market sizes. Solid understanding of marketing segments, size, consumer purchasing behavior, demographics, market structure and competitor positioning.

- Skilled in evaluating market conditions and implementing strategies and products to capitalize on market trends.
- Effective in communicating with marketing staff, brand planners, category business managers and strategic planners.
- Computer literate (PC and Macintosh; Word, Excel, PowerPoint, FileMaker, Internet applications).

Experience

AVIA CORPORATION – Issaquah, Washington

Manager, Market Intelligence / Global Consumer Insights Department (3/92-12/98)
As integral member of marketing team, conducted research that provided insights on market structure and dynamics, competitors' positioning strategies and consumer purchasing behavior. Prepared presentations and reports that analyzed strengths and weaknesses of current marketing plans; identified opportunities and threats posed by competitors.

- Developed global network of research managers and oversaw the preparation of market share reports.
- Evaluated, compared and recommended research methodologies.
- Analyzed and recommended custom and syndicated research to foster in-depth understanding of sports participation in the U.S. and other key countries.

Senior Market Research Analyst (2/89-3/92)
Researched, compiled and published global competitor and industry profiles. Managed marketing library and directed the preparation of quantitative studies, surveys and secondary research projects to support athletic footwear marketing.

- Compiled and published annual *Marketing Insights Compendium.*
- Advised senior managers and played a key role in strategic planning company-wide.

Earlier Positions:
- Information Specialist / Information Analyst (6/87-2/89)
- Product Line Manager (5/84-6/87)
- Forecasting Analyst (2/82-5/84)

Education

PORTLAND STATE UNIVERSITY – Portland, Oregon
B.S. Business Administration (1982)

29

Combination. *Pat Kendall, Aloha, Oregon*
Lines enclosing contact information make it easy to see. The Profile paragraph shows experience, and bullets point to skills. Later bullets show achievements. See Cover Letter 237.

SHANNON R. STANFORD

17 Hillside Avenue • Smithfield, Rhode Island 12345 • (555) 555-5555

KEY QUALIFICATIONS

- BS in Business Management, Boston University.
- Proven expertise in planning, coordinating and implementing all facets of multilayered projects, including industry analyses and promotional strategies.
- Superb interpersonal, presentation, and communication skills, both oral and written.
- Flexible and adaptable; team task oriented; strong fashion sense.
- Willing to relocate.

ACHIEVEMENTS

- Proposed, organized and implemented all aspects of first citywide fashion show in Smithfield, Rhode Island. Created stage design, recruited sponsors, selected garments and accessories, and hired models. Generated profits for all merchandisers involved.
- Winner of Congressman Ronald Little Community Leadership Award.
- Selected as an Orientation Counselor for this highly competitive program at Boston University. Led group of twenty-two students through a four-day orientation program. Facilitated workshops that helped new students transition to campus life.

PROFESSIONAL EXPERIENCE

PAN GLOBAL AIRLINES   XXXX- present
Flight Attendant -- Maintain positive relationships with passengers on both domestic and international flights. Ensure a safe and comfortable flight for crew and passengers. Successfully resolve any passenger complaints.
- Act as Chief Purser: make all announcements and act as intermediary in passenger disputes.
- Received many "Going the Extra Mile" awards for superb service.

AMERICAN AIRBORNE AIRLINES   XXXX - XXXX
Flight Attendant -- Provided excellent customer service to passengers and crew.
- Received several commendations as a result of passenger satisfaction review cards.

THE ULTIMATE EXPRESS   SUMMER XXXX
Sales Associate -- Assisted customers and store managers with daily floor operations. Created, coordinated, and set up special displays for store.

EDUCATION

BOSTON UNIVERSITY -- BOSTON, MASSACHUSETTS
BS in Business Management, XXXX.
Major: Management   Concentration: International Business
- Produced an in-depth automobile industry analysis as part of a Seniors' Management Team project

AWARDS / MEMBERSHIPS / VOLUNTEER EXPERIENCE

- First Runner Up -- Miss Teen Rhode Island, XXXX
- First Runner Up -- Rhode Island Young Woman of the Year, XXXX
- Member, International Business Society
- Volunteer, Rhode Island Association for Retarded Citizens

30

Combination. *Mary Sward Hurley, Smithfield, Rhode Island*
Centered headings enable you to look down the middle of the page and size up the resume.
Superb, strong, and *excellent* are effective power words. See Cover Letter 239.

JANET R. SALES

33333 Woodmere Avenue ● Kansas City, Kansas 66666
HM: (913) 555-5555 ● Email: JSales@aol.com

EXECUTIVE SALES / MANAGEMENT

10+ years' successful experience demonstrated by a solid history of achievements, steady advancements, and increased accountabilities. Results-oriented dependable professional with a strong work ethic and management style that reflect a "Can do!" attitude. Confident and competent decision maker. Effective team developer, leader, and contributor working with all levels of management , staff, and customers. Areas of expertise include:

National / Key Account Management ● **Sales Training / Development** ● **Market / Account Analysis**
Field Supervision ● **Merchandising** ● **Promotions / Special Events Coordination**

PROFESSIONAL HISTORY

FISHER PRICE, INC. - International toy manufacturer with over $350 million in US operations.   1986 to Present

Regional Operations Manager – St. Louis, MO, and Kansas City, KS (01/96 to Present)
Senior field sales position with $97 million central region in highly competitive retail toy markets. Development of senior middle managers of national accounts. Liaison to National Account Executives and Regional Sales Managers. Extensive training of District Sales Representatives. Account analysis and sales forecasting. Train and direct Regional Promotional Coordinator; oversee special events and promotions.
- Drove regional sales to a 19% increase Year-to-Date '98 versus '97.
- National account development and management for Kmart (854 stores), Wal-Mart (665 stores), Target (461 stores), Toys R Us (268 stores).
- Implemented new promotional programs to optimize high-volume account sales.

Market Manager – St. Louis, MO (07/93 to 01/96)
Multifunctional accountabilities:
Southwest Regional Trainer: Hired, trained, and developed 9 Sales Representatives in all aspects of territory management, middle management development, independent and key account management, and merchandising.
Merchandiser Coordinator: Hired, trained, and directed 35 full-time and 15 seasonal Merchandisers. Controlled promotional budget.
- Maintained high employee retention due to quality training and positive personnel management.
- Significantly reduced turnover as a direct result of restructuring duties, benefits, and pay.

Territory Manager – St. Louis, MO (07/90 to 07/93)
Plan, control, and direct $10 million, four-state sales territory.
- Grew key account to $2.1m from $925,000 within 5 years.
- Awarded Regional M. V. P. for outstanding territory management and execution of company objectives.
- "High Flyer Award" (out of 12 Territory Managers nationwide) based on demonstrated leadership abilities.
- Named "Head Trainer"- Southwest Region.
- Received "Vendor of the Year" award (Venture Stores) based on maintaining excellent buying staff relations, managing flow of goods, promotional program management, and contribution to sales.

Territory Representative – St. Louis, MO (08/87 to 07/90)
Managed three-state sales territory - key accounts and middle management development.
- Took start-up account from $0 to $120k in retail sales.
- Grew and managed Independent accounts to $125k from $45K.
- Awarded Southwest Region M. V. P. Award, 1989.

(Continued...)

Combination. *Karen D. Wrigley, Round Rock, Texas*
Thick-thin lines are used for the page borders and to enclose the opening section, which is a profile that also indicates areas of expertise. These are listed horizontally and separated by

JANET R. SALES

PROFESSIONAL HISTORY... (Continued)

FISHER PRICE, INC. - Continued

Sales Representative Trainee / Sales Representative – St. Louis, MO (02/86 to 08/87)
- Start-up of two-state sales territory and 90 retail accounts – recruiting, hiring merchandising staff, developing two middle managers, and developing 15 independent accounts.

INDEPENDENT EUROPEAN TRAVEL   1985 to 1985
- Gained international experience while backpacking independently through England, Greece, Eastern Germany, and Spain.

ABC TEMPORARIES - Contract employment agency.   1984 to 1984

Accounts Manager – Houston, TX
- Developed branch from start-up and doubled revenues in three months.

NOLANDE CORPORATION - Contract employment agency.   1983 to 1984

Territory Manager – Houston, TX   (11/83 to 07/84)
- Achieved 120% of annual sales quota.

Sales Representative - Houston, TX (05/83 to 11/83)
- Promoted to Territory Manager within six months.

EDUCATION
Bachelor of Science in Business Administration – UNIVERSITY of KANSAS, XXXX

Honors: President of Upsilon Upsilon Upsilon Social Sorority
National Honor Society
Business Placement Council

PROFESSIONAL / CIVIC AFFILIATIONS
Fund-raising Committee Chairperson 'XX to 'XX for Court Appointed Special Advocate (CASA)

Excellent References Provided on Request

bullets. If you read the person's professional history from end to beginning, you can trace her career from some successful temporary jobs, to some travel, and then to her place of permanent employment, where her career record is one of steady growth with promotions almost every three years. See Cover Letter 250.

Judith Thompson
P. O. Box 10045
Fall City, Washington 90000
(000) 000-0000

Highlights of Qualifications

- *Master of Education in Guidance and Counseling with a GPA of 3.38.*
- *Experience working with at-risk youth and chemically dependent clients on an individual and group setting basis.*
- *Intuitive, perceptive, and nonjudgmental; ability to inspire client trust and motivation.*
- *Use creativity, resourcefulness, and knowledge of community resources to problem-solve and help clients implement goals.*
- *Understand and encourage each client's fundamental need to communicate honestly about life experiences.*
- *Work to identify, acknowledge, and cultivate clients' strengths and abilities.*
- *Team-oriented; work well with diverse personalities and cultures at all economic levels.*
- *Accurate, organized, and reliable; basic familiarity with computers.*

Education

City University, Bellevue, WA; *Master of Education in Guidance & Counseling, xxxx*

Antioch University, Seattle, WA; *Bachelor of Arts in Psychology, xxxx; course work in CDC*

Registration & Certification

Registered Counselor, Washington State--effective through xxxx (RC00000000)

Educational Staff Associate Certification in Counseling K-12

Relevant Experience

Somewhere School District, Somewhere, WA; *Counselor Intern*   9/94-6/96
- Provided counseling services for at-risk youth and families in a culturally diverse setting.
- Through interviewing, screening, and assessment, determined a need for anger management groups; subsequently implemented and facilitated these successful groups which were especially tailored for at-risk youth. All students experienced growth at some level.
- Routinely worked with students and families who had issues surrounding:

| – Chemical dependency | – Low academic skills | – Suicidal tendencies |
| – Violence and abuse | – Divorce/Single parenting | – Aggression and anger |

- Earned respect and trust of students, parents, and staff.

> *"(Judith) brings depth and honesty and outstanding guidance skills to her work as a Counselor. . . Judith . . . interacts with students in an understanding and empathic way. She is a person who truly cares about the well being of others and is delightfully courteous and professional in all her dealings."*
> -Joseph Jones, M.A., M.S., Counselor/Supervisor, Somewhere High School, June 1996

32

Combination. *Kathryn Vargo, Issaquah, Washington*
The contact information, the Education and Certification sections, and the testimonials are more easily seen because of their enclosure within borders or horizontal lines. Shading

Judith Thompson

Page 2

Relevant Experience, continued

Cedar Branch Treatment Center, Somewhere, WA; *Counselor Intern*   2/93-6/93
  Completed 250 hours toward certification for Chemical Dependency Counseling
- In this culturally and economically diverse environment, provided counseling services for a population in crisis with issues surrounding chemical dependency.
- Working under direction of a counselor, co-facilitated groups with dual diagnoses (MICA).
- Counseled individuals of all ages (from 18 through 70s) who had extremely traumatic backgrounds with issues surrounding:

– Chemical dependency	– Homelessness	– Posttraumatic stress disorder
– Violence / Abuse	– Unemployment	– Sexual orientation
– Mental illness	– Physical illness	– Vocational training

- Routinely interacted with and gained assistance for clients through State and County agencies including CPS, ADC, DSHS, and King County DASAS.
- Earned clients' respect and trust by approaching each person as an individual. Used perception, empathy, and a broad knowledge of counseling methods to begin the healing process.
- Communicated consistently with psychiatrist so medication effects could be monitored and dosages adjusted for optimum benefit.

Additional Experience includes

Caterer/Lead Cook/Manager for various Pacific Northwest restaurants (7 years)
  – Experience included supervision of a teenage crew.

Nutrition Consultant, Mrs. Webster's, Los Angeles, CA, 1986-1989
  – Created new recipes and taught cooking classes.

Private Household Chef, employed by World Renowned Celebrities, Malibu, CA, 1983-1986
  – Created / prepared healthful gourmet cuisine; cared for celebrity couple's children.

> *"Miss Thompson was at all times courteous, thoughtful and responsible, and she was exceedingly gentle with our children." –*World Renowned Celebrities, 1984

Community Activities

Coordinator and Facilitator for AA and ACA groups in the Somewhere Valley, 1983-Present

References are readily available.

directs attention to the bulleted "issues" in the Relevant Experience section. The Highlights of Qualifications section serves as a profile of the individual. Although testimonials don't provide much information, their influence can be exceptionally helpful, especially in nonchronological resumes. See Cover Letter 274.

Britain Jesse Walker

P.O. Box 555 □ Blue River, WI 55555 □ (555) 555-5555

Qualifications

- Over a decade of sales success, consistently the company's best in sales
- Project management experience with multimillion-dollar projects
- Easily learn new product lines, highly technical data, design specifications
- Experienced presenter, conducting seminars as well as product demonstrations and contract negotiations
- Analytical thinker with incredibly productive problem-solving abilities
- Resolute and determined; proactive in all areas, particularly in sales
- Intensely loyal and unfailingly dependable; flawless reputation for high ethical standards, honesty, and service after the sale

Career Highlights

- Designed and implemented a customized selling system that increased job gross profits from 7% to 150%
- Built company's outside sales division from zero to $3 million annually
- Negotiated an annual $6 million national contract with Union Carbide ($1.5 million annually for West Virginia)
- Over five years, developed and negotiated exclusive contract covering all state universities
- Consistently ranked as company's top salesperson for the past eight years

Professional Experience

Holyman Manufacturing, Richland Center, WI   1986-Present
Manufacturer's Representative for Craigo Scientific
Sales Representative for all of Wisconsin

- Market high-end line of chemical fumehoods, cabinets and countertops; service fixtures and alarm systems for chemical laboratories
- Consult with architects and engineers in design, layout, ordering, and installation; a typical project averages two years, with a contract sales price in excess of $400,000
- Develop new leads and complete bid specifications while simultaneously managing 15 to 20 ongoing projects across the state
- Outstanding communication skills at all levels: make presentations to upper management, negotiate contracts, consult with design teams, and coordinate installation process
- Successfully close high-bid contracts with incomparable customized service

Education

- Wisconsin Career College, Secretarial Sciences Diploma, 1985-1986
- In-house and manufacturer training, including:
  - Project Management Training
  - Product Specifications and Installation Design
  - Sales Training

33

Combination. *Barbie Dallmann, Charleston, West Virginia*
White-on-black section headings running vertically at the left margin leap from the page to catch your attention and direct your eye to the person's name. See Cover Letter 263.

ARTHUR C. BARRY

220 Newbrand Store Road
Athens, Georgia 30000
(222) 222-2222

PROFILE:

Excellent communication, interpersonal, and counseling skills with significant background in problem identification, problem solving, and strategy development. Capable of coordinating activities and contributing effectively to team efforts focused on the improvement of life. Ability to manage multiple responsibilities, set priorities, and achieve goals.

EXPERIENCE:

COMMUNITY TREATMENT CENTER, Athens, Georgia

Court Services Worker / Youth Services Counselor   *1981 to Present*

- Supervise a caseload of 30 + youths who have been committed to the State of Georgia through the Juvenile Court System.
- Develop and implement an individualized plan of care for each youth which includes an intensive, structured format involving individual, peer group, family, and substance abuse counseling. Secure residential treatment for chemically dependent youth.
- Correlate community efforts with schools, private counselors, employers, D.F.C.S., Department of Mental Health, and the Council on Child Abuse.
- Implement positive recreational programs and activities, lead peer groups, multifamily groups, and family counseling sessions.
- Assist clients in formulation of behavior contracts and appropriate resolution of emergency or crisis situations.
- Maintain current narratives on each client, ensuring that mandatory state government forms and legal records from the Juvenile Court are compiled and updated.

THE UNITED METHODIST CHILDREN'S HOME, Decatur, Georgia

Maintenance Supervisor Assistant   *1977 to 1981*

- Performed upkeep, general repairs, and preventive maintenance for campus facilities.
- Assisted in the coordination and implementation of a children's work program, including C.E.T.A. employment opportunities.

Additional employment history and references available upon request.

EDUCATION:

GEORGIA STATE UNIVERSITY, Atlanta, Georgia
Bachelor of Science, Human Resources/Youth Agency Administration, 1981

34

Combination. *Carol Lawrence, Savannah, Georgia*
A resume for a person wanting to help economically deprived families care for a new home. Maintenance work during college provided useful skills for this goal. See Cover Letter 276.

Barbara Patterson
74 Hometown Lane
Town, State 33333
(555) 555-5555
e-mail: barpat1@aol.com

SUMMARY: *Skilled educator with 20+ years experience creating curricula and delivering instruction, evaluating students, developing and implementing strategic plans, and managing projects. Seeking opportunity to transition existing instructional, organizational, and human relations skills into a training or human resource position in a corporate environment.*

QUALIFICATIONS:

Instruction:
- **State Permanent Teaching Certification (N - 6).**
- Prepare lesson plans in Social Studies, Science, Math, and Language Arts.
- Instruct 25 elementary students, addressing individual needs and learning styles.
- Evaluate students' performance and implement plans for improvement, as appropriate.
- Train students, parents, and staff in the use of computer systems.
- Fulfill on-site "Help Desk" role for students and staff using computers.

Planning:
- Serve on numerous District Planning and Building Planning Committees that address ongoing concerns of staff and the community, identifying problems and solutions.
- Chair Positive School Climate Committee that promotes a comfortable learning environment and workplace for students and staff, respectively.
- Participated in developing five-year technology plan for Newark district.
- Wrote technology plan for Suburb School District and monitored implementation.
- Implemented computers in the classroom for Rural School District.
- Chaired committee that pioneered school yearbook at a time when the district had none.

Additional Skills:
- Wrote grant proposal that resulted in $7,000 in funding from State government for purchase of capital equipment (computers) at Rural Central School.
- Proficient in Windows 95, Microsoft Office / Mac, ClarisWorks, Word Processing, Spreadsheets, and the Internet.
- Coached Cheerleading Squad at Suburb Central School; Ski Club Advisor (Rural).

PROFESSIONAL EXPERIENCE:

1989 - Present **Elementary Teacher, Rural Central School District; Rural, State.**

1976 - 1989 **Elementary Teacher, Suburb Central School District; Suburb, State.**

EDUCATION:

1981 **Master of Science, Education**
State University College at Lakeside; Lakeside, State.
GPA: 3.77 / 4.00.

1976 **Bachelor of Science, Education**
State University College at Lakeside; Lakeside, State.
Dean's List.

PROFESSIONAL ENRICHMENT:

Creative Learning Styles   Portfolio Assessment
Cooperative Learning   Gender Equity
Annual Computer Conference   Grant Writing
Essential Elements of Instruction

35

Functional. *Arnold G. Boldt, Rochester, New York*
The goal of this individual is placed at the end of the Summary. Information in the Qualifications section is grouped according to three criteria for easy access. See Cover Letter 145.

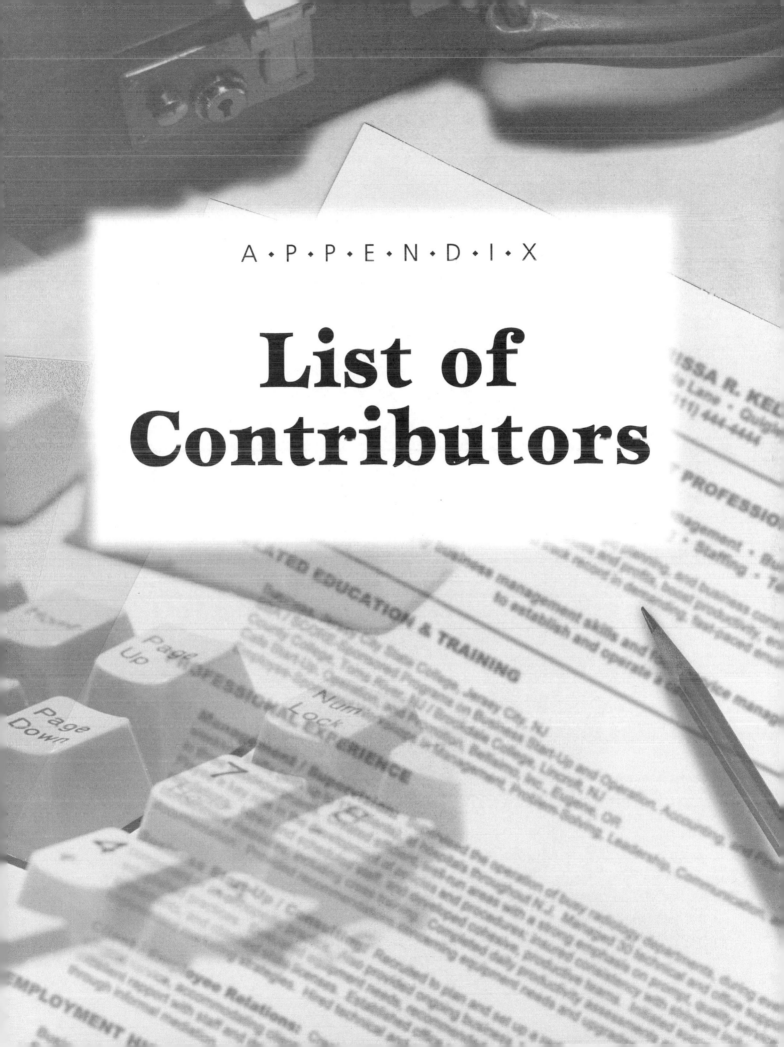

A·P·P·E·N·D·I·X

List of Contributors

—List of Contributors

The following persons are the contributors of the resumes and cover letters in this book. All of the contributors are professional resume writers. To include in this appendix the names of these writers and information about their business is to acknowledge with appreciation their voluntary submissions and the insights expressed in the letters that accompanied the submissions. Cover letter numbers and resume numbers after a writer's contact information are the numbers of the writer's cover letters and resumes included in this book, not page numbers.

Alabama

Montgomery

Donald Orlando
The McLean Group
640 South McDonough
Montgomery, AL 36104
Phone: (334) 264-2020
Fax: (334) 264-9227
E-mail: orlandores@aol.com
Member: PARW
Certification: MBA, CPRW
Cover Letters: 5, 8, 26, 37, 44, 88, 99, 105, 146, 153, 188, 198, 200, 203, 209, 210, 247
Resumes: 5, 14, 18, 22

California

Anaheim

Denise C. Ross
More than Just Words
9852 W. Katella Ave., #187
Anaheim, CA 92804
Voice/Fax: (714) 828-8220
E-mail: mtjwords@aol.com
Member: PARW, NRWA
Cover Letter: 52

Campbell

Georgia Adamson
Adept Business Services
180-A West Rincon Ave.
Campbell, CA 95008
Phone: (408) 866-6859
Fax: (408) 866-8915
E-mail: georgiaa@ix.netcom.com
Web site: www.adeptbussvcs.com
Member: NRWA, PARW, PASS
Certification: CPRW
Cover Letter: 251

Fremont

Carl L. Bascom
American Marketing Associates
555 Mowry Ave., Unit D
Fremont, CA 94536
Phone: (510) 713-7133
E-mail: ama_dtp@hotmail.com
Member: PARW
Cover Letters: 80, 81, 123, 157, 205

Fresno

Susan Britton Whitcomb
Alpha Omega Services
1255 W. Shaw Ave., #100A
Fresno, CA 93711
Phone: (559) 222-7474
Fax: (559) 222-9538
E-mail: topresume@aol.com
Web site: www.careerwriter.com
Member: NRWA, PARW
Certification: NCRW, CPRW
Cover Letter: 21

Menlo Park

Sydney J. Reuben
854 Coleman Ave., #L
Menlo Park, CA 94025
Phone: (650) 323-2643
E-mail: SReubenMA@aol.com
Member: NRWA, PARW
Certification: CPRW, MA
Cover Letters: 25, 48, 93, 96, 150, 155, 225, 235
Resume: 28

Orange

Christine Edick
Action Résumés
1740 W. Katella Ave., Ste. J
Orange, CA 92867
Phone: (714) 639-0942
Fax: (714) 639-3262
E-mail: Christine@actionresumes.com
Web site: actionresumes.com
Member: NRWA, PARW, CDP
Certification: CPRW
Cover Letters: 278, 279

Santa Monica

Sonja A. Wittich
Résumés (with a little help from a friend)
58 Village Park Way
Santa Monica, CA 90405
Phone: (310) 392-1682
Member: PARW
Certification: CPRW
Cover Letters: 199, 288

Valley Glen

Vivian Van Lier
Advantage Resume and Career Services
6701 Murietta Ave.
Valley Glen (Los Angeles), CA 91405
Phone: (818) 994-6655
Fax: (818) 994-6620
E-mail: vvanlier@aol.com
Member: PARW, NRWA
Certification: CPRW
Cover Letters: 4, 33, 196, 212

Connecticut

Enfield

Louise Garver
Career Directions
115 Elm St., Ste. 104
Enfield, CT 06082
Phone: (860) 623-9476
Fax: (860) 623-9473
E-mail: CAREERDIRS@aol.com
Web site: www.resumeimpact.com
Member: PARW, NRWA, IACMP, NCDA, ACA
Certification: CPRW, CMP, MA
Cover Letters: 45, 76, 86, 87, 128, 142, 185, 257

Florida

Ft. Lauderdale

Shelley Nachum
Career Development Services
4801 South University Dr., Ste. 201
Ft. Lauderdale, FL 33328
Phone: (954) 434-0989
Fax: (954) 434-4284
E-mail: cardevsv@bellsouth.net
Web site: www.ExpertResumes.com
Member: PARW, NRWA, SHRM, NCDA
Cover Letters: 10, 30, 82, 101, 102

Middleburg

Valerie Roberts
Roberts' Keyboard Connection
1803 Dahlia Ct.
Middleburg, FL 32068
Phone: (904) 269-9226
Fax: (904) 908-0986
E-mail: valerie@kbdconnection.com
Web site: www.kbdconnection.com
Member: PARW
Cover Letter: 281

Tampa

Anne-Marie Carroll
Carroll's Professional Service
7530-O W. Waters Ave.
Tampa, FL 33615
Phone: (813) 249-7407
Fax: (813) 249-6062
E-mail: amcresume@aol.com
Web site: cpsjoblink.com
Member: PARW
Cover Letter: 221

Gail Reynolds Frank
Frankly Speaking
Tampa, FL
Phone: (813) 289-0919
Fax: (813) 288-8604
E-mail: gailfrank@post.harvard.edu
Web site: www.callfranklyspeaking.com
Member: PARW, NRWA
Certification: NCRW
Cover Letter: 206

Diane McGoldrick
Business Services of Tampa Bay
2803 West Busch Blvd., #103
Tampa, FL 33618
Phone: (813) 935-2700
Fax: (813) 935-4777
E-mail: mcgoldrk@ix.netcom.com
Member: PARW, NAJST, *Who's Who Among
  Professionals*
Certification: CPRW
Cover Letters: 19, 156, 231, 238
Resume: 26

Valrico

Cynthia Kraft
Executive Essentials
P.O. Box 336
Valrico, FL 33595
Phone: (813) 655-0658
Fax: (813) 685-4287
E-mail: cprw@exec-solutions.com
Web site: www.exec-essentials.com
Member: PARW, NRWA
Certification: CPRW
Cover Letters: 50, 159, 229, 236
Resume: 17

Georgia

Buford

Kimberly Wright
The Wordwright Shop
115 N. Alexander St.
Buford, GA 30518
Phone: (770) 932-0178
Fax: (770) 645-5281
E-mail: wordwrightshop@mindspring.com
Member: PARW
Certification: CPRW
Cover Letter: 57

Savannah

Carol Lawrence
P.O. Box 9826
Savannah, GA 31412
Phone: (912) 832-4438
Certification: CPRW
Cover Letters: 63, 90, 169, 214, 276
Resume: 34

Illinois

Arlington Heights

Joellyn Wittenstein
A-1 Quality Résumés & Career Services
2786 Buffalo Grove Rd., Ste. 206
Arlington Heights, IL 60004
Phone: (847) 255-1686
Fax: (847) 255-7224
E-mail: joellyn@interaccess.com
Web site: a-1qualityresumes.com
Member: NRWA, PARW
Certification: CPRW
Cover Letters: 202, 208

Chicago

Cathleen M. Hunt
Write Works
6645 North Oliphant Ave., Ste. H
Chicago, IL 60631
Phone: (773) 774-4420
Fax: (773) 774-4602
E-mail: cmhunt@ibm.net
Member: PARW, NRWA, Board of
  Edison Park C of C
Certification: CPRW
Cover Letters: 94, 107, 148, 227, 267

Jacksonville

Sally McIntosh
Advantage Resumes
35 Westfair Dr.
Jacksonville, IL 62650
Phone: (217) 245-0752
Fax: (217) 243-4451
E-mail: sally@reswriter.com
Web site: www.reswriter.com
Member: NRWA
Certification: NCRW, CPRW, JCTC
Cover Letters: 14, 54, 178

Lincolnshire

Christine L. Dennison
Dennison Career Services
16 Cambridge Lane
Lincolnshire, IL 60069
Phone: (847) 405-9775
Fax: (847) 405-9775
E-mail: chrisdennison@hotmail.com
Member: PARW
Certification: CPC
Cover Letters: 174, 176

Troy

John A. Suarez
Executive Career Fitness
519 Nottingham
Troy, IL 62294
Phone: (888) 521-3483
E-mail: JASUAREZ@aol.com
Member: PARW
Certification: CPRW, MA
Cover Letters: 65, 192
Resumes: 9, 21

Indiana

Hebron

Susan K. Schumm
The Printed Page
805 S. County Line Rd.
Hebron, IN 46341
Phone: (219) 996-6110
E-mail: theprintedpage@email.com
Web site: http://theprintedpage.cjb.net/
Cover Letter: 75

Kentucky

Danville

Debbie Ellis
Career Concepts
Danville, KY 40422
Phone: (606) 236-4001
       (800) 876-5506
Fax: (606) 236-4001
E-mail: resume@searnet.com
Member: PARW
Cover Letters: 55, 71

Lexington

David Adler
Reliable Résumé
243 Chinoe Rd.
Lexington, KY 40502
Phone: (606) 269-8229
Fax: (606) 266-4337
E-mail: relresume@aol.com
Member: PARW, NRWA
Cover Letter: 172

Maryland

Columbia

Diane Burns
Career Marketing Techniques
5219 Thunder Hill Rd.
Columbia, MD 21045
Phone: (410) 884-0213
E-mail: Bburns7385@aol.com
Member: PARW
Certification: CPRW
Cover Letters: 170, 191, 197

Ms. Earl M. Melvin
The Executive Desktop Publishing & Résumé
    Services, Inc.
8955 Guilford Rd., Ste. 140
Columbia, MD 21046
Phone: (410) 290-8277
Fax: (410) 290-7077
E-mail: careers@execdtp.com
Web site: www.execdtp.com
Member: PARW
Cover Letter: 16

Massachusetts

Needham

Wendy Gelberg
Advantage Résumés
21 Hawthorn Ave.
Needham, MA 02492
Phone: (781) 444-0778
Fax: (781) 444-2778
E-mail: wgelberg@aol.com
Member: NRWA
Certification: CPRW, JCTC
Cover Letters: 29, 66, 141, 215
Resume: 4

Michigan

Battle Creek

Peggy Weeks
CompuPage
3914 W. Michigan Ave.
Battle Creek, MI 49017
Phone: (616) 964-7533
Fax: (616) 964-7843
E-mail: Peggy_Weeks@glfn.org
Member: PARW, NRWA, ABSSI
Cover Letters: 61, 154, 180, 184, 216, 217,
    222, 228, 269, 271
Resumes: 8, 24

Jackson

Jan Passmore
Premium Word Processing Services
1030 S. Grinnell St.
Jackson, MI 49203
Phone: (517) 796-1717
Fax: (517) 784-7494
E-mail: jlpassmore@dmci.net
Member: PARW, BPW
Cover Letters: 127, 246, 280, 286

Novi

Lorie Lebert
Résumés for Results
P.O. Box 267
Novi, MI 48376
Phone: (248) 380-6101
         (800) 870-9059
Fax: (248) 380-0169
E-mail: llebert@aol.com
Web site: www.resumes4results.com
Member: PARW, *Who's Who for Entrepreneurs*
Certification: CPRW
Cover Letters: 6, 100
Resumes: 1, 6

Trenton

Maria E. Hebda
Premier Résumé Writing Service, LLC
Trenton, MI 48183
Phone: (734) 676-9170
         (877) 777-7242
Fax: (877) 777-7307
E-mail: maria@writingresumes.com
Web site: www.writingresumes.com
Member: PARW
Certification: CPRW
Cover Letters: 106, 124, 173

Vicksburg

Betty A. Callahan
Professional Results
11331 Schoolhouse Dr.
Vicksburg, MI 49097
Phone: (616) 649-4955
Fax: (616) 649-4910
E-mail: oops2000@net-link.net
Member: PARW
Certification: CPRW, PC
Cover Letter: 2

Minnesota

Rochester

Beverley Drake
CareerVision Resume & Job Search Systems
3936 Highway 52N, #224
Rochester, MN 55901
Phone: (507) 252-9825
Fax: (507) 252-1525
E-mail: bdcprw@aol.com
Member: PARW, NAJST
Certification: CPRW
Cover Letters: 23, 117, 121, 194, 204, 262

Sartell

Connie Hauer
Hauer Word Processing
P.O. Box 232
Sartell, MN 56377
Phone: (320) 240-2355
Fax: (320) 253-5245
E-mail: chauer5234@aol.com
Web site: http://members.aol.com/chauer5234/
    hauer.html
Member: NRWA
Cover Letter: 132

New Jersey

Brick

Carol Rossi
Computerized Documents
4 Baywood Blvd.
Brick, NJ 08723
Phone: (732) 477-5172
Fax: (732) 477-5172
E-mail: comp-docs@juno.com
Web site: http://members.aol.com/compdocsCR
Member: PARW
Certification: CPRW
Cover Letters: 36, 179, 182, 224, 252, 253
Resumes: 20, 25

Fair Lawn

Vivian Belen
The Job Search Specialist
1102 Bellair Ave.
Fair Lawn, NJ 07410
Phone: (201) 797-2883
Fax: (201) 797-5566
E-mail: vivian@jobsearchspecialist.com
Web site: www.jobsearchspecialist.com
Member: NRWA, AJST, CPADN,
    Five O'Clock Club
Certification: NCRW, CPRW, JCTC
Cover Letter: 249

Lawrenceville

Susan Guarneri
Guarneri Associates
1101 Lawrence Rd.
Lawrenceville, NJ 08648
Phone: (609) 771-1669
Fax: (609) 637-0449
E-mail: resumagic@aol.com
Member: PARW, NRWA, Middle Atlantic
    Career Counselors Assn.
Certification: CPRW, NCC, NCCC, JCTC
Cover Letters: 18, 60, 147, 158, 266, 275, 292

Marlboro

Beverly Baskin
Baskin Business & Career Services
6 Alberta Dr.
Marlboro, NJ 07746
Other offices:
    120 Wood Ave. S, Iselin, NJ, 08830;
    116 Village Blvd., Princeton, NJ 08540
Phone: (800) 300-4079
Fax: (732) 974-8846
E-mail: bbcs@att.net
Member: NRWA, PARW, NCDA, NECA, ACA
Certification: MA, NCC, CPRW
Cover Letter: 103

Rochelle Park

Alesia Benedict
Career Objectives
151 West Passaic St.
Rochelle Park, NJ 07662
Phone: (800) 206-5353
Fax: (800) 206-5454
E-mail: careerobj@aol.com
Web site: www.getinterviews.com
Member: PARW (Board), Career
    Masters Institute (Board), NAJST
Certification: CPRW, IJCTC
Cover Letters: 89, 160, 195, 207, 240

Toms River

Nina K. Ebert
A Word's Worth Résumé & Writing Service
808 Lowell Ave.
Toms River, NJ 08753
Phone: (732) 349-2225
    (609) 758-7799
Fax: (732) 286-9323
E-mail: wrdswrth@gbsias.com
Member: PARW
Certification: CPRW
Cover Letters: 9, 95, 151, 171

West Paterson

Melanie A. Noonan
Peripheral Pro
560 Lackawanna Ave.
West Paterson, NJ 07424
Phone: (973) 785-3011
Fax: (973) 785-3071
E-mail: PeriPro1@aol.com
Member: PARW, NRWA, ABSSI, IAAP
Certification: CPS
Cover Letters: 20, 43, 46, 70, 97, 115, 122, 211,
    213, 223, 272, 277, 282, 285, 289
Resumes: 7, 23

New York

Brooklyn

Rebecca Weissner
Word for Word
189 Penn St., #4
Brooklyn, NY 11211
Cover Letter: 291

East Greenbush

Elizabeth M. Daugherty
1st Impressions Business & Resume Services
2 Columbia Dr.
East Greenbush, NY 12061
Phone: (518) 477-8753
Fax: (518) 477-8753
E-mail: Elizabeth@capitalConcierge.com
Member: PARW
Cover Letters: 56, 136

Elmira

Betty Geller
Apple Résumé & Typing Service
456 W. Water St., Ste. 1
Elmira, NY 14905
Phone: (607) 734-2090
Fax: (607) 734-2090
E-mail: bgellerres@aol.com
Member: NRWA, PARW
Certification: CPRW
Cover Letters: 1, 111, 256

Jackson Heights

Kim Isaacs
Advanced Career Systems
34-41 85th St., Ste. 6-G
Jackson Heights, NY 11372
Phone: (888) 565-9290
Fax: (718) 565-1611
E-mail: support@resumesystems.com
Web site: http://www.resumesystems.com
Member: NRWA, PARW
Certification: CPRW, NCRW
Cover Letters: 35, 72, 118, 129, 164, 254, 259, 273

Lindenhurst

Jackie Connelly
Prestige Résumé Service
302 Grand Ave.
Lindenhurst, NY 11757
Phone: (888) 248-7188
Fax: (516) 888-7814
E-mail: ResumePro1@aol.com
Web site: www.resumes1.com
Member: NRWA
Cover Letter: 32

Medford

Deborah Wile Dib
Advantage Résumés of New York
77 Buffalo Ave.
Medford, NY 11763
Phone: (516) 475-8513
Fax: (516) 475-8513
E-mail: gethired@advantageresumes.com
Web site: http://www.advantageresumes.com
Member: NRWA, PARW, NAJST, CPADN
Certification: NCRW, CPRW, JCTC
Cover Letters: 73, 112, 114, 161, 187, 233,
   258, 264, 268
Resumes: 10, 12, 27

Mt. Morris

Salome Randall Tripi
The Office Outsource
3123 Moyer Rd.
Mt. Morris, NY 14510
Phone: (716) 658-2480
Fax: (716) 658-2480
E-mail: srttoo@frontiernet.net
Web site: http://www.frontiernet.net/ ~ srttoo/
Member: PARW
Cover Letter: 186

New York

Judith Friedler
CareerPro Résumé Services
150 Nassau St., 1624
New York, NY 10038
Phone: (212) 227-1434
Fax: (212) 766-2772
E-mail: JudyCPro@aol.com
Member: Founding Member of NRWA
Certification: NCRW, CPRW, IJCTC
Cover Letter: 24

Poughkeepsie

Kristin Mroz Coleman
Custom Career Services
44 Hillcrest Dr.
Poughkeepsie, NY 12603
Phone: (914) 452-8274
Fax: (914) 452-7789
E-mail: kcoleman@idsi.net
Member: PARW, NRWA
Cover Letters: 62, 67, 78, 116, 126, 131, 193, 201
Resume: 13

Rochester

Arnold G. Boldt
Arnold-Smith Associates
625 Panorama Trail, Bldg. 2, Ste. 200
Rochester, NY 14625
Phone: (716) 383-0350
Fax: (716) 387-0516
E-mail: Arnoldsmth@aol.com
Member: PARW
Certification: CPRW
Cover Letters: 7, 11, 13, 31, 41, 42, 64, 74, 104, 134,
   139, 140, 145, 175, 177
Resume: 35

Scotia

Barbara M. Beaulieu
Academic Concepts
214 Second St.
Scotia, NY 12302
Phone: (518) 377-1080
Fax: (518) 382-8462
E-mail: barbra2@banet.net
Member: PARW, NRWA
Certification: CPRW
Cover Letter: 22

Victor

Kim Little
Fast Track Resumes
1281 Courtney Dr.
Victor, NY 14564
Phone: (716) 742-2467
E-mail: ServPCR@aol.com
Web site: www.fast-trackresumes.com
Member: NRWA
Certification: JCTC
Cover Letters: 91, 108, 189

North Dakota

Fargo

Mary Laske
ExecPro Résumé Service
1304 23rd St., SW
Fargo, ND 58103
Phone: (701) 235-8007
Fax: (701) 235-7983
E-mail: mlaske@aol.com
Member: PARW, NRWA
Certification: CPRW
Cover Letters: 39, 51, 110, 232, 243, 260

Jeffrey Thompson
4311 15th Ave. SW
Fargo, ND 58103
Phone: (701) 281-8840
E-mail: jThom7248@aol.com
Cover Letters: 143, 144
Resume: 15

Ohio

Delaware

Gwen Haggerty
Willow Résumé & Word Processing
135 Hawthorn Blvd.
Delaware, OH 43015
Phone: (740) 362-8021
Fax: (740) 369-6231
E-mail: willowgh@aol.com
Member: PARW
Certification: CPRW
Cover Letter: 12

Oregon

Aloha

Pat Kendall
Advanced Résumé Concepts
18580 S.W. Rosa Rd.
Aloha, OR 97007
Phone: (503) 591-9143
Fax: (503) 642-2535
E-mail: reslady@aol.com
Web site: www.reslady.com
Member: NRWA
Certification: JCTC, NCRW
Cover Letters: 163, 237
Resume: 29

Pennsylvania

Wellsboro

Deborah S. Edwards
Résumé Connection
33 Waln St., P.O. Box 361
Wellsboro, PA 16901
Phone: (570) 724-3610
Fax: (570) 724-5492
E-mail: resume@epix.net
Web site: http://members.tripod.com/
    dedwardsgroup/resume.htm
Member: NRWA, PARW, The Five
    O'Clock Club
Certification: NCRW, CPRW
Cover Letters: 84, 92, 98, 119

Rhode Island

Smithfield

Mary Sward Hurley
Best Impression
P.O. Box 17271
Smithfield, RI 02917
Phone: (401) 231-7551
Fax: (401) 231-7510
E-mail: Resume99@aol.com
Member: NRWA
Certification: NCRW
Cover Letter: 239
Resume: 30

South Carolina

Greenwood

Gwen P. Noffz
110 Satcher Dr.
Greenwood, SC 29646
Phone: (864) 227-3771
Fax: (864) 229-6377
Member: PARW
Certification: CPRW
Cover Letters: 68, 244, 245

Tennessee

Hendersonville

Carolyn Braden
Braden Resume & Secretarial
108 La Plaza Dr.
Hendersonville, TN 37075
Phone: (615) 822-3317
Fax: (615) 826-9611
Member: PARW
Certification: CPRW
Cover Letters: 83, 190, 219, 241, 248, 261, 290

Knoxville

Lynda Lowry
Absolutely Write
8240 Hunter Hill Dr.
Knoxville, TN 37923
Phone: (423) 690-1489
Fax: (423) 531-7083
E-mail: ResWritr@aol.com
Member: NRWA
Cover Letters: 168, 218

Texas

Denton

Dorothy E. Smith
Resumes, Etc.
3309 N. Bonnie Brae
Denton, TX 76207
Phone: (940) 566-3343
Fax: (940) 565-0776
Member: PARW
Cover Letter: 137

El Paso

Shari Favela
342 Vista Del Rey
El Paso, TX 79912
E-mail: afavela1@worldnet.att.net
Certification: NCC
Cover Letter: 283

Fort Hood

Jackie Sexton
P.O. Box 6322
Fort Hood, TX 76544
Phone: (254) 547-4260
E-mail: jackiecprw@yahoo.com
Member: PARW
Certification: CPRW
Cover Letters: 28, 284
Resume: 3

Houston

Rosa St. Julian
Aicron Career & Resume Services
9597 Jones Rd., #189
Houston, TX 77065
Phone: (888) 209-6577
Fax: (281) 894-6214
E-mail: info@aicron.com
Web site: www.aicron.com
Member: PARW, NRWA
Certification: CPRW
Cover Letters: 3, 58, 149

Round Rock
Karen D. Wrigley
AMW Résumé Service
3102 Scarlet Oak Cove
Round Rock, TX 78664
Phone: (512) 246-7423
        (800) 880-7088
Fax: (512) 246-7433
E-mail: amwrig@ibm.net
Member: PARW, NRWA
Certification: CPRW
Cover Letters: 34, 40, 220, 234, 250
Resume: 31

Virginia
Lynchburg
Rebecca Stokes
The Advantage, Inc.
1330 Walnut Hollow Rd.
Lynchburg, VA 24503
Phone: (800) 922-5353
Fax: (804) 384-4700
E-mail: advresume@aol.com or
        advanresume@earthlink.net
Web site: www.advantageresume.com
Member: PARW
Certification: CPRW
Cover Letters: 226, 255, 265

Richmond
Betty H. Williams
BW Custom Résumés
Richmond, VA
Phone: (804) 359-1065
Fax: (804) 359-4150
E-mail: VaBHW@aol.com
Member: PARW, NRWA
Certification: CPRW, NCRW
Cover Letters: 47, 85, 130, 183
Resume: 16

Virginia Beach
Anne G. Kramer
Alpha Bits
4411 Trinity Ct.
Virginia Beach, VA 23455
Phone: (757) 464-1914
E-mail: akramer@livenet.net
Member: PARW, Phi Theta Kappa, contributing
    writer to womenCONNECT.com
Certification: CPRW
Cover Letters: 59, 69, 79, 113, 120, 125, 138, 162,
    165, 166, 167, 242

Washington
Issaquah
Kathryn Vargo
Words at Work
P.O. Box 83
Issaquah, WA 98027
Phone: (425) 392-2577
Fax: (425) 391-2604
E-mail: Ticonder@aol.com
Certification: CPRW, NCRW
Member: PARW
Certification: CPRW, NCRW
Cover Letters: 133, 270, 274
Resume: 32

Woodinville
Carole S. Barns
Barns & Associates, Complete Career Services
22432-76th Ave. SE, Ste. 201
Woodinville, WA 98072
Phone: (425) 487-4008
        (800) 501-4008
Fax: (425) 489-1995
E-mail: BarnsAssoc@aol.com
Member: PARW, NRWA, ICF, PSCDA
Cover Letters: 27, 53, 77, 109, 135, 152, 181, 230
Resume: 19

West Virginia
Charleston
Barbie Dallmann
Happy Fingers Word Processing & Résumé Service
1205 Wilkie Dr.
Charleston, WV 25314
Phone: (304) 345-4495
Fax: (304) 343-2017
E-mail: BarbieDall@mindspring.com
Member: PARW, NRWA
Certification: CPRW
Cover Letters: 15, 38, 49, 263, 287
Resumes: 2, 11, 33

Wisconsin
Milwaukee
Tina Merwin
Consultancy In Action, Ltd.
152 W. Wisconsin Ave., Ste. 531
Milwaukee, WI 53203
Phone: (414) 272-3151
Fax: (414) 272-2747
E-mail: cialtd@naspa.net
Web site: www.naspa.net/members/cialtd
Member: PARW, APCC
Cover Letter: 17

For those who would like to contact the Professional Association of Résumé Writers (PARW), its address is as follows:

Professional Association of Résumé Writers
3637 Fourth Street North, Suite 330
St. Petersburg, FL 33704
Phone: (727) 821-2274
Fax: (727) 894-1277
E-mail: parwhq@aol.com
Web site: www.parw.com

For those who would like to contact the National Résumé Writers' Association (NRWA), call Jackie Connelly, (516) 884-2507, or inquire by e-mail: resumepro@aol.com. NRWA's Web site is www.nrwa.com.

Occupation Index

Cover Letters

Note: The following entries are, in most cases, target positions for the job seekers. (If the target position is not stated clearly, the current or most recent position is listed here.) The numbers are cover letter numbers in the Gallery, not page numbers.

Resumes

Note: The following occupations represent the current or most recent position of the job seekers. The numbers are resume numbers in the Exhibit of Resumes, not page numbers.

Gallery of Best Resumes

A Collection of Quality Resumes by Professional Resume Writers

By David F. Noble, Ph.D.

This is the best collection of resumes and cover letters you'll ever find! Members of the Professional Association of Resume Writers offer the best of the best in this wide collection. Sample more than 200 great resumes with an expansive range of styles, formats, designs, occupations, and situations—all arranged in easy-to-find groups. You also get the author's 101 best resume tips—tips on design, layout, papers, writing style, mistakes to avoid, and more than 25 sample cover letters!

ISBN: 1-56370-144-8 • $17.95 • Order Code: LP-GBR

Professional Resumes for Accounting, Tax, Finance, and Law

A Special Gallery of Quality Resumes by Professional Resume Writers

By David F. Noble, Ph.D.

Showcasing resumes in the fields of Accounting, Tax, Finance, and Law, plus other related fields including Information Systems/Information Technology, this book displays a new collection of the best 201 resumes and 22 cover letters from 91 professional writers across the United States.

ISBN: 1-56370-605-9 • $19.95 • Order Code: LP-J6059

Professional Resumes for Executives, Managers, and Other Administrators

A New Gallery of Best Resumes by Professional Resume Writers

By David F. Noble, Ph.D.

A great collection of 342 new professionally designed resumes assembled to meet the needs of anyone seeking an upper-management position. Resumes were submitted by members of the Professional Association of Résumé Writers and the National Résumé Writers' Association. Each resume contains a professional analysis explaining when and how to use a specific format.

ISBN: 1-56370-483-8 • $19.95 • Order Code: LP-J4838

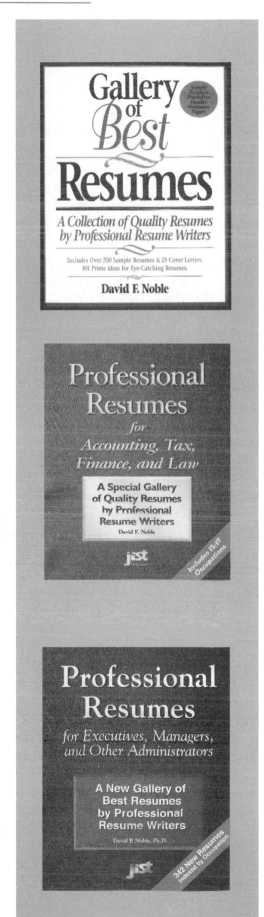

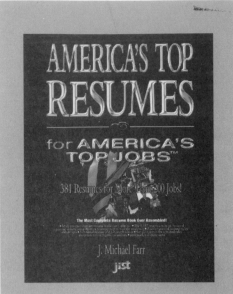

America's Top Resumes for America's Top Jobs™

By J. Michael Farr

Introducing the ONLY book with sample resumes for all major occupations covering 85% of the workforce! Here you'll find nearly 400 of the best resumes submitted by members of the Professional Association of Resume Writers, grouped according to occupation and annotated by the author to highlight their best features—PLUS career planning and job search advice from Mike Farr!

ISBN: 1-56370-288-6 • $19.95 • Order Code: LP-J2886

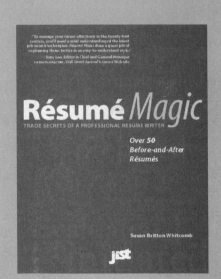

Résumé Magic

Trade Secrets of a Professional Résumé Writer

By Susan Britton Whitcomb

Make your ordinary resume extraordinary by following the proven techniques presented in this excellent resource. Many resume books only offer a finished product of how a resume should look. *Résumé Magic* presents examples that will teach you *why* certain techniques work and shows you how to produce a powerful, effective resume. Techniques include

- ✦ Using advertising strategies to gain an audience with your boss-to-be
- ✦ Choosing the most flattering format
- ✦ Writing great copy
- ✦ Resume-style editing

ISBN: 1-56370-522-2 • $18.95 • Order Code: LP-J5222

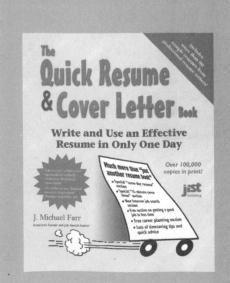

The Quick Resume & Cover Letter Book, Second Edition

Write and Use an Effective Resume in Only One Day

By J. Michael Farr

A hands-on, total job search guide! The author understands you don't have a lot of valuable time to waste preparing your job search. This award-winning title offers tips on

- ✦ Writing a "same-day resume"
- ✦ Job searching
- ✦ Interviewing
- ✦ Cover and follow-up letters
- ✦ And much, much more!

ISBN: 1-56370-634-2 • $14.95 • Order Code: LP-J6342